Banking and Financial Sector Reforms in India

Banking and Financial Sector Reforms in India

Asha Singh
M.S. Gupta
T.K. Shandilya

SERIALS PUBLICATIONS
NEW DELHI (INDIA)

First Published – 2010

ISBN: 978-81-8387-361-1

Published by

SERIALS PUBLICATIONS
4830/24, 1st Floor, Ansari Road
Darya Ganj, New Delhi-110002 (India)
Phone : 23245225. Fax : 91-11-23272135
E-mail: serials@satyam.net.in

CONTENTS

PREFACE

Banking system in the country is undergoing momentous change. It is gearing up itself to meet the global competitiveness. Indian banking sector comprises of an impressive network of banks, committed to planned economic development within the framework of a mixed economy under a federal political setup. Significant developments have taken place in Indian banking in the post Independence period and especially since the beginning of the reform process in the country.

In modern economy, bankers are to be considered not merely as dealers in money but more realistically the leaders in development. Banks are not just the store house of the country's wealth but are reservoirs of resources necessary for economic development. In the perspective of the history of economic development of developed countries, banking was necessary for development. The new philosophy, at least in our country, regards banking as a trinity, pre-requisite, requisite and concomitant, all taken together. Banking as a tool for development is multi-purpose tool and depending upon the value system of the society, its uses are capable of wide variations. Economic development of developed as well as underdeveloped countries is based on the process of investment. The banking structure provides simple intermediation in the process of investment. Banks encourage investment and thereby help capital formation. Banks can stimulate capital formation and promote productivity and trade by providing credit and a more generous supply of money in the form of bank notes deposits. Banks are the purveyors of money and credit to the factors of production and they help in the acceleration of growth. Banking, when properly organized aids and facilitates the growth of trade and industry and hence of the national economy. Today banks are instruments of economic change to maximize social good.

The economic reforms launched by the Government of India since 1991 are designed to accelerate the overall growth and help India realize its full productive potential. The rapid growth requires a sustained effect at mobilizing savings and resources and deploying these in ways which encourage efficient production. For this, reforms in the financial sector, particularly in the banking system, which has the prime responsibility of mobilizing and allocating financial resources, is a pre-requisite.

There are some unique aspects of banking sector reform in India. There has been no banking crisis in the Indian economy. The reform process can best be described as gradual rebalancing of the banking sector to enhance efficiency and stability. The overhang problems were managed internally without recourse to Asset Reconstruction Company (ARC). Some to the salient aspects of the banking sector reforms in India are briefly enumerated here.

First, the reform measures were initiated and sequenced to create and enable environment for banks to overcome the external constraints–which were related to administered interest rate regime, high levels of pre-emption through reserve requirements, and credit allocation to certain sectors. The interest rates in the banking system have been largely deregulated except for a few categories, viz., savings deposit accounts, non-resident Indian (NRI) deposits, small loans up to Rs. 200 thousand and export credit. However, the administered interest rates prevail in small savings schemes of the Government. The statutory reserve requirements have also been progressively reduced while the norms for priority sector lending have been rationalized.

Second, as against the overwhelming dominance of the Public Sector Banks in the banking system in the pre-reform period, the share of the public sector banks in the aggregate assets of the banking sector has declined from 90 per cent in 1991 to around 75 per cent in 2000, while the share of wholly Government-owned public sector banks declined sharply from about 90 per cent to less than 10 per cent of aggregate assets of all scheduled commercial banks during this period. Diversification of ownership has led to greater market accountability and improved efficiency.

Third, with a view to enhance efficiency and productivity in the banking sector through competition, the private sector and the foreign-banks were allowed more liberal entry. Since 1993, twelve new private sectors towards enhancing competition in the banking sector, foreign direct investment in the private sector banks is now allowed up to 74 per cent, subject to conformity with the guidelines issued from time to time.

Fourth, consolidation in the banking sector has been another feature of the reform process, which also encompassed the Development Financial Institutions (DFIs), which have been providers of long-term finance. The Reserve Bank enabled the reverse-merger of a large DFI with its commercial-banking subsidiary, which was a major initiative towards universal banking. Subsequently, another large term-lending institution has been converted into a bank. The mergers between non-banking financial companies and banks as also between private sector banks are now permitted, subject to the Reserve Bank guidelines. The underlying principles for consolidation would also apply, as appropriate, to the public sector banks, subject to the provisions of the relevant legislation.

Fifth, impressive institutional and legal reforms have been undertaken in relation to the banking sector. In 1994, a Board for Financial Supervision (BFS) was constituted comprising select members of the Reserve Bank Board with a variety of professional expertise to exercise 'undivided attention to supervision'. The BFS ensures an integrated approach to supervision of commercial banks, development finance institutions, non-banking finance companies, urban cooperatives banks and primary dealers. It provides direction on a continuing basis on regulatory policies including governance issues and supervisory practices.

A Board for Regulation and Supervision of Payment and Settlement Systems (BPSS) has also been recently constituted to prescribe policies relating to the regulation and supervision of all types of payment and settlement systems, set standards for existing and future systems, authorize the payment and settlement systems and determine criteria for membership to these systems.

The Credit Information Companies (Regulation) Act, 2005 and the Government Securities Act, 2004 have been enacted. Certain amendments are also being considered by the Parliament to enhance Reserve Bank's regulatory and supervisory powers.

Sixth, a number of measures for enhancing transparency in the banking sector, through disclosures standards, have been instituted. Illustratively, all cases of penalty imposed by the Reserve Bank on the banks as also directions issued on specific matters, including those arising out of inspection, are placed in the public domain.

Seventh, in the regulatory framework and supervisory practices, which have almost converged with the best international practices, two points are noteworthy. First, the minimum capital to risk assets ratio (CRAR) has been kept at nine per cent, i.e., one percentage point above the international norm; and separate Investment Fluctuation Reserve (IFR) out of profits, towards interest rate risk. The IFR has helped in cushioning the valuation losses require to be booked by the banks in a rising interest rate environment.

As regards the implementation of Basel II framework for capital adequacy, a differentiated approach has been adopted in respect of commercial, cooperative and Regional Rural Banks (RRBs) – keeping in view the significant divergence in their size, operational complexity, their criticality for the financial sector and the need to achieve greater financial inclusion. Thus, the capital adequacy norms applicable to these entities have been maintained at varying levels of stringency and one might say that we are adopting a three-track approach with regard to capital adequacy rules. On the first track, the commercial banks are required to maintain capital for both credit and market risks as per the Basel I framework; on the second track, co-operative banks are required to maintain capital for credit risk as per the Basel I framework and surrogates for market risk; on the third track, the RRBs have a minimum capital requirement, which is, however, not no par with the Basel I framework.

As regards the timeframe for implementation of Basel II framework, the foreign banks operating in India and the Indian banks with foreign branches are required to adopt the Standardized Approach for credit risk and the Basic Indicator Approach for the operational risk, with effect from March 31, 2008. All other commercial banks are required to adopt these approaches not later than March 31, 2009.

Eighth, the regulatory framework in India is increasingly focusing on ensuring good governance through 'fit and proper' owners, directors and senior managers of the banks. Transfer of shareholding of 5 per cent and above requires acknowledgement from the Reserve Bank and such significant shareholder are put through a 'fit and proper' test. Banks are required to screen the nominated and elected directors through a nomination committee to satisfy 'fit and proper' criteria. The directors are also required to sign a covenant indicating their roles and responsibilities. The Reserve bank has issued detailed guidelines on ownership and governance in private sector banks emphasizing diversified ownership. The listed banks are also required to comply with governance principles laid down by the SEBI – the securities-markets regulator.

The historical experience of developing countries, in most of which the state has played a predominating and active economic role, suggests that both the nature and the intensity of government intervention will change over time. As the economy reshapes itself in response to an initial set of interventions, it can develop undesirable tendencies that perhaps require a completely different set of interventions, or even a total withdrawal of them. It is this change in the nature of state intervention that has come in the form of economic restructuring. Countries that have recognized the need for restructuring and effectively implemented it, for the most part, have maintained their tempo of growth and development. Countries that have failed to respond to such needs have found themselves in a situation of crisis, their choices and actions dictated by the priorities of those who would bail them out. Effective restructuring would depend on the prevailing state of the economy, the nature and intensity of the original interventions as well as their overall success or failure, global economic tendencies, the fundamental goals of the society and on so many other important factors.

Restructuring process in Indian economy typically began in a situation of macro-economic crisis, with the high inflation, escalating fiscal deficits and widening balance of payments deficits. It is generally accepted that such environment is not conducive to the success of any restructuring programme. Thus, the first step should be to tackle the macro-economic problem. This is done with a combination of fiscal, monetary and exchange rate policies.

While a stable macro-economy may provide an essential backdrop for growth, the impetus for growth is most likely to come from a fundamental reallocation of the economy's resources in a way that maximizes their productivity. In order to induce this reallocation, the structure of incentives in the economy has to change, and the barriers to the movement of capital and labour have to be lowered. The change in incentives and the lowering of barriers is brought about through financial sector reforms. These reforms constitute the growth components of a restructuring package.

Banking and financial sector reforms have been assessed with following concluding points:

(a) The area of banking and financial reform has been, as yet, mainly confined to functional aspect of the institutions. Sickness of commercial banks has been tried to be corrected by reducing their irrational lending and restricting the directional credit. The improvement of functioning of the nationalized commercial banks is recently evident from their regaining strength in respect of capital norm and profitability. A few of nationalized banks have turned round currently.

(b) The interest rate flexibility has not induced any sufficient competition in the system. Interest rate, exchange rate and capital asset yield rate are important components of interest rate syndrome. Low interest rate discourages intermediation and ultimately reduces investment via reduction of savings. This repression hypothesis is supported by fiscal compulsion of the government.

Over last few years, the external value of Rupee in terms of dollar has been sliding. The alignment between exchange rate and the other trade and capital account variables are not convincing. The trade account of the country shows no sign of improvement and the export growth is disappointing. On the other hand, the capital flow has been quite unsatisfactory, after an initial spurt. In our balance sheet account, capital account convertibility has made no progress although expectation of foreign capital for economic development has been one important factor for globalization.

(c) Financial reform has two components – fiscal policy and monetary policy. Government has to make budgetary balance so that it does not depend much on market borrowing or ad hoc finance from the banking system. It frustrates the objectives of monetary policy of liquidity control in our country; government budgetary position is yet to be compressed.

(d) As for the approach to external sector reforms, Report of the High Level Committee on Balance of Payments (Chaired by C. Rangarajan) is relevant. It has recommended the market determined exchange rate, current account convertibility and regulation of commercial borrowings. On the recommendations of this committee, the capital loss has been managed and there has been a gradual move from administered exchange rate to market determined exchange rate. But, as stated above, capital flow has been sluggish and exchange rate has been unfavourable. Compared to China, another big foreign capital recipient, capital flow in India has been very insignificant. As against the recommendations of the Rangarajan Committee, the exchange rate volatility has become an endemic feature even with incipient capital flow and RBI appears to be shaky against the uncertainty of international currency markets.

(e) This leads to the central macro-economic issue of foreign investment and economic crises of Asian and Mexico type. In view of these experiences, the slow process of our financial sector reform, particularly in the external sector, is a step in the right direction.

(f) Compulsion of external sector and financial sector globalization generally comes from two sources – the private multinational debtor and the IMF- World Bank. However, if the country continuously avoids too much borrowing from these sources, the crises from MNC investment and IMF compulsion can be avoided. This requires reform in a big way on the domestic front, which we are lacking.

Hence, financial markets play an important role of collecting savings and channeling them into productive investments. Efficient functioning of financial markets can induce savers to save in the form of financial assets rather than in the form of physical assets such as land, gold, etc. Thus, the level of investment, and hence the growth rate of the economy, can be increased. But there is considerable controversy regarding policies that can lead to well functioning of financial markets. The main policy issue in this regard is whether the structure and ownership of banking, the interest rates and the allocation of credit should be market determined or controlled, to some extent, by the government.

Some economists have pointed to various market imperfections that may make government intervention desirable. For example, Keynes argues in favour of keeping the interest rates low to stimulate investments. More recently, Stiglitz and Weiss and Cho have argued that as the interest rates on loans go up, so does the risk of default; this may hamper the markets' ability to allocate credit efficiently. It may also lead to excessive build-up of non-performing loans. Some economists have argued that the state may be able to speed up the long-term growth rate of the economy be directing credit to strategic industries.

The proponents of financial liberalization have asserted that the higher interest rates following liberalization lead to more of the savings being kept in the form of financial assts, thus making more funds available for investments. They also argue that the markets can allocate credit more efficiently by supplying it to the highest interest paying, and therefore, the most productive borrower. Thus, financial liberalization is claimed to increase both the amount and productivity of investments and hence, the rate of growth of the economy.

Considering the importance of the subject in the context of economic reform process in India, a National Seminar, sponsored by the University Grants Commission, was organized at Magadh Mahila College, Patna University, Patna on this issue. This book is a compilation of the research papers presented by dedicated scholars, academicians, bankers, financial experts and research scholars in the said Seminar.

We are appreciative of the efforts made by various contributors who adhered to our request and undertook the tedious task of preparing papers in spite of their busy schedule. There are no words adequate to express our gratitude. We are grateful to the University Grants Commission, Eastern Regional Office, Kolkata for extending financial support to organize the Seminar and prepare a ground for materializing the present book.

Thanks are due to the Office staff, Librarian, Computer Operator and some of the students without whom the work would have been very difficult. They deserve our gratitude for their unconditional support.

Lastly, we extend our gratitude to all who have supported and helped us directly or indirectly in this endeavour.

Thanks

Asha Singh
M.S. Gupta
T.K. Shandilya

LIST OF CONTRIBUTORS

Mahesh Chandra Prasad, Senior Lecturer, Department of Applied Economics and Commerce, Patna University, Patna

M.S. Gupta, Department of Commerce, R.K.D. College (Magadh University), Patna

Bipin Kumar, Head, Department of Economics, R.R.S. College (Magadh University), Mokama

Asha Singh, University Professor and Head, Department of Economics, Magadh Mahila College, Patna University, Patna

Pushpa Sinha, Department of Economics, Patna Women's College (Patna University), Patna

Ratna Mitra, Department of Economics, Patna Women's College (Patna University), Patna

Tapan Kumar Shandilya, Department of Economics, College of Commerce (Magadh University), Patna

Md. Reyazuddin, Reader, Vanijya Mahavidyalaya, Patna University, Patna.

Zafar A. Sultan, P.G. Department of Economics, L.S. College, B.R.A. Bihar University, Muzaffarpur

Priti Kashyap, Department of Economics, A.N. College, Patna

Anju Jain, Department of Economics, R.P.M. College, Patna City

Syed Eqbal Afzal, Department of Commerce, Oriental College, Patna City

Naqui Mohammad, Department of Commerce, Oriental College, Patna City

Kumari Veena, Department of Economics, A.N. College, Patna

Nagendra Kumar Jha, Department of Applied Economics and Commerce, Patna University, Patna

Kamini Jha, Department of Economics, Patna Women's College (Patna University), Patna

S.K. Khandelia, Research Scholar & Guest Faculty, Department of Commerce, Magadh Mahila College, Patna University, Patna

Meera Ranjan Lal, Department of Economics, B.D. Evening College, Patna

Reeta Kumari, Department of Economics, B.S. College, Danapur

Rashmi Akhoury, Department of Economics, College of Commerce (Magadh University), Patna

M.M. Nazri, Department of Commerce, Karim City College, Jamshedpur

Md Imteyaz Hassan, Department of Commerce, College of Commerce, Patna

Bhagwan Prasad Singh, Professor of Economics, Patna University, Patna

Arjun Kondamani, Vice President (Finance), Merill Lynch, USA

Indradeo Sharma, A.N. Sinha Institute of Social Studies, Patna

Renu Sinha, A.N. Sinha Institute of Social Studies, Patna

Bipul Vikash, Faculty, Department of Economics, Magadh Mahila College, Patna (Bihar)

Chapter 1

BANKING SECTOR REFORMS IN INDIA AND THE CHALLENGES AHEAD

Asha Singh

INTRODUCTION

Finance and growth are closely correlated. As the economy grows and becomes more vibrant, the banking sector has to develop accordingly in a way that it supports and stimulates such growth. With increasing pace of globalization, the Indian banking system has also to be strengthened to make it competitive. India has had more than a decade of banking sector reforms during which there has been considerable changes. It is, therefore, appropriate to assess the efficacy of the reform process in banking sector. It may be mentioned that the path of reforms in India has been different from most other developed economies. It has been a gradual, cautious and steady process.

The banking system in India consists of commercial and cooperative banks, of which the former account for around 98 per cent of banking system assets. Based on the ownership pattern, the commercial banks can be in grouped into three types–state owned or public sector banks (PSBs), private banks under Indian ownership, and foreign banks. The 27 PSBs dominate the commercial banking system of India, accounting for a little more than 80 per cent of commercial banking assets.

The rest of the paper is organized as follows. Section II includes a brief review of the strategy of banking development in India. Section III provides bird's-eye view of the banking sector reforms. Section IV covers the analysis of the impact of reform on banking industry. Section V outlines the broad areas of challenges before the banking sector. Section VI concludes.

STRATEGY OF BANKING DEVELOPMENT

In the last over five decades since independence, Banking in India has evolved through broadly four distinct phases *viz.*, (a) Foundation phase (1950-1969); (b) Expansion phase (1969-1984); (c) Consolidation phase (1985-1990); and (d) Reform phase (1991 onwards). During the foundation phase, the accent of the strategy was on development of the necessary legislative framework for facilitating reorganization and consolidation of the banking system. The expansionary process culminated with the nationalization of the 14 largest commercial banks in 1969 and subsequently of other six major commercial banks in 1980. A distinct transformation of far reaching significance occurred in the banking system during the decade and a half following the bank nationalization in 1969. Banking in India acquired a broad mass base and emerged as an important instrument of socio-economic change. A series of policy initiatives were taken in third phase aimed mainly at consolidation and diversification in the banking system. The consolidation measures, *inter alia*, included–a slowdown in branch expansion, comprehensive action plan of individual banks covering organization and structure, credit management, recovery, staff productivity, profitability and computerization.

However, the pre-reform period witnessed major regulatory constraints on the banking sector which not only distorted the efficiency of the interest rate mechanism but also adversely affected the viability and profitability of banks such as-large pre-emptions–both in terms of the statutory holding of Government securities (statutory liquidity ratio, or SLR as high as 38.5 per cent) and cash reserve ratio (CRR) as high as

15 per cent; and complex structure of administered interest rates.

BANKING SECTOR REFORMS

In order to support the major changes that took place in trade and industrial policies in the wake of the macroeconomic crisis in 1991, to protect the interest of depositors and investors, and also to enhance competitiveness and efficiency, a thorough review of the financial system including banking sector was felt necessary. Consequently, the Narasimham Committee was set up by the Government of India in 1991. The main goal in the early phase of reforms (1991-first generation) was to create an efficient, productive and profitable financial service industry operating within the environment of operating flexibility and functional autonomy. The objective of the second phase of reforms (Narasimham Committee II - 1998 - second generation) has been the strengthening of the financial system and introduction of structural improvements. Noteworthy developments in the banking system over the period were– (a) financial repression through statutory pre-emptions were lowered. Illustratively, at end-March 2006, the CRR stood at 5 per cent (legal minimum is 3 per cent) and SLR at 25 per cent (legal minimum); (b) The administered interest rate regime was dismantled, allowing banks the freedom to choose their deposit and lending rates based on the prevailing market conditions; (c) Competition was infused by allowing more liberal entry of foreign banks and permitting functioning of new private banks; (d) A set of micro-prudential measures (capital adequacy requirements, income recognition, asset classification and provisioning norms for loans, exposure norms, accounting norms) was stipulated; (e) The banking system has also witnessed greater levels of transparency and standards of disclosure; (f) As the banking system has liberalized and become increasingly market-oriented, the financial markets have been concurrently developed, while the conduct of monetary policy has been tailored to take into account the realities of the changing environment (switch to indirect instruments); (g) allowing foreign direct investment in the private sector banks; (h) Strengthening Bank regulation and supervision towards international best practices; (i) Streamlining supervision process through combination of on-site and off-site surveillance along with external auditing; (j) Introducing Risk based supervision; (k) Introducing process of structured and discretionary intervention for problem banks through a prompt corrective action mechanism; and (l) Measures have also been taken to broaden the ownership base of PSBs by enhancing the role of public shareholders in nationalised banks by gradual reduction of Government shareholding in these banks. Ownership in public sector banks is now well diversified. As at end-March 2005, the holding by general public in six banks ranged between 40 and 49 per cent and in 12 banks between 30 and 49 per cent. Only in four banks, the Government holding was more than 90 per cent (Table 1). It may be mentioned that one of the major objectives of banking sector reforms has been to enhance efficiency and productivity, which were achieved over the years, *inter alia*, through above measures.

Table 1
Private Shareholding in Public Sector Banks*
(As on March 31, 2005)

Shareholding (in per cent)	*Number of Banks*
Up to 10	4
More than 10 and up to 20	–
More than 20 and up to 30	5
More than 30 and up to 40	6
More than 40 and up to 49	6

* : Including 19 nationalised banks, State Bank of India and IDBI Ltd.

– : Nil/Negligible

Source: Report on Trend and Progress of Banking in India, Reserve Bank of India.

IMPACT OF BANKING SECTOR REFORM

The cumulative impact of these measures is that banks have been accorded greater discretion in sourcing and utilisation of resources albeit in an increasingly competitive environment. These reform measures have also had a major impact on the overall efficiency and stability of the banking system in India.

Table 2
Banking Industry Profile - 1990-91 to 2004-05

	1990-91			*1995-96*			*2004-05*		
Year/Bank Group	*PSB*	*Private*	*Foreign*	*PSB*	*Private*	*Foreign*	*PSB*	*Private*	*Foreign*
1. No. of banks	28	25	23	27	35	29	28	29	31
2. Share (%) of									
(a) Assets	91.4	3.7	4.9	84.5	6.5	7.9	75.3	18.2	6.5
(b) Deposits	92.0	4.0	4.0	85.4	6.6	6.7	78.2	17.1	4.7
(c) Credit	93.0	4.0	3.0	82.4	6.8	8.9	74.2	19.2	6.5
(d) Income	89.4	3.3	7.3	82.5	8.2	9.4	76.4	16.9	6.7
(e) Expenses	90.0	3.3	6.8	84.1	7.5	8.4	76.7	16.9	6.4
(f) Profit	68.5	4.1	27.4	-33.3	55.6	77.8	74.2	16.4	9.4

PSB: Public Sector Banks
Source: Report on Trend and Progress of Banking in India, Reserve Bank of India.

The present capital adequacy of Indian banks is comparable to those at international level. There has been a marked improvement in the asset quality with the percentage of gross non-performing assets (NPAs) to gross advances for the banking system reduced from 14.4 per cent in 1998 to 7.2 per cent in 2004. The reform measures have also resulted in an improvement in the profitability of banks. The Return on Assets (RoA) of the banks rose from 0.4 per cent in the year 1991-92 to 1.2 per cent in 2003-04. Considering that, globally, the RoA has been in the range 0.9 to 1.5 per cent for 2004, Indian banks are well placed. The banking sector reforms also emphasized the need to review the manpower resources and rationalize the requirements by drawing a realistic plan so as to reduce the operating cost and improve the profitability. During the last five years, the business per employee for public sector banks more than doubled to around Rs.250 lakh in 2004. A summary profile of the banking sector since 1991 is set out in Table 2.

Albeit, there could be many ways of analysing the impact of reform on the banking sector, but select indicators that have been analysed in this paper are - non-performing assets as percentage to total advances; non-interest income as percentage to total assets; burden as percentage to total assets; spread as percentage to total assets; productivity (*viz.*, business per employee and profit per employee); net profit as percentage to total assets; relative share of bank stock and pace of technology.

Despite the gradual tightening of prudential norms, the ratio of NPAs to total assets, which was at a high of 24.8 per cent for PSBs at end-March 1994, has declined to 5.5 per cent at end-March 2005 (Table 3). Net NPAs also witnessed a significant decline, driven by the improvements in loan loss provisioning and improved recovery management, which comprises over half of the total provisions and contingencies. Capital adequacy of the banking sector also recorded a marked improvement and reached 12.8 per cent at end-March 2005, well above the stipulated level of 9 per cent.

Table 3
Non-performing Assets (NPAs) in Banking Sector - 1994-2005
(As % to Total Advances)

Year (End-March)	*PSB*	*Old Private Banks*	*New Private Banks*	*Foreign Banks*
1994	24.8	–	–	–
1995	19.5	–	–	–
1996	18.0	–	–	–
1997	17.8	10.7	2.6	4.3
1998	16.0	10.9	3.5	6.4
1999	15.9	13.1	6.2	7.6
2000	14.0	10.8	4.1	7.0
2001	12.4	10.9	5.1	6.8
2002	11.1	11.0	8.9	5.4
2003	9.4	8.9	6.7	5.3
2004	7.8	7.6	5.0	4.6
2005	5.5	6.0	3.6	2.8

-: Not available.
Source: Statistical Tables relating to Banks in India, Reserve Bank of India.

Table 4
Non-interest Income in Banking Sector - 1992-2004
(As % to Total Asset)

Year (End-March)	*Public Sector Banks*	*Private Banks*	*Foreign Banks*
1992	1.2	1.0	3.4
1993	1.2	1.1	1.0
1994	1.3	1.3	2.2
1995	1.3	1.4	2.5
1996	1.4	1.7	2.4
1997	1.3	1.6	2.5
1998	1.3	1.9	3.0
1999	1.2	1.4	2.5
2000	1.3	1.7	2.6
2001	1.2	1.3	2.5
2002	1.4	1.6	2.9
2003	1.7	2.5	2.6
2004	1.9	2.1	3.0

Source: Statistical Tables relating to Banks in India, Reserve Bank of India.

Since the second half of the 90s, both interest income and interest expenditure of banks as proportions of total assets have declined due to the benign interest rate regime. Interest expenditure declined faster than interest income, resulting in an increase in net interest income. However, non-interest income, which emanates mostly from fee-based activities, has been increasing consistently in the post-reform period. For example, non-interest income as a proportion of total assets of PSBs increased from 1.2 per cent in 1992 to 1.9 per cent in 2004 (Table 4). It may be mentioned that public sector banks, are yet to catch-up fully with their foreign counterparts.

Table 5
Burden in Banking Sector- 1992-2004
(As % to Total Asset)

Year (End-March)	*Public Sector Banks*	*Private Banks*	*Foreign Banks*
1992	1.4	1.9	-1.1
1993	1.4	1.6	1.7
1994	1.4	1.2	0.4
1995	1.6	0.9	0.3
1996	1.6	0.8	0.4
1997	1.6	0.7	0.5
1998	1.3	0.2	0.0
1999	1.4	0.7	0.9
2000	1.2	0.2	0.5
2001	1.5	0.6	0.7
2002	0.9	-0.1	0.1
2003	0.6	-0.5	0.1
2004	0.3	-0.1	-0.2

Note: Burden means non-interest expense *minus* non-interest income.
Source: Statistical Tables relating to Banks in India, Reserve Bank of India.

Improvements in efficiency of the banking sector are expected to be reflected, *inter alia*, in a reduction in operating expenditure, interest spread and cost of intermediation (*i.e.* ratio of operating expense to total assets). Intermediation cost in general witnessed a gradual reduction in the post reform era across bank groups excepting foreign banks but still remained higher than those in developed economies. This intermediation cost needs to be seen in conjunction with non-interest income. Till 2001, the burden (*i.e.* excess of non-interest expenditure over non-interest income as a percentage to total assets) of public sector banks hovered in the range of 1.2-1.6 per cent. It may be mentioned that the burden reflects the extent to which non-interest expenses are recovered through non-interest income. The gap between intermediation cost and income from fee-based activities (*i.e.* non-interest income) has narrowed considerably in recent years. The burden in public sector banks declined from 1.4 per cent in 1992 to 0.3 per cent in 2004 (Table 5). The improvement in respect of private banks has been remarkable in recent years and it has surpassed their intermediation cost and has resulted in a negative burden.

Table 6
Spread in Banking Sector - 1992-2004
(As % to Total Asset)

Year (End-March)	*Public Sector Banks*	*Private Banks*	*Foreign Banks*
1992	3.2	4.0	3.9
1993	2.4	2.9	3.6
1994	2.4	3.0	4.2
1995	2.9	3.1	4.3
1996	3.1	3.1	3.8
1997	3.2	2.9	4.1
1998	2.9	2.5	4.0
1999	2.8	2.1	3.5
2000	2.7	2.1	3.8
2001	2.8	2.3	3.6
2002	2.7	1.6	3.2
2003	2.5	2.0	3.4
2004	3.0	2.2	3.5
2005	2.9	2.3	3.3

Note: Spread means interest income (earned) *minus* interest expenditure (paid).

Source: Report on Trend and Progress of Banking in India, Reserve Bank of India.

Analysing Spread (*i.e.* excess of interest income over interest expense as ratio to total bank assets; lower ratio is an indicative of higher efficiency) as yet another indicator of efficiency of banks, it is observed that spread (also called net interest margin) was at 3.2 per cent in 1992 and thereafter, it recorded a relatively modest decline to around 3.0 per cent in recent years (Table 6). It may be mentioned that it is the foreign banks, which by virtue of their ability to mobilise low-cost deposits, have the highest net interest margin, whereas those for private banks have been the lowest in recent years. In case of developed economies, banks have net interest margin in respect to total assets of about 2 per cent.

The labour productivity indicators such as business per employee and profit per employee may be assessed to work out the productivity in banking sector. The business per employee of banking sector increased about three times from Rs.54 lakh in 1992 to Rs.163 lakh in 2004 while the profit per employee increased more than seven-fold from Rs.20,000 to Rs.1.50, lakh over the same period (Table 7). There has been a distinctive productivity improvement in the banking sector during the reform period on account of technological improvement and a catching up effect (*i.e.* competitiveness compelling banks to raise productivity levels).

Table 7
Productivity Indicators of Scheduled Commercial Banks

(Rs. lakh)

Year	*Business Per Employee*	*Profit Per Employee*
1992	54	0.20
1993	54	-0.50
1994	54	-0.40
1995	56	0.20
1996	60	0.10
1997	66	0.40
1998	75	0.50
1999	84	0.30
2000	97	0.50
2001	115	0.50
2002	137	0.90
2003	150	1.20
2004	163	1.50

Source: Statistical Tables relating to Banks in India, Reserve Bank of India.

Net profit of the public sector banks increased over three-fold, from 0.28 per cent of total assets in 1992 to 0.89 per cent in 2005 while it increased by almost one and half-fold for the private banks during the same period (Table 8). This ratio, however, declined in case of foreign banks from 1.57 per cent in 1992 to 1.30 per cent in 2005. The public sector banks are favourably impacted by the consolidation and reform process since 1992.

Table 8
Net Profit in Banking Sector
(As % to Total Assets)

Year (End-March)	*Public Sector Banks*	*Private Banks*	*Foreign Banks*	*Scheduled Commercial Banks*
1992	0.28	0.57	1.57	0.39
1993	-0.99	0.34	-2.88	-1.08
1994	-1.15	0.56	1.51	-0.85
1995	0.25	1.06	1.66	0.41
1996	-0.07	1.21	1.58	0.16
1997	0.57	1.13	1.19	0.67
1998	0.77	1.04	0.97	0.82
1999	0.42	0.68	0.69	0.47
2000	0.57	0.88	1.17	0.66
2001	0.42	0.70	0.93	0.49
2002	0.72	0.66	1.32	0.75
2003	0.96	1.00	1.56	1.01
2004	1.12	0.95	1.65	1.13
2005	0.89	0.83	1.30	0.91

Source: Report on Trend and Progress of Banking in India, Reserve Bank of India.

In an increasingly market oriented environment, banks need to continuously raise capital to sustain the growth in their operations. Several banks, therefore, accessed the capital market during 2004-05 to strengthen their capital base. The progress of the banking sector reforms along with improvement in bank's balance sheets resulted in increased interest in bank stocks. These also benefited from several other positive factors such as the implementation of the Securitisation and Reconstruction of Financial Assets and Enforcement of Security Interest Act, permission to foreign banks to acquire up to 75 per cent in the weaker private sector banks and the news about the Union Cabinet's approval to amend the

Banking Regulation Act, 1949 to lift the 10 per cent voting rights cap in private sector banks and to amend the law to enable banking companies to issue preference shares. Satisfactory financial performance by public sector and new private sector banks despite rise in interest rates was another factor that led to increased interest in bank stocks. Market participants, in general, revised upward their expectations of future earnings by banks. Reflecting this, the banking sector stocks outperformed the market during 2004-05. Bank stocks now constitute a significant portion of market capitalisation of the Indian equity market, even though there was some slide in their share at end-March 2005 in comparison with end-March 2004 (Table 9).

Table 9
Relative Share of Bank Stocks –Turnover and Market Capitalisation

(Per cent)

Year	*Share of Turnover of Bank Stocks in Total Turnover*	*Share of Capitalisation of Bank Stocks in Total Market Capitalisation*
2003-04	4.96	9.09
2004-05	7.35	8.64

Source: Report on Trend and Progress of Banking in India, Reserve Bank of India.

CHALLENGES AHEAD IN BANKING SECTOR

The enhanced role of the banking sector in the Indian economy, the increasing levels of deregulation along with the increasing levels of competition have facilitated globalisation in the banking system and placed numerous demands on banks. Operating in this demanding environment has exposed banks to various challenges. The recent years have witnessed considerable changes in the financial sector - new banks, new financial institutions, new instruments, new windows and new opportunities–and along with all this, new challenges. While deregulation has opened up new vistas for banks to augment revenues, it has entailed greater competition and consequently greater risks. Demand for new products, particularly derivatives, has required banks to diversify their product mix and also effect rapid changes in their processes and operations in order to remain competitive in the globalised environment. A few broad challenges faced by the banks in the integrated economies could be-enhancement of customer service; application of technology; implementation of Basel II; improvement of risk management systems; implementation of new accounting standards; enhancement of transparency and disclosures; compliance with Know Your Customers (KYCs) aspects, enhancing corporate governance and outsourcing risks.

Customer Service

It is no longer applicable for banks to provide only traditional banking services. Apart from providing the conventional banking services, banks have begun offering a bouquet of financial services to their clients, including cross selling of financial products. The ultimate aim is to offer a one-stop-shop for meeting varied customers' financial needs. Some banks have begun employing customer relationship management systems to not only retain the existing customers but also to attract new customers. The establishment of new private sector banks and foreign banks has rapidly changed the competitive landscape in the consumer banking industry and placed greater demands on banks to gear themselves up to meet the increasing needs of customers. It is not only relevant to offer a wide menu of services to bank customers but also provide these in an increasingly efficient manner in terms of cost, time and convenience. It would, therefore, be reasonable to expect banks to focus on the above aspects while designing their products for customers.

Technology

This is one area where perhaps banks need to do significant 'catching up', notwithstanding the rapid strides made over the last few years, though data on this score are difficult to obtain. Some available figures indicate that the percentage of customers using online banking is little over 1 per cent in India, compared with anywhere in the range of 5.5-29.5 per cent in developed economies. It may be mentioned that despite India happens to be the hub of the information technology, its usage in the banking industry is negligible. It is, therefore, important for the banking sector to exploit this high-tech expertise available to their maximum advantage. In this endeavour, banks have been investing to computerise their branches and in new delivery channels such as Automated Teller Machines (ATMs), phone banking, internet banking and mobile banking. As on March 31, 2005, public sector banks had incurred an expenditure of Rs.9,487 crore on computerisation and development of communication networks. Computerisation of banking business has received high importance in recent years. While new private sector banks, foreign banks and a few older private sector banks have already put in place 'core banking solutions', public sector banks are adopting similar systems. The directive by the Central Vigilance Commission (CVC) to achieve 100 per cent computerisation has resulted in renewed vigour in these banks towards fulfilment of this requirement which could go a long way to improve customer service. All PSBs, except eight, had achieved 100 per cent fully/partially computerisation of their branches. As at end-March 2005, more than 90 per cent branches of public sector banks were fully or partially computerised (Table 10). Out of 27 public sector banks, as many as nine public sector banks had 100 per cent computerised branches. Nineteen banks had more than 50 per cent computerised branches.

Table 10
Computerisation in Public Sector Banks
(As on March 31, 2005)

(Per cent)

Branches already Fully Computerised #	60.0
Branches Under Core Banking Solution	11.0
Fully Computerised Branches (i + ii)	71.0
Partially Computerised Branches	21.8

: Other than branches under Core Banking Solution.

Source: Report on Trend and Progress of Banking in India, Reserve Bank of India.

Total number of ATMs installed in the country was 17,642 at end-March 2005. New private sector banks constituted the largest share of ATMs, followed by the State Bank of India (SBI) group, nationalised banks, old private sector banks and foreign banks. While nationalised banks and old private sector banks had more on-site ATMs than off-site ATMs, SBI group, new private sector banks and foreign banks had more off-site ATMs than on-site ATMs. Off-site ATMs as percentage to total branches was the highest in the case of foreign banks, followed by new private sector banks, SBI group, old private sector banks and nationalised banks. Although cash continues to be used heavily in retail transactions in India, the use of cheques and several other payment instruments such as credit cards, debit cards and smart cards, on the whole, has been increasing in recent years. The use of payment cards, both in volume and value terms, more than doubled in 2004-05. The use of electronic payments in the form of Electronic Clearing Service (ECS), Electronic Funds Transfer (EFT) and Special Electronic Funds Transfer (SEFT) is also on increase. As a result of sharp increase in Real Time Gross Settlement System (RTGS) and other electronic transactions, the proportion of electronic transactions both in volume and value terms has increased sharply (Table 11). Electronic payments are cheaper as they have lower production cost than paper-based instruments. They can also be carried out faster in comparison with paper-based transactions. The increased use of electronic payments has, thus, increased the efficiency of the payment system.

Risk Management

Banking in modern economies is more concerned about risk management. The successful implementation of Basel II Accord (to be implemented with effect from March 31, 2007) is likely to lead to an even sharper focus on the risk measurement and risk management at the institutional level. It may be mentioned that the Basel Committee has, through its various publications, provided useful guidelines on managing the various facets of risk in banking. With the introduction of capital charge for market risks with effect from March 31, 2005, banks in India

Table 11

Paper-based *Versus* Electronic Transactions

Year	*Volume (in million)*			*Value (Rs. crore)*		
	Paper-based	*Electronic*	*Total*	*Paper-based*	*Electronic*	*Total*
2002-03	1,014	173	1,187	1,34,24,313	37,536	1,34,61,849
2003-04	1,023	224	1,247	1,15,94,976	67,352	1,16,62,328
2004-05	1,125	432	1,557	1,10,47,052	42,24,746	1,52,71,798

Source: Report on Trend and Progress of Banking in India, Reserve Bank of India.

are compliant with all elements of Basel I. Basel II is the revised framework for capital adequacy for banks and implementation of Basel II will require more capital for banks in India due to the fact that operational risk is not captured under Basel I. The institution of sound risk management practices would be an important pillar for staying ahead of the competition. Banks can, on their part, formulate 'early warning indicators' suited to their own requirements, business profile and risk appetite for better monitoring and managing risks.

Corporate Governance

The quality of corporate governance in the banks becomes critical as competition intensifies, banks strive to retain their client base and regulators move out of controls and micro-regulation. It is relevant to note that there is nothing like an 'optimal' level of governance for banking industry to be satisfied with. The objective would be to continuously strive for excellence. The improved corporate governance practice would also provide an opportunity to accord greater freedom to the banks' boards and move away from micro regulation to macro management.

International Accounting Standards

One of the prime international standards considered relevant for ensuring a safe and sound banking system is the 'Core Principles for Effective Banking Supervision' issued by the Basel Committee on Banking Supervision (BCBS). Accounting standards are now a part of the set of twelve standards that have been identified by the Financial Stability Forum as conducive to a robust financial infrastructure. Financial reporting and prudential supervision have slightly different perspectives. While the former is oriented towards capturing the historical position, the latter has a forward looking element particularly with reference to measurement of impairment and capital. An important challenge, therefore, would be to ensure that accounting standards and prudential frameworks are mutually consistent.

Outsourcing Risks

Banks are increasingly using outsourcing for either reducing operational costs or tapping expertise which is not available internally. Outsourced financial services include applications processing, document processing, investment management, marketing and research, supervision of loans, data processing and back office related activities. It is worth noting that outsourcing might give rise to several risks including, strategic risk, compliance risk, operational risk, access risk, concentration risk and systemic risk. The failure of a service provider to provide a specified service, ensure security or confidentiality, comply with legal and regulatory requirements can lead to financial losses or reputational risk for the bank and could also lead to systemic risks for the entire banking system in a country. It would, therefore, be important for the bank outsourcing its activities to ensure effective management of such risks.

CONCLUDING OBSERVATION

With the increasing levels of globalisation of the Indian banking industry, evolution of universal banks and bundling of financial services, competition in the banking industry is likely to intensify further. The banking industry has the potential and the ability to follow and implement the rapid pace of automation which has already had a profound impact on raising the standard of banking services. Strong capital positions and balance sheets (*i.e.* financial strength) place banking industry in a better position to deal with any external shocks. Banking sector needs to supplement financial strength with sound risk management practices to face future challenges for achieving and sustaining high banking operating standards. Thus, consolidation, competition and risk management would be critical to the future of banking industry in the context of India economy.

REFERENCES

—Reserve Bank of India (1991), *'Report of the Committee on the Financial System'* (Chairman: M Narasimham), Reserve Bank of India.

Jalan, B. (1992) (Ed), *'The Indian Economy-Problems and Prospects'*, Penguin Books India Ltd.

Jadhav, N. (1996) (Ed), *'Challenges to Indian Banking–Competition, Globalization and Financial Markets'*, Second Edition, Macmillan India Ltd.

Subramanian, K and Velayudham, T.K. (1997), *'Banking Reforms in India – Managing Change'*, Tata McGraw Hill Publishing Company Ltd.

Joshi, V.C. and Joshi, V.V. (1998), *'Managing Indian Banks–The Challenges Ahead'*, Response Books.

—Government of India (1998), *'Report of the Committee on Banking Sector Reforms'* (Chairman: M Narasimham), Government of India.

Banerjee, A and Singh, S.K. (2001) (Ed), *'Banking and Financial Sector Reforms in India'*, Deep & Deep Publications Pvt. Ltd.

Rangarajan, C. (1998), *'Banking Sector Reforms: Rationale and Relevance'*, SICOM Silver Jubilee Memorial Lecture, Mumbai.

Jalan, B. (2000), *'Agenda for Banking in the New Millennium'*, Reserve Bank of India Bulletin, March.

Ram Mohan, T.T. (2002), *'Deregulation and Performance of Public Sector Banks'*, EPW, February 2.

Bhide, M G; Prasad, A and Ghosh, S. (2002), *'Banking Sector Reforms–A Critical Overview'*, EPW, February 2.

Mohan R. (2005), *'Financial Sector Reforms in India–Policies and Performance Analysis'*, EPW, March 19.

Das, A; Nag, A and Ray, S. C. (2005), *'Liberalization, Ownership and Efficiency in Indian Banking– A Nonparametric Analysis'*, EPW, March 19.

Jalan, B. (2002), *'Indian Banking and Finance- Managing New Challenges'*, Speech, Bank Economists Conference, Kolkata, January 14.

Reddy, Y.V. (2004), *'Banking Sector in Global Perspective'*, Speech, Bankers' Conference.

Reddy, Y.V. (2005): *'Banking Sector Reforms in India- An Overview'*, Speech, Institute of Bankers of Pakistan, Karachi, May 18.

Mohan, R. (2005), *'Reforms, Productivity and Efficiency in Banking – The Indian Experience'*, Speech, 21st Annual General Meeting and Conference of the Pakistan Society of Development Economists, Islamabad, December.

Leeladhar, V. (2006), *'Indian Banks and the Global Challenges'*, Speech, Seminar, Indian Merchants' Chamber and Indian Banks' Association, Mumbai, January 31.

—Reserve Bank of India: *'Report on Trend and Progress of Banking in India'*, Various Issues.

—Reserve Bank of India: *'Statistical Tables Relating to Banks in India'*, various issues.

—Reserve Bank of India: Monthly Bulletin, various issues.

CHAPTER 2

BANKING SECTOR REFORMS AND RTGS MECHANISM

M. S. Gupta

INTRODUCTION

Payment and settlement systems constitute the backbone of the financial economy. The objective of an efficient payment system is to minimize systemic risk. Moreover, operating in a globally competitive environment requires a high level of technology development. The oversight of payment system is an essential function of central bank, aiming to ensure the smooth functioning of payment system and seeking to contribute to financial stability. The payment system is also important for the integration of financial markets, which in turn facilitates transmission of monetary policy impulses. The payment system influences the speed, financial risk, reliability and cost of domestic and international transactions.

The Reserve Bank of India has made concerted efforts at developing a safe, secure and efficient payment and settlement system to enhance financial stability. In the process of improving the overall efficiency of the payment and settlement systems in the country, the Reserve Bank, apart from performing the regulatory and oversight functions, has also undertaken promotional and institutional activities. During 2004-05, the thrust of Reserve Bank's policy initiatives was on widening the range electronic payment products and building a sound institutional framework for regulation and supervision. The stabilization of the Real Time Gross Settlement (RTGS) System is a significant development.

CONCEPT OF RTGS

The Real Time Gross Settlement (RTGS) System has been launched by the Reserve Bank of India on 26th March 2004 in Indian Financial Market after a comprehensive audit and review of the software and also by conducting extensive training of users at commercial banks. The RTGS provides for an electronic based settlement of inter-bank and customer based transactions with intra-day collateralized liquidity (IDL) support from the Reserve Bank of India to the participants of the system. It is a system of transferring funds from one Bank/ Financial Institution to another on an immediate basis. In this system, the inter-bank payment instructions are processed and settled, transaction-by-transaction, one-by-one, continuously, i.e. in real time. In other words, these transactions are settled individually without netting debits against credits. It is fully integrated with the Accounting System of the Reserve Bank of India and other settlement services such as Deferred Net Settlement (DNS) System, the settlement of which is performed as RTGS transactions through a facility for Multi Lateral Net Settlement batch processing.

The RTGS System has several unique features. It is a single, all-India system, with the settlement being effected in Mumbai. The payments are settled transaction by transaction. The settlement of funds is final and irrevocable. The settlement is done in real time; the funds settled can be further used immediately. It is a fully secure system, which uses digital signatures and Public Key Infrastructure (PKI) based encryption for safe and secure message transmission. It provides for intra-day collateralized liquidity support for the member-banks to smoothen the temporary mismatches of fund flows and thereby ensuring smooth settlements. Under the

RTGS System, inter-bank transactions; customer based inter-bank transactions and net-clearing transactions can be settled. Both high value and retail payments can be effective through the RTGS System. Thus, it provides less risk-based fund transfers for both banks and for their customers apart from providing for more efficient funds management at the treasuries of banks. Thus, the RTGS arrangement enables banks to ensure transfer of funds instantaneously among the member banks of the system all over the country through electronic transfer mechanism availing the benefit of pooling of funds at different centers for optimum utilization. The system has also enabled for straight through processing (STP) of customer transaction without manual transaction.

SALIENT FEATURES OF RTGS

The RTGS System will be fully integrated with the Accounting System of the Reserve Bank of India and other settlement services, such as, Deferred Net Settlement (DNS) Systems, the settlement of which would be performed as RTGS transactions through a facility for Multi Lateral Net Settlement (MLNS) Batch Processing.

In modern age, technology has been the driving force for all the banking transactions all over the world. Not surprisingly, the present RTGS System also makes use of the state-of-the-art solution by using INFINET as its secure communication backbone, Structured Financial Messaging Solutions (SFMS) as the secure messaging system, IBM's S/390 mainframe system as the robust platform at the back-end for implementation, Quaestor, a product from the solution developer, Logical India, to be customized and used as the front end for solution, while MQ series would act as the (gluing) interface between the various components of the solution.

The RTGS System has several unique features. It is a single, all-India system, with the settlement being effected in Mumbai. The payments are settled transaction by transaction. The settlement of funds is final and irrevocable. The settlement is done in real time; the funds settled can be further used immediately. It is a fully secure system, which uses digital signatures and Public Key Infrastructure (PKI) based encryption for safe and secure message transmission. It provides for intra-day collateralized liquidity support for the member-banks to smoothen the temporary mismatches of fund flows and thereby ensuring smooth settlements. Under the RTGS System, inter-bank transactions; customer based inter-bank transactions and net-clearing transactions can be settled. Both high value and retail payments can be effective through the RTGS System. Thus, it provides less risk-based fund transfers for both banks and for their customers apart from providing for more efficient funds management at the treasuries of banks.

Business Process Re-engineering – A Pre-requisite for Banks

Further, the introduction of the RTGS System will require business process re-engineering in the banks. Therefore, banks will require to re-visit the existing procedures/processes in their respective organizations. The recycling of the existing procedures/processes in the unfolding RTGS environment will not help banks optimally realize benefits from the RTGS System.

The RTGS System will provide 'real time on-line gross settlement' of the payment transactions depending upon the availability of sufficient liquidity in banks' Settlement Accounts and therefore, proper liquidity management will assume significantly greater importance and acquire real time dimensions for each banks.

This will require process re-engineering to be addressed by each bank individually and the procedural changes will have to be duly communicated and in-grained in field functionaries, the front line interface with the ordinary customers.

The whole customer banking will have to be re-oriented and the customers will also require to be educated by each banks, as the RTGS System will be a credit transfer system only as against the current cheques/instruments based systems, which are debit transfer systems.

The implementation of the RTGS System will also open up newer avenues for product innovation, arising out of Intra-day liquidity management and the consequential financial support to be extended to other RTGS participants with inferior liquidity management infrastructure.

Further, the fee based RTGS services extended to the customers will also provide a source of additional revenue. Banks will also require to focus on these areas to optimally benefit from the introduction of the RTGS System.

Essential Components of RTGS

For using RTGS mechanism, following are the essential components which needs to be addressed by banks:

- Membership of Indian Financial System Network (INFINET)
- Establishment of Payments Gateway
- Branch connectivity with Payments Gateway
- Use of Structured Financial Messaging System (SFMS) as a common message format
- Use of Electronic Coding and Decoding Technology
- Unique Identification of Bank's Branch for RTGS

Types of Transaction Covered Under RTGS

RTGS System covers the payment and settlement transactions of the following types:

- Inter-bank Payments
- Customer-to-Customer Transfers
- Own Account Transfers
- Multilateral Net Settlement Batches

Technological Components of RTGS

RTGS System uses the state of art technology in processing the payment and settlement requests. The important components and technologies used in the process are INFINET, SFMS, PKI. These are explained in detailed below:

Indian Financial Network (INFINET)

The RBI has established The Institute for Development and Research in Banking Technology (IDRBT) at Hyderabad. IDRBT has taken initiative to setup a communication backbone Indian financial Network (known as INFINET) using both V-SATs and terrestrial leased line technology to provide wide area network connectivity exclusively for the use of a closer user group – the entities in the Indian banking and financial sector. The earth station is located at Hyderabad and almost all the banks and financial institutions are members in the network. This being a network of closer user group and is being managed by IDRBT, other public will not have access. INFINET becomes a reliable communication backbone and the transactions or messages passed through this network are safe and secure.

Structured Financial Messaging System (SFMS)

Banking community is familiar with the use of SWIFT messages and formats in case of international financial messages. IDRBT has developed a secure messaging backbone for the Indian Banking and Financial Sector and named it Structured Financial Messaging System (SFMS). IDRBT has studied the various applications requiring messaging, reviewed the existing message formats and designed various standard message formats for communicating message across the banks. As the messages mainly relate to financial transactions, taking into consideration the security aspects, the messaging system is further fortified, by providing facilities such as encryption and digital signatures.

Public Key Infrastructure (PKI)

In the physical world, the signature of a person is used and associated to establish identity and credibility of the individual. 'Creating trust' in an electronic environment involves assuring the transacting entities about the confidentiality of the transaction, along with authentication of the sending and receiving entities such that both entities cannot repudiate the transaction. The technology used to achieve this trust is Public Key Infrastructure (PKI).

PKI is an online infrastructure using encryption, digital signatures and digital certificates. The paper based concepts of identification, declaration and proof are carried out through the use of digital signatures in electronic environment. Digital signatures are created and verified using Public Key Cryptography. The combinations of many factors are taken and two pairs of keys–Public Key and Private Key are generated using the algorithm. The two pairs will remain unique – i.e. no two pairs will be similar.

The keys are generated once and the private key is directly downloaded on to the smart card or system. Either the issuer or the owner or anybody cannot view and read the private key written on the smart card. The owner of a smart card is expected to take care of its protection. Public key is stored in the repository of the issuer and is available to everyone.

How does a digital signature work?

The private key is used for digitally signing a document while the public key is used for verifying the digital signature. The keys are generated using such a complicated algorithm that knowing the public key; one cannot compute the private key belonging to the owner.

Digital signature is more a process than just affixing of a signature. When a document is digitally signed, the digital software scans the document and creates a calculation, which represents the document. The calculation becomes part of the digital signature. When the recipient authenticates the signature, a similar process is carried out. The sender's and the receiver's calculations are then compared. If the results are the same, the signature is treated as valid. If they are different, the signature is treated as invalid.

How will RTGS function?

- Any scheduled bank can be a member of RTGS which is connected to Central HUB of RBI through INFINET via Payments Gateway of each Bank. The branches identified for RTGS will have connectivity to their Payments Gateway, viz., Treasury Branch.

- Communication will be based on Structured Financial Message System (SFMS) formats and the messages will flow as shown in the Chart-1.

MSG No. 1– Branch of Bank 'A' receives instructions from customer to remit the funds to beneficiary who is maintaining account with Branch of Bank 'B' which is also connected under RTGS. The user inputs the SFMS message and on authorization, the message will land in Branch Controller.

MSG No. 2– Branch Controller of Bank 'A' codifies the message and forwards it to Gateway of Bank 'A'.

MSG No. 3– Gateway of Bank 'A' receives the message in Incoming Q and routes to Central HUB.

MSG No. 4 & 5– Central Hub receives the messages at its Incoming Q and after processing forwards to the Gateway of Bank 'B' and also sent delivery message to Gateway of Bank 'A' (Refer MSG No.10).

MSG No. 6– Gateway of Bank 'B' receives message from Central HUB in its Incoming Q and puts in Out Q for destination Branch and also sends delivery message to Central HUB (Refer MSG No. 9)

MSG No. 7– Branch controller of destination Branch of Bank 'B' receives messages and after validations forward to branch user PC for application of funds. Thus, beneficiary's account gets credited.

MSG No. 8– This is an acknowledgement message from Incoming Q to Outgoing Q at Gateway of Bank 'B'.

. *MSG No. 9*– Acknowledgement message from Gateway of Bank 'B' to Central HUB.

MSG No. 10– Acknowledgement of delivery received by Bank 'B' is sent from Out Q of Central HUB to Gateway of Bank 'A'.

MSG No. 11– Acknowledgement message from Central HUB passed on to Branch Controller of remitting Bank.

PRESENT POSITION OF RTGS

The system was initially started with four banks besides the Reserve Bank of India. The RTGS facility is increasing day by day. At the end of June 2006, 96 banks including the Reserve

Table 1
Paper Based Vs RTGS Transaction

(Amount in Rs. Crore)

Year-End June	*Instrument-based Inter-bank Transactions*		*RTGS Inter-bank Transactions*		*RTGS Customer Transactions*		*Total RTGS Transactions*	
	Volume	*Value*	*Volume*	*Value*	*Volume*	*Value*	*Volume*	*Value*
1	2	3	4	5	6	7	8	9
2004	2,61,796	4,74,268	23,996	2,05,806	955	3,370	24,951	2,09,175
2005	–	–	2,04,290	18,39,311	67,504	2,06,796	2,71,794	20,46,107
2006	–	–	3,14,472	27,30,945	4,89,106	14,27,971	8,03,578	41,58,916

Source: RBI, Report on Trend and Progress of Banking in India, 2005-06, Table VI.4, p202.

Bank at over 21,916 branches in 2,793 centres in 469 districts have provided the facility. As at the end of July 2005, the number of branches providing this facility has touched 8200 at 418 centres. The growth of transactions under RTGS registered a substantial increase during 2005-06 covering both inter-bank and customer originated fund transfers. The value of transactions under RTGS during 2005-06 was Rs. 1,15,40,836 crores in which share of inter-bank transfer was Rs. 89,70,624 crores and customer originated transfer was Rs. 25,70,212 crores.

Chart 1
RTGS Message Flow
CENTRAL HUB

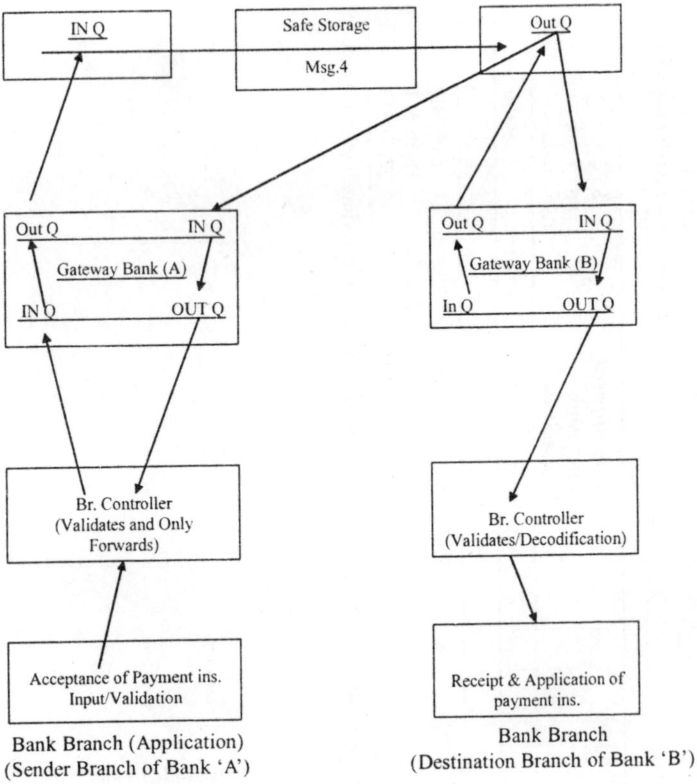

Source: Bank Quest, The Journal of Indian Institute of Banking & Finance, Vol. 76, No.1, January-March, 2005, p. 22

Paper Based Transaction Vs RTGS Transaction

A major development from the perspective of financial stability was the introduction of the RTGS in large-value funds transfer systems. As final settlement of individual inter-bank fund transfers is effected on a gross real time basis during the processing day, a major source of systemic risk in the financial system has been reduced substantially. RTGS transactions, both in terms of volume and value, have increased sharply in a short span of its operation as is evident from Table-1. The value of transactions being settled in the RTGS system is more than total amount of cheques, which were being settled earlier by the individual inter-bank clearings held in different centres.

Payment Systems

The Reserve Bank plays a proactive role in facilitating the payment systems initiatives of banks in providing various services like internet banking, mobile banking as other innovative services to their customers. While permitting such initiative by banks, the Reserve Bank prescribes minimum safeguards which the bank should put in place before implementing such channels for payments. The overall turnover in various payment and settlement systems rose by 35 per cent during the year 2005-06 on top of 67 per cent during 2004-05. The turnover in respect of RTGS transactions increased sharply. In terms of value, turnover in RTGS now constitutes the largest component, followed by foreign exchange clearing and high value clearing among the Systemically Important Payment Systems (SIPS) as evidenced from Table-2.

BENEFITS OF RTGS

RTGS offers various benefits to banks, branches and clients. Banks are benefited by optimum use of infrastructure already placed, better management of liquidity and cost saving, improvement in customer service while branches have benefits like funds transfer through electronic message system saving a lot of time and labour in work like issuance of Demand Draft, good source for improvement in non-interest income, faster disposal of customer's remittances giving an edge over the

Table 2

Payment System Indicators: Annual Turnover

	Volume (000s)			*Value (Rupees in Crores)*		
	2003-04	2004-05	2005-06	2003-04	2004-05	2005-06
Systemically Important Payment Systems (SIPS)						
Inter-bank Clearing	1,142	808	–	30,46,666	9,91,436	–
High Value Clearing	13,172	13,077	18,748	30,23,290	46,07,208	49,75,477
Negotiated Dealing System (NDS)	265	185	151	25,18,323	26,92,126	25,59,260
Forex Clearing	331	466	490	23,18,530	40,42,435	52,39,674
RTGS	67	460	1,767	1965	40,66,184	1,15,40,836
Total SIPS (1 to 5)	14,977	14,996	21,156	1,09,08,774	1,63,99,389	2,43,15,247
Others						
MICR Clearing	6,24,360	9,41,693	10,34,539	20,35,934	90,18,073	94,82,300
Non-MICR Clearing	3,34,039	2,25,392	2,52,911	30,05,139	11,02,643	18,54,763
Electronic Clearing	31,352	57,900	83,241	29,606	77,702	1,06,599
Cards	1,86,558	3,61,517	10,45,319	36,176	77,266	2,36,994
Total Others (6 to 9)	11,76,309	15,86,502	24,16,010	51,06,855	1,02,75,684	1,16,80,656
Grand Total (1 to 9)	11,91,286	16,01,498	24,37,166	1,60,15,629	2,66,75,073	3,59,95,903

Source: Reserve Bank of India, Annual Report, 2005-06,Table 8.1, p.205

Note:

1. Paper-based inter-bank was closed at Mumbai with effect from November 1, 2004 and subsequently at other centers in phases. By June 2005, it was discontinued at all the centers. Inter-bank transactions are now settled through settled through RTGS became operational on March 26, 2004
2. High value clearing refers to cheques of Rs. 1 lakh and above.
3. Settlement of NDS and Forex clearing is through Clearing Corporation of India Limited (CCIL).
4. At the end of March 2006, the MICR clearing was at 53 centres. Non-MICR clearing refers to all paper based clearings at the centers where MICR cheque processing centers have not been set up.
5. Electronic clearings comprise Electronic Clearing service (ECS), Electronic Funds Transfer (EFT), Special Electronic Funds Transfer (SEFT) and National Electronic Funds Transfer (NEFT).
6. Cards include Credit and Debit Cards.

competition and competitors. Lastly, customer is the real beneficiary under RTGS as he gets the funds almost simultaneously when remitter intends to remit. Hence, both the beneficiary as well as the remitter is delighted.

Apart from the above, the RTGS system has benefited the Indian financial system in several other ways such as (i) enhanced customer service by facilitating instantaneously and irrevocable funds transfer as against a day's lag in the case of instrument based inter-bank clearing; (ii) straight-through processing of payment transactions which include customer transactions; and (iii) mitigation of payment system risks inherent in deferred net settlement such as high value clearing and MICR clearing. Hence, it is an urgent need here to study the impact of RTGS operations on the financial sector.

RTGS Operations–Impact on Financial Sector

The RTGS system has brought about some significant benefits to the Indian financial system. Apart from enhancing the stability of the financial system, it has improved the efficiency of the system in terms of efficient cash management by banks, immediate transfer to the customer's account and reduction in transaction cost. In the pre-RTGS regime, banks settled their inter-bank obligations by issue of paper based instruments, which used to be cleared in a net clearing system called 'inter-bank clearing'. Efficiency of the inter-bank clearing was highly dependent on efficient transportation of paper instrument and uses of a good number of staff either to collect or to handover the instruments. Fragmented inter-bank clearing settlement taking place at different centres in the country also interfered with efficient cash management system in banks and placed an additional burden of pooling of funds at a centralised account. The RTGS system ensures settlement finality in the books of the Reserve Bank on a real time basis, thereby providing a confidence to the sending bank as well as the receiving bank that the payment transaction has been completed and the receiving bank can make use of the funds so received immediately. The RTGS also altered the scenario by providing a platform of settling all inter-bank transactions at Mumbai. The window for settling inter-bank transactions has also been widened from earlier position of 'within the banking hours' to the RTGS operating hours of '9.00 am to 5.00 pm on week days and 9.00 am to 2.30 pm on Saturday'.

The RTGS system is also used for customer transactions. No minimum or maximum limit has been fixed on such transactions so far. Technically, time critical transactions of similar value can also be routed through the RTGS.

RTGS AND FUTURE AGENDA

The implementation of Real Time Gross Settlement system has revolutionized the large value payment system in the country by facilitating faster movements of funds across accounts. In chain of its further improvement, the Integrated Accounting System (IAS) of the Reserve Bank is being integrated with the RTGS system. The full fledged operation of the RTGS-IAS system would begin shortly. The benefits of implementation of RTGS-IAS are as follows:

- Automated Start-of-Day funding of the RTGS Settlement Account i.e., transfer of funds on the basis of standing instruction from the current account to the settlement account.
- Automated End-of-Day flushing of the RTGS Settlement Account i.e., transfer of funds from the settlement account to the current account to make the settlement account zero.
- Message-based Own account Transfer (OAT) between the RTGS Settlement Account and the current account in IAS or two current accounts in IAS in Deposit Accounts Department (DAD) of the Reserve Bank at Mumbai.
- Multilateral Net Settlement Batch-Settlement of the Net Clearing Batches such as MICR, EFT, ECS from NCC, Government securities, foreign exchange, CBLO and NFS-ATM from CCIL and the net clearing batches originated from BSE and NSE.

- Automated Intra-day Liquidity (IDL) facility including automated request for grant of IDL, automated reversal of outstanding IDL with incoming credits and intra-day addition/withdrawal of un-encumbered securities offered for IDL availment.
- Gridlock Resolution Mechanism.

CONCLUSION

Thus, a secure and efficient payment and settlement system is necessary and a major pre-condition for the stability of the financial system and successful implementation of monetary policy of the country. RTGS is a project of national importance and therefore necessary awareness about the proposed RTGS System has to be built up. For this purpose, the RBI is still conducting RTGS Awareness Programmes for various target groups in the banks, Treasury In-charges, IT Heads, Operation Staff, Faculty Members of the Banks' Training Institutes, Business Development Teams, etc. RBI officials are regularly meeting with banks RTGS Nodal Officers to take stock of banks preparedness for participation in the RTGS System. In this context, all the bankers have to make coordinated and concerted efforts to ensure that the entire nation optimally benefits from the introduction of the RTGS System. Its buzzword should be 'cooperation' and not 'competition'. Bankers should gear up and make preparation for taking up the challenges in global scenario to make the most of the revolutionary change and thus make dream a reality in banking and finance fraternity.

REFERENCES

—RBI, Annual Report, Mumbai (Various Issues)

—RBI, Report on Trend and Progress of Banking in India, Mumbai (Various Issues)

—RBI, Report on Currency and Finance, Mumbai (Various Issues)

Shroff, F.T. (2005), 'Implementation of Real Time Gross Settlement (RTGM)' On-line Real Time Payment and Settlement Mechanism – Preparedness and Roll-out Strategy for Banks, Bank Quest, The Journal of Indian Institute of Banking & Finance, January-March.

CHAPTER 3

BANKING SECTOR REFORMS IN INDIA: PROGRESS, IMPACT AND TASKS AHEAD

Tapan Kumar Shandilya

INTRODUCTION

In India, the banking and financial sector reforms were initiated during the last decade of the 20th century as a part of general economic reforms with a view to improving the soundness of the public sector banks and other financial institutions. Pubic sector banks achieved spectacular success during the post nationalization period but such spectacular progress was witnessed in the spread of branch network of banks, mobilization of savings and in creating employment opportunities rather than in the improvement of the services to the customers. Frauds, corruption and misutilisation of public money were discovered. The vast expansion and spread of the banking sector resulted in surfacing of several internal deficiencies in the system. Due to these difficulties the customer service was affected badly, work technology remained stagnant and the transaction cost kept on increasing over the years.

Thus, in spite of positive achievements and meeting various socio-economic goals, the banking system in India experienced several problems-mainly of the profitability and viability of banks. The major factors affecting the profitability of public sector banks included higher SLR and CRR requirements, sick industrial advances, growing non-performing assets (NPAs), deterioration in the quality of assets, priority sector advances, political and administrative interference etc. While these factors were responsible for realization of far less income by public sector banks, their expenditure, especially, the administrative costs increased at a higher pace. Besides branch expansion by public sector banks into rural and semi-urban areas, lack of improvement in operational methods and procedures, slower computerization of various operations leading to higher transaction costs etc. also contributed to the lower profitability of public sector banks. Lack of proper disclosure norms led many banks to keep their teething problems under cover. Besides these internal factors, there were also certain external factors like high levels of preemption in reserve ratios, administered structure of interest rates and directed credit allocations to certain schemes and sections at distorted interest rates that were responsible for the banking crises.

Thus, under the above circumstances the viability of a number of public sector banks became a matter of grave concern. Some of them were incurring huge losses. The systematic and effective supervision and regulation of the banking and non-banking financial system did not keep pace with the developments in these areas. In order to support the major changes that took place in trade and industrial policies and to protect the depositors and investors a thorough review of the financial system was felt necessary. In this background, the government of India appointed a high level committee under the chairmanship of M. Narashimham - a former Governor of the Reserve Bank of India in August 1991 to go into all aspects relating to structure, organisation and functioning and procedures of the public sector banks and other financial institutions.

The Narasimham Committee's recommendations constitute a landmark in the evolution of the banking policy in the country and deal with transforming Indian banking from highly regulated to a more-market-oriented system. Many of the recommendations are in line with the banking policy reforms implemented in a number of developing economies since the seventies. The Committee made separate recommendations for reforms of (i) the banking sector, (ii) public sector financial institutions and (iii) money and capital markets.

The major banking sector reforms suggested by the Narasimham Committee are: reduction in SLR and CRR, transparent guideline or norms for entry and exit of private sector banks, direct access to capital markets to mobilize funds from the public, simplification and rationalization of interest rates, movement of interest yield on government securities towards market-related rates, liberalisation of branch licensing policy, accounting and prudential norms related to income recognition, provisioning and capital adequacy etc.

The government of India initiated the first phase of banking and financial sector reforms in 1992 on the basis of recommendations of CFS. The reform measures led to the improvement in several of the quantitative indices (such as gross and net profits, gross and net NPAs etc.) but there were many areas in which weaknesses still persisted. These include customer services, technological upgradation, improvement in house keeping in terms of reconciliation of entries and balancing of books. It was against this backdrop that the government considered it necessary to appoint a committee in November 1997 under the chairmanship of M. Narasimham himself to review the progress of banking sector reforms to date and chart a programme for further reforms necessary to strengthen India's financial system so as to make it internationally competitive. The Narasimham Committee II submitted its report in April 1998 which set the pace for the second generation of banking sector reforms.

PROGRESS OF BANKING SECTOR REFORMS

On the basis of the recommendations of both the Narasimham Committee I and II, several banking sector reform measures have been implemented since 1991. The major banking and financial reform measures initiated are broadly outlined below:

Reduction in SLR and CRR

A major factor affecting the profitability and functioning of commercial banks was massive pre-emption of bank resources in the form of high Statutory Liquidity Ratio (SLR) and Cash Reserve Ratio (CRR). The affecting CRR has been progressively reduced from 16.5 percent to 14.5 percent in November 1995, 10 percent in May 1999, 8.5 percent in April 2000, 7.5 percent in May 2001 and further to 4.75 percent in November 2002. The elective SLR on incremental net demand and time liabilities has been reduced from 38.5 percent in 1991 to 25 percent at present. These reductions have helped both in augmenting loanable resources of the banks and in improving profitability of banks.

Increase in Competition and Transparency

Transparent guidelines or norms of entry and exit of private sector banks have been stipulated. An element of competition has been ought to be fostered in financial sector by permitting new private sector banks and more liberal entry of branches of foreign banks. Local area branches have also been encouraged to foster competition in rural and semi-urban areas. Except in maturity pattern of assets and liabilities, movements in provision account and Non-Performing Assets (NPAs), transparency and disclosures standards have been enhanced to meet international standards.

Prudential Norms

Based on the recommendations of CBSR, prudential norms comparable to international standards have been initiated in relation to capital adequacy, income recognition and asset provisioning as per guidelines issued by the Reserve Bank of India in April 1992. With a view to improving the financial health and credibility of banks, capital adequacy ratio has been marked up and risk weights have been assigned to different government approved securities.

Measures have been taken for reclassification of the NPAs and improvement of the soundness of commercial bank functions. Assets have been classified in four categories-standard, substandard, doubtful and loss.

As for capital adequacy, banks were expected to reach 8 percent capital to risk-weighted asset ratio by March 1996. The State Bank of India and other nationalized banks had reached this norm in 1995-96. In line with the recommendations of the CBSR, commercial banks had been advised to raise minimum capital to risk-weighted asset ratio from 8 percent to 10 percent from the year ended March 2000.

Deregulation of Interest Rates

The deregulation of the structure of administered interest rates has been one of the major reform measures undertaken in India. Starting April 1992, the structure of interest rates has become more free and simpler. The bank deposit rates have been deregulated subject to a ceiling rate. The number of lending rates has been reduced from six to three rates with two concessive rates and a floor rate for all advances above Rs. 2 lakhs. Banks are now free to set interest rates with two concessive rates on all term deposits of maturity of over 30 days. Prescription of rates of all term deposits and conditions for premature withdrawal have been completely dismantled. The deregulation of interest rates has given a high degree of freedom to banks in determining deposit and lending rates.

Direct Access to Capital Market

Public sector banks have been allowed direct access to capital markets to mobilize funds from the public, though they will remain in the control of the government which will retain 51 percent of the equity. The government of India has amended the Banking Companies (Acquisition and Transfer of Undertakings). Act to enable the nationalized banks to access markets for capital funds.

Functional Improvement of Public Sector Banks

Important issues in respect of functional improvement of public sector banks are credit delivery system, priority sector lending and risk management. As regards credit control and credit delivery system, several measures have been implemented. Banks have been given freedom to decide on their own the levels of holdings of inventory and receivables of various industries while assessing credit requirements of borrowers. Considerable flexibility has been introduced with regard to credit delivery system for borrowers. There has been some progress in respect of simplification of procedure in regard to agriculture and small- scale industry. All selective credit controls on sensitive commodities except for sugar have been abolished. To some extent advances have been made to introduce market-oriented control and delivery system.

Priority Sector Lending

So far as directed credit/priority sector lending is concerned, Narasimham committee suggested to redefine the priority sector and to limit the bank credit for the redefined priority sector to 10 percent of total bank credit. The priority sector has been redefined which includes advances to software industry, transport operators, housing, plantation crops, investment on special bonds of SIDBI, NABARD, HCSDCO, SFCs and Rural Electrification Corporation. This extension of priority sector has facilitated banks to make loans to commercially viable units. Thus, the priority sector has been redefined but for the time being advances to the priority sector has not been drastically reduced because of growing dependence of weaker section population on these advances. The administered rate of interest has been adopted only in the most desirable cases. Subsidies too have declined for certain forms of advances. Now the beneficiaries under Government-sponsored programmes are required to depend more on bank credit at market-determined rate of interest and less on subsidies.

Risks in Market-oriented Lending

Narasimham Committee II (1998) has elaborately examined the risk-issue in the respect of market-oriented lending. Banks have been advised to introduce effective risk management system to cover credit risk, forex risk, market risk and operational risk. Comprehensive Asset Liability Management

Systems are being introduced to take care of these risks. For reducing operational risks also several measures have been introduced. One such measure is implementation of Jilani Committee recommendations for strengthening the internal inspection and audit system in banks. Apart from that, intensive monitoring of inter-branch, inter-bank accounts too have been introduced. Other steps taken in this respect are setting up of Audit Committee of Board and provision of compliance officers.

Money Market Reform

The Reserve Bank of India has recently taken measures to develop money market through issue of new instruments such as Commercial Paper and Certificate of Deposits in which banks and financial institutions are allowed to operate on a limited scale. Another Market Operations has become stronger and now it includes Treasury Bills of varying maturities. Some important changes have been introduced in the Government securities market also. Tap-T Bills were replaced by 14 days intermediate T-Bills and 182 days T-Bills were withdrawn. A new set of Satellite Dealers were also registered. Besides, some policy measures were also implemented. Instruments eligible for repo/reverse repo transactions were expanded; non-banking entities were permitted to enter into reverse repo transactions security market. These efforts are in the line of making the government debt market competitive as suggested by Chakraborty Committee.

The bond market and corporate securities markets are also coming up. Some important PSU bonds and other bonds are traded in this market whereas Securities and Exchange Board of India (SEBI) regulates the non-government securities in the secondary market through stock exchange. The debt market development is, therefore, a significant part of the financial reform as it plays a very important role in the financial flow of the economy and its investment pattern.

Regulation of Non-Banking Financial Companies (NBFCs)

Another development in the financial market has been the regulation of non-banking financial companies (NBFCs). A comprehensive frame work for NBFCs has been introduced in January 1998 in order to determine their prudential norms and deposit acceptance activities.

Supervision

Following the recommendations of the Narasimham Committee, Reserve Bank of India has set up in 1994 a Board for Financial Supervision (BFS). The four components of BFS supervisory strategy are: (i) restructuring system of inspection, (ii) setting up of offsite surveillance, (iii) enhancing the role of external auditors and (iv) strengthening corporate governance, internal controls and audit function. Thus, the present supervisory strategy covers both off-site and on-site inspection. The key elements of on-site inspection of the performance of the banks are under the CAMELS system, i.e. capital adequacy, asset quality, management earnings, liquidity and internal audit system. This new system has been in force since July 1997 and by now most of the Basle Core Principles for effective banking supervision are met by Indian supervisory authority. The implementation phase of the risk-based supervision project started in June 2000, for which project implementation group has been set up in RBI to address the transitional and change management issues for facilitating a smooth switch over to risks-based supervision.

Institutional Strengthening

A major effort has been taken to strengthen the banking system in general and public sector banks in particular, through appropriate institutional building measures such as (i) recapitalization, (ii) improving the quality of loan portfolio, (iii) instilling a greater element of competition and (iv) strengthening the supervisory process.

IMPACT OF BANKING REFORMS

The banking and financial reform measures taken as per the recommendations of the Narasimham Committee I & II have not only changed the face and prospects of the public sector banks but also the entire banking system and other financial institutions and intermediaries. The prospects of immense business opportunities are also opening up in the liberalized atmosphere. While prospects in the financial sector thus seem attractive, the operating-environment in the industry has also changed qualitatively. In the last few years the performance of the Indian Banking and Financial System and especially of our public sector banks has shown a measure of improvement judged by the parameter of operating profits along with other indicators of soundness, such as enhancement of capital funds and a reduction in the percentage level of non-performing assets.

(a) By mid 1997, the reform process had started yielding results. For instance, the net profit of public sector banks as percentage of their total assets has been turned around from a negative figure of –1.0% on an average between 1992-93 and 1993-94 to a positive figure of 0.57 percent in 1996-97. The ratio of net profit to total assets of these banks rose to 0.77 percent in 1997-98, though it declined to 0.42 percent in 1998-99, but again rose to 0.72% in 2001-02. The percentage of net profit in respect of all commercial banks also indicated a similar trend (Table-1).

    Operating profit of public sector banks showed a marked increased from Rs. 8887 crores in 1996-97 to Rs. 10577.5 crores in 1998-99 and further to Rs. 21672.93 crores in 2001-02. Similarly, the ratio of operating profit to total assets in respect of these banks had risen to 1.60 percent in 1996-97 but declined to 1.34 percent in 2001-02 but again rose to 1.88 percent in 2001-02. The ratio of operating profits in respect of all commercial banks had increased to 1.84 percent in 1997-98, but declined to 1.47 in 2000-01 and again rose to 1.94 percent in 2001-02.

(b) Reform measures had positive impact also on gross and net NPAs of Public sector banks. The gross and net NPAs of public sector banks as percentage of advances declined to 16 percent and 8.2 percent

Table 1
Profitability of Public Sector Banks

(Rs. Crores)

Year	Operating Profit				Net Profit			
	SBI Group	Nationalized Banks	Public Sector Banks	All Commercial Banks	SBI Group	Nationalized Banks	Public Sector Banks	All Commercial Banks
1996-97	4457.81	4429.37	8887.18	12239.49	1707.05	1445.12	3152.17	4504.24
	(2.18)	(1.26)	(1.60)	(1.82)	(0.84)	(0.41)	(0.57)	(0.67)
1997-98	4732.84	5541.38	10273.50	14640.15	2459.77	2569.90	5029.67	6501.84
	(2.03)	(1.33)	(1.58)	(1.84)	(1.6)	(0.62)	(0.77)	(0.82)
1998-99	4648.06	5929.44	0577.501	13992.31	1465.66	1792.43	3258.09	4659.50
	(1.63)	(1.22)	(1.37)	(1.47)	(0.51)	(0.37)	(0.42)	(0.49)
1999-2000	5839.14	7203.15	13042.29	18306.57	2679.18	2437.00	5116.1	7245.25
	(1.74)	(1.30)	(1.46)	(1.66)	(0.80)	(0.44)	8(0.57)	(0.66)
2000-01	5739.62	6266.98	13801.68	19756.78	2221.85	2095.09	4316.94	6403.48
	(1.42)	(1.29)	(1.34)	(1.53)	(0.55)	(0.33)	(0.42)	(0.49)
2001-02	8719.68	11160.17	21672.93	29814.20	3449.49	4857.75	8301.24	11572.46
	(1.94)	(1.83)	(1.88)	(1.94)	(0.77)	(0.69)	(0.72)	(0.75)

Figures in brackets are percentage to total assets.
Source: Compiled from Reserve Bank of India, Report on Trend and Progress of Banking in India 1998-99.
Reserve Bank of India, Report on Trend and Progress of Banking in India 2001-02.

respectively in March 1998 and further to 11.1% and 5.5 percent respectively in March 2002. In terms of percentage to total assets, gross and net NPAs of these banks went down to 7.0 percent and 3.3 percent respectively in March 1998 and further to 4.9 percent and 2.4 percent respectively in March 2002 (Table-2).

Table 2
Gross and Net NPAs of Public Sector Banks

(Rs. Crores)

Year End March	*Gross NPAs*	*Percent to Gross Advances*	*Percent of Gross NPAs to Total Assets*	*Net NPAs*	*Percent to Net Advances*	*Net NPAs as Percent to Total Assets*
1	2	3	4	5	6	7
1993	39,253	23.2	11.7	–	–	–
1994	41,041	24.8	10.8	–	–	–
1995	38,385	19.5	8.7	17,567	10.7	4.0
1996	41,661	18.0	8.2	18,297	8.9	3.6
1997	43,577	17.8	7.8	20,285	9.2	3.6
1998	45,653	16.0	7.0	21,232	8.2	3.3
1999	51,710	15.9	6.7	24,211	8.1	3.1
2000	53,033	14.0	6.0	26,187	7.4	2.9
2001	54,672	12.4	5.3	27,977	6.7	2.7
2002	56,507	11.1	4.9	27,985	5.8	2.4

1. Reserve Bank of India, Report on Currency & Finance, 1998-99.
2. Reserve Bank of India, Report on Trend & Progress of Banking in India 2001-02.

(c) With the progress of reform measures, one can discern some other positive developments also. One of the significant areas of improvement has been the greater accuracy and transparency in respect of bank's financial statements. The financial statements of banks have been rendered more credible and transparent as a result of acceptance of the recommendations with regard to bringing Indian accounting standards closer to internationally accepted norms as also the requirements of fuller disclosure on sensitive aspects of operations. The refinement of accounting practices and disclosing requirements to bring them at par with internationally accepted norms will have to be a continuous process.

(d) Reform measures have helped to bring about some improvement in the operation of the banking system. Asset management, soundness in capital structure, technological upgradation are some important changes that have come about in the banking operations. Private sector banks have been permitted to compete with public sector banks while some public sector banks have also been selected for autonomous status to enable them to operate in the competitive market. Besides, the government is persuading banks to raise funds from the capital market and ceasing to provide fund for recapitalisation of sick banks.

(e) The Indian banking and financial system has entered in the domain of information technology with the setting up of the Indian Financial Network (INFINET), and a technology-based Wide Area Network (WAN).

(f) Reform measures have led to the deepening and widening of financial market. Certain new institutions like PDs and MMF, foreign institutional investors, banks and corporates have become players of the financial market. Securities market has become more versatile.

(g) The technological upgradation has been an important step forward. Introduction of internet and on-line credit is a significant step which will serve as a big push forward in trade and commerce and resource management.

(h) Banking reform measures have made the public sector banks aware of their inefficiency, poor management and profitability. Entry of private banks and foreign banks, which are more efficient and profitable, has injected some element of competition at certain levels of operations.

THE UNFINISHED TASK

Inspite of several positive effects of the banking sector reform measures, the banking system still faces many policy issues and problems. The unfinished agenda of the banking and financial sector reforms in India may be analysed in respect of the banking policy, management of NPAs of commercial banks, norms of capital adequacy, overall supervision of banks, deregulation of interest rate structure and safety of customers' interests and risk management.

BANKING POLICY

Entry deregulation in the banking sector during the post reform period has resulted in emergence of dualism in the banking sector. The public sector banks with large accumulated NPAs, exposure to the priority sector, considerable presence in rural and semi-urban areas with a large number of unremunerative branches are definitely not at par with the new technology savvy metropolis-based private sector banks. Besides, the intended privatization of public sector banks will lead to the adoption of a policy of class banking with the possible adverse consequences on the economy of rural India. It would therefore, be essential to evolve a local banking structure to cater to the needs of rural and semi-urban areas along with the provision of full managerial and financial autonomy to the public sector banks.

HIGH LEVEL OF NPAS

The public sector banks are afflicted with a high proportion of NPAs. As on 31st March 2002, the public sector banks had a huge gross NPAs to the true of Rs. 56;507 crores. The accumulation of huge amount of NPAs has been the out come of two factors: (i) exposure of the public sector banks to the priority sector with high incidence of overdues and (ii) unwillingness of many large borrowers to repay in view of the lax legal environment. Although the gross NPAs as a percentage of gross advances declined from 23.2 percent in March 1993 to 11.1 percent in March 2002 (Table-2), it is still high in comparison to other countries. This situation is not sustainable. The Indian commercial banks cannot afford to have NPA ratios beyond 5 percent in view of intensification of competitiveness and the associated decline in interest spreads.

CAPITAL ADEQUACY

The Basle Norm of capital adequacy has been reintroduced in Indian following the recommendations of the Narasimham Committee (1991). The Narasimham Committee -I suggested that a bank must hold at least 8 percent of its assets when multiplied by appropriate risk weights. The committee on Banking Sector Reforms (1998) suggested further tightening of the capital adequacy norms after which the CRAR norm was revised upward to 9 percent.

In view of the present scenario, the CRAR norm has become terribly unsatisfactory owing to two reasons. Firstly, the present norm does not take into account market risks, rather it considers only the credit risk. While the credit risk estimates the potential loss in future earnings resulting from changes in the prices of assets, the importance of market risk in the sphere of banking has grown manifold in recent years due to the introduction of market system of valuation. This is likely to increase even further once illiquid assets are scrutinised. Secondly, the arbitrarily assigned risk weights do not reflect the true risk contents of the various types of securities. Thus, the present capital adequacy formula provides a misleading picture of the financial health of the commercial banks. In view of the emerging scenario, capital adequacy norm in the Indian context needs substantial modification.

BANK SUPERVISION

Some important change took place in respect of bank supervision in the nineties following the recommendations by the committee on the Financial System (1991) and the Working Group on the Review of the System of Banking Supervision (1995), but the Indian banking system exhibited several weaknesses in this respect: (i) illiquidity of assets and lack of transparency in trading; (ii) high beverage; (iii) asset liability mismatch and (iv) primitive knowledge of risk management. These problems are further compounded due to the existence of legal environment that promotes moral hazards since recovery of dues is a difficult proposition.

The importance of bank supervision has increased manifold in recent years in view of the deregulation of financial markets and a greater role for the private sector. Broadly speaking, the emerging issues relating to bank supervision are as follows.

(i) *Interest Rate Regulation, Market Risk and Investor Safety:* As is well known, interest rate deregulation has increased market risks considerably. Repo market liberalisation is likely to intensify the problem even further. As such, it is essential to ensure that the commercial banks adopt market risk management system so that systematic bank failures may be avoided.

(ii) *Problem of Moral Hazard:* The privatization of the banking sector without proper regulatory safeguards can lead to the problem of moral hazard. It is, therefore essential to develop a regulatory system that would take care of such problem.

(iii) *Fixing Exposure Norms:* As per the market exposure norm, a bank's exposure to an individual concern should not exceed 25 percent and to a group of business concern 50 percent of a bank's capital funds. The problem with the current exposure norm is that it does not discriminate between banks depending on the individual situations. There are several problems in this regard. Firstly, smaller banks need on enhanced upper limit to cater to medium/large borrowers who have grown with the bank and new find it difficult to get bank loan only due to the fact that their bank has reached the upper exposure limit. Secondly, the exposure norms for larger banks appear far from prudent.

LACK OF WISDOM ON DOMESTIC FRONT

The banking sector reform has exhibited lack of wisdom and courage on domestic front. The entire rural financial sector requires radical reform, both in respect of structure and function of the financial institutions. Throughout the reform process agricultural sector is languishing and public investment in this vital sector has perceptibly declined. Banking sector reform has been particularly against the primary sector.

LACK OF PROGRESS IN PERSONNEL MANAGEMENT

There has been no progress in the personnel management of financial institutions. The entire nationalized banking structure suffers from low customer service and inefficiency. As such personnel management in banking sector needs to be given proper attention so that services to the customers improve and banks may turn sickness into efficiency.

TASKS AHEAD

Implementation of the banking and financial sector reforms following the recommendations of the Narasimham Committee I & II, has largely been successful in respect of raising awareness of the Government, the banking and financial staff and the people for changing the inefficient and lethargic banking and tinancial structure into a morel efficient, effective and vibrant system. Such a system will be able to better serve the people and the economy at home and acquire the strength to complete in the global market. As such the ongoing reform process and the agenda for further reforms would have to focus on making the banking and financial system more viable and efficient so that it could contribute to enhancing the competitiveness of the real economy and face the challenges of an increasingly integrated global financial architecture. Thus, the tasks for banking and financial sector reform would have to address the following:

(i) Effective steps should be taken to strengthen the foundation of the banking system by clearing the assets, accounts and capital structure. One of the challenging problems faced by the banking sector at present is the high level of NPAs. Different options are available for tackling this critical problem. Existing NPAs should be reduced and their further build-up should be curbed. Avenues should be explored for recovering NPAs-especially for recovering small loans. Revenue Recovery Act should be strictly enforced for recovering the dues of banks and DFIs and the number of Debt Recovery Tribunals should be increased. A complete ban should be imposed on generalized loan waivers.

(ii) Another problem of banking sector is a large number of unremunerative branches, low productivity, overstaff and archaic methods of operations which have adversely affected the profitability of public sector banks. To enable the bigger banks to gear up to face global competition from foreign banks and Indian private banks, the Government should pave the way for universal banking with a three-tier structure for the banking system as recommended by the Narasimham Committee- I and reiterated by the Narasimham Committee-II.

(iii) Management of credit risk would have to be accorded a very high priority. Since a high level of NPAs is a symptom of poor credit management, banks with high NPAs would need to put in place an effective credit appraisal and management system. The approach to NPA management by the banks has to be multi-pronged necessitating varied strategies suited to different stages of the passage of credit facility. Close monitoring of accounts, particularly the large ones, is of prime importance.

(iv) Banks would have to move away from excessive concentration on asset management and adopt a more general approach of asset liability management aimed at modifying their liability structure in consonance with the desired-asset structure.

(v) The accounts and balance sheet of the banks and financial institutions have to be brought under stricter scrutiny so as to plug loopholes of corruption and prevent further scams. Measures taken in this respect have to be uniformly applied in banks and financial institutions. With globalisation of the financial system, transnational transactions and off-shore operations of banks may involve bigger financial fraud than before. All banks and financial institutions should follow the standard norms of maintaining the adequate proportion of their assets in liquid form. The RBI is also moving toward risk-based supervision and has adopted a rating model CAMELS (Capital adequacy, Asset quality, Management, Earnings and Liquidity) approach. Ultimately a separate body of financial supervision has to be developed as the RBI panel suggested.

(vi) Banks would have to equip themselves to operate in an increasingly deregulated interest rate environment. There is a need for further rationalization of interest rates and in particular it is desirable to evolve a Reserve Bank Reference Rate of Interest which could be effective, has to earn its place in the market and develop a pivotal role in the system overtime. But there is the need for a cautious step-by-step approach rather than a rapid deregulation of all interest rates in the system as it can be destabilizing as has been experienced in a number of countries.

(vii) The financial sector reform on the domestic front lacks wisdom and courage. The entire rural financial sector requires radical reform, both in respect of structure and function of financial institutions. While there is a strong case for reviewing the targets of the priority sector lending, it must be emphasized that some directed credit is imperative in the development process. The Narasimham Committee I & II have suggested to redefine priority sector and to reduce credit to this sector to 10 percent of bank credit. But the redefined priority sector leaves many below poverty line marginal people. The growth of NGOs (Non-Government Organisations) and the so-called Self Help Groups (SHGs) are now filling the vacuum. The sickness of RRBs, co-operative banks and branches of commercial banks has to be corrected. It has be noted that agricultural and small scale industries account for a significant proportion of national income and it would not be proper to starve these sectors of credit. Even now the biggest productive potential lies in the rural sector and rejuvenated rural financial structure is the biggest push factor for accelerating growth rate. A sharper thrust on agricultural production necessitates expansion and diversification in the operations of agricultural credit delivery agencies to improve the quality of rural lending.

(viii) Modern financial system at global level has become largely technology-based. On customer's side one outcome is the move towards relationship banking which is cost effective, profitable and customer-friendly. But this virtual banking has made only small beginning in India. As such next step of banking and financial sector reform should concentrate on technological upgradation throughout the financial sector. Vasudevan Committee (1999) has made important recommendations for upgradation of technology in the banks. A robust management information system based on date ware housing and date mining at individual bank level is essential for implementing various guidelines including asset liability management.

(ix) There has been no progress in personnel management of financial institutions. The entire nationalised banking structure suffers from low customer service and inefficiency. At present customer service is the first casualty and corruption is rampant. It is, therefore, necessary that serious attention be paid to the personnel management so that services to the customers improve.

(x) The entire banking system needs to be restructured and of 27 nationalised banks at last 4 to 6 banks should be elevated to the international standard. At present only State Bank of India is of international standard. Indian economy and our financial system are getting increasingly aligned with international economy and international financial system where multinational firms dominate the word trade. Indian financial institutions should improve in such a way as to become global players. Merger and acquisition should be guided so that international and national banks are strengthened.

CONCLUSION

The pace of reforms in banking sector in India is definitely encouraging and giving positive signals of structural change in the financial sector. The reforms will be successful if the banking sector can reduce drastically the ratio of NPAs. There is a need for appropriate and effective legal reforms to tackle the problem of NPAs. While analysing the success of economic restructuring in India' initiated amidst wide diversity of conditions, the effectiveness of banking sector reforms to achieve sustained economic progress needs to be monitored vigorously. The implications of full scale financial reforms in the economy are difficult to predict on account of several structural rigidities that still remain in its operations. But one can possibly expect that the second generation financial sector reforms, if taken in the right direction and with the right speed, may strengthen not only the monetary and financial parameters, but also stimulate higher and less vulnerable growth in the medium and long run.

We can expect the emergence of a completely changed scenario of the Indian banking and financial market characterised by: (i) a banking system dominated by private sector banks, (ii) flexible interest rates and assets prices leading to the prevalence of considerable market risks, (iii) increasing integration of the various segments of the financial markets with significant spillover effects; (iv) presence of transparent and uniform trading practices across the secondary markets, (v) increased influence of global capital market etc. Thus, in the years to come, the Indian financial system will grow not only in size but also in complexity with competition gaining further momentum. As such the further financial and banking reforms have important and radical tasks ahead.

Under the above circumstances, the Indian banking system is required to acquire adequate competitive strength to be able to meet the new challenges. In particular, the situation demands enhancement of credit appraisal and monitoring skill, adoption of scientific risk management practices and provision of customer services of international standard. Banks will have to evolve appropriate mechanism and procedures to evaluate credit risk and to equip themselves to operate in an increasing deregulated interest rate environment. Imaginative corporate planning combined with organizational restructuring are necessary prerequisites to achieve greater efficiency and better results. Banks and financial institutions will have not only to upgrade their product system, technology and procedures but also bring about a qualitative change in the work culture ad secure the willing participation of people in the changed process.

There is a need to further strengthen the audit structure, to improve the content and nature of regulation and to remove the constraints of legal inadequacies to improve the corporate governance systems in banks. Risk management to strengthen banking regulation and supervision, more transparency in operation, fixing accountability and to strengthen the public policies relating to moral hazards in banking sector. The Reserve Bank of India must play a new role in the liberalized environment and its guidance and intervention must take into account both the micro and macro aspects of the banking and financial sector liberalisation.

REFERENCES

Rangrajan, C. (1998), Indian Economy-Essays on Money Finance, UBS Publishers & Distributors Ltd. New Delhi.

Tarapore, S.S. (1998), "Need for Second Generation Banking Sector Reforms" in Raj Kapila and Umakapila (ed.), Banking and Financial Sector Reforms in India, Academic Foundation, New Delhi.

Sen, Kurnal and Rajendra R. Vaidya (1998), The Process of Financial Liberalisation in India, Oxford University Press, New Delhi.

Chelliah, Raja J. (1996), Towards Sustainable Growth-Essay in Fiscal and Financial Sector Reforms in India, Oxford University Press, New Delhi.

Reddy, Y.V. (1999), "Financial Sector Reforms: Review and Prospects", RBI Bulletin, January 98.

—Reserve Bank of India (1991), Committee on the Financial System (Narasimham Committee-I).

Patel, UR (1997), Emerging Reforms in Indian Banking: Economic & Political Weekly October 18.

—Reserve Bank of India (1998), Report of Committee on Banking Sector Reforms, (Narasimham, Committee II).

—Reserve Bank of India, Report Currency and Finance Various issues.

—Reserve Bank of India, Report on Trend and Progress of Banking in India, various issues.

Kulkarni, P. B., (1998), "Banking Sector Reforms", Journal of Indian School of Political Economy (Oct. & Dec.) Bombay.

Dev Raj, "Banking and Financial Sector Reforms in India," "Rationale Efficiency & Future Agenda," in Banking and Financial Sector Reforms in India. Deep & Deep Publications, New Delhi.

Banerjee, Amalesh (2001), "Second Generation of Financial Reforms" in Second Generation Economic Reforms in India (ed.) Rudra Datta, Deep & Deep Publications, New Delhi.

Passah, P.M. (2001), "Banking and Financial Sector Reforms in India-Rationale Progress Efficacy and Future Agenda" in Banking and Financial Sector Reforms in India (ed. Amalesh Banerjee) Deep & Deep Publications, New Delhi.

CHAPTER 4

BANKING SECTOR REFORMS AND FINANCIAL PERFORMANCE: THE INDIAN EXPERIENCE

Zafar A. Sultan

One of the most significant developments in the world economy, since the 1980s, has been structural adjustments and macro-economic reforms introduced by a number of developing countries. India, too, was not an exception to this trend. Trends towards liberalization in the Indian economy were apparent during 1980s, but took concrete shape in mid-1991 when economic condition of the country, especially external sector, turned unmanageable. The Indian government had no option but to resort to macroeconomic reform and structural adjustment in order to bring the economy back on track. Economic reforms initiated in India during mid 1991 were broad based and comprehensive. They embraced all the vital sectors of the economy including the banking sector.

NEED FOR REFORMS

The Indian financial system of the pre-reform period essentially catered to the needs of planned development in a mixed-economy framework where the Government sector had a predominant role in economic activity. As part of planned development, the macro-economic policy in India moved from fiscal neutrality to fiscal activism (Reddy 2000). Such activism meant large developmental expenditures, much of it to finance long-gestation projects requiring long-term finance. The sovereign was also expected to raise funds at fine rates, and understandably at below the market rates for private sector. In order to facilitate the large borrowing requirements of the Government, interest rates on Government securities were artificially pegged at low levels, which were unrelated to market conditions. The government securities market, as a result, lost its depth as the concessional rates of interest and maturity period of securities essentially reflected the needs of the issuer (Government) rather than the perception of the market. The provision of fiscal accommodation through *ad hoc* treasury bills (issued on tap at 4.6 per cent) led to high levels of monetisation of fiscal deficit during the major part of the eighties. In order to check the monetary effects of such large-scale monetisation, the cash reserve ratio (CRR) was increased frequently to control liquidity.

The environment in the financial sector in these years was thus characterised by segmented and underdeveloped financial markets coupled with paucity of instruments. The existence of a complex structure of interest rates arising from economic and social concerns of providing concessional credit to certain sectors resulted in "cross subsidisation" which implied that higher rates were charged from non-concessional borrowers. The regulation of lending rates, led to regulation of deposit rates to keep cost of funds to banks at reasonable levels, so that the spread between cost of funds and return on funds is maintained. The system of administered interest rates was characterised by detailed prescription on the lending and the deposit side leading to multiplicity and complexity of interest rates.

By the end of the eighties, the financial system was considerably stretched. The directed and concessional availability of bank credit with respect to certain sectors resulted not only in distorting the interest rate mechanism, but also adversely affected the viability and profitability of banks. The lack of recognition of the importance of transparency, accountability and prudential norms in the operations of the banking system led also to a rising burden of nonperforming assets.

In sum, there was a *de facto* joint family balance sheet of Government, RBI and commercial banks, with transactions between the three segments being governed by plan priorities rather than sound principles of financing interinstitutional transactions (Reddy, November 2000). There was a widespread feeling that this joint family approach, which sought to enhance efficiency through co-ordinated approach, actually led to loss of transparency, of accountability and of incentive to measure or seek efficiency.

The policies pursued did have many benefits, although the issue of the higher costs incurred to realize the laudable objectives remains. Thus, the post nationalisation phase witnessed significant branch expansion to mobilise savings and there was a visible increase in the flow of bank credit to important sectors like agriculture, small-scale industries, and exports. However, these achievements have to be viewed against the macro-economic imbalances as well as gross inefficiencies at the micro level in the financial sector compounded by non-transparent accounting of intra-public sector financial transactions. A number of these banks were plagued with poor profitability. Most of the banks were undercapitalized with a high proportion of non-performing assets i.e. bad loans. The quality of customer service was unsatisfactory. Khusro Committee (1989) too felt that the rise in operational cost, lack of efforts in manpower planning, employees welfare package, career plan, and training and performance appraisal system were not conducive to the efficient functioning of the Indian banking system. These maladies called for an urgent need of reforms in the banking sector.

REFORMS

The basis for banking reforms was provided by the Committee on financial system (Narasimham Committee), which made recommendations in first report in November 1991; and in second report in 1998. These recommendations are a landmark in the evolution of banking policy in the country, as these transformed the Indian banking system from a highly regulated to a more market-oriented system. The main reforms introduced on the basis of two reports of Narasimham Committee may be summarized as follows:

Statutory Liquidity Ratio (SLR)

For a long time the government intervention in India's banking sector was in form of high SLR and CRR. In this manner, the Government pre-empted bank resources at below market rate. This policy benefited the government as it reduced the cost of borrowing. But it was directly responsible for eroding the profits of the banks. The Narasimham Committee, therefore, recommended a reduction in SLR to 25 per cent and unspecified reduction in CRR. As such SLR on incremental net demand time liabilities (DTL) has been outstanding net domestic demand and time liabilities have been reduced gradually from 38.5 per cent to 27 per cent in 1997 and further to 25 per cent in October 1997 and it is the minimum stipulated level under section 24 of Banking Regulation Act, 1949.

Cash Reserve Ratio (CRR)

Originally, it was the intention of RBI to bring down the cash reserve ratio (CRR) from the statutory 15 per cent. In fact it was brought down to 14 per cent in May 1993. At the same time, the incremental cash reserve ratio (ICRR) of 10 per cent was abolished. When condition eased and money growth started slowing down during 1995-96 and 1996-97, RBI reduced CRR gradually from 15 per cent by March 1997 and further to 7.5 per cent in May 2001. It was then reduced to 5.5 percent in December 2001, and further to 5 percent. The purpose of reducing CRR was to release funds locked up with RBI for lending to the industrial and other sectors, which were starved of bank credit.

Interest Rate Deregulation

Interest rate slabs were gradually reduced from 20 to 2 by 1994-95. The important changes in the interest rates since 1991-92 are as follows:

- Interest rate on domestic term deposits above one year and on non-residential non-reportorial NRNR) rupee deposits have been decontrolled.
- The prime lending rate of SBI and most other banks on general advanced of over Rs.2 lakh has been reduced.
- Rate of interest on bank loan above Rs.2 lakh has been fully decontrolled.
- The interest rates on deposits and on advances of banks) have been deregulated subject to a minimum lending rate of 13 per cent (earlier it was 12 per cent).
- The purpose of deregulating of interest rate on the high slab of bank advances was to stimulate healthy competition among the banks and encourage their operational efficiency. Scheduled commercial banks have now the freedom to set interest rates on their deposits subject to minimum floor rates and maximum ceiling rates.

Prudential Norms

In an attempt to maintain profitability, banks developed a tendency to over-extend their lending by accepting debtors of low credit worthiness, which has come to be known as "adverse selection." In 1992, prudential norms and regulations were introduced in order to ensure safety and soundness of banks and impart greater transparency and accountability in operations. Prudential norms introduced relate to income recognition, provisioning for bad and doubtful debts and capital adequacy. Prudential norms have helped to serve two purposes: (i) they have brought out the true position of the banking system's loan portfolio, and (ii) the norms have helped to arrest its deterioration. The norms have been progressively tightened since their introduction.

Capital Adequacy Norms

In 1992, RBI fixed capital adequacy norms at 8 per cent and the banks had to comply with them over a three-year period. By the end of March 1996, all public sector banks had attained capital to risk weighted assets ratio of 8 per cent. The full norm of 8 per cent was also attained by foreign banks in India and by some Indian banks.

A new capital framework was introduced for Indian scheduled commercial banks based on the Basle Committee recommendations presenting two tiers of capital for the banks.

Tier 1 or core capital, considered the most permanent and readily available support against unexpected losses, includes paid-up capital, statutory reserves, share premium and capital reserve; *and* Tier II capital consisting of undisclosed reserves, fully paid-up cumulative perpetual preference shares, revaluation reserves, and general provisions and loss reserves, etc.

It was also prescribed that Tier II capital should not be more than 100 percent of the Tier I capital.

The Government of India has amended the Banking Companies (Acquisition and Transfer of Undertakings) Act to enable the nationalized banks to access the market for capital funds through public issues, subject to the provision that the holding of Central Government would not fall below 51 per cent of the paid-up capital.

Strengthening the Institutional Framework

It is another key element of banking reforms. A more competitive environment has also been created for banks so as to raise their efficiency and performance. Efficiency is not just operational or allocation efficiency but functional efficiency as well. Banks already face competition form non-banking finance companies (NBFCs), mutual funds and from within the industry itself. While existing banks have been allowed greater flexibility, new banks are now being set-up in the private sector to provide increased competition. In January 1993, RBI announced guidelines for the entry of new private sector banks. Approvals have been given for the establishment of new foreign banks to set-up their operations in India and existing foreign banks have been allowed to expand their branch network.

Strengthening of Supervisory Mechanism

It is essential for a sound banking system. There has to be an alert mechanism for monitoring compliance with prudential norms and directives of RBI and other regulatory agencies. The establishment of the Board Financial Supervision, with the operational support of the Department of Banking Supervision of RBI, has revamped the system of external supervision. In tune with international practice of supervision, a three-tier supervisory model comprising on-site inspection, off-site monitoring and a periodical external auditing based on CAMELS (capital adequacy, assets quality, management, earnings, liquidity and system controls) has been put in place.

Development finance institutions and non-banking finance institutions were also brought into the regulatory ambit of RBI. In terms of the Khanna Committee (1995) a three-tier supervisory framework was introduced in respect of non-banking finance companies (NBFCs). The CAMELS approach has been made applicable to NBFCs also. A department of non-banking supervision has been created to exclusively supervise NBFCs only.

Directed Credit

After nationalisation of commercial banks a strong case was made out in favour of directed credit on the grounds of both efficiency and equity. In practice, however, the directed credit not only undermined the profitability of the banks but also failed to promote efficiency and equity. Hans Binswanger and S.R. Khandker stated that directed credit has only a mildly positive effect on output and a zero effect on employment in the agricultural sector.[55] The effects of directed credit on equity have not been encouraging. In the agricultural sector medium and large farmers have pre-empted a large part of such credit and have thus received large subsidies.

The small-scale industries have received subsidized credit on 'market failure' grounds for more than 25 years. This period is long enough to overcomes market failures. Hence, there is no justification to provide subsidized credit to this sector under the change circumstances.

The Narasimham Committee that noted that the case for directed credit under existing conditions is quite weak recommended a phasing of the direct credit programme. As it would need some time, some credit support was recommended in the medium-term some credit support was recommended in the medium-term to the priority sector, which has been redefined. Further, the committee suggested that the credit target for this sector is to be reduced from 40 per cent to 10 per cent of the aggregate. The government, however, seems to be lacking political will to implement this recommendation. Over the ears large farmers, transporters and small industrialists have greatly benefited form directed credit programmes. These economic groups have powerful lobbies and would not allow the government easily to phase out directed credit programmes.

Competition

Until 1991 there was little competition in the banking sector. The public sector banks dominating the banking industry in terms of size. The government has now recognized the need to make banking industry more competitive. It has thus made certain policy changes such as deregulation of interest rates and dilution of consortium lending requirements. Moreover, banking has been opened up to the private sector, both domestic and foreign. Response to this policy has been quite encouraging. Ten new private sector banks have started functioning, out of the thirteen in principle approvals given for setting up of new banks in the private sector. The RBI has pursued a restrictive policy as regards allowing the new banks to open branches.

Freedom of Operation

Scheduled commercial banks have now been given freedom to open new branches and upgrade extension counters, after obtaining capital adequacy norms and prudential accounting standards. They are also permitted to close non-viable branches other than in rural areas. Bank lending norms have been liberalized and banks have been given freedom to decide levels of holding of individual items of inventories and receivables.

Recovery of Debts

The Government of India passed "Recovery of Debts due to banks and Financial Institutions Act, 1993" in order to facilitate and speed up the recovery of debts due to banks and financial institutions. Six Special Recovery Tribunals have been set-up at Calcutta, New Delhi, Jaipur, Ahmedabad, Bangalore and Chennai to facilitate quicker recoveries of loan arrears (within six months and Appellate Tribunal has also been set-up in Mumbai.

FINANCIAL PERFORMANCE OF THE BANKING SECTOR

These reforms have made an impressive impact on the overall efficiency and stability of the banking system. In recent times, a significant body of literature has evolved which explores the performance of financial institutions in the wake of financial liberalisation. The link between deregulation and efficiency are established on the ground that deregulation is expected to unleash competitive forces. Such competition would, in turn, enable banks to alter their input and output mix, which when combined with technological developments facilitates increase in output that raises overall bank productivity and efficiency. Further, liberal entry of private and foreign banks as a part of the deregulation process is expected to raise bank efficiency, productivity and technology levels, because private/foreign banks are associated with superior management practices and technology, which can be fruitfully imbibed by those which are not.

Competition and Profitability of Indian Banks

Beginning from 1992, Indian banks were gradually exposed to the rigours of domestic and international competition.

Newly opened banks from the private sector and entry and expansion of several foreign banks resulted in greater competition in both deposit and credit markets. Consequent to these developments, there has been a consistent decline in the share of public sector banks in total assets of commercial banks. Notwithstanding such transformation, the public sector banks still remain the mainstay, accounting for nearly three-fourths of assets and income. For example, its share declined from 87.8 percent in 1992-93 to 69.1 percent in 2005-06 in terms of assets and 86.6 percent and 72.4 percent during the corresponding period in terms of income.

One of the important outcomes of the reforms in the banking sector is the increase in profitability of public sector. The public sector banks have positively responded to the new challenges of competition. This is evident from the increase in the share of these banks in the overall profit of the banking sector. From the position of net loss in the mid-1990s, the bank has started making profits. For the first time, the public sector banks registered a positive profit in 1994-95 of the amount Rs.1116 crores and that increased to Rs.16539 crore in 2005-06 at an annual compound rate of 27.8 percent. In recent years the share of public sector banks in the profit of the commercial banking system has become broadly commensurate with their share in assets (67.2 percent) indicating a broad convergence of profitability across various bank groups during the reform period. This suggests that, with operational flexibility, public sector banks are competing relatively effectively with private sector and foreign banks. The 'market discipline' imposed by the listing of most public sector banks has also probably contributed to this improved performance. Public sector bank managements are now probably more attuned to the market consequences of their activities (Mohan, 2005).

Since the late1990s, in line with the benign interest rate regime, both interest income and interest expenditure of banks as proportions of total assets have declined (Table 2). However, interest expenditure declined faster than interest income, resulting in an increase in net interest income. As percent of total assets, the interest spread of public sector has increased from 2.3 percent in 1992-93 to 3.0 percent in 2005-06. However, non-interest income, which emanates mostly from fee-based activities, has not been increasing consistently in the post-reform period. It hanged around 1.2 to 1.4 percent. In this context, it is also appropriate to mention that Indian banks, in particular the public sector banks, are yet to catch-up fully with their foreign counterparts.

Efficiency of Indian Banks

Improvements in efficiency of the banking system are expected to be reflected, inter alia, in a reduction in operating expenditure, interest spread and cost of intermediation in general. Several indicators have been employed in the literature to compare banking production costs across time. Illustratively, intermediation cost, defined as the ratio of operating expense to total assets, witnessed a gradual reduction in the post reform period across various bank groups barring foreign banks. This decline in intermediation cost needs to be weighed against the large expenditures incurred in upgradation of information technology and institution of 'core banking' solutions. Admittedly, intermediation costs of banks in India still tend to be higher than those in developed banking markets. (Mohan 2005)

Rakesh Mohan has found that 5 Indian banks have improved their efficiency in the post reform period. The per unit cost of output of these banks, irrespective of the choice of outputs has declined over the period. The operating cost per unit of earning assets declined from 2.1 per cent in 1992 to 1.8 percent in 2004; similarly, operating cost per unit of total volume of business declined from 3.4 per cent to 2.6 per cent during the same period. Among the components of operating expenses, employee cost per unit of output witnessed a noticeable decline in the post-reform period. This decline is discernible across all bank groups, and especially for public sector banks in the post 2001 period consequent to the voluntary retirement scheme across several nationalised banks. On the other hand, the change in physical capital cost per unit of output has been marginal, reflecting the fact that Indian banks maintained a steady flow of investments towards physical capital formation, especially on automation and information technology (Mohan 2005).

From the efficiency standpoint, the intermediation cost needs to be viewed in conjunction with non-interest income. Till 2000-01, the burden (the excess of non-interest expenditure over non-interest income as a percentage to total assets) of commercial banks hovered around 1 to 1.5 per cent. This gap between intermediation cost and income from fee-based activities has narrowed considerably in recent years. For example, the burden of Indian commercial banks declined from 1.5 percent in 1992-93 to 0.5 percent in 2005-06. Moreover, there has been a lowering of the burden across bank groups in recent years. The improvement in respect of Indian private banks and foreign banks has been remarkable; their burden has declined from about 1.7 percent to 0.2 percent. However the burden of public sector banks could decline only to 1.0 percent in 2005-06 from 1.3 percent in 1992-93.

The cost income-ratio (defined as the ratio of operating expenses to total income less interest expense) of Indian banks showed a declining trend during the post reform period. For example, Indian banks paid roughly 50.9 per cent of their net income towards managing labour and physical capital in 2005-06 as against nearly 72.6 per cent in 1992-93. In other words, Indian banks recorded a net cost saving of nearly 22 per cent of their net income during the post reform period. According to the data reported in The Banker 2004, the cost-income ratio of world's largest banks varied markedly from a low of 48 per cent to a high of 116 percent and the ratio around 60 per cent is an indicative benchmark (RBI, 2005, quoted in R.Mohan). In that respect, the cost-income ratio of Indian banks is now comparable internationally. Among various ownership patterns, public sector banks have tended to have relatively higher cost-income ratio as against private banks and foreign banks. But this too has improved its efficiency level during the reform period. Its cost-income ratio has declined from 74.4 percent to 51.5 percent, coming very close to private banks, during the reform period.

Table 1

Financial Indicators of Scheduled Commercial Banks

(Rupees Crores)

	Public Sector Banks			*Foreign Banks*			*Private Sector Banks*			*Schedule Commercial Banks*		
Items	*1992-93*	*2000-01*	*2005-06*	*1992-93*	*2000-01*	*2005-06*	*1992-93*	*2000-01*	*2005-06*	*1992-93*	*2000-01*	*2005-06*
Income	36089	103499	160946	4009	11984	17435	1595	9091	11729	41693	132078	222209
InterestIncome	32111	90984	137614	3700	9471	12236	1410	8052	10359	37221	114951	184510
Other Income	3978	12515	23332	309	2513	5199	185	1039	1370	4472	17127	37698
Expenditure	39457	99182	144407	4851	11039	14367	1520	8568	10852	45828	125654	197616
Interest Expenditure	24112	61693	80272	2570	5768	5150	987	5932	6236	27669	78152	106919
Intermediatation Cost	8908	28013	41532	858	3111	5625	417	1679	3123	10183	34179	58729
Provision and Cotingencies	6437	9476	22603	1423	2160	3592	116	957	1493	7976	13323	31968
Operating Profit	2969	13793	39142	581	3105	6661	191	1480	2369	3841	19747	56560
Net Profit	-3368	4317	16539	-842	945	3069	75	523	876	-4135	6424	24593
Net Interest Income (Spread)	7999	29291	57342	1130	3703	7086	423	2120	4123	9552	36799	77591
Total Assets	336181	1029770	1926334	31678	101824	201586	15111	84605	149749	382970	1294974	2787892

Source: Economic Survey, Ministry of Finance, Government of India, Delhi, Various issues.

Table 2
Financial Indicators of Scheduled Commercial Banks

(Percent of Total Assets)

	Public Sector Banks			*Foreign Banks*			*Old Private Sector Banks*			*Schedule Commercial Banks*		
Items	*1992-93*	*2000-01*	*2005-06*	*1992-93*	*2000-01*	*2005-06*	*1992-93*	*2000-01*	*2005-06*	*1992-93*	*2000-01*	*2005-06*
Income	11.7	10.1	8.4	12.7	11.2	8.6	10.6	9.5	7.6	10.9	10.2	8.0
InterestIncome	10.2	8.8	7.1	11.7	9.3	6.1	9.3	8.2	5.8	9.7	8.9	6.6
Other Income	1.4	1.2	1.2	1.0	2.5	2.6	1.2	1.4	1.8	1.2	1.3	1.4
Expenditure	11.5	9.6	7.5	15.3	10.8	7.1	10.1	8.7	6.6	12.0	9.7	7.1
Interest Expenditure	6.4	6.0	4.2	8.1	5.7	2.6	6.5	6.0	3.6	7.2	6.0	3.8
Intermediatation Cost	2.5	2.7	2.2	2.7	3.1	2.8	2.8	1.7	2.0	2.7	2.6	2.1
Provision and Cotingencies	2.5	0.9	1.2	4.5	2.1	1.8	0.8	0.9	1.0	2.1	1.0	1.1
Operating Profit	0.8	1.3	2.0	1.8	3.1	3.3	1.3	1.7	2.0	1.0	1.5	2.0
Net Profit	-1.0	0.4	0.9	-2.7	0.9	1.5	0.5	0.8	1.0	-1.1	0.5	0.9
Net Interest Income (Spread)	2.3	2.8	3.0	3.6	3.6	3.5	2.8	2.1	2.1	2.5	2.8	2.8
Total Assets	100	100	100	100	100	100	100	100	100	100	100	100
Operating Expenses as % of net income	74.4	67.0	51.5	59.6	50.0	45.8	68.6	53.2	50.2	72.6	63.4	50.9

Source: Economic Survey, Ministry of Finance, Government of India, Delhi, Various issues.

Another important indicator of efficiency of banks is interest spread or net interest margin (NIM), defined as the excess of interest income over interest expense, scaled by total bank assets. Broadly speaking, this ratio reflects the allocative efficiency of financial intermediation. It is quite reasonable to believe that the decline in deposit rates ushered by the deregulation process will be manifested in the lending behaviour of banks. In practice, however, lending rates have tended to be sticky downwards and seem to operate with a time lag. Historically, the NIM of Indian banks is rather high. Around the onset of the reform process in 1992-93, the NIM of Indian banks was about 2.3 percent. Thereafter, it recorded a relatively modest rise to around 3 per cent in recent years. And traditionally, it is the foreign banks, which by virtue of their ability to mobilise low-cost deposits, have the highest NIMs, whereas those for private banks have been the lowest in recent years. These comparisons are not watertight: typically, small and medium banks had high NIM until 1997. Thereafter, NIM for big banks recorded a rise. Contextually, it may be mentioned that banks in most developed countries and several emerging economies have NIM (as a percentage to total assets) of around 2 per cent. This provides some indication that competition in banking still has some way to go in India (Mohan, 2005 ,Internet).

Non-Performing Assets (NPAs)

Non-performing assets constitutes a source of deadweight loss to the commercial banks and thwart downward movement in lending rates. Despite the gradual tightening of prudential norms, the ratio of non-performing loans (NPL) to total loans has been continuously declining (Table 3). which was at a high of 14.7 per cent for scheduled commercial banks (SCBs) at end-March 1999, has declined by more than two thirds to 3.3 per cent at end-March 2006. Net NPLs also witnessed a significant decline, driven by the improvements in loan loss provisioning and improved recovery management, which comprises over half of the total provisions and contingencies.

Table 3
Gross Non-Performing Assets of Schedule Commercial Banks (SCBs)

	% to Gross Advances			*% to Total Assets*		
Bank Group	*1998-99*	*2000-01*	*2005-06*	*1998-99*	*2000-01*	*2005-06*
Public Sector	15.9	12.4	3.7	6.7	5.3	2.1
Private Sector	10.8	8.5	2.4	4.5	3.7	1.4
Foreign	7.6	6.8	1.9	3.1	3.0	1.0
All SCBs	14.7	11.4	3.3	6.2	4.9	1.9

Source: Economic Survey, Ministry of Finance, Government of India, Delhi, Various Issues.

Capital adequacy of the banking sector also recorded a marked improvement and reached 12.8 per cent at end-March 2005, well above the stipulated level of 9 per cent. Banks have also been sensitised to develop robust risk management systems for credit and operational risks and focus on their asset-liability maturity profile to withstand adverse movements in market risk parameters such as interest rates and take corrective measures.

CONCLUSION

Thus we find that the reform implemented since 1991 have had significant favourable changes in India's highly regulated banking sector. Liberalising the sector for private sectors, both domestic and foreign, by easing the condition of entry led to reduction in concentration of the banking sector and improving the performance. The profitability and efficiency of the public sector steadily improved over the reform period, and the gap in performance compared with foreign banks has diminished. Further, foreign banks (and private domestic banks in some cases) have generally performed better than other banks in terms of profitability and income efficiency. This suggests that ownership matters and foreign entry has a positive impact on banking sector restructuring.

SELECT REFERENCES

—Government of India, 'Economic Survey', *Ministry of Finance,* Delhi, various issues.

Jalan, B (2000), 'Finance and Development-Which Way Now?' *RBI Bulletin*, January, 29-45.

Jalan, B (2001), 'Banking and Finance in the New Millennium', *RBI Bulletin*, February, 215-232.

Joshi, Vijay and I.M.D. Little (1996), *India's Economic Reforms: 1991-2001* (Oxford, Clarendon Press).

Mohan, Rakesh (2005), 'Reforms, Productivity and Efficiency in Banking: the Indian Experience', downloaded from Internet.

Reddy, Y.V. (2000), 'Monetary and Financial Sector Reforms in India: A Central Banker's Perspective', UBS Publishers, New Delhi.

Reddy, Y.V. (November 2000): 'Fiscal and Monetary Policy Interface: Recent Developments in India', *RBI Bulletin*, pp.1257-72.

—Reserve Bank of India (1991), *'Report of the Committee on the Financial System'*, (Chairman Shri M.Narasimham).

—Reserve Bank of India (1997), *'Report of the Committee on Banking Sector Reform'*, (Chairman Shri M.Narasimham).

Tarapore S.S. (2000), Issues *in Financial Sector Reforms*, UBS Publishers.

CHAPTER 5

INDIAN BANKING SECTOR REFORMS: AN APPRAISAL

Md. Reyazuddin

INTRODUCTION

Indian economy took a new direction when the Government announced its new industrial policy in the Parliament in July 1991. Since then, the economic reforms process has encompassed all areas of the economy. The wide-ranging reforms, initiated and implemented since 1991, have induced greater efficiency and competitiveness in all spheres of economic activity and placed the economy on a higher growth path.

The last decade of the 20th century was momentous in the economic history of India as it witnessed a successful transition of India from a controlled, inward looking and slow growing economy to a liberalised and open economy that has now found a place amongst the fastest growing economies in the world.

Indian economy has shown the potential to achieve and even surpass the 8 per cent growth rate stipulated in the Tenth Five Year Plan (2002-07). However, this achievement hinges critically on improvement of the domestic savings rate (including public savings), increased public investment, efficient, reliable and affordable infrastructure, higher inflow of foreign capital, better credit delivery system, labour reforms and export competitiveness.

India is now Asia's third largest economy and has the world's fourth largest foreign exchange reserves.

Financial institutions and financial markets of a country are the channels for transferring resources from the surplus sectors to deficit sectors. Financial intermediaries play an important role in the growth process by encouraging saving and investment and improving the allocative efficiency of resources. In India, the main conduits of credit are commercial and co-operative banks, Development Finance Institutions (DFIs) and Non-Banking Financial Companies (NBFCs). Banks and NBFCs provide short-term credit whereas DFIs specialise in extending medium-term and long term loans. Prior to reforms, the mutual fund industry suffered a lot. Because there was only one institution, UTI which dominated the market for long and faced no competition, resulting in a seller oriented market condition.

It was in this backdrop that wide-ranging financial sector reforms were introduced as an integral part of the economic reforms initiated in mid-1991.

Considering the strategic importance of the financial sector, the Government of India set up a Committee on Financial system in 1991 under the Chairmanship of Mr. M. Narasimham. It was asked to examine all aspects relating to the structure, organisation, functions and procedures of the Indian financial system. The Committee submitted its report in November 1991 which was presented to the Parliament in December 1991.

The banking system forms the core of the financial sector of an economy. The role of commercial banks is particularly important in underdeveloped countries. Through mobilisation of resources and their better allocation, commercial banks play an important role in the development process of underdeveloped countries. By offering attracting saving schemes and ensuring safety of deposits, commercial banks encourage willingness to save among the people. By reaching out to people in rural areas, they help convert idle savings into effective ones. Commercial banks improve the allocation of resources by lending money to priority sectors of the economy. These banks provide a meeting ground for the savers and the investors. Savers may not invest either because of inadequate savings and/or lack of risk-taking spirit.

INFORMATION TECHNOLOGY IN BANKING

Today the financial sector has been a large user of information technology (IT). Banks, in particular, has been increasingly using IT in their day to day operations. It is being viewed as an excellent tool for providing a fairly exhaustive range of products and extending banking facilities to the vast multitude of population. Over the years, banks have extended the reach of Core Banking Solutions (CBS) to more branches so as to facilitate anywhere banking, introduced technology based products and services such as mobile banking and expanded the internet banking facilities. Banks have been increasingly using the National Electronic Fund Transfer (NEFT) for ensuring wider reach for electronic funds movement.

Nationalised banks have three reasons to adopt information technology. First, Central Vigilance Commission's instructions for computerization of 70% of their operation. Second, reduction of government holding to 33%, which will make them compatiable to private banks. Third, severe competition from new private sector banks which are 100% computerized and keep on adopting latest technologies. Now, growth of banks, both public and private depends purely on their performance as well as willingness and capability to capitalize on information technology.

Indian banking sector has taken a quantum leap forward in terms of switching over from paper-based transactions, which include use of currency notes, cheques or challans, to electronic means, which include Real Time Gross Settlement (RTGS), National Electronic Fund Transfer (NEFT) and other electronic modes. Computerisation in banking business received high importance in 2005-06. For this purpose, banks invested heavily in technology upgradation.

Table 1 shows the expenditure incurred on computerisation and development of communication network by public sector banks.

Table 1
Expenditure Incurred on Computerisation and Development of Communication Networks by Public Sector Banks

(Amount in Rs. Crore)

Name of the Bank	*Expenditure Incurred During Half Year Ended March 2006*	*Expenditure Incurred Between September 1999 and March 2006*
Public Sector Banks (I+II)	1,054.45	10.676.12
I. Nationalised Banks	613.57	6,599.87
Bank of Baroda	86.72	473.90
Bank of India	97.72	1,008.40
Canara Bank	59.03	703.92
Punjab National Bank	51.44	768.07
II.State Bank Group	440.88	4,076.25

Source: RBI, Report on Trend and Progress of Banking in India, Appendix Table III, 32, p.310.

Between September 1999 and March 2006, Public Sector Banks incurred an expenditure of Rs. 10,676 crore on computerization and development of communication networks in which share of nationalized banks and State Bank group were Rs. 6599.87 crores and Rs. 4076.25 crores respectively. The top rankers among nationalized banks were Bank of India, Punjab National Bank, Canara Bank and Bank of Baroda while State Bank Group was led by State Bank of India followed by State Bank of Bikaner and Jaipur. The number of branches providing Core Banking Solutions (CBS) has increased significantly in recent years. The CBS provides a host of benefits such as anywhere banking, anywhere access and quick funds movement at optimal costs and in an efficient manner. While new private sector banks, foreign banks and a few old private sector banks have already put in place core banking solutions, public sector banks are increasingly adopting similar systems. The total number of branches providing CBS increased from 11.0 per cent as on March

31,2005 to 28.9 per cent as on March 31, 2006 as is showed in Table 2.

Table 2
Computerisation in Public Sector Banks
(As on March 31, 2006)

	(Per cent)
Branches already Fully Computerised*	48.5
Branches Under Core Banking Solutions	28.9
Fully Computerised Branches (I+II)	77.5
Partially Computerised Branches	18.2

* Other than branches under Core Banking Solutions.

Source: RBI, Report on Trend and Progress of Banking in India, Table III, 48, p.97.

Table 3
Computerisation of Branches – Public Sector Banks

(As on March 31, 2006)

Extent of Computerisation	*Number of Banks*
Nil	–
Upto 10 per cent	1
More than 10 and up to 20 per cent	–
More than 20 and up to 30 per cent	2
More than 30 and up to 40 per cent	2
More than 40 and up to 50 per cent	–
More than 50 and up to 60 per cent	3
More than 60 and up to 70 per cent	2
More than 70 and up to 80 per cent	2
More than 80 and up to 90 per cent	–
More than 90 and up to 100 per cent	5
Fully Computerised	10
Total*	27

* Excludes IDBI Ltd.

Source: RBI, Report on Trend and Progress of Banking in India, Table III, 49, p.97.

It is clear from Table 2 that 77.5 per cent of the branches are fully computerized in which the share of branches under core banking solutions was 28.9 per cent while percentage of partially computerized branches were 18.2 per cent at the end of March 2006. It means that more than 95 per cent branches of public sector banks were either fully or partially computerized at the end of March 2006.

Table 4
Branches and ATMs of Scheduled Commercial Banks
(As at End-March 2006)

Bank Group	Number of Branches					Number of ATMs			
	Rural	*Semi-urban*	*Urban*	*Metro-politan*	*Total*	*On-site*	*Off-site*	*Total*	*Percent of off-site to total ATMs*
Nationalised Banks	12992	7120	7056	7017	34185	4812	2353	7165	32.8
State Bank Group	5229	4043	2449	2110	13831	1775	3668	5443	67.4
Old Private Sector Banks	936	1447	1236	947	4566	4054	493	1547	31.9
New Private Sector Banks	97	322	674	857	1950	2255	3857	6112	63.1
Foreign Banks	–	1	37	221	259	232	648	880	73.6
Total	19254	12933	11452	11152	54791	10128	11019	21147	52.1

Source: RBI, Report on Trend and Progress of Banking in India, Table III, 50, p.97.

An attempt has also been made to study the bank-wise computerization of branches. Table 3 shows that out of 27 public sector banks, branches of as many as ten public sector banks were 100 per cent computerized, while branches of another 12 banks were more than 50 per cent computerized.

Table 4 reveals the total number of ATMs installed by the banks were 21147 at end-March 2006. Nationalised banks accounted for the largest share of installed ATMs, followed by the new private sector banks, SBI group, old private sector banks and foreign banks. While SBI group, new private sector banks and foreign banks had more off-site ATMs, nationalized and old private sector banks had more on-site ATMs.

Off site ATMs as percentage to total ATMs were the highest in case of foreign banks followed by SBI group, new private sector banks, nationalized banks and old private sector banks as is clear from Table 4.

PERFORMANCE APPRAISAL

The emerging scenario is very dynamic and the biggest challenge before the banking sector is the management of change. Banking sector have not only to upgrade their products, systems, procedures and technology but also bring about a qualitative change in the work culture and ensure the willing participation of our people in the change process.

Table 5
Retail Electronic and Card-Based Payments
(Volume in thousand: Value in Rs. Crores)

	Retail Electronic @		*Card-based #*		*Total*	
Year	*Volume*	*Value*	*Volume*	*Value*	*Volume*	*Value*
2001-02	178	6123	N.A.	N.A.	178	6123
2002-03	237	10222	N.A.	N.A.	237	10222
2003-04	290	29606	1862	35889	2152	65496
2004-05	579	77702	3615	77267	4194	154969
2005-06	832	106599	10543	236994	11286	343593

N.A. : Not Available.
@ : ECS (Debt and Credit), EFT and SEFT/NEFT.
# : Credit cards, debt cards and smart cards.
Note : Volume represents number of transactions.
Source: RBI, Report on Trend and Progress of Banking in India, Table III, 50, p.98.

Convenience and easy acceptability of credit cards and technological advances have resulted in a continuous rise in retail electronic and card-based mode of payments. Table 5 shows the volume and value of card and electronic based payments more than doubled in 2006 from the previous year.

Reflecting the increasing use of electronic and card-based payments in retail transactions, their share in total transactions constituted 46.7 per cent in terms of volume and 51.2 per cent in terms of value in 2006. The use of electronic mode of payment increased both in terms of volume and value during 2005-06 compared with the previous year (Table-6).

Table 6
Paper-Based Versus Electronic Transactions

Year	*Paper-based*	*Electronic*	*Total*
	Volume (in lakhs)		
2002-03	10139	1730	11869
2003-04	10228	2152	12380
2004-05	11671	4200	15871
2005-06	12895	11300	24195
	Value (Rs. crore)		
2002-03	13424313	37536	13461849
2003-04	11595960	67461	11663421
2004-05	10120716	4221153	14321869
2005-06	11337062	11884429	23221491

Source: RBI, Report on Trend and Progress of Banking in India, Table III, 52, p.98.

The RTGS was operationalised on March 26, 2004. Its usage for transfer of funds, especially for large values and for systematically important purposes, has increased since then. The inter bank paper based clearing was discontinued at all the RBI centres from June 2005. All inter-bank transactions are now settled through RTGS. Apart from inter-bank funds transfer, the RTGS system facilitates customer transactions. As at end-March 2005, the number of RTGS branches reached about 23,000. The volume crossed 200,000 transactions a month by March 2006.

CONCLUSION

In the years to come, the Indian financial system will grow not only in size but also in complexity as the forces of competition start gaining further momentum. Banks have to prepare themselves to grapple with these challenges and convert them into opportunities. In the changed context, banks will have to move away from excessive concentration on asset management and adopt a more general approach of asset liability management aimed at modifying their liability structure in consonance with the desired asset structure. Banks will have to equip themselves to operate in an increasing deregulated interest rate environment. A significant improvement in customer service by banks can no longer be ignored.

Thus, Information Technology (IT) has made steady inroads into the financial sector. In fact, IT has brought about a significant change in many aspects relating to financial stability. Banks, customers and the regulators have benefited alike from the increasing use of information technology by the banking sector. Computerisation of transaction processing at banks has enabled the availability of audit trails which could be used for analysis. The greatest benefit of use of IT in the banking sector is the payment and settlement systems. With the migration of traditional paper-based fund movement to quick and more efficient electronic mode fund transfers have become easy and efficient to perform. More importantly, these systems have ensured settlement finality being achieved within time frames which are much smaller than was possible under the manual system. Quicker funds settlement has a direct impact on availability of money, which has a positive impact on liquidity management.

IT has also provided for better asset liability management, which was a relatively difficult task in manual based system spanning a large number of branches of banks, geographically spread across the country. This has helped banks in better fund management, thereby improving profitability for banks. Concepts such as core banking system, internet banking, anytime banking and anywhere banking have all been made possible with the help of IT. All these have made banking transactions to be performed in a manner, which is beneficial not only for the customer and his banker but for the economy as a whole.

The emerging technological development and the global competition have made the banking sectors to recognize the significance of human resource value for the advanced developments introduced in the Banking services. Before the Banking Industry can reap the Internet advantages fully, the employees should be trained with proper tools depending upon the nature of the job they have been assigned to undertake. Various skills for the computerization should be brought out in the banks with the advanced technology.

REFERENCES

Banerjee, A. and S.K. Singh (2001), Banking and Financial Sector Reforms in India, Deep & Deep Publications, New Delhi.

Bhasin, T.M., (2001), E-Commerce in Indian Banking, IBA Bulletin, April-May.

Bhide, M.G., et al., (2002), Banking Sector Reforms: A Critical Overview, Economic and Political Weekly, February 2.

Chopra, V.K., (2001), Emerging Challenges, Strategies and Solutions in Indian Public Sector Banks, IBA Bulletin, March.

Deivikaran, M.P. (1999), Virtual Banking, The Journal of the Indian Institute of Bankers, July-September.

Girija, U., (2001), Technology and Banking : Challenges Ahead, IBA Bulletin, March.

Gupta, M.S. (2006), "Towards Banking Excellence Under Reforms: Some Issues" in Indian Banking and Financial Sector Reforms (Ed. Ravishankar Kumar Singh), Abhijeet Publications, Delhi.

Kurup, M.P. (1996), Banking Sector Reforms and Transparency, Economic and Political Weekly, March 23.

Singh, Asha and M.S. Gupta (2006), "Financial Stability under Reforms" in Indian Banking and Financial Sector Reforms (Ed. Ravishankar Kumar Singh), Abhijeet Publications, Delhi.

Verma, D., (2000), Banking on Change, The Economic Times, April 4.

—RBI (2005-06), Report on Trend and Progress of Banking in India, Mumbai.

—RBI (2005-06), Report on Currency and Finance, Mumbai.

—RBI (2005-06), Annual Report, Mumbai.

CHAPTER 6

IMPACT OF BANKING SECTOR REFORMS ON PRODUCTIVITY AND EFFICIENCY OF BANKING IN INDIA

Priti Kashyap

Financial sector management and reform is a process rather than an event. It has no separate identity than the reform in real sector. Both are mutually reinforcing, sustaining and also sustained by each other. In the last few years reforms in the real sector, particularly in the area of industrial and trade policies have moved ahead of reforms in financial sector. In the changing scenario, there would be a need for a dynamic response from the banking and financial sector to match the evolving and diversified needs of the real sector as the real sector has become market driven, outward looking and with a premium on competitive efficiency.

Financial sector is treated as to be the backbone of the economy. The Quality of functioning of the financial sector can be expected to affect the functioning and productivity of all sectors of the economy. Efficient Financial intermediation should help in improving economy-wide resource allocation thereby promoting all round productivity growth. Thus the discussion on economic efficiency and productivity should involve analysis of developments in the financial sector.

Improvements in financing of physical and human capital, both in terms of allocative efficiency, should raise efficiency and productivity across the economy.

Financial intermediation is essential for the promotion of both extensive and intensive growth. The efficient intermediation of funds from savers to users enables the application of available resources in their most productive uses. The more efficient a financial system is in such resource generation and its allocation, the greater is its contribution to productivity and economic growth. As resource allocation improves and real return increase, savings would presumably respond and higher resource generation should result. Thus development of financial system is essential to the generation of higher productivity and economic growth.

IMPACT OF BANKING SECTOR PRODUCTIVITY ON THE REST OF THE ECONOMY

Economic history has established the fact that the financial development has played a crucial role in the promotion of industrialization in developed countries by facilitating the mobilization of capital for large investments in physical plants and equipments and the research and development of new technologies. A basic indicator of financial development is the contribution of finance related activities to G.D.P..

Table 1
Share of Real G.D.P.

Period	*Share of Banking andInsurance in G.D.P.(Percent)*	*Share of Banking andInsurance in Services (Percent)*
1970 – 71 to 1974 – 75	1.8	4.6
1975 – 76 to 1979 – 80	2.2	5.4
1980 – 81 to 1984 – 85	2.5	5.9
1985 – 86 to 1992 – 93	3.9	8.5
1993 – 94 to 1998 – 99	5.8	11.8
1999 – 00 to 2003 – 04	6.7	12.3

*Source:*National Accounts Statistics, Central Statistical Organization.

Table shows that the share of real GDP from finance related activities in India tripled from just 2% during 1970s to around

6% in 1990s and further 7% during the first half of this decade. Within the service sector the share of finance rose from less than 5% to more than 12% over the same period.

When we expose the liquidity and credit based indicators of financial development we find that the ratio of aggregate deposits to G.D.P. exceeded 50% during the first half of the current decade. At a slightly more disaggregated level, while bank credit to government has witnessed some tapering off in the second half of 1990s, credit to the commercial sector averaged over 30% of GDP during the first half of the current decade.

Table 2
Liquidity and Credit Based Indicators
(As Per G.D.P. at Current Market price)

Period	*Aggregate Deposit*	*M3 (Broad Money)*	*Bank Credit to Government*	*Bank Credit to Commercial Sector*
1970 – 71 to 1974 – 75	16.4	25.9	13.3	15.6
1975 – 76 to 1979 – 80	24.1	33.0	14.0	21.8
1980 – 81 to 1984 – 85	30.0	39.1	18.7	26.9
1985 – 86 to 1989 – 90	36.1	45.4	22.9	30.3
1990 – 91 to 1994 – 95	39.6	49.3	23.6	29.0
1995 – 96 to 1999 – 00	43.8	53.8	21.9	28.6
2000 – 01 to 2004 – 05	54.7	65.3	24.9	33.5

Source: Reserve Bank of India.

This suggests that the enhanced freedom of banks since the liberalization process has provided them with the flexibility in resource mobilization and deployment which has manifested itself in the uptrend in these ratios. Thus financial deepening has been taking place continuously in India and is still in progress.

REFORMS IN THE FINANCIAL SECTOR

The financial sector reforms have affected all three sectors: Capital Market, Banking and Insurance. The most striking development in capital markets was the abolition of the office of the Controller of Capital Issues, which regulated the pricing of initial public offerings. Firms were now free to price their

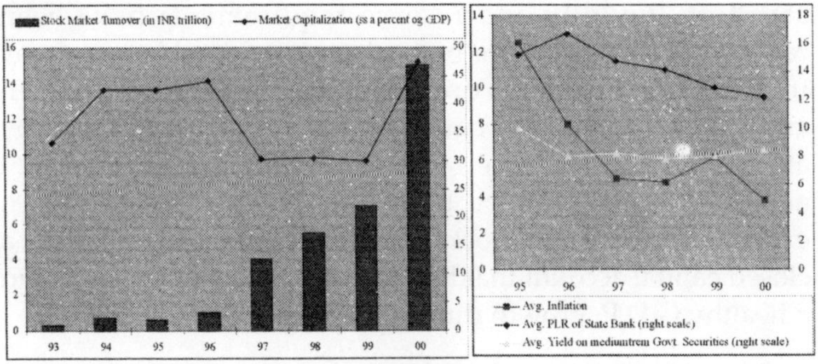

Figure 1

own equity. The simultaneous setting up of Securities and Exchange Board of India *(S.E.B.I.)* as the regulator of capital markets, of the National Stock Exchange *(N.S.E.)* a fully electronic order book driven exchange with a clearing corporation and a share depository introduced a great degree of transparency in the operations. The India Stock Exchange of N.S.E. and B.S.E. now boast of the second lowest transaction costs among all the major stock exchanges of the world. In addition to this mutual fund operators and Indian firms were allowed to raise funds from offshore markets through global depository rights and the capital market was opened for Foreign Institutional Investors.

Private players have now been allowed in insurance with foreign equity capped at 26% with an additional provision of 14% for non resident Indian investors.

The reforms in the banking sector are also very significant. As in most developing economies, the Indian government had used the implicit taxation of financial intermediation as a means of deficit financing. This was done by several means including, domestic borrowing by the government at below market rates, a high cash reserve ratio, and a statutory liquidity requirement. This enabled the government to preempt almost half of all bank credit. Interest rates were protected by ceilings on deposit rates and floors on lending rates. Banks are also required to lend 40 per cent of their deposits to the priority sector. The reform process has seen all of the above slowly dismantled. Interest rates are now largely deregulated, statutory liquidity and reserve requirements have been reduced, and banks have been given considerable autonomy in their operations. Foreign equity holding has been encouraged. All the deregulation has been accompanied by an application of more stringent prudential and capital adequacy norms. In fact it was the stringent restriction on exposure of banks to stocks and real estate, coupled with a closed capital account that has been credited for the success in a healthy G.D.P. growth during the Asian crisis of 1997–98.

BANKING SECTOR REFORMS

The banking sector reforms in India, initiated since 1992, have provided the necessary platform to operate on the basis of operational flexibility and functional autonomy, thereby enhancing efficiency, productivity and profitability. These reforms helped in bringing out structural changes in the financial sector, eased external constraints in their working, introduced transparency in reporting procedures, restructuring and recapitalization of banks and have increased the competitive element in the market.

A couple of reforms in the banking sector since liberalization are as under:

- *Phasing out of Statutory Pre-emption:* The SLR requirement has been brought down from 38.5% to 25% and the C.R.R. requirement from 7.5% to 5.75%.
- *De-regulation of Interest Rates:* All lending rates, except lending to small borrowers, and a part of export finance, have been de-regulated. Interest on all deposits are determined by banks, except on savings deposits.
- *CAR:* Capital Adequacy Ratio
- *Debt Recovery Tribunals (DRT):* 22 DRTs and 5 DRATs have already been set up and 7 more DRTs will be set up during this current financial year. The Act has been comprehensively amended to make the provisions for adjudication, enforcement and recovery more effective.

- *Other Prudential Norms:* Income recognition, asset classification and provisioning norms has been made applicable. The provisioning norms are more prudent, objective, transparent, uniform and designed to avoid subjectivity.
- *Transparency in Financial Statements:* Banks have been advised to disclose certain key parameters such as CAR, percentage of NPAs, provisions for NPAs, net value of investment, return on assets, profit per employee and interest income as a percentage to working funds.
- *Functional Autonomy:* The minimum prescribed government equity has been brought down to 51%. The boards of banks have been given more powers in operational matters such as rationalization of branches, credit delivery and recruitment of staff.
- *Hiving Off Regulatory and Supervisory Control:* The board for financial supervision was set up under the RBI in 1994, bifurcating the regulatory and supervisory functions.
- *Private Sector Banks:* A lot of new private sector banks have been set up with a view to induce greater competition and for improving operational efficiency of the banking system.
- *Payment System:* Significant progress has been made in the payment system by introducing modern payment media, such as smart cards, electronic funds transfer, debit/credit clearing and e-banking. RBI will soon put in place Real Time Gross Settlement *(RTGS)* to facilitate efficient funds management and mitigating settlement risks.
- *Interest Rate Decontrol:* Interest rates on time deposits, including 15–day deposits, were freed. Only the rate on savings deposits remains controlled by RBI.
- *Non-Performing Assets (NPA):* The government has cleared the Securitization Bill, as per which lenders can send notices to defaulters giving them a period of 60 days. If borrowers fail to pay during this period,

the bill allows them to take possession of their properties and the personal properties of promoters/ directors pledged with the bank.

Table 3
Non–Performing Loans of Different Bank Groups: 1994-2005
(Per cent to Total Advances)

Year (End–March)	*PSB*	*Old Private Banks*	*New Private Banks*	*Foreign Banks*	*Memo: NPL/Total loans(percent)–2004*
1994	24.8	NC	NC	NC	China: 15.6
1995	19.5	NC	NC	NC	Indonesia: 13.4
1996	18.0	NC	NC	NC	Korea: 1.7
1997	17.8	10.7	2.6	4.3	Malaysia: 11.6@
1998	16.0	10.9	3.5	6.4	Argentina: 17.5@
1999	15.9	13.1	6.2	7.6	Brazil: 3.9
2000	14.0	10.8	4.1	7.0	US: 0.8
2001	12.4	10.9	5.1	6.8	UK: 2.2
2002	11.1	11.0	8.9	5.4	Japan: 2.9
2003	9.4	8.9	6.7	5.3	
2004	7.8	7.6	5.0	4.6	
2005	5.5	6.0	3.6	2.8	Global range: [0.3 to 30.0]

@: Relates To 2005; NC: Not Compiled.
Source: Computed from Statistical Tables relating to Banks in India, RBI, various years.

The macro approach to financial monitoring has enabled policy makers to fine-tune their regulatory stance in consonance with the changing market and institutional dynamics so as to balance growth and stability concerns. For instance, despite the gradual tightening of prudential norms, the ratio of Non-Performing Loans *(NPL)* to total loans, which was at a high of 15.7 per cent for Scheduled Commercial Banks *(SCBs)* at end–March 1997, has declined by more than two thirds to 5.2 per cent at end–March 2005. Net NPLs also witnessed a significant decline, driven by the improvements in loan loss provisioning and improved recovery management, which comprises over half of the total provisions and contingencies. Capital adequacy of the banking sector also recorded a marked improvement and reached 12.8 per cent at end-March 2005, well above the stipulated level of 9 per cent. Banks have also been sensitized to develop robust risk management systems for credit and operational risks and focus on their asset-liability maturity profile to withstand adverse movements in market risk parameters such as interest rates and take corrective measures.

Another heartening development in bank's balance sheets, driven by the twin forces of international accounting irregularities and regulatory initiatives has been the increasing focus on corporate governance. As part of their Annual Report, banks presently disclose, under the head 'Report on Corporate Governance', details of their boards of directors, number of board meetings attended by members, details of the various sub-committees of the boards and provided the banks are listed, information on their stock price movements. This is complemented with the banks' philosophy on corporate governance and the enabling mechanisms undertaken by the banks to achieve their philosophy.

EFFICIENCY AND PRODUCTIVITY ANALYSIS IN BANKING

In recent times, a significant body of literature has evolved which explores the performance of financial institutions in the wake of financial liberalization. These studies are essentially micro-economic in nature and seek to analyze the efficiency and productivity of banking systems. Such analysis is of relevance from the policy standpoint, because as the finance-growth literature suggests, if banks become better-functioning entities, this is expected to be reflected in safety and soundness of the financial system and ultimately, lead to increases in the rate of economic growth. More importantly, such analysis is useful in enabling policymakers to identify the success or failure of policy initiatives or, alternatively, highlight different strategies undertaken by banking firms which contribute to their successes.

A priori, deregulation is expected to unleash competitive forces. Such competition would, in turn, enable banks to alter their input and output mix, which when combined with technological developments facilitates increase in output that raises overall bank productivity and efficiency. Second, liberal entry of de novo private and foreign banks as a part of the deregulation process is expected to raise bank efficiency, productivity and technology levels, because de novo private/ foreign banks are associated with superior management practices and technology, which can be fruitfully imbibed by those which are not. A third strand of thinking, borrowing from the public choice framework, contends that different ownership structures may engender different efficiency levels. The theoretical argument is straightforward: lack of capital market discipline weakens owners' control over management, enabling the latter to pursue their own interests, and provides fewer incentives for them to be efficient. Finally, as banking in the current world is technology driven and technological progress itself is scale augmenting; the relationship between bank size and efficiency becomes important. Skeptics, on the contrary, argue that deregulation is, in general, accompanied by an increase in banks' operational cost and could induce financial fragility due to over-expansion of banking activity. Thus, productivity gains after deregulation could be temporary and not sustainable in the long run. As a result, evidence in support of a unidirectional relationship between deregulation and efficiency/productivity is not conclusive.

EFFICIENCY OF INDIAN BANKS

Improvements in efficiency of the banking system are expected to be reflected, inter alia, in a reduction in operating expenditure, interest spread and cost of intermediation in general. Several indicators have been employed in the literature to compare banking production costs across time. Illustratively, intermediation cost, defined as the ratio of operating expense to total assets, witnessed a gradual reduction in the post reform period across various bank groups barring foreign banks *(Table–4)*. This decline in intermediation cost needs to be weighed against the large expenditures incurred in up gradation of information technology and institution of 'core banking' solutions. Admittedly, intermediation costs of banks in India still tend to be higher than those in developed banking markets.

Table 4
Intermediation Cost* of Scheduled Commercial Banks:1992 – 2004
(As Percentage to Total Asset)

Year (End-March)	*Public Sector Banks*	*Indian Private Banks*	*Foreign Banks*	*All Scheduled Commercial Banks*
1992	2.60	2.97	2.26	2.59
1993	2.64	2.71	2.70	2.65
1994	2.65	2.49	2.65	2.64
1995	2.83	2.35	2.73	2.79
1996	2.99	2.47	2.78	2.94
1997	2.88	2.36	3.04	2.85
1998	2.66	2.14	2.99	2.63
1999	2.65	2.04	3.40	2.65
2000	2.52	1.85	3.12	2.48
2001	2.72	1.87	3.05	2.64
2002	2.29	1.45	3.03	2.19
2003	2.25	1.99	2.79	2.24
2004	2.20	2.01	2.76	2.20

* Intermediation Cost = Operating Expenses.

Source: Computed from Statistical Tables relating to Banks in India, RBI, various years.

At a more disaggregated level, it is evident that Indian banks have improved their efficiency in the post reform period which is evidenced from the declining trend in per unit cost of output, irrespective of the choice of outputs *(Table–5)*. The operating cost per unit of earning assets declined from 2.1 per cent in 1992 to 1.8 per cent in 2004; similarly, operating cost per unit of total volume of business declined from 3.4 per cent to 2.6 per cent during the same period. Among the components of operating expenses, employee cost per unit of output witnessed a noticeable decline in the post-reform period. This decline is discernible across all bank groups, and especially for public sector banks in the post 2001 period consequent to the voluntary retirement scheme across several nationalized banks. On the other hand, the change in physical capital cost per unit of output has been marginal, reflecting the fact that Indian banks maintained a steady flow of investments towards physical capital formation, especially on automation and information technology.

Table 5
Operating Expense and Its Components of ScheduledCommercial Banks: 1992-2004

(Percent)

Year (End-March)	*Operating Expense/ Earning Assets@*	*Labour Cost/ Earning Assets@*	*Non-Labour Cost/ Earning Assets@*	*Operating Expense/ Total Business**	*Labour Cost/ Total Business**	*Non-Labour Cost/ Total Business**
1992	2.08	1.40	0.68	3.42	2.30	1.12
1993	2.14	1.43	0.72	3.51	2.34	1.17
1994	2.22	1.44	0.78	3.56	2.31	1.25
1995	2.32	1.54	0.78	3.74	2.48	1.26
1996	2.48	1.73	0.75	4.01	2.80	1.22
1997	2.36	1.60	0.76	3.84	2.60	1.24
1998	2.16	1.46	0.70	3.51	2.37	1.14
1999	2.21	1.47	0.74	3.55	2.35	1.20
2000	2.05	1.37	0.68	3.22	2.15	1.06
2001	2.16	1.47	0.69	3.36	2.28	1.07
2002	1.82	1.18	0.64	2.73	1.77	0.96
2003	1.81	1.13	0.69	2.65	1.65	1.00
2004	1.78	1.08	0.71	2.61	1.58	1.03

@ Earning Assets = Credit + Investment
* Total Business = Deposit + Credit
Source: Computed from Statistical Tables relating to Banks in India, RBI, various years.

From the efficiency standpoint, the intermediation cost needs to be viewed in conjunction with non-interest income. Till 2001, the burden *(the excess of non-interest expenditure over non-interest income as a percentage to total assets)* of commercial banks hovered around 1 to 1.5 per cent *(Table–6)*. This gap between intermediation cost and income from fee-based activities has narrowed considerably in recent years. For example, the burden of Indian commercial banks declined from 1.2 per cent in 1992 to 0.2 per cent in 2004. Moreover, there has been a lowering of the burden across bank groups in recent years. The improvement in respect of Indian private banks has been remarkable; their non-interest income in recent years has surpassed their intermediation cost and has resulted in a negative burden.

Table 6
Burden* of Scheduled Commercial Banks: 1992-2004
(As Percentage to Total Asset)

Year (End-March)	*Public Sector Banks*	*Indian Private Banks*	*Foreign Banks*	*All Scheduled Commercial Banks*
1992	1.37	1.94	-1.14	1.21
1993	1.45	1.57	1.70	1.48
1994	1.39	1.16	0.42	1.30
1995	1.57	0.92	0.27	1.43
1996	1.60	0.78	0.43	1.44
1997	1.56	0.72	0.50	1.40
1998	1.33	0.19	0.03	1.11
1999	1.44	0.69	0.94	1.32
2000	1.24	0.18	0.53	1.05
2001	1.51	0.59	0.59	1.32
2002	0.86	-0.14	0.12	0.63
2003	0.59	-0.46	0.15	0.38
2004	0.29	-0.07	-0.22	0.19

*Burden = Non-Interest Expense Less Non-Interest Income. It reflects the extent to which non-interest expenses are recovered through non-interest income.

Source: Computed from Statistical Tables relating to Banks in India, RBI, various years.

The cost income-ratio *(defined as the ratio of operating expenses to total income less interest expense)* of Indian banks showed a declining trend during the post reform period. For example, Indian banks paid roughly 45 per cent of their net income towards managing labour and physical capital in 2004 as against nearly 72 per cent in 1993 *(Table–7)*. In other words, Indian banks recorded a net cost saving of nearly 27 per cent of their net income during the post reform period. According to the data reported in The Banker 2004, the cost-income ratio of world's largest banks varied markedly from a low of 48 per cent to a high of 116 percent and the ratio around 60 per cent is an indicative benchmark *(RBI, 2005)*. In that respect, the cost-income ratio of Indian banks is now comparable internationally. Among various ownership patterns, public sector banks have tended to have relatively higher cost-income ratio as against private banks and foreign banks.

Table 7
Cost–Income Ratio of Scheduled Commercial Banks:1992-2004

(Percent)

Year (End-March)	*Public Sector Banks*	*Indian Private Banks*	*Foreign Banks*	*All Scheduled Commercial Banks*
1992	58.4	58.9	30.9	55.3
1993	73.7	66.8	59.2	71.9
1994	73.1	57.3	41.2	68.1
1995	67.6	52.2	40.6	63.5
1996	66.7	51.5	45.6	63.3
1997	64.3	51.3	45.6	61.0
1998	62.7	48.5	43.1	58.9
1999	65.9	58.9	56.9	64.3
2000	63.2	48.6	48.5	59.9
2001	67.0	51.8	50.0	63.4
2002	54.9	45.6	49.1	53.1
2003	47.8	45.1	46.5	47.2
2004	45.1	46.6	42.8	45.1

Cost-Income Ratio = Ratio Of Operating Expenses To Total Income Less Interest Expense. It measures the extent to which non-interest expense devours net total income.

Source: Computed from Statistical Tables relating to Banks in India, RBI, various years.

This explanation needs to be viewed in conjunction with the differential ownership profile of banks. Early studies *(Sarkar et al., 1998)* found somewhat weak evidence to suggest that ownership was an important determinant of performance. More recent studies exhibit mixed evidence: while certain studies *(Keova, 2003)* suggest ownership to have some effect on bank performance, others *(e.g., Bnaumik and Dimova, 2004)* veer around the view that competition induced public sector banks to eliminate the performance gap that existed between them and both domestic and foreign and private sector banks. More recent research reported differences in the efficiency of Indian commercial banks with different ownership status, level of non-performing loans, size and asset quality *(Das and Ghosh, 2006)*. More importantly, their study uncovered evidence that Public Sector Banks *(PSBs)* recorded higher efficiency gains in the post-reform period. Clearly, the evidence here is not conclusive, because comparisons are beset with several difficulties. Given the size and variety of PSBs, it is possible to find banks that could equal the good private sector banks as well as bad ones. In addition, PSBs have to reckon with 'legacy' problems, such as many of the non-performing assets that they have been saddled with. Some PSBs operate in relatively backward areas with limited discretion to pull out from such areas. The question still remains: whether there is a better payoff in enabling PSBs to improve their performance while promoting private sector banks, as compared with an alternative policy that provides for transfer of ownership and control from the public to the private sector. Will greater scope for mergers and acquisitions within and between public and private sector add to greater efficiency?

Another important indicator of efficiency of banks is Net Interest Margin *(NIM)*, defined as the excess of interest income over interest expense, scaled by total bank assets. Broadly speaking, this ratio reflects the allocative efficiency of financial intermediation, a lower ratio being indicative of higher efficiency. It is quite reasonable to believe that the decline in deposit rates ushered by the deregulation process is manifested in the lending behaviour of banks. In practice, however, lending rates have tended to be sticky downwards and seem to operate with a time lag. Historically the NIM of Indian banks is rather high. Around the onset of the reform process in 1992, the NIM of Indian banks was about 3.3 percent *(Table–8)*. Thereafter, it recorded a relatively modest decline to around 3 per cent in recent past. And traditionally, it is the foreign banks, which by virtue of their ability to mobilize low-cost deposits, have the highest NIMs, whereas those for private banks have been the lowest in past years. These comparisons are not watertight: typically, small and medium banks had high NIM until 1997. Thereafter, NIM for big banks recorded a rise. Contextually, it may be mentioned that banks in most developed countries and several emerging economies have NIM *(as a percentage to total assets)* of around 2 per cent. This provides some indication that competition in banking still has some way to go in India.

Table 8
Spread @ Of Scheduled Commercial Banks: 1992-2004
(As Percentage to Total Asset)

Year (End-March)	*Public Sector Banks*	*Indian Private Banks*	*Foreign Banks*	*All Scheduled Commercial Banks*
1992	3.22	4.01	3.90	3.30
1993	2.39	2.92	3.57	2.51
1994	2.36	3.01	4.20	2.54
1995	2.92	3.07	4.27	3.03
1996	3.10	3.10	3.76	3.15
1997	3.16	2.95	4.13	3.22
1998	2.91	2.46	3.97	2.95
1999	2.81	2.11	3.51	2.79
2000	2.70	2.13	3.85	2.72
2001	2.84	2.33	3.64	2.84
2002	2.73	1.58	3.25	2.57
2003	2.52	1.96	3.36	2.48
2004	2.97	2.24	3.47	2.87

@ Spread = Interest Earned – Interest Paid
Source: Report on Trend and Progress of Banking in India, RBI, various years.

PRODUCTIVITY

Studies on productivity in Indian banking have only begun to emanate of late. A recent study found that total factor productivity growth has improved marginally in the post deregulation period, but there was little evidence of narrowing of productivity differentials across ownership categories following deregulation *(Kumbhakar and Sarkar, 2003)*. Among various productivity indicators, labour productivity indicators like business per employee and profit per employee are most commonly used. In addition, business per branch is also used to judge branch-level productivity. The business per employee of Indian banks increased over three-fold in real terms from Rs.5.4 million in 1992 to Rs.16.3 million in 2004, exhibiting an annual compound growth rate of nearly 9 per cent *(Table–9)*. At the same time, the profit per employee increased more than five-fold: from Rs.20,000 to Rs. 150,000 over the same period, implying a compound growth of around 17 per cent. Branch productivity also recorded concomitant improvements.

Overall, the balance of evidence suggests distinctive productivity improvements in the banking sector over the reform period. The extant literature suggests that such improvements could be driven by two factors: "technological improvement," which expands the range of production possibilities and a "catching up effect," as peer pressure amongst banks compels them to raise productivity levels. In the context of gradual deregulation of financial sector, several factors could have been at work: a significant shift of the best-practice frontier, driven by a combination of technological advances, financial innovation and different strategies pursued by banks suited to their business philosophy and risk-return profile, changing composition of banks' input–output, and reduction in total cost due to improvements in overall efficiency. While it is difficult to pinpoint the relative mix of these factors in raising productivity, the bottomline is clear: Indian banks witnessed significant productivity improvements, in the post-reform era.

In a wider framework, cross-country studies of deregulation and productivity growth of banks report divergent views. Typically, cross-country comparisons are often fraught with difficulties, not only because of the different regulatory and economic regimes encountered by financial entities, but also owing to the differential quality of services associated with deposits and loans in different countries. Maudos and Pastor *(2001)* analyzed the cost and profit efficiency across 14 EU economies, as well as Japan and the USA. The results uncovered the evidence that, since the start of the 1990s increasing competition has led to gains in profit efficiency in the USA and Europe but not so in the Japanese banking system. Their results also show that the variance of profitability between countries would be considerably reduced if inefficiencies were eliminated, efficiency gains thus being a very important source of improvement in profitability. A recent study in the Asian context analyzed various efficiency measures of South-East Asian *(Indonesia, Korea, Malaysia, Philippines and Thailand)* banks in the context of corporate governance *(Williams and Nguyen, 2005)*. Although the motivation of the study was different, their empirical results found economic justification for the policy of bank privatization.

Table 9
Select Productivity Indicators of Scheduled Commercial Banks
(Rs. Million at 1993-94 Prices)

Year	*Business Per Employee*	*Profit Per Employee*	*Business Per Branch*
1992	5.4	0.02	109.9
1993	5.4	-0.05	110.4
1994	5.4	-0.04	109.2
1995	5.6	0.02	113.0
1996	6.0	0.01	119.6
1997	6.6	0.04	129.0
1998	7.5	0.05	144.9
1999	8.4	0.03	158.7
2000	9.7	0.05	179.4
2001	11.5	0.05	196.2
2002	13.7	0.09	214.9
2003	15.0	0.12	234.8
2004	16.3	0.15	254.5

Source: Statistical Tables relating to Banks in India

Let me encapsulate this section by making some general comments on the efficiency and productivity growth of Indian banks vis-à-vis leading Asian nations like China and Korea. As far as real growth *(adjusted for price movement and exchange rate fluctuations)* in banking business is concerned, Indian banks are favourably placed. In recent years, the real growth of deposits and of loans of Indian banks was noticeably higher than those of other Asian countries such as China and Korea. At the same time, profitability of Indian banks, as determined by the return on assets, is also much higher *(Tables–10, 11, 12, and 13)*. The intermediation cost of Indian banks seems to be relatively higher than that of Korea and China. Nonetheless, higher operating cost in India is well compensated by the higher non-interest income, as compared to other Asian countries. Finally, the labour productivity of the top 4 banks in India *(which includes one de novo private bank)* and the four state-owned Chinese banks indicates that except the private

Table 10
Spread (Net Interest Margin) of Banks of Major Asian Countries (As Percentage to Total Asset)

Year	*China*	*Indonesia*	*Korea*	*Malaysia*	*Philippines*	*Thailand*	*India*
1996	1.86	2.92	1.70	2.91	4.07	2.57	3.07
1997	2.27	2.76	1.80	2.94	4.21	3.00	2.83
1998	2.16	-9.38	1.69	3.32	4.52	0.74	2.66
1999	1.83	-3.11	2.03	2.67	3.16	0.69	2.56
2000	1.76	2.21	2.06	3.02	2.54	1.43	2.74
2001	1.78	3.16	2.12	2.83	2.60	1.69	2.54
2002	1.78	3.61	2.33	2.70	2.29	1.84	2.74
2003	1.87	4.22	2.50	2.61	2.30	1.99	2.84

Source: Bank Scope

Table 11
Intermediation Cost (Operating Expense) of Banks of Major Asian Countries (As Percentage to Total Asset)

Year	*China*	*Indonesia*	*Korea*	*Malaysia*	*Philippines*	*Thailand*	*India*
1996	1.23	2.39	2.24	1.42	3.52	1.50	2.77
1997	1.24	4.50	2.55	1.49	3.28	2.05	2.60
1998	1.40	4.04	2.53	1.68	3.67	2.54	2.58
1999	1.18	2.83	1.53	1.50	3.38	2.20	2.41
2000	1.12	2.72	1.46	1.70	3.32	1.98	2.57
2001	1.10	2.36	1.42	1.80	3.30	2.01	2.21
2002	1.05	2.73	1.39	1.73	3.16	1.78	2.22
2003	1.01	2.94	1.38	1.61	3.00	1.71	2.19

Source: Bank Scope

Table 12
Non-Interest Income of Banks of Major Asian Countries (As Percentage to Total Asset)

Year	*China*	*Indonesia*	*Korea*	*Malaysia*	*Philippines*	*Thailand*	*India*
1996	0.26	0.99	1.06	0.98	2.12	0.68	1.44
1997	0.24	2.97	0.93	1.10	1.73	1.00	1.49
1998	0.13	1.31	0.20	1.16	1.96	1.03	1.38
1999	0.17	1.96	0.99	1.00	1.95	0.97	1.47
2000	0.22	1.51	0.74	1.01	1.59	0.62	1.33
2001	0.22	1.08	1.28	1.15	1.73	0.73	1.49
2002	0.25	1.30	0.91	1.11	2.11	0.93	1.83
2003	0.25	1.46	0.80	0.94	2.16	0.95	1.97

*Source:*Bank Scope

bank, the top three public sector banks in India recorded much lower employee productivity. However, in the absence of data on employment for banks in other countries, it is difficult to ascertain the degree of labour productivity differentials across countries.

Table 13
Net Profit of Banks of Major Asian Countries
(As Percentage to Total Asset)

Year	*China*	*Indonesia*	*Korea*	*Malaysia*	*Philippines*	*Thailand*	*India*
1996	0.29	1.01	0.17	1.40	2.06	-0.56	0.71
1997	0.30	-0.39	-0.84	1.03	1.63	-1.17	0.90
1998	0.20	-46.92	-3.10	0.04	0.85	-5.57	0.54
1999	0.17	-9.20	-1.40	0.96	0.10	-5.88	0.70
2000	0.21	0.46	-0.37	1.29	-0.03	-0.15	0.48
2001	0.20	0.87	0.76	0.68	0.48	1.46	0.69
2002	0.20	1.30	0.60	1.03	0.60	0.21	0.97
2003	0.12	1.61	0.15	1.08	1.08	0.63	1.14

Source: Bank Scope

A clear message emanating is the role of technology in driving productivity and efficiency improvements. In today's world of banking, technology is considered as the basic tool of the 'process engineer's of the organization. It is crucial for the design, control, and execution of service delivery in banks. Therefore, a key driver of efficiency and productivity in the banking industry today is the effective use of technology. This is a crucial pre-requisite for capitalising on future opportunities for the banking sector. In effect, it has become the key to servicing all customer segments–offering convenience to retail customer, corporates and government clients. The increasing sophistication, flexibility and complexity of products and servicing offerings makes the effective use of technology critical for managing the risks associated with banking business. However, the 'technological penetration' in India has been quite modest. According to data reported in the World Development Indicators database, as of 2002, the number of computers per 1000 persons was about 7 in India compared to anywhere between 70-500 in most emerging markets and even higher in most developed economies. Wide disparities exist within the banking sector as far as technological capabilities are concerned: the percentage of 'computer literate' employees as percentage of total staff in 2000 was around 20 per cent in public sector banks compared with 100 per cent in new private banks and around 90 per cent in foreign banks *(Reserve Bank of India, 2002)*. Data reported by the RBI suggests that nearly 71 per cent of branches of public sector banks are fully computerized. However, computerization needs to go beyond the mere 'arithmeticals', to borrow a term from the Report of the Committee on Banking Sector Reforms *(Government of India, 1998)*, and instead, "needs to be leveraged optimally to achieve and maintain high service and efficiency standards". In fact, a recent research on the role of technology in driving productivity improvements in banking demonstrates that computer employees and IT capital exhibit higher productivities than their respective non-computer employees and non-IT capital, respectively *(Huang, 2005)*. The challenge, therefore, remains three fold: acquiring the 'right' technology, deploying it optimally and remaining cost-effective whilst delivering sustainable returns to shareholders. In effect, 'managing' technology so as to reap the maximum benefits remains a key challenge for the Indian banks.

CONCLUSION

The above elaborations have been focused on the efficiency and productivity changes in Indian banking. The patterns of efficiency and technological change witnessed in Indian banking can be viewed as consistent with expectations in an industry undergoing rapid change in response to the forces of deregulation. In reaction to evolving market prospects, a few pioneering banks might adjust quickly to seize the emerging opportunities, while others respond cautiously. As deregulation gathers momentum, commercial banks would need to devise imaginative ways of augmenting their incomes and more importantly their fee-incomes so as to raise efficiency and productivity levels.

REFERENCES

Bell, C and P. Rousseau (2001), "Post Independence India: A Case of Finance-led Industrialization?", Journal of Development Economics, 65, 153-175.

Berger, A.N and D.B. Humphrey (1992), "Measurement and Efficiency Issues in Commercial Banking" in Z. Griliches *(ed.)*: Output Measurement in the Services Sector, Chicago: University of Chicago Press, 245-279.

Bhaumik, S.K. and R.Dimova (2004), "How Important is Ownership in a Market with Level-Playing Field? The Indian Banking Sector Revisited", Journal of Comparative Economics, 32, 165-180.

Bhide, M.G., A. Prasad and S.Ghosh (2001), Emerging Challenges in Indian Banking, Working Paper No.103, Centre for Research in Economic Development and Policy Reform, Stanford University.

Das, A. and S. Ghosh (2006), "Financial Deregulation and Efficiency: An Empirical Analysis of Indian Banks during the Post-Reform Period", Review of Financial Economics *(forthcoming).*

Demirgúc-Kunt, A., & V. Maksimovic (1998), "Law, Finance and Firm Growth", Journal of Finance, 53, 2107-37.

Frexias. X and J.C. Rochet (1997), Microeconomics of Banking, Cambridge MA: MIT Press.

Government of India (1998), Report of the Committee on Banking Sector Reforms *(Chairman: Shri M Narasimham)*, New Delhi.

Huang Tai-Hsin (2005), "A Study on the Productivities of IT Capital and Computer Labor: Firm-level Evidence from Taiwan's Banking Industry", Journal of Productivity Analysis, 24, 241–257.

Koeva, P. (2003), The Performance of Indian Banks During Financial Liberalization. IMF Working Paper No.150, Washington DC.

Kumbhakar, S. and S. Sarkar (2003), "Deregulation, Ownership and Efficiency Change in Indian Banking: Evidence from India", Journal of Money, Credit and Banking, 35, 403-414.

Maudos, J. and J.M. Pastor (2001), "Cost and Profit Efficiency in Banking: An International Comparison of Europe, Japan and USA", Applied Economics Letters, 8, 383-387.

Mohan, R. (2005), "Financial Sector Reforms: Policies and Performance Analysis", Economic Political Weekly, Special Issue on Money, Banking and Finance (March), 40, 1106-1121.

Mohan Rakesh, Deputy Governor, RBI: Reforms, Productivity, and Efficiency in Banking: The Indian Experience.

Rajan, R.G., and L. Zingales (1998), Financial Dependence and Growth. American Economic Review, 88, 559-86.

Rangarajan, C and N. Jadhav (1992), "Issues in Financial Sector Reforms", In B. Jalan *(ed.)*: The Indian Economy, Delhi: Penguin Books India.

Ray, P. and I. Sengupta (2004), "Systemic Restructuring of Banks: The Indian Experience", Journal of the Indian Bankers Association.

Reserve Bank of India (2000), Report on Currency and Finance 1999-2000, RBI: Mumbai.

Reserve Bank of India (2002), 'Expenditure Pattern and IT Initiatives of Banks', RBI Bulletin, December.

Reserve Bank of India (2005), Report on Trend and Progress of Banking in India, 2004-2005, RBI: Mumbai.

Sarkar, J., S. Sarkar and S.K. Bhaumik (1998), "Does Ownership Always Matter? Evidence from the Indian Banking Industry", Journal of Comparative Economics, 26, 262-281.

Stiglitz, J.E. (1998), "More Instruments and Broader Goals: Moving Towards the Post-Washington Consensus", WIDER Annual Lecture, Helsinki.

Tandon B.B. (2002), 'Financial Sector Reforms, Book on Financial Sector Reforms.

Williams, J. and Nguyen, N. (2005), "Financial Liberalization, Crisis, and Restructuring: A Comparative Study of Bank Performance and Bank Governance in South East Asia", Journal of Banking and Finance, 29, 2119–2154.

CHAPTER 7

BANKING SECTOR REFORMS IN INDIA: CHALLENGES AHEAD

Anju Jain

INTRODUCTION

A strong and efficient financial system is critical to the attainment of the objective of creating a market driven, productive and competitive economy to support higher investment levels and accentuate growth. Banking is the most dominant segment of the financial system and plays a crucial role in the development of a sound economy.

Banking today has transformed into a technology intensive and customer friendly mode with a focus on convenience. The sector is yet to witness the emergence of financial super markets in the form of universal banks providing a suite of services from retail to corporate banking and industrial lending to investment banking. While co-operate banking is clearly the largest segment, personal financial services is the highest growth segment.

Banking sector reforms is a part and parcel of financial sector reforms which initiated in 1991 to remove the deficiencies in the financial sector, particularly in the banking sector to strengthen the economic reform. Almost two decades is enough to evaluate and assess the performance of banking sector reforms.

INDIAN BANKING REFORM–AN OVERVIEW

The transformation of the banking sector in India needs to be viewed in light of the overall economic reform process along with the rapid changes that have been taking place in the global environment within which banks operate. The global forces of change include technological innovation, the deregulation of financial services internationally, our own increasing exposure to international competition and equally important, changes in corporate behaviour such as growing disinter mediation and increasing emphasis on shareholder value. Recent banking crises in Asia, Latin America and elsewhere have accentuated these pressures.

India embarked on a strategy of economic reforms in the wake of a serious balance of payments crisis in 1991; a central plank of the reforms was reform in the financial sector and with banks being the mainstay of financial intermediation, the banking sector. The objective of the banking sector reforms was to promote a diversified, efficient and competitive financial system with the ultimate objective of improving the allocative efficiency of resources through operational flexibility, improved financial viability and institutional strengthening. A summary profile of the banking industry over the last 15 years is presented in Table 1.

The financial system in India by the late 1980s was characterized by dominant government ownership of banks and financial institutions, widespread use of administered and variegated interest rates and financial repression through forced financing of government fiscal deficits by banks and through monetisation. Thus, although a great degree of financial deepening had indeed taken place and financial savings had increased continuously, financial markets were not really functioning and there was little price recovery in terms of the cost of money, i.e., interest rates. The efficiency and productivity enhancing function of the financial system was severely handicapped. Hence, a widespread financial sector reform effort has been underway since 1991.

Table 1
Summary Profile of the Banking Industry: 1990-91 to 2004-05

	1990-91			*1995-96*			*2004-05*		
Year/Bank Group	*PSB*	*Private*	*Foreign*	*PSB*	*Private*	*Foreign*	*PSB*	*Private*	*Foreign*
No. of banks	28	25	23	27	35 (8)	29	28	29 (9)	31
Listed	None	None	NA	2	9 (3)	NA	20	18 (7)	NA
Non-listed				25	26 (5)	NA	8	11 (2)	NA
Share (in per cent) of									
Assets	91.4	3.7	4.9	84.5	6.5 (1.5)	7.9	75.3	18.2 (12.5)	6.5
Deposits	92.0	4.0	4.0	85.4	6.6 (1.3)	6.7	78.0	17.3 (10.9)	4.7
Credit	93.0	4.0	3.0	82.4	6.8 (1.9)	8.9	73.2	20.0 (13.9)	6.8
Income	89.4	3.3	7.3	82.5	8.2	9.4	76.4	16.9	6.7
Expenses	90.0	3.3	6.8	84.1	7.5	8.4	76.7	16.9	6.4
Profit	68.5	4.1	27.4	-33.3	55.6	77.8	74.2	16.4	9.4
Memo									
Bank asset / GDP (per cent)		56.3			50.4			80.4	

PSB: public sector banks; NA: Not applicable; Listed: Banks listed on recognised stock exchanges.
Figures in bracket under Private pertain to *de novo* private banks.
Source: Reserve Bank of India

A basic indicator of financial development is the contribution of finance-related activities to GDP. The share of real GDP originating from finance-related activities in India tripled from just around 2 per cent during the 1970s to around 6 per cent during the 1990s and further to 7 per cent during the first half of this decade. Within the services sector, the share of finance rose from less than 5 per cent to more than 12 per cent over the same period.

Table 2

Share of Real GDP Originating in Banking and Insurance

(Per cent)

Period	*Share of Banking and Insurance in GDP*	*Share of Banking and Insurance in Services*
1970-71 to 1974-75	1.8	4.6
1975-76 to 1979-80	2.2	5.4
1980-81 to 1984-85	2.5	5.9
1985-86 to 1992-93	3.9	8.5
1993-94 to 1998-99	5.8	11.8
1999-2000 to 2003-04	6.7	12.3

Source: Computed from *National Accounts Statistics*, Central Statistical Organisation.

Major areas of banking sector reforms can be summed up as follows:

- Financial repression through statutory pre-emptions has been reduced, while stepping up prudential regulations at the same time.
- Interest rates have been progressively deregulated on both the deposit and lending sides.

Restoration of the health of the banking system has involved:

- Restoration of public sector banks' net worth achieved through recapitalisation where needed (total cost less than one per cent of GDP).
- Competition increased through entry of new private sector banks and foreign banks.
- Higher levels and standards of disclosure achieved to enhance market transparency.

- Bank regulation and supervision strengthened towards international best practice.
- Micro prudential measures instituted.
- Supervision process streamlined with combination of on-site and off-site surveillance along with external auditing.
- Risk based supervision introduced.
- Process of structured and discretionary intervention introduced for problem banks through a prompt corrective action mechanism.
- Ownership of public sector banks has been broadened through disinvestment up to 49 per cent.
- Mechanism for greater regulatory coordination instituted for regulation and supervision of financial conglomerates.
- Measures taken to strengthen creditor rights.

As the banking system has been liberalised and become increasingly market-oriented and financial markets have developed concurrently, the conduct of monetary policy has also been tailored to take into account the realities of the changing environment.

IMPLEMENTATION OF RTGS

With the commencement of the operations of the Real Time Gross Settlement (RTGS) system form 26th March 2004, India crossed a major milestone in the development of Systemically Important Payment Systems (SIPS) and complied with the Core Principles framed by the Bank for International Settlements (BIS). It was a 'soft' launch with four banks, besides the Reserve Bank as participants. In addition to the service provider, the Reserve Bank is also a participant in the RTGS System. Currently, there are 71 direct participants in the RTGS system. Scheduled banks, primary dealers and clearing houses numbering around 125 are the targeted members.

The RTGS system started with pure inter-bank transactions. Customer based inter-bank transactions were permitted to be settled through the system, effective April 29, 2004. The RTGS system will be fully integrated with the accounting system of the Reserve Bank and other payment systems and services.

Salient features of the RTGS system are:

- Payments are settled transaction by transaction for high value and retail payments;
- Settlement of funds in final and irrevocable;
- Settlement is done on a real time basis and the funds settled can be further used immediately;
- It is a fully secure system which uses digital signatures and Public Key Infrastructure (PKI) based encryption for safe and secure message transmission;
- There is a provision for intra-day collateralized liquidity support for member banks to smoothen the temporary mismatch of fund flows.
- RTGS provides for transfer of funds relating to inter-bank settlement and also for customer related fund transfers. More than 75 percent of the value of inter-bank transactions, which was earlier being settled through the Deferred Net Settlement Systems (DNSS) based Inter-bank clearing, is not being settled under the RTGS. Requirements for settlement of transactions under the RTGS system are met through intra-day liquidity support to the members by the Reserve Bank on a collateralized repo basis.

BASEL II AND INDIA

The RBI's association with the Basel Committee on Banking Supervision dates back to 1997 as India was among the 16 non-member countries that were consulted in the drafting of the Basel Core Principles, The Reserve Bank of India became a member of the Core Principles Liaison Group in 1998 and subsequently became a member of the Core Principles Working Group on Capital, Within the Working Group, the RBI has been actively participating in the deliberations on the New Accord and had the privilege to lead a group of six major non-G-10 supervisors which presented a proposal on a simplified approach for Basel II to the Committee.

Commercial banks in India will start implementing Base II with effect from March 31, 2007, They will adopt the standardised approach for credit risk and the basic indicator approach for operational risk initially. After adequate skills are developed, both at the banks and also at supervisory levels, some banks may be allowed to migrate to the Internal Rating Based (IRB) Approach. The RBI had announced in its annual polity statement in May 2004 that banks in India should examine in depth the options available under Basel II and draw a road- map by end-December 2004 for migration to Basel II and review the progress made at quarterly intervals.

CHALLENGES AHEAD

Improving Profitability

The most direct result of the above changes is increasing competition and narrowing of spreads and its impact on the profitability of banks. The challenge for banks is how to manage with thinning margins while at the same time working to improve productivity which remains low in relation to global standards. This is particularly important because with dilution in banks' equity, analysts and shareholders now closely track their performance. Thus, with falling spreads and interest rates, and rising provision for NPAs, greater attention will need to be paid to reducing transaction costs. This will require tremendous efforts in the area of technology and for banks to build capabilities to handle much bigger volumes.

Technology

Technology has thus become a strategic and integral part of banking, driving banks to acquire and implement world class systems that enable them to provide products and services in large volumes at a competitive cost with better risk management practices. The pressure to undertake extensive computerisation is very high as banks that adopt the latest in technology have an edge over others. Customers have become very demanding and banks have to deliver customised products through multiple channels, allowing customers to access the bank round the clock.

Risk Management

The deregulated environment brings in its wake risks along with profitable opportunities and technology plays a crucial role in managing these risks. In addition to being exposed to credit risk, market risk and operational risk, the business of banks would be susceptible to country risk, which will be heightened as controls on the movement of capital are eased. In this context, banks are upgrading their credit assessment and risk management skills and retraining staff, developing a cadre of specialists and introducing technology driven management information systems.

Sharpening Skills

The far-reaching changes in the banking and financial sector entail a fundamental shift in the set of skills required in banking. To meet increased competition and manage risks, the demand for specialised banking functions using IT as a competitive tool is set to go up. Special skills in retail banking, treasury, risk management, foreign exchange, development banking, etc., will need to be carefully nurtured and built. Thus, the twin pillars of the banking sector i.e. human resources and IT will have to be strengthened.

Greater Customer Orientation

In today's competitive environment, banks will have to strive to attract and retain customers by introducing innovative products, enhancing the quality of customer service and marketing a variety of products through diverse channels targeted at specific customer groups.

Corporate Governance

Besides using their strengths and strategic initiatives for creating shareholder value, banks have to be conscious of their responsibilities towards corporate governance. Following financially liberalisation, as the ownership of banks gets broad based the importance of institutional and individual shareholders will increase. In such a scenario, banks will need to put in place a code for corporate governance for benefiting all stakeholders of a corporate entity.

International Standards

Introduction of internationally followed best practices and observing universally acceptable standards and codes is necessary for strengthening the domestic financial architecture. This includes best practices in the area of corporate governance along with full transparency in disclosures. In today's globalised world, focusing on the observance of standards will help smooth integration with world financial markets.

High Capital Inflows

While we have an all time high foreign exchange reserves of more than US $ 140 billion, high capital inflows pose a big challenge to monetary and exchange rate management. In this context, operationalisation of Market Stabilization Scheme (MSS) has given an additional instrument for liquidity and monetary management.

Digital Divide

We have all heard of the digital divide which is a challenge to be overcome by the banking industry as well. While the average Indian customer may be as technology sauvy or even better than the western counterpart the cultural aspects of his relationship may necessitate a personal touch to the offering of banks.

Further, all the technology based offering by banks have a bias towards the major town and cities and the need for reaching the mid size cities as well as large rural population assumes significance.

BANKING SECTOR REFORMS AND INDIA'S EXPERIENCE

There was a significant degree of deregulation in the Indian economy since 1991. Many of the reforms introduced were aimed at integrating India more closely with the rest of the world and quite a number of those reforms directly affected in the banking sector.

Although liberalisation of financial services and competition has improved customer services, experience shows that customers' interests are not always accorded priority. More importantly, concerns have been raised with regard to banking practices that tend to exclude vast segments of the population. In this context, the Reserve Bank has announced its intention to implement policies to incentivise banks to provide extensive services responsive to the needs of the under-privileged. As part of the process, the Reserve Bank has recently advised all banks to make available a basic banking 'no frills' account either with 'nil' or very low minimum balances as well as charges that would make such accounts accessible to vast sections of population. The nature and number of transactions in such accounts could be restricted, but made known to the customer in advance in a transparent manner. Banks have been urged to give wide publicity to this facility so as to ensure greater financial inclusion.

Over the reform period, more and more banks have begun to get listed on the stock exchange, which in its wake, has led to greater market discipline and concomitantly to an improvement in their governance aspects as well. This has led to a broadbasing of the ownership of PSBs. Such diversification of ownership has also led to a qualitative difference in their functioning, since there is induction of private shareholding as well as attendant issues of shareholder's value, as reflected by the market capitalisation, board representation and interests of minority shareholders. The issue of mixed ownership as an institutional structure where government has controlling interest is a salient feature of bank governance in India. Such aspects of corporate governance in PSBs are important, not only because PSBs dominate the banking industry, but also because it is likely that they would continue to remain in banking business. To the extent, there is public ownership of PSBs, the multiple objectives of the government as owner and the complex principal-agent relationships needs to be taken on board. Given the increased technical complexity of most business activities including banking and the rapid pace of change in financial markets and practices, PSBs would need to devise imaginative ways of responding to the evolving challenges within the context of mixed ownership. This is an exciting phase for PSBs to grow and prosper, and it is up to these banks to respond to the challenges.

CONCLUSION

The face of banking is changing rapidly. Competition is going to be tough and with financial liberalization under the WTO. Banks in India will have to benchmark themselves against the best in the world. It also means institutional co-operation among regulators is of increasing importance. The reforms introduced in the banking sector in the 1990s were far reaching, but the world of business and banking is changing rapidly. For a strong, resilient banking and financial system, banks need to go beyond peripheral issues and tackle significant issues like improvement in profitability, efficiency and technology. While achieving economics of scale through consolidation and exploring cost effective solution, Indian banks should be capable of competing with the best in the world. Given the size of domestic market, it should be possible for Indian Banks to become truly global players.

REFERENCES

Purwar, A.K. – Sector 2: Industry Review.

Reddy, Y.V. Governor, R.B.I., (2004), Banker's Conference.

Krueger, Anne O, - Keynote Address by First Deputy Managing Director IMF–Banking Needs of a Global Economy.

Leeladhar, V. (2005), Reserve Bank of India Bulletin, July.

Gopinath. S. (2005), Reserve Bank of India Bulletin, February.

Muju, N.A.– Former Principal of Reserve Bank of India. Indian Institute of Banking & Finance – Monthly Column.

—(1997), Financial Sector Reform & the BRI's Balance Sheet Management– Address at the Vysya Bank's IInd Annual Lecture on Banking, Bangalore, 14 November.

Reddy, Y.V. (2005), Banking Sector Reforms in India – An Overview – Reserve Bank of India Bulletin, June.

Leeladhar, V. (2005), Emerging Challenging before the Indian Banks – Reserve Bank of India Bulletin, June.

Ranade, A. – Chief Economist of India– A Decade of India's Economic Reforms

Udeshi, K.J. (2005), Reserve Bank of India Bulletin, May.

—(2004), R.B.I., Annual Report.

—Reforms, Productivity and Efficiency in Banking: The Indian Experience.

CHAPTER 8

BANKING SECTOR REFORMS: A DECADE

Pushpa Sinha
Ratna Mitra

The decade of 1991-2001 is a decade of challenges and criteria changes of the whole economic scenario. It was the period which became a milestone in the pack of economic transaction of the presently so called super market of Asia. The Indian economy faced a distinct slow down during the fiscal year 1991-92 after a decade of relatively high growth. The dominant failures in this low growth were stagnation in the industrial output and a decline in the agricultural production. The process of fiscal correction and adjustment set in motion during 1990-91.

It was the year when various reforms were started in India in order to renovate the Indian economy with the implementation of the New Economic Policy. The country witnessed set of reforms in each and every sector of the economy and banking sector was not an exception. In order to bring correction in the balance of payment position and stabilization in the economy, this sector needed certain adjustments. Consequent to these reforms, the financial system has been transformed from a planned and administered regime to a market oriented financial system.

By the time, India had witnessed a phenomenal expansion in the geographical coverage and functional spread of our banking and financial system since nationalization in 1969. Despite impressive quantitative achievements in resource mobilization and in extending the credit reach, several distortions over the years had crept into the banking and financial system. As a result, productivity and efficiency of the system had suffered, its portfolio quality had badly deteriorated, profitability had been decreasing in several public sector banks and financial institution had been incurring losses year after year. Their customer service was poor, their work technology outmoded and they were unable to meet the challenges of a competitive environment. It was under these circumstances that the Government of India set up a High Level Committee with Mr M. Narasimham, former Governor of Reserve Bank of India as Chairman to examine all aspects relating to the structure, organization, function and procedures of the financial system. This committee on the financial system submitted its report in November, 1991.

The Narasimham Committee recommendations were aimed at:-

(1) Ensuring a degree of operational flexibility.

(2) Internal autonomy for public sector banks in their decision making process and

(3) Greater degree of professionalism in banking operations.

These recommendations of Narasimhan Committee I in 1991 provided the blueprint for the first generation reforms of financial sector. The period 1992-97 witnessed the laying of the foundations for reforms in banking system (Rangarajan 1988). Despite stiff opposition from bank unions and political parties in the country, the Government of India accepted all the major recommendations of Narasimham Committee and started implementing them straightway as follows:-

(1) Statutory Liquidity Ratio (SLR) on incremental net demand and time liabilities has been reduced from 38.5% to 25% and SLR on outstanding net domestic

demand and time liabilities were reduced gradually from 38.5% to 25% in October 1997. This was the minimum stipulated under section 24 of the Banking Regulation Act, 1949

(2) Financial regulation through statutory preemptions has been lowered while stepping up prudential regulations at the same time. Prudential norms required banks to make 100% provision for all non-performing assets (NPAs). As for funding this purpose was placed at Rs. 10,000 crores, it was phased over in two years. Bank had to make at least 30% provision against doubtful and bad debts during 1992-93 and balance 70% in 1993-94.

(3) The incremental cash reserve ratio (CRR) of 10% was near to be abolished. But RBI could not reduce CRR immediately. It was done in a phased manner and was marked at 5% during 2005 to 2006.

(4) Interest rate slabs were gradually reduced.

(5) Capital adequacy norms were fixed at 8% by RBI in April 1992 and banks had to comply with them over a period of three years. By end of March 1996 all PSBs had obtained capital to risk assets ratio of 8%. The new norm of 8% was also obtained by foreign banks in India and by some Indian banks.

(6) Measures have also been taken to broaden the ownership base of PSBs. Consequently, the private shareholding in PSB's has gone up ranging from 23% (Bank of India) to 43.7% (State Bank of India).

(7) Scheduled commercial banks have now been given freedom to open new branches and upgrade extension counters.

(8) Ten new private sector banks have started functioning and were allowed to raise capital contribution. In 1996-97 budget, the Government of India announced the setting up of new private local banks with jurisdiction over three continuous districts.

(9) Supervision of commercial banks is being tightened by R.B.I.

(10) The Government of India passed "Recovery of Debts due to Banks and Financial Institution Act, 1913" in order to speed up the recovery of debts.

The above recommendations laid down and the implementation of prudential norms pertaining to capital adequacy, income recalling recognition asset, classification and provisioning exposure norms, etc. during 1992-97. Due to the difficulties faced during this period and the changes in global scenario, the report of Narasimham Committee II in 1998 provided the roadmap for second generation reform.

It seems important at this stage and refers to another development: the growing significance of the economic sector has per se, also impacted the sphere of political economy. Principles of economic governance appears to be gaining ground vis-à-vis considerations of political expediency. On a broader plane, the nature of social conflict also appears to be changing. It seems that the classical mode of conflict between the haves and the have-nots is being overtaken by conflict between the price-taker and the price-maker. These are much broader issues and a debate thereon is outside the scope of this paper. A careful note, however, needs to be taken to these changes by the financial system.

1998 Recommendations	*1991 Recommendations*
More strong banks	Merge banks to reduce numbers
Free bank boards from Government interference	Free bank boards from Government interfere
Move to three tier structure	Move to three tier structure
Review capital adequacy norms	Fix capital adequacy at 8%
Consider whether autonomy is consistent with public ownership finance ministry.	Ensure autonomy of banks wind up banking division of the

Source: Ruddar Datt & Sunderam, Ed. 2005

The set of measures, coupled with many others, have their positive impact on the system. There has been considerable improvement in profitability of the banking system measured in terms of operating and net profits. What is equally important is the fact that the intermediation process has improved, as is evident from the fact that the ratio of net interest income to total assets of PSBs has declined from 3.22 in 1990-91 to 2.84 in 2000-01.

The profile of asset portfolio and also the extent of the net non-performing loans (NPLs) as percentage of total assets have shown improvement during 1993-2001 (Table 1). During this period, the supervisory strategy has undergone a change, moving from opacity towards transparency. A positive externality of the reform process has been the building up of the institutional architecture in terms of markets, and creation of enabling environment through technological and legal infrastructure and improving the managerial competence, etc.

WHAT ARE THE SHORTCOMINGS?

Does this mean that there are no areas of shortcoming? The answer to this question would not be in the affirmative.

INTEREST RATE DEREGULATION

In the area of interest on deposit/savings, there does not appear any systematic architecture of the interest rate structure. To substantiate, no defined time path or defined preconditions have been identified in the area of deregulation of saving bank rates. It is apparent that banks, especially public sector banks are not ready for this reform since there is a potential for instability in the forth of shifts in saving bank deposits between banks, depending on the interest rates that emerge. Thus, this is essentially a structural issue and conditional on improvements in operational efficiency of the public sector banks rather than an overall interest rate issue in the macroeconomic sense. Furthermore, on the overall interest rate structure in the financial system, with different authorities setting different interest rates, it might impinge upon the signaling mechanism of the bank rate.

NON-PERFORMING ASSETS

The improvement in the position regarding NPAs in viewed as more superficial than real. The root problem is that there is a sizeable overhang component arising.

From the weak debt recovery processes, inadequate legal structure, weakness in underlying security, inadequate risk management techniques, etc. Any solution to the overhang problem of large magnitude requires well-crafted medium to long-term actions, devoted to specific definition of goals and negotiation of the process rather than ad hoc approaches.

Operationally, it seems imprudent to treat all non-performing loans as a single 'catch-all' category. Broadly, they can be categorized as loans to agricultural sector directed lending, loans to small enterprises and loans to corporate sector. Many of the directed loans are subsistence loans, where default rates are high and recovery prospects not bright. As regards loans to agricultural borrowers, legal impediments often prove to be challenging proposition for banks to recover their dues. Loans to small enterprise become difficult to recover due to inordinate judicial delays. Even if court decrees can be obtained towards recovery, by the time the charge of the assets is taken, its realizable value is significantly diminished because of several reasons including depreciation of the asset, lack of borrowers' cooperation, limited market value of asset, with the concomitant effect that such decrees are not executed.

Table 1
Non-Performing Assets of Public Sector Banks

End-March	*NPAs (Rs Billion)*	*Gross NPAs As Per Cent*	*Gross NPAs As Per Cent*	*Net NPAs As Per Cent*	*Net NPA As Per Cent*
1993	392.5	23.2	11.8	NA	NA
1994	410.4	24.8	10.8	NA	NA
1995	383.8	19.5	8.7	10.7	4.0
1996	416.6	18.0	8.2	8.9	3.6
1997	435.8	17.8	7.8	9.2	3.6
1998	456.5	16.0	7.0	8.2	3.3
1999	517.1	15.9	6.7	8.1	3.1
2000	530.3	14.0	6.0	7.4	2.9
2001	247.7	12.4	5.3	6.5	2.6

Note: NA – Not Available

Source: Report on Trend and Progress of Banking in India, various years (ref: EPW, February, 2-8, 2003 pp. 399-408

As regards corporate loans, suits pending/referred to the Board for Industrial and Financial Reconstruction leaves little headroom for banks to affect recovery. Inadequate corporate governance practices coupled with problems of fixation of accountability leaves little maneuverability for banks towards an all-out recovery drive.

DIRECTED LENDING

The issue of directed lending is also an area of concern. In a developing economy with a democratic policy and a large section of the populace below poverty line, while the policies are to the left of center, the implementation somehow is to the right of center. For instance, despite the definitional changes for eligibility under priority sector lending that have been effected consistently, the share of priority sector advances total non-food gross bank credit of commercial banks (SCBs) has come down from 40.3 per cent in December 1980 to 35.9 per cent in March 2001. The direct agricultural lending accounts of all PSBs also show a declining trend (2.13 crore in 1994 versus 1.59 crore in 2000). The story of regional rural banks (RRBs), also paints the same picture. Although during 1993 to 1998, their credit-deposit (C-D) ratio has declined from 67 per cent to 44 percent (42 per cent in 2001), the share of agriculture loans has come down from 52.4 per cent to 44.4 per cent during the corresponding period.

It is also interesting to note that the capital formation in agriculture is decelerating. Compared to the growth of 5.4 per cent in Gross Capital Formation (GCF) during 1950-96, GCF during this period has been 3.69 percent. This growth during 1981-96 has only been 1.87 per cent as compared to 5.51 per cent in 1966-80 and 3.18 per cent in 1950-65. What is even more disturbing is the fact that the public sector capital formation has displayed negative growth of – 3.49 per cent during 1981-96 as against 6.86 per cent during 1966-80 and 7.37 percent during 1950-65. Decline in flow of funds to agriculture can be of serious consequence to the growth process.

OWNERSHIP STRUCTURE

Another serious weakness is in the area of ownership and control. The existing and the continued government ownership has proved to be problematic. While there was a merit in the public sector model when it was adopted, a time has come for the government to review its position. In any case, it must follow the norms of good governance. It is also imperative to review the position of the Reserve Bank of India (RBI) in this context as the regulator and the majority owner of State Bank of India (SBI), the largest state-owned bank in the country (in terms of branches and assets).

The Reserve Bank in its Monetary and Credit Policy statement of April 2001 has announced the intention to divest its ownership in SBI. The RBI also has its nominee director on the boards of all banks, including SBI. Overlap of ownership and regulatory functions can lead to problems of regulatory forbearance with its attendant impact on financial stability.

CORPORATE GOVERNANCE

Last, but not the least of the problem areas is the weak corporate governance practices in banks in general, and PSBs, in particular. It must be appreciated that the reform process is only an enabling mechanism; leveraging it fully is possible only if the institutional players in the system are receptive to good governance. Good governance practices are 'coping mechanism' for an institution. Lack of such mechanism can prove to be major source of weakness among financial institutions and banks, in India.

CHALLENGES

The areas of weakness mentioned above help to bring into light the following issues -

Consolidation

With the emergence of new players and deepening of markets, the structure of the banking system has come into sharp focus. In particular, it is necessary, to take a critical view of the structure of the PSBs which still play and are expected to play a dominant role in the foreseeable future. The NCR-II highlighted the need for re-structuring of these banks. The pressure on their bottom lines is growing and the business profile is getting overtly complex, making higher demands on the personnel, more so, in the face of the Voluntary Retirement Schemes that have been offered by these banks. A rethinking is necessary as to whether the financial sys-tem is 'optimal' in terms of number of banks. There also appears to be a strong case for branch rationalization. In the absence of full-fledged reforms in the labour sector, which notwithstanding recent budget announcements, still suffers from high levels of rigidities. A degree of mergers/acquisitions moves among the new private sector banks is being witnessed in the banking sector. It is evident that the new private sector banks with institutional parentage are making tremendous strides. They are also performing well in terms of enhancing shareholder value. While they could be seen in the root to distant future to consolidate their operations further either by merging with their parent institutions or with other banks, it is the PSBs that need to evaluate the opportunities to consolidate as bigger players. Currently, the overwhelming presence of SBI in every segment of the market makes it a virtually uniplayer market. Such a market is also unidirectional and does not lend dynamic stability to the system. The emergence of another large player in Indian banking is necessary for healthy development of the market. It must be reckoned that what is required is not merger of a weak bank with a strong one, but of two strong banks.

Mere prescription of prudential norms is not enough: 'stress testing' of the figures is required.

Recapitalisation

The recapitalisation of PSBs also is coming into sharp focus. The Reserve Bank has estimated that, given the present growth rate of the economy and the extent of capital adequacy norms, the PSBs (barring the three weak banks) would need Rs 100 billion as additional capital in the coming five years [Jalan 2000]. With the government indicating that when privatised, the PSBs would retain their 'public sector character', the equity in such weakly privatised banks might become an unattractive proposition. Besides, there remains the problem of raising such a large quantum of funds on equity markets due to lack of

Table 2
Profitability, Capitalization & Soundness of Public Sector Banks

Year/Bank	*1999-2000*				*2000-2001*			
	CAR	*ROE*	*Net NPA*	*NP (Rs Crore)*	*CAR*	*ROE*	*Net NPA*	*NP*
Nationalised Bank								
Allahabad bank	11.51	7.97	12.17	-5	10.50	4.42	11.21	-34
Bank of Baroda	12.10	16.40	6.95	488	12.80	8.33	6.77	260
Bank of India	10.57	7.03	8.61	-2	12.23	9.69	6.72	78
Canara Bank	9.64	9.43	5.28	131	9.84	10.54	4.84	180
PNB	10.31	19.42	8.52	354	10.24	18.76	6.69	409
Stat bank Groups								
SBI	11.49	18.20	6.41	–	12.79	12.53	6.03	–
State bank of Hyderabad	10.86	22.94	7.30	–	12.28	21.77	7.83	–

Notes: CAR Capital Adequacy Ratio, ROE Return on Equity, Net NPA to Net Advance.
Source: Report on Trend and progress of Banking of India.

depth and liquidity. Performance of some of the public sector banks which have divested their equity has not been very encouraging.

It would be pertinent at this juncture to sound a note of caution. While recapitalisation of banks is a necessary condition for dealing with weaknesses in the banking industry, it is, by no means, a sufficient condition.

Prudential Regulation

When there is a boom, banks tend to increase their lending in pursuit of higher profits, making themselves vulnerable to adverse selection. During periods of bust it is the same loans that turn bad and require larger provisioning, which will impact the already sagging balance sheets. A choice before the regulator is to tighten the prudential norms during the boom and to impose tighter provisioning requirements, thereby dampening the profits.

Weak Banks

Treatment of weak banks is another issue of importance. Currently, there are three major nationalized banks identified as 'weak' banks. Managerial inadequacies and existence of high levels NPAs have been cited as the ostensible causes of such weakness. In spite of the huge quantum of write offs, the stock of NPAs has intended to remain at a high level. It however needs to be recognized that there are two main drawbacks. This might engender moral hazard problems and the loan assets covered by such funds are so weak that there would be a large gap between the fund and the realised value (which again would require government funding). Another solution is the extreme step of closure of these banks.

NON-PERFORMING LOANS

The most vexed issue in Indian Banking is that of NPLs. In Indian Banks, the problem of NPLs is not only because of unfriendly legal structure and low marketable value but also due to regulatory provision for loan. The problem is further compounded by the rationalization norms for the loan classification.

Legal Framework

Legal framework is closely connected with the NPLs. The current legal framework is loaded in favour of defaulting clients. The introduction of the Board for Industrial and Financial Reconstruction (BIFR) and Debt Recovery Tribunals (DRTs) has not yielded the desired results. As at end-March 1999, out of the total number of 21,781 cases involving a sum of 18 billion transferred to/filed with the DRT the number of cases decided was 3,774 (17.3 per cent of the total) accounting for 10 percent of the total. The status of cases at BIFR also presents a sober picture, with as many as 3,296 companies with accumulated losses amounting to Rs 552 billion being locked up as on December 31, 2000. In fact, there have been instances where an undertaking has been anxious to have itself declared as covered by the provisions of BIFR and labelled as 'sick' to perpetuate defaults or negotiate a more favourable term. A thorough and complete change in the legal system is urgently called for.

OWNERSHIP ISSUES

Another issue that needs early resolution is one of potential conflicts as owner/supervisor. RBI has their nominee directors on the board of SBI where it holds a major portion of the equity as also on the board of most PSBs.

REGULATION AND SUPERVISION

Another set of issues of significance that is now coming to the fore and meriting urgent attention relates to the area of supervision. The major issues among them are (a) whether the supervision should remain with the monetary authority or separated and (b) whether there should be fragmented, function-specific supervisors functioning independent of each other or should there be a super coordinating regulator and that function residing with the RBI.

CORPORATE GOVERNANCE

Another area which has received little operational importance is corporate governance. Good governance enables an organization to reap full benefits of the reform and acts as a coping mechanism in containing the risks. Many of the problems in the banking sector in India can be fundamentally traced to the lack of sound corporate governance practices. The rights of private shareholders of SBI/nationalised banks are very considerably abridged. At present, they do not enjoy the basic rights of adoption of annual accounts or approving dividends. There is also a lack of equality among different group of share-holders. In the private sector, voting rights of individual shareholders are restricted to no more than 10 per cent of the bank's equity, even though they may own more than 10 per cent of the equity. The com-position, functioning and lack of autonomy of the boards call for a major reform. The manifestation of the relationship between the government as owner and banks also needs to be reviewed and restated.

IMPACT OF REFORMS

After the study of the reforms, the weakness and the emerging challenges of the reforms that had started in the banking sector, now we are in position to see the importance of future agenda. As we have already discussed, we are now in a position to summarise the impact of reforms on the Indian banking sector:-

(i) To analyze this we focus on comparative performance of major bank group's in the Reform period.

(ii) The availability of bank credit semi reforms.

(iii) The impact of reforms on the interest rate structure.

(iv) The trends in banking sector intermediation in the light of the development of the non bank finance intermediaries and capital market.

(v) The impact of deregulation on competition and efficiency in the banking sector.

Comparative Performance of Major Bank Groups Semi Reforms

The structure of the Indian Banking system has undergone significant changes in terms of the shape of private sector bank operation. This is shown in the Table 3 which shows that the

Table 3
Number of Schedule Commencing Banks
1991-92 and 1995-96 Banks

	1991-92	*1995-96*
SBI & Associates	8	8
Nationalised Banks	20	19
Domestic Pvt Sector Banks	23	25
New Domestic Pvt Sector Banks	0	9
Foreign Banks	23	27

Data based on performance highlights of Banks 1991-92 IBA and Indian Banking Review 1995-96.

Source: Data based on performance highlights of banks 1991-92 IBA and Indian Banking Review 1995-96.

number of scheduled private sector banks has increased from 46 to 63 between 1991-1992 to 1995 -96.

Growth Rates of Deposits and Advances: The annual compound growth rates of deposits and advances for the pre reforms and reform period for commercial banks as a whole as well as disaggregated by the bank group are presented in the fig. below. The deposits and advances of PSB in reform period is slightly lower than those prevailing in the pre reform period. The main reason for sluggish growth of bank deposits in the reforms period is the growth of NBFCs mutual funds. Moreover deposit mobilization by the commercial banks has been affected by "saturation factor".

Non Interest Income of Banks- An increasing proportion of non interest income also entails a diversification of banks

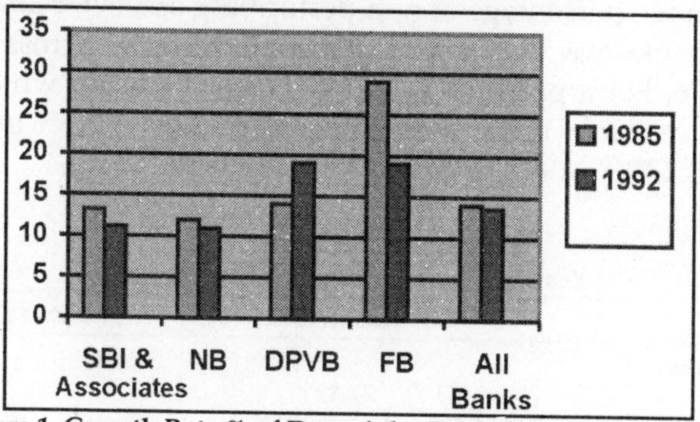

Figure 1: Growth Rate % of Deposit by Bank Groups 1985 to 1992

Source: Statistical Table Relating to Banks in India, RBI

activity from its core intermediation business and consequently a reduction in the interest risk faced by the banks. As shown in the figure foreign banks have the highest proportion of non interest income to the total income and there is considerable divergence between the share of FBS and that of domestic banks. However, since the reforms such divergence has considerably narrowed down. The trends in the non interest income indicate that domestic banks are diversifying away from there core intermediation business and are providing increased competition to the foreign banks in the provision of fee based services.

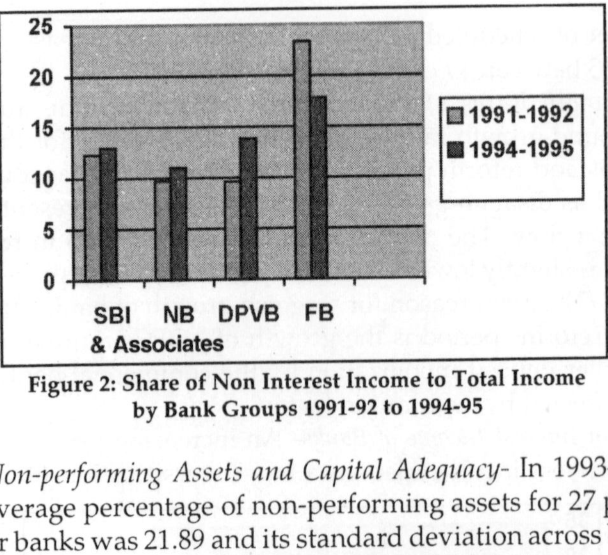

Figure 2: Share of Non Interest Income to Total Income by Bank Groups 1991-92 to 1994-95

Non-performing Assets and Capital Adequacy- In 1993-1994, the average percentage of non-performing assets for 27 public sector banks was 21.89 and its standard deviation across banks was 7.76. For a panel of 17 Public Sector Bank for which the data is available, the average of NPA fall from 20.15% in 1993-94 to 16.13% in 1994-95 to 14.88% in 1995-96.

Table 4
Year NPL as Percentage of Total Loans

	Average	*Standard Deviation*
All 23 Banks		
1993-94	21.89	7.76
1994-95	17.46	6.93

Contd.

	Average	*Standard Deviation*
Panel of 17 Banks		
1993-94	20.15	7.41
1994-95	16.13	6.82
1995-96	14.88	4.91

Source: Estimates based on data from performance highlights of Banks IBA several issues and IBR 1995 IBA, EPW February, 2002

Profitability: RBIs Annual Report on Trend and Progress of Banking in India as well as GOI, Economic Survey give the profitability of different types of banks in the country as follows:-

State Bank of India and its seven associate banks have recorded steady rise in the profits. In case of 19 nationalised banks viz. other public sector banks, profitability has always been quite low as during 1992-93. These banks poised severe loss due to Harshad Mehta scam. In case of Indian Private Sector Bank, net profit had increased from Rs. 77 crores to Rs. 1179 Crores between 1991-92 to 2001-2002. The profitability of the foreign banks has always been excellent.

Table 5
Net Profit of Schedule Commercial Banks

Reporting Banks	*1991-92*	*1992-93*	*1993-94*	*1995-96*	*2000-01*
State Bank Group	224	280	356	793	3450
Nationalised Banks (19)	599	-3648	-4779	-1160	4851
Private Sector Banks (30)	77	60	149	557	1779
Foreign Banks (40)	320	-842	573	749	1492

Source: Economic Survey

AVAILABILITY OF CREDIT

Availability of credit to the private sector as a proportion of the total deposits of the banking sector is indicated by the Credit Deposit Ratio. Following the reforms, the CDR of the commercial banks as a whole declined substantially from 60.6% in 1991-1992 to 52.2% in 1993-94 following recession. Subsequently, the CDR has recovered to 58.6% in 1995-1996. The decrease in the CDR since reforms has been accompanied by corresponding increase in the proportion of risk free government securities in Banks, major earning assets i.e. loans and advances and investments.

PRIORITY SECTOR CREDIT

There has been appreciable reduction in the proportion of bank credit going to the priority sector since the reforms. This has taken place in spite of the fact that the priority sector requirement for the foreign banks has been increased.

Table 6
Public Sector Banks Advances to Priority Sector: Amount Outstanding (Rs. in Crores)

Priority Sectors	*June 1960*	*June 1971*	*March 2002*
Agriculture	160	340	63,080
S.S.I.	260	440	49,740
Other Priority Sector	20	130	53,710
Total Priority Sector Advance	440	910	1,71,190
Total Bank Credit	3020	4080	3,96,950
% of Priority Sector Advances to Total Bank Credit	12	25	43

Source: RBI Report on Trends and Progress of Banking in India, 2001-2002

INTEREST RATE TRENDS

Interest rates were gradually reduced from 20% to 2% by 1994-1995. The important changes in the interest rate since 1991-1992 are as follows:-

(a) Interest rate on domestic term deposits has been decontrolled.

(b) The prime lending rate of SBI and most other banks on general advances of over 2 lakhs has been reduced.

(c) Rate of interest on bank rate above 2 lakhs has fully been decontrolled.

(d) Interest rates on deposit and on advances of all co-operative Banks have been deregulated subject to a minimum lending rate of 13%.

This has been done to stimulate healthy competition among the banks and encourage their operational efficiency. It would also help banks better adjust their lending rates to the track record and risk perception with regard to their customers.

Scheduled commercial banks have now the freedom to set the interest on their deposits subject to minimum floor rates and maximum ceiling rates.

In recommending liberalized entry and expansion for private sector banks including the foreign banks, N.C.Fs observed that while in the short run, such a policy could create a problem for Indian banks over a period of time. Indian banks would reorganize their operations to improve the dynamic efficiency and meet the increased competition and it happened so in case of Indian banks. Presently they are more efficient as a result of competition which means more customers and their benefits like ATM, tele-banking, increased number of branches, Credit Cards, computerization and improved hours of working in banking, etc.

CONCLUSION

Thus, the outcome of our analysis is that there should be a balanced approach between intervention and complacent belief in the ability of banking system to self which rectifies its deficiencies because in the ideal world, there are always disturbances. Whatsoever, these changes were necessary to make Indian banking efficient and to accept challenges for moving ahead with a strict vigil on the changes and happenings in the economies of the world.

REFERENCES

Dutt and Sundaram, (2001,2002,2005), Indian Economy.

—(1991-1992), Economic Review: Report on Currency and Finance Vol. I .

—(1997), India Development Report.

Ahluwalia. M.S., (1993), India's Economic Reforms.

Reddy. Y.V. (2000), Monetary and Financial Sector Reforms in India.

—(1991 and 2001), Reserve Bank of India Bulletin

—(1991, 2001, 2002), Economic Survey (Government of India)

—Reserve Bank of India Report on Trend and Progress of Banking in India

Jalan. B. (2000), Agenda for Banking in New Millennium.

—(2002), Economic and Political Weekly, February 2-8.

CHAPTER 9

DEPOSIT MOBILISATION BY COMMERCIAL BANKS IN BIHAR UNDER REFORMS

Naqui Mohammad
Syed Eqbal Afzal

INTRODUCTION

Commercial banks play vital role in economic development of a country. They hold a significant position among the financial institutions which help in the canalization of saving for productive investment with a view to accelerating the process of economic growth. Commercial banking implies creation of purchasing power in the form of deposit money through acceptance of deposits, granting of overdrafts and other forms of credit, withdrawal by cheques. This power distinguishes the banks from other non-banking financial intermediaries.

Deposits are the basic raw material for banks operations and deposit mobilisation is one of the basic innovations. The growth of deposits reflects a greater degree of sophistication in financial and trading customs and practices. It is an important index of the growth of banking business, essential for mobilization of resources. Effectiveness of banking operations depends as much on the efficient management and service attitude and on adequate financial resources of banks. Deposits constitute the most significant share of their total resources. Attempt is, therefore, made in this paper to visualize the role of bank deposits under reform period. In this study, we shall make discussion about the deposit growth in commercial banks in Bihar during reform period. Hence, a study of their growth is very essential.

FACTORS AFFECTING BANK DEPOSITS

The study of the factors affecting bank deposits is not only important to banks for evolving an efficient deposit mobilization scheme but also important to the central bank of the country for formulating a proper monetary policy because the bank deposits form a part of monetary aggregates on which the central bank wants to have control. There are some highly important factors which during the process of development promote the growth of deposits. They are mentioned below:

(a) The fact that during a period of fast growth the marginal propensity to consume may decline because (i) consumers for some time cling to the conventional consumption habits and (ii) business, particularly in corporate form, withhold for some time a greater portion of the increased income from the consumer and reinvest it. In this connection Nurkse Ragnar correctly observes that "on the supply side, there is a small capacity to save, resulting from the low level of real income. The low real income is a reflection of low productivity, which in its turn is due largely to lack of capital. The lack of capital is a result of the small capacity to save".

(b) Banking habits and methods of discharging debts;

(c) Leakages,

(d) Monetary policies,

(e) Availability of banking facilities and

(f) Efficiency and outlook of banking institutions.

R.S. Sayers has enumerated certain more important factors that affect the volume of bank deposits. The relevant factors are:

(1) The volume of national debt of all kinds (including cash, Treasury bills, and short and long bonds) created by the Government (more created, more bank deposits).

(2) The public willingness to hold cash (more cash outside the banks, less bank deposits).

(3) The public willingness to hold Treasury Bills and other government obligations short and long (more held, less bank deposits).

(4) the willingness of the discount houses to hold short bonds (the more wiling, the less effect will reduced availability of Treasury Bills have in restricting the banks liquid assets, since the banks can lend to enable discount houses to hold short bonds).

(5) The cash and other liquidity ratios of the banks (higher ratios, lower bank deposits).

(6) The public relative preferences for bank deposits and claims on other financial intermediaries (higher preference, more bank deposits).

(7) The public relative preferences for borrowing from banks or from other financial intermediaries (more from banks, more bank deposits).

(8) The liquidity reserve requirements of non-bank intermediaries (higher requirements of government obligations, lower bank deposits).

Thus, the bank deposits at any particular point of time are determined by supply aspects as well as factors influencing demand for it by the public. Supply of bank deposits by the banking industry and the monetary authority of the country generally are governed by the components like government budget operations, foreign exchange assets, monetary policy, open market operations, bank rate, cash-reserve ratio, etc. Demand for bank deposits are determined by factors like income or wealth, interest rate and some times, even by service variables like banking network or per capita bank branches etc. Apart from the traditional variables like income/wealth and interest rates, institutional factors like monetization, financial sophistication, etc. also affect demand for bank deposits. Thus, we may observe that the volume of national income, rate of savings, growing monetization of the economy, encouragement of banking habits among the people, price level changes, interest rate, bank's liquidity, efficiency in the banking personnel, structural change in the banking institutions, the volume of trade and commerce and the availability of banking services in the economy are some of the relevant and more important factors which influence the volume and pattern of bank deposits in the economy.

DEPOSIT GROWTH PATTERN

In this section, an attempt has been made to analyse the deposit growth pattern of scheduled commercial banks in Bihar. The study has been made on the basis of population group-wise bank deposits, bank group-wise bank deposits, bank deposits of Bihar with deposits of other states and bank deposits of Bihar with bank deposits of scheduled commercial bank of India.

Population Group-wise Bank Deposits

We have examined population group-wise deposits of scheduled commercial; banks in Bihar. This aspect of deposit growth has been studied on the basis of three population groups: rural, semi-urban and urban which has been shown in Table 1.

Table 1 reveals the picture of population group-wise deposits of scheduled commercial banks in Bihar since 1990. In quantitative terms, the share of deposits of rural population in total deposits of scheduled commercial banks in the year 1990 was Rs. 2,604 crores which increased to Rs. 5,534 crores in 1995, Rs. 8,533 crores in the year 2000, Rs. 13,749 crores in the year 2005 and finally to Rs. 14,817 crores in the year 2006. In percentage terms, the share of deposits of rural population to total deposits which was 29.6 per cent in the year 1990, increased to 32.0 per cent in 1995, 34.6 per cent in 2000 and went up to 35.1 per cent in 2002. After 2002, it started declining and went down to 33.1 per cent in the year 2005 and finally to 29.8 per cent in the year 2006.

Table 1
Population Group-wise Deposits of Scheduled Commercial Banks in Bihar (At the end of the year)

(Rs. in Crores)

Year	*Rural*	*Semi-urban*	*Urban*	*Total*
1990	2,604 (29.6)	2,705 (30.8)	3,484 (39.6)	8,793 (100.0)
1991	2,937 (30.7)	2,895 (30.3)	3,730 (39.0)	9,562 (100.0)
1992	3,326 (31.6)	3,114 (29.6)	4,089 (38.8)	10,529 (100.0)
1993	3,923 (32.4)	3,532 (29.1)	4,662 (38.5)	12,117 (100.0)
1994	4,535 (32.2)	4,087 (29.0)	5,456 (38.8)	14,078 (100.0)
1995	5,534 (32.9)	4,852 (28.9)	6,417 (38.2)	16,803 (100.0)
1996	6,312 (31.9)	5,996 (30.3)	7,496 (37.8)	19,804 (100.0)
1997	7,595 (32.4)	7,151 (30.5)	8,683 (37.1)	23,429 (100.0)
1998	9,264 (32.6)	8,638 (30.3)	10,566 (37.1)	28,468 (100.0)
1999	11,040 (32.7)	10,168 (30.1)	12,531 (37.2)	33,739 (100.0)
2000	8,533 (34.6)	7,017 (28.5)	9,092 (36.9)	24,642 (100.0)
2001	9,803 (34.9)	8,169 (29.1)	10,114 (36.0)	28,086 (100.0)
2002	10,551 (35.1)	8,635 (28.7)	10,900 (36.2)	30,086 (100.0)
2003	11,677 (34.9)	9,631 (28.8)	12,167 (36.3)	33,475 (100.0)
2004	12,614 (33.8)	10,908 (29.2)	13,778 (37.0)	37,300 (100.0)
2005	13,749 (33.1)	12,075 (29.0)	15,756 (37.9)	41,580 (100.0)
2006	14,817 (29.8)	12,424 (25.0)	22,509 (45.2)	49,750 (100.0)

Source: RBI, Banking Statistics–Quarterly Handout, Various Issues.

The share of deposits of semi-urban population in total deposits in Bihar has also an increasing trend during all the years taken under study. The share of semi-urban in total deposits which was Rs. 2,705 crores in the year 1990, increased to Rs. 4,852 crores in 1995, Rs. 7,017 crores in the year 2000, Rs. 12,075 crores in 2005 and finally to Rs. 12,424 crores at the end of the year 2006.However; in percentage terms, the share of semi-urban deposits in total deposits maintained almost a declining trend in all the years taken under study except few years. The percentage of semi-urban deposits in total deposits was recorded at 30.8 per cent which decreased to 28.9 per cent in the year 1995. It started increasing and reached up to 30.5 per cent in the year1997 and again recorded a declining trend and went down to 28.5 per cent in the year 2000 and finally came down to 25.0 per cent in the year 2006 with an improved figure in the previous year 2005 with 29.0 per cent.

The share of deposits of urban population in total deposits has also maintained an increasing trend in the years taken under study. In quantitative terms, its share in total deposits was recorded at Rs. 3,484 crores at the end of 1990 which increased to Rs. 6,417 crores in 1995, Rs. 9,092 crores in the year 2000, Rs. 15,756 crores in 2005 and finally to Rs. 22,509 crores at the end of the year 2006. In percentage terms, the share of deposits of urban population in total deposits was recorded at 39.6 per cent at the end of the year 1990 which decreased to 38.2 per cent in the year 1995, 36.9 per cent in the year 2000 but it increased to 37.9 per cent in 2005 and finally to remarkable 45.2 per cent in the year 2006.

Bank Group-wise Bank Deposits

Another important aspect of the discussion about the growth of bank deposits in Bihar is the analysis of deposit growth pattern bank group-wise. This is an important aspect for analysis of the changing pattern in the growth of bank deposits in Bihar.

Table 2 provides the figures of bank group-wise distribution of deposits in Bihar from 1990 to 2006 thus, covering the period of reforms. The bank group-wise figures have been classified into five groups viz., State Bank of India and its associates, nationalized banks, foreign banks, regional rural banks and other scheduled commercial banks. One group consists of State Bank of India and its seven associates. State Bank of India was established in 1955 by the Special Act of Parliament and in subsequent years, its subsidiaries were established. The operation of State Bank of India covers also the operation of its subsidiaries. In this table also, we have compiled the figures of total deposits of State Bank of India along with its seven subsidiaries banks. Another group consists of 14 major banks which were nationalized on 19th July1969 and other 6 banks nationalized on 15th April 1980. Thus, these bank-group deposits cover the total deposits with 20 nationalized banks. The establishment of Regional Rural Banks is another landmark in the history of banking in the country. The main purpose of establishing these RRBs was to make innovative efforts in the rural areas. The regional rural banks play a significant role in extending banking facilities in the rural areas of the country. The first regional rural bank was established in 1976. Till 1980, these regional rural banks could not contribute significant figures but in recent years, the share of these banks in bank deposits during nineties and till 2006 has been considerably increased. The fifth group consists of other scheduled commercial banks.

As evident from the figures in the table, there has been constant increase in the volume of bank deposits in all these bank-groups during the reform period. It is not of much significance to analyse the figures year-wise during all the years to justify the trend of growth in bank deposits with the different bank groups. Therefore, we have contended the analysis for the period ending December 1990, 1995, 2000, 2005 and 2006. The analysis of the figures of the bank deposits at the interval of five years will show the comparative figure of different bank groups and thus, will serve the purpose of our analysis.

In quantitative terms, the deposits of State Bank of India and its associates in total deposits was marked at Rs. 3,044 crores in the year 1990 which increased to Rs. 5,687 crores in 1995, Rs, 7,716 crores in 2000, Rs. 13,900 crores in 2005 and finally to Rs. 16,267 crores in the year 2006. Though the figure has been increased in all the years, its percentage in total deposits achieved a mixed trend. Its percentage in total deposits was marked at 34.6 per cent in 1990 which has declining trend till 2000 and marked at 31.3 per cent. It again increased to 33.4 per cent in the year 2005 and finally came down to 32.7 per cent in the year 2006. The same condition is with the nationalized banks. The deposits of nationalized banks was registered at Rs. 5,105 crores at the end of 1990 which increased to Rs. 9,581 crores in 1995, Rs. 13,358 crores in 2000, Rs. 21,484 crores in 2005 and finally to Rs. 25,855 crores in the year 2006. In percentage terms, it also has maintained a declining trend during the year under study except the year 2006. Its percentage in total deposits was marked at 58.1 per cent in the year in 1990 which came down to 57.0 per cent in 1995, 54.2 per cent in 2000 and 51.7 per cent in 2005 but it improved a very little to 52.0 per cent in the year 2006.

Table 2
Bank Group-wise Distribution of Deposits of Scheduled Commercial Banks in Bihar (At the end of the year)

(Rs. in Crores)

Banks	*1990*	*1995*	*2000*	*2005*	*2006*
State Bank of India & its associates	3,044 (34.6)	5,687 (33.8)	7,716 (31.3)	13,900 (33.4)	16,267 (32.7)
Nationalised Banks	5,105 (58.1)	9,581 (57.0)	13,358 (54.2)	21,484 (51.7)	25,855 (52.0)
Foreign Banks	–	–	–	43 (0.1)	55 (0.1)
Regional Rural Banks	630 (7.2)	1,475 (8.8)	3,468 (14.1)	5,613 (13.5)	6,720 (13.5)
Other Scheduled Commercial Banks	14 (0.1)	60 (0.4)	100 (0.4)	540 (1.3)	853 (1.7)
All Scheduled Commercial Banks	8,793 (100.0)	16,803 (100.0)	24,642 (100.0)	41,580 (100.0)	49,750 (100.0)

Source: RBI, Banking Statistics – Quarterly Handout, Various Issues.

However, the performance of foreign banks in Bihar is negligible. In quantitative terms, the share of foreign banks in total deposits in the years 1990, 1995 and 2000 was nil while this figure was marked at Rs. 43 crores in 2005 which increased up to Rs. 55 crores in the year 2006. But in percentage terms, there was no improvement as its percentage was marked at 0.1 per cent in both the years 2005 and 2006. Hence, the performance of foreign banks in a state like Bihar was dismal.

In this paragraph, a study has been made to analyse the deposits of regional rural banks in total deposits of Bihar. In quantitative terms, the deposits of regional rural banks was marked at Rs. 630 crores in the year 1990 which increased to Rs. 1,475 crores in 1995, Rs. 3,468 crores in 2000, Rs. 5,613 crores in 2005 and finally to Rs. 6,720 crores in the year 2006. In percentage terms, it was marked at 7.2 per cent in the year 1990 which increased to 8.8 per cent in 1995 and 14.1 per cent in 2000 but it declined to 13.5 per cent in 2005 and remained unchanged in 2006. However; other scheduled commercial banks maintained an increasing trend in both quantitative and percentage terms.

In quantitative terms, the deposits of other scheduled commercial banks was recorded at Rs. 14 crores in 1990 which increased to Rs. 60 crores in 1995, Rs. 100 crores in 2000, Rs. 540 crores in 2005 and finally to Rs. 853 crores in the year 2006. In percentage terms, its percentage in total deposits increased from 0.1 per cent in 1990 to 0.4 per cent in the years 1995 and 2000, 1.3 per cent in 2005 and finally to 1.7 per cent in the year 2006.

Thus, it can be concluded that the deposits of State Bank of India and its associates multiplied by 5.3 times, nationalized banks by 5.1 times, regional rural banks by 10.7 times, other scheduled commercial banks by 61 times while the overall deposits of scheduled commercial banks multiplied by 5.7 times during the period under study.

Bank Deposits of Bihar vs Deposits of Other States

Deposits growth is one of the indices to measure the performance of commercial banks. There has been tremendous increase in the volume of deposits of scheduled commercial banks since 1990. Various deposit mobilization schemes launched by the banks, expansion of branch network, development of banking habits among population are the important reasons for increasing bank deposits in the various states.

In this section, an attempt has been made to study the state-wise bank deposits in the country followed by the share and position of bank deposits of Bihar in total bank deposits of India. It is also important to mention that the figure of bank deposits of Bihar was united till 1999. From the year 2000, the figure of Bihar has been bifurcated with the formation of new state Jharkhand.

It was not possible to break-up the figures in comprehensive manner. Thus, we have contended ourselves by providing the figures of bank deposits state-wise for some selected years. We have proceeded on analyzing the state-wise figures of scheduled commercial banks for the periods at the interval of five years by taking the figures at the end December 1990, 1995, 2000, 2005 and finally 2006 to arrive at certain conclusion on the basis of trends of state-wise deposits during all these years. It may be pointed out that one of the major objectives of the nationalization of the banks in the country was to provide monetary base for economic development in the country with social justice. Thus, the government policy has always been in favour of encouraging branch expansion in hilly and economically backward states so that unbanked and underbanked areas in the country would be covered by branch network. According to figures in Table-3, one can observe that in December 1990, the economically backward states like Bihar, Orissa, Madhya Pradesh, Rajasthan, Andhra Pradesh and the hilly states like Assam, Himachal Pradesh, Jammu and Kashmir, Nagaland, Tripura had very low profile in the sphere of bank deposits. To the contrary, the industrially and economically developed states like Gujarat, Maharashtra, West Bengal and Tamil Nadu maintained very high profile of bank deposits in the country. The main reason was that during that period,the banks in the country were doing business with urban clientle and these states were industrially advanced and consequently, there was greater volume of bank deposits in those states. However; during reform period, there was a shift in the emphasis and the economically backward states as well as the hilly states accounted for increasing amount of bank deposits during the post-reform period. In Andhra Pradesh, the total bank deposits was only Rs. 10,012 crores in December 1990 which increased to Rs. 20,642 crores in 1995, Rs. 49,843 crores in 2000, Rs. 1,08,602 crores in 2005 and finally to Rs. 1,30,459 crores by the end of December 2006. It means that the deposit of Andhra Pradesh has become double in every five years. The study shows that the deposits of Andhra Pradesh have increased by more than 13 times during the period under study. Similarly, the states like Assam, Bihar, Orissa, Karnataka, Kerala, Madhya Pradesh also maintained the increasing trend of bank deposits during the years under study. The deposits of Karnataka was marked at Rs. 8,790 crores in 1990 which increased to Rs. 21,394 crores in 1995, Rs. 49,795 crores in 2000, Rs. 1,20,338 crores in 2005 and finally to Rs. 1,50,965 crores in the year 2006, registering an overall increase by more than 17 times during the period under study. In case of Bihar (united), the deposit was marked at Rs. 8793 crores in the year 1990, which increased to Rs. 16803 crores in 1995. Later on, Jharkhand was separated from Bihar. The deposits of Bihar excluding Jharkhand was marked at Rs. 24,642 crores in 2000 which increased to Rs. 41,850 crores in 2005 and further to Rs. 49,750 crores in the year 2006. While the deposits of Jharkhand, which was marked at Rs. 14,323 crores in 2000, increased to Rs. 28,997 crores in 2005 and further to Rs. 33,520 crores in the year 2006. The same situation is with Madhya Pradesh and Chattisgarh. As regards to the hilly states like Himachal Pradesh, Jammu and Kashmir, Manipur, Tripura, Meghalaya, Nagaland and Union Territories of Dadar Nagar and Haveli, Goa, Daman and Diu, Pondicherry, etc. also have increasing trend of bank deposits. The increase in the deposits of Dadar and Nagar Haveli was about 35 times during the period under study.

Though there was emphasis on development of banking business in economically backward areas and also the government followed the policy of bank expansion in those areas, the industrially advance states like Gujarat, Maharashtra, Tamil Nadu, West Bengal, still dominate over the deposits of scheduled commercial banks in India. These states and union territory of Delhi are maintaining the high share of total bank deposits. The backward states have still to go for a long way in boosting their deposits when we compare it with the industrially developed states.

Table-3
State-wise Deposits of Scheduled Commercial Banks
(At the end of the year)

(Rs. in Crores)

States/Union Territories	*1990*	*1995*	*2000*	*2005*	*2006*
Haryana	3,746	8,372	18,688	41,908	53,418
Himachal Pradesh	1,314	2,854	6,983	13,060	15,379
Jammu & Kashmir	1,769	3,786	10,007	17,172	19,783
Punjab	9,530	19,007	41,713	69,718	80,456
Rajasthan	5,071	11,336	25,739	46,052	54,108
Chandigarh	1,271	3,589	6,960	13,931	18,973
Delhi	16,513	40,507	98,113	2,57,195	3,19,703
Arunachal Pradesh	116	314	510	1,169	1,383
Assam	2,031	4,124	9,210	19,136	22,959
Manipur	91	200	391	1,004	1,091
Meghalaya	297	651	1,523	3,200	3,445
Mizoram	69	166	319	798	927
Nagaland	179	336	731	1,519	1,854
Tripura	251	510	1,339	3,048	3,480
Bihar	8,793	16,803	24,642	41,580	49,750
Jharkhand			14,323	28,997	33,520
Orissa	2,444	5409	13,708	29,129	37,120
Sikkim	99	180	646	1233	1,507
West Bengal	17,724	29706	64,808	1,18,205	1,38,033
Andman & Nicobar Islands	54	137	359	793	936
Chattisgarh			6,782	18,611	21,591
Madhya Pradesh	7,324	14464	26,969	52,613	59,844
Utter Pradesh	19,198	38767	78,936	1,42,747	1,67,641
Uttranchal			8,605	21,502	26,759
Goa	1,392	2920	6,815	12,480	19,796
Gujarat	11,063	23959	49,056	1,00,379	1,09,917
Maharashtra	35,979	83815	1,61,486	4,37,580	5,80,159
Dadar & Nagar Haveli	15	61	209	412	522
Daman & Diu	59	154	403	802	921
Andhra Pradesh	10,012	20642	49,843	108602	1,30,459
Karnataka	8,790	21394	49,795	120338	1,50,965
Kerala	7,200	18819	42,178	75039	88,244
Tamil Nadu	12,266	27667	59,015	1,21,426	1,49,456
Lakshadweep	8	22	49	125	132
Pondicherry	291	685	1,520	3,118	3,738
All-India	1,84,961	4,01,358	8,22,373	19,24,624	23,67,968

Source: RBI, Banking Statistics–Quarterly Handout, Various Issues.

The study further shows that bank deposits are still coming in greater proportion from urban and metropolitan population. The urban and metropolitan populations due to their banking habits contribute substantially to the growth of bank deposits. The rural population is still ignorant of banking habits and the rural economy is half-monetised and the bank deposits could not have progressive trend in those areas with high expectation. In the hilly states, the rural population could not have easily access to the bank offices located at far distance places. Besides, there is low saving in the rural areas and the rural population is reluctant to deposit saving in to the banks. However, the state-wise analysis of the deposit growth may provide a satisfactory picture that there has been increase in the volume of bank deposits in all the states in the country. There is further need for launching some especially designed attractive and more effective bank deposit schemes by the banks in the backward and hilly states to encourage bank deposits. The bank personnel should also be motivated with enthusiasm towards rural population for proper care and attention so that rural population may develop bank habits.

Deposits of Scheduled Commercial Banks–Bihar vs India

After state-wise study of bank deposits, the study has further been extended to analyse the share and place of deposits of Bihar total bank deposits of India. Table-4 shows that the volume of bank deposits of Bihar was recorded at Rs. 8,793 crores at the end of the year 1990 which increased to Rs. 16,803 crores in 1995. These figures were united. After formation of Jharkhand, this figure has been divided in the year 2000. The bank deposits of bifurcated Bihar was recorded at Rs. 24,642 crores at the end of 2000 which increased to Rs. 41,580 crores in 2005 and finally to Rs. 49,750 crores in the year 2006. Thus, it has been observed that bank deposits in Bihar have registered an increasing trend throughout the period under study despite of division of the state. But in percentage term, the story is different. The percentage of deposits of Bihar in total deposits of India registered at 4.8 per cent in the year 1990 which decreased to 4.2 per cent in 1995, 2.8 per cent in 2000, 2.2 per cent in 2005 and finally to 2.1 per cent in the year 2006.

Table 4
Deposit of Scheduled Commercial Banks–Bihar and India
(At the end of the year)

(Rs. in Crores)

Year	*Bihar**	*India*
1990	8793 (4.8)	184961
1991	9562 (4.4)	219539
1992	10529 (4.0)	261588
1993	12117 (4.0)	303088
1994	14078 (4.0)	356360
1995	16803 (4.2)	401358
1996	19804 (4.3)	464460
1997	23429 (4.2)	551562
1998	28468 (4.4)	652664
1999	33739 (4.4)	765790
2000	24642 (2.8)	882373
2001	28086 (2.8)	1021130
2002	30086 (2.5)	1206620
2003	33475 (2.4)	1386001
2004	37300 (2.3)	1637053
2005	41580 (2.2)	1924624
2006	49750 (2.1)	2367968

*Percentage in total (India)
Source: RBI, Banking Statistics–Quarterly Handout, Various Issues.

CONCLUSION

Hence, it may be concluded that despite of increase in volume of bank deposits of scheduled commercial banks in Bihar, its percentage share in bank deposits of scheduled commercial banks of India is declining continuously. The division of Bihar in to Jharkhand is among the visible factors of this situation. But the main reason is the backwardness of the state in all respect including the less development of banking habits among the rural population in Bihar. This is the prime reason which affected the bank deposits in Bihar especially in percentage terms. The year-wise growth of bank deposits shows that there has been constant increase in the volume of bank deposits during the reform period which is due to expansion of branch network and deposit mobilization schemes launched by the banks. The policy of the government encouraged the expansion of banking facilities to rural and unbanked areas and there has been tremendous increase in bank offices in economically backward and hilly states. But the results are below expectation and the urban population still shares the major portion of bank deposits. It needs more attention in economically backward states where banking habit is lacking. Deposit mobilisation efforts must be planned in the sense that they must have specific objectives and must be directed towards specific groups of potential depositors. Banks as well as the government should make effort to increase banking habits among rural population which ultimately will result in fresh deposits in place of window-dressing deposits. Finally, the success fully depends up on the joint effort of banking personnel, government and local customers.

REFERENCES

Desai, V. (1979), Indian Banking: Nature and Problems, Himalaya Publishing House, Bombay.

—(1949), The Banking Regulation Act.

Gerg, K.N., Banking, Kitab Mahal, Allahabad.

Sharma, B.P. (1974), The Role of Commercial Banks in India's Developing Economy, S. Chand & Co., New Delhi.

Sayers, R.S (1967), Modern Banking (7th Edition), Oxford University Press.

Sundaram, K.P.M. (1976), Modern Banking, Sultan Chand & Co., New Delhi.

Vasudevan, S.V. (1977), Theory of Banking, S. Chand & Co., Delhi.

Maheshwari, S.N. (1988), Banking Law and Practice, Kalyani Publishers, (5th Revised and Enlarged Edition), 1988.

Gupta, M.S. (2006), "Towards Banking Excellence under Reforms: Some Issues" in *Indian Banking and Financial Sector Reforms* (Ed. Ravishankar Kumar Singh), Abhijeet Publications, Delhi.

—RBI, Banking Statistics – Quarterly Handout, Various Issues.

—RBI, Report on Trend and Progress of Banking in India, Various Issues.

—RBI, Report on Currency and Finance, Various Issues.

CHAPTER 10

BANKING SECTOR REFORMS AND MICRO-FINANCE: A STUDY IN CONTEXT OF SELF HELP GROUPS

Kumari Veena

INTRODUCTION

The banking sector policy reforms, generally attempts at improving the financial health of the banks and for this provide better services to the customers. But for a poor country like India, the dire need of making banks useful for the poor and asset less customers has been felt since long. The situation prompted the policy makers to go for development friendly banking, social banking and certain banking sector reforms (particularly, friendly to poor) like agricultural credit, rural banking, and micro-credit for encouraging small entrepreneurs through group mechanism, particularly those who are asset-less and also encouraging savings among such people. Micro finance or micro-credit is the latest outcome of this approach. Micro-finance has emerged as one of the most sustainable and effective tool for enabling the poor and disadvantaged sections of our society to access institutional credit. The Indian banking system on its part has shown a willingness and resilience to experiment and join the 'micro-finance movement'. The experiences of last ten years of its working in shape of micro-financing to Self Help Groups (SHGs), has resulted in both the 'sweet and sour tastes'[1]. The studies show that Asian countries like Bangladesh, Indonesia and other have recorded greater positive result in comparison to that of India.[2] In case of intra-national variation, entire eastern region and particularly Bihar has been placed at low parameters of success scale, especially in terms of the credit flow to SHGs from all kinds of bank in this region. This makes an urgent imperative to examine the nature and pace of the 'micro-finance movement' vis-à-vis attitude of banks in this context despite set priorities of banking sector reforms in favour of SHGs. With this major objective in mind the paper intends to have a brief overview of banking sector reforms and policies of NABARD in context of micro-finance. It goes to examine the attitude of all kinds of banks towards lending to these SHGs. Finally, it attempts to suggest strategies for banking sector reforms in order to make the micro-finance more proliferated in the poor regions of India.

BANKING SECTOR REFORMS: AN OVERVIEW

The Indian financial system in the pre-reform period (prior to Gulf crisis of 1991) essentially catered to the needs of planned development in mixed economy framework where the public sector had a dominant role in economic activity. The strategy of planned economic development required huge development expenditure, which was met through Government's dominance of ownership of banks, automatic monetization of fiscal deficit and subjecting the banking sector to large preemptions–both in terms of the statutory holding of Government securities and cash reserve ratio. But in the changed situation it has been attempted to make the bank development-friendly. The Government of India and the Reserve Bank of India, realizing the importance of credit in the development processes, have taken various steps since independence to encourage banks to (i) make timely, adequate and uninterrupted finance available to the poor for agriculture and allied activities and (ii) emancipate the rural masses from the clutches of the money-lenders at the grassroots level. These major objectives prompted the developments in Indian banking system to take steps like creation of special development finance institutions like NABARD, IDBI, State Financial Corporations, Regional Rural Banks and policies like aggressive branch licensing by RBI, mandating credit or priority sector (agricultural, small scale industries, housing, small business, education, professionals etc. Besides, steps were taken to control the interest rates. These steps were supply driven and intended to convert the banking system from "class banking to mass banking'[3] modes, in other words, social banking.

The contour of banking reforms in India in post 1990 periods reflect certain drastic changes in the banking system like initiating to create an enabling environment for banks to overcome the external constraints, policy environment of public ownership, enhancing efficiency and productivity through competition, consolidation of the banking sector with non-banking financial institutions and institutional and legal reforms relating to banking. For these various steps were taken like formation of boards of experts like Board of Financial Supervision (1994), and passage of the Credit Information Companies (Regulation) Bill 2004 and Government Securities Bill 2004. The reform measures emanate out of such series of reports, the pioneering ones being–Report of the Committee on the Financial System (Chairman: M. Narsimham) in 1991, Report of the High Level Committee on Balance of Payments (Chairman: C Rangarajan) in 1992 and the Report of the Committee on Banking Sector Reforms (Chairman M Narsimham) in 1998. It will be out of place to explain the findings of these reports, however, it has been found that the banking sector reforms also emphasized the need to review the manpower resources and rationalize the requirements by drawing a realistic plan so as to reduce the operating cost and improve the profitability with achieving the cherished goal of accelerating the pace of development in the country.[4] The mid-term reviews reflect that progress has been made in various developmental and regulatory measures in banking sector.[5]

Here our concern is centered on the micro-finance, which is meant for the poor. The Annual Policy Statement of April 1999 and the mid-term Review in October 1999 emphasised the importance of Micro-credit Institutions and Self Help Groups (SHGs) as important vehicles for credit delivery to self-employed persons, particularly women in rural and semi-urban areas. The Reserve Bank's objective was to accelerate the flow of bank credit to micro-finance institutions while maintaining their decentralised, voluntary and non-bureaucratic character. RBI issued comprehensive guidelines to banks for mainstreaming micro-credit and enhancing the outreach of micro-credit providers. Banks were permitted to treat micro-finance extended by them as part of their priority sector lending. Banks were also allowed to classify their credit under the SHG-bank linkage programme as advances to weaker sections. As a result of these initiatives, significant strides have been made in purveying of micro-finance across the country and in providing micro-finance intermediaries substantial access to bank credit.

Recently, the Governor of Reserve Bank of India himself underlines the tenets of banking sector policies in favour of the poor, he said, "The annual policy statement for the current year reiterates the concern for the common person, while enunciating a medium term framework, for development of money, forex and government securities markets; for enhancing credit flow to agriculture and small industry; for action points in technology and payment systems; for institutional reforms in cooperative banking, non-banking financial institutions and regional rural banks and for ensuring availability of quality services to *all* sections of the population. The most distinguishing feature of the policy statement relates to the availability of banking services to the common person..."[6] Again the review document states, "However, there are legitimate concerns in regard to the banking practices that tends to exclude rather than attract vast sections of population, in particular poor ones, self-employed and those employed in unorganized sector. While commercial considerations are no doubt important, the banks have been bestowed with several privileges, especially of seeking public deposits on highly leveraged basis and consequently they should be obliged to provide banking services to all segments of the population on *equitable* basis."[7] To Mr. Reddy, 'Operationally, it has been made that RBI to implement policies to encourage banks which provide extensive services while dis-incentivising those which are not responsive to the banking needs of the community, including the unprivileged".[8] Again, some of the strategies recommended by the Advisory Committee on Flow of Credit to Agriculture and Related Activities (chairman: Prof. V. S. Vyas) in 2004 had emphasized the following striking features that go to the extent like - (i) mandatory lending by commercial banks to the rural people, (ii) restriction of direct lending of SACP (Special Agricultural Credit Plan) and extension to private sector, (iii) raising the share of small and marginal farmers in agricultural credit, (iv) expanding the outreach of retail lending to rural areas, (v) enhancing the cost effectiveness for agricultural loans and (vi) flowing the credit to disadvantaged borrowers[9].

The whole gamut of discussions regarding the priorities of banking sector reforms particularly towards the rural disadvantaged sections suggests that the micro-finance is not only vital to development but essential for the banks also.

MICRO FINANCE AND SELF HELF GROUPS

Micro finance is a more comprehensive concept than micro-credit since it includes the provision of loans, savings, micro insurance and other financial innovations aimed at serving the very poor. Micro credit is the extension of very small loans to unemployed, poor entrepreneurs and others living in poverty who are not *bankable*. These individuals lack collateral, steady employment and a verifiable credit history and therefore cannot meet even the most minimum qualifications to gain access to traditional credit. Micro credit is a financial innovation, which originated in developing countries where it has successfully enabled extremely impoverished people (mostly women) to engage in self-employment projects that allow them to generate an income and, in many cases, begin to build wealth and exit poverty. Due to the success of micro credit, many in the traditional banking industry have begun to realize that these micro credit borrowers should more correctly be categorized as *pre-bankable*; thus, micro credit is increasingly gaining credibility in the mainstream finance industry and many traditional large finance organizations are contemplating micro credit projects as a source of future growth. Although almost everyone in larger development organizations discounted the likelihood of success of micro credit when it was begun in its modern incarnation as pilot projects.[10]

The SHG-bank linkage programme has proved that the banking with the poor is a viable proposition. It also benefited the banks by externalising the credit delivery process and ensuring more than 95 per cent recoveries, besides being cost effective. When National Bank for Agricultural and Rural Development (NABARD) had originally got into SHGs, the sole idea was to improve outreach of the banking sector. It tried to create a financial infrastructure in the rural areas where banking had not yet reached.[11]

According to Economic Survey Report 2004-2005 SHGs contribute to development of human and social capital. The number of SHGs linked to banks under the SHG-bank linkage programme aggregated 1079091 as on March 31 2004 of which 90 per cent were exclusively women groups. The cumulative disbursement of the bank loans to SHGs amounted to Rs. 3904 crore as in the March 31 2004 to around 16 million families. This translates to an average loan per SHG at Rs. 38179 and the average loan per family at Rs. 2412. The RBI stepped up to mature micro finance initiatives.[12] Based on the recommendations of the four Groups on issues relating to structure and sustainability, funding, regulation and capacity building of micro finance institutions, banks were advised to provide adequate incentives to their branches for financing SHGs establishing linkages and adopting simple and easy procedures to suit local conditions. The ambit of micro finance was extended to include consumption expenditure. Banks were also advised that the group dynamics of the SHGs did not need be regulated. There was also no need to impose or insist upon formal structures. Micro finance institutions are not allowed to accept public deposits unless they comply with the extent regulatory framework of the Reserve Bank.

Shibu Jagdevan of NABARD finds that the SHGs-bank linkage programme has some noble elements that worked it to success. To quote him, "We did a lot of social engineering to make this concept work. The bank only matched the contribution of the group. So if there was a bad debt, then people lost their money too. So the members essentially owned the corpus and not surprisingly recovery was 99%. And this is true in all parts of the world where microfinance is practiced. It is like mixing warm money with cold money so that in the end it is all one money and the group feels that they own it. There is a lot of convenience in this scheme as well. When a person has to go to the city for loan, he has to spend time and money on the visit. If he has to go more than once for the same work, it adds to his costs".[13] Thus the SHGs are the most viable and potential institutional set up that serves the individual's financial needs. Not only this, it makes the unable persons able and vibrant to work for themselves.

THE SOUR TASTE

But the distribution of such SHGs is not universal throughout the country. The data shows that out of the 17 lakh groups today, nearly 10 lakh are from southern states of Andhra, Tamil Nadu, Kerala and Karnataka. The rest of the states contribute to 6.5 to 7 lakh SHGs. But if looked at the SHGs formed in 2004-2005, 51 per cent were formed in other states and 49 per cent in southern states. Initially the concentration was in the southern states. Now there is an emphasis to look at the poorer states. Initially the planning commission had suggested 150 poor districts to be taken up on priority, which was later, made to 200 districts. A large number of these districts have less than 100 SHGs. We need to focus on these districts now. In short, there have been regional disparities in the number of SHGs in different Indian regions. It can be argued that the number does not decide the success of plight. The credit flow can be the criteria for the success of the SHGs. It can only be judged by the figures relating to disbursement and credit flows to the SHGs through banks.

FINANCIAL PERFORMANCE OF SHGS-BANK LINKAGES

Amrit Patel[14] finds that the number of poor people who benefited from Micro Credit Programmes has grown more than four times from 1997 to 2001. It has been a cause of dismay that India's performance has been the most unsatisfactory despite the fact that India has a large number of poor people and rural financial intermediaries are quite capable if they demonstrate their willingness and commitment in the area. He further finds that while commercial banks have been improving their working results as reflected through net profits in particular, the momentum of providing credit to farm sector and rural development, has sharply declined and the performance under micro-credit, leave alone micro-finance, has abysmally poor. The following table 1 will tell the situation.

At present, banks are required to limit their commitment by way of unsecured advances in such a manner that 20 per cent of banks' outstanding unsecured guarantees together with total of outstanding unsecured advances should not exceed 15 per cent of their total outstanding advances. Banks generally lend to SHGs against group guarantee without insisting on any security. Considering the high recovery rate in respect of banks' advances to SHGs and that this programme helps the poor, it has been decided that unsecured advances given by banks to SHGs against group guarantees would be excluded for the purpose of computation of the prudential norms on unsecured guarantees and advances until further notice. But banks are not interested in dealing with 20 lakh or 30 lakh SHGs. The transaction cost to reach out to individual groups is too great and may not be profitable for banks. If 1000 SHGs form a federation, then they can leverage a better deal from the financial sector and even banks will be interested in monitoring the health of the federation. Federations can help one another with funds and with expertise. However, as soon as federations gain control, SHG will become weak. So this has to be a natural process where SHGs come together by themselves. Government or external agencies should not force federations on SHGs. The figures in above Table 1 show that Bihar and Eastern region of the country has been the loser in this programme. But again the data of Reserve Bank Report fortifies the propositions that SHGs have not been performing uniformly well. The following Table 2 describes the performance of banks in providing loans to self-help groups.

Table 1
Intra-national Disparities in Credit Linking SHGs with Banks

States	*No. of SHGs*	*Cumulative Disbursement (in million Rupees)*
Andhra Pradesh	281000 (50.7)	9753.8 (57.2)
Tamil Nadu	98410 (17.8)	4255 (24.9)
Uttar Pradesh	53696 (9.7)	874.6 (5.2)
Maharstra	28065 (5.0)	697.5 (4.2)
Orissa	42272 (7.7)	510 (3.0)
Bihar	8161 (1.6)	120.9 (0.7)
Rajasthan	22742 (4.1)	462.5 (2.7)
Madhya Pradesh	15271 (2.7)	307.4 (1.8)
North Eastern Region	4069 (0.7)	60 (0.3)

Source: Amrit Patel, "Micro Credit and Role of Banks", Kurukshetra, February, 2004, pp. 4-10

The above Table 2 shows that the performance of commercial banks in flowing out funds to the SHGs has been inadequate in northern, northeast, central and eastern regions in the country as compared to southern and western regions by and large. The number of SHGs has also been variable in regions of the country. A natural question arises – why south Indian states are better at SHG-Bank linkages programme? The

Table 2
Disparities in SHGs and Bank Linkages (Bank Loans in Crore Rupees)

Region/Stat	*Commercial Banks*		*Regional Rural Banks*		*Cooperative Banks*		*Total Banks*	
	No. SHGs	*Bank Loans*	*No. of SHGs*	*Bank Loans*	*No. of SHGs*	*Bank Loans*	*No. SHGs*	*Bank Loans*
Northern Region	19796	49.4	21421	51.6	11173	31.4	52396	132.4
Northeast Region	2279	7.8	9521	11.7	478	0.7	12278	20.2
Eastern Region	49678	95.5	73174	121.0	35385	43.0	158237	260.5
Central Region	45297	108.8	71951	150.5	9761	17.7	127009	276.3
Western Region	28803	81.3	17109	40.0	8903	19.6	54815	140.9
Southern Region	392569	1911.1	212816	903.4	68971	259.4	674356	3073.9
Bihar	5197	13.7	10916	16.6	133	0.4	16246	30.8
Grand Total	538422	2254.8	405998	1278.3	134671	371.1	1079091	3904.2

Source: Computed on the basis of National Bank for Agriculture and Rural Development (NABARD)

reason behind it can be the lackluster attitude of commercial banks working in the region. Other attributable factors are concerned with the lack of qualified leadership among women, prevalent patriarchal norms, lack of voluntarism and enthusiasm among them.

CONCLUDING REMARKS

There is need of simplifying operating procedure and credit delivery loan products. Standardized loan programmes are essential with adequate flexibility in respect of loan purposes, maturities and necessity of the borrower. Besides, borrowers' training, orientation and prospects of loan programmes should be imparted. For all these, the voluntary organizations should be involved. The loan collection policies and procedure should be flexible and the concerned officials should take responsibility. The borrowers should be motivated for benefits of good repayment record. Proper propaganda is required for developing the saving habits among rural poor. There is urgent need to impart need-based intensive training to the borrowers and the character of borrowers' capacity of their enterprise to generate sufficient income.

REFERENCES

—(2004), See Kurukshetra, (special number on Rural Credit Scenario in India SHGs Empowering Women), February.

Amrit Patel, (2004), "Micro Credit and Role of Banks: Need for Initiative and Commitment", Kurukshetra, February.

J. C. Mishra and R.K. Thanvi (2004), "Indian Banking System and Micro Finance", Kurukshetra, February, pp.12-15.

—On the Basis of Various Annual Reports of the Reserve Bank of India

Y.V. Reddy (2005), Banking Sector Reforms in India: An Overview, Address at the Institute of Bankers of Pakistan, Karachi delivered by the Governor of Reserve Bank of India (Mr. Reddy).

—Y. V. Reddy, op cit, p.1

—As quoted by Y.V.Reddy, op cit, p.6

—*Ibid.*

—(2004), Reserve Bank of India, "Report of the Advisory Committee on Flow of Credit to Agriculture and Related Activities From Banking System", RBI Bulletin, August.

—Downloaded from Internet

Shibu Jagadevan (2005), November, downloaded from Internet

—(2004-2005), Reserve Bank of India, Economic Survey, p. 135

—*Ibid.*

Amrit Patel, op cit, pp. 4-10

FOOTNOTES

1. See Kurukshetra, (special number on Rural Credit Scenario in India SHGs Empowering Women), February, 2004
2. Amrit Patel, "Micro Credit and Role of Banks: Need for Initiative and Commitment", Kurukshetra, Feb. 2004
3. J. C. Mishra and R.K. Thanvi, "Indian Banking System and Micro Finance", Kurukshetra, February, 2004, pp.12-15
4. On the basis of various annual reports of the Reserve Bank of India
5. Y.V. Reddy, Banking Sector Reforms in India: An Overview, Address at the Institute of Bankers of Pakistan, Karachi delivered by the Governor of Reserve Bank of India (Mr. Reddy) on 18-5-2005
6. Y. V. Reddy, op cit, p.1
7. As quoted by Y.V.Reddy, op cit, p.6
8. *Ibid.*
9. Reserve Bank Of India, "Report of the Advisory Committee on Flow of Credit to Agriculture and Related Activities From Banking System", RBI Bulletin, August 2004
10. Downloaded from Internet
11. Shibu Jagadevan, November 10, 2005, downloaded from Internet
12. Reserve Bank of India, Economic Survey 2004-2005, p. 135
13. *Ibid.*
14. Amrit Patel, op cit, pp. 4-10

CHAPTER 11

BANKING SECTOR REFORMS IN INDIA–PROGRESS, EFFICACY AND FUTURE AGENDA

Nagendra Kumar Jha

FINANCIAL SECTOR REFORMS-AN INITIATIVE

We are moving in the age of globalization which has created certain challenges before the Indian economy and India is bound to meet such challenges. This is why India has initiated certain economic reforms in which banking sector reforms is one of them. My present paper has been divided into four sections, first section gives detailed informations about the progress of B.S reforms, second is concerned with its positive achievements, third says about its limitations and fourth highlights some important areas of future reforms.

The Government had appointed a committee on August 14, 1991 under the Chairmanship of Shri M. Narasimham to examine all aspects relating to the structure, organization, functions and procedures of the financial system. The Committee submitted its final report to the Government on November 16, 1991. Shri M. Narasimham chaired another committee on banking reforms. It submitted its report on April 23, 1998. This committee is also known as the Narasimham Committee II.

The RBI has initiated action on the recommendations of Narasimham Committee Reports.

Goals of Reforms

- To correct and improve the macro-economic policy setting within which banks operate. This involves monetary control reforms, including rationalisation of interest rates, redesigning direct credit programmes, and bringing down the levels of resource pre-emptions;
- To improve the financial health and condition of banks, by recapitalising banks, restructuring the weaker ones and improving the incentives under which banks function;
- To build financial institutions and infrastructure relating to supervision, audit, technology and legal framework;
- To improve the level of managerial competence and the quality of human recruitment, training, placement, etc;
- To improve access to financial savings;
- To reduce intermediation costs and distortions in the banking system;
- To promote competition through a level playing field and free entry and exit in the financial sectors;
- To develop transparent and efficient capital and money markets.

Principles of Reforms

The approach towards financial sector reforms in India is based on five principles:

- Cautious and appropriate sequencing or reform measures.
- Introduction of norms that are mutually reinforcing.
- Introduction of complementary reforms across sectors (most importantly, monetary, fiscal and external sector).
- Development of financial institutions.
- Development if financial markets.

BANKING SECTOR REFORMS- AN INTRODUCTION

Banking sector reforms were introduced in India in order to improve efficiency in the process of financial intermediation. The RBI has initiated too many measures for the creation of a competitive environment. With the deregulation measures, prudential norms were instituted to strengthen safety and soundness of the banking system.

Since January 1992, the Government has been implementing the recommendations of the Narasimham committee on financial system. The objective is to improving the competitiveness and transparency of the banking system.

(1) Reduced barriers to entry of private sector banks.

(2) Liberalisation of branch regulations for both public and private sector banks.

(3) Partial deregulation of interest rates on deposits and advances.

(4) Introduction of capital adequacy norm of 8 percent.

(5) Transparent, prudential and income recognition norms.

(6) Allowing public sector banks to access to capital market to raise equity.

(7) Reducing the pre emption of lonable funds through reduction of cash reserve ratio and statutory liquidity ratio.

DIFFERENT ASPECTS OF BANKING SECTOR REFORMS

Organization of Banking Structure

In the organisation of banking structure, it is proposed to reduce the number of public sector banks by mergers and acquisition. The broad pattern should consist of 3 or 4 national banks could become international in character; 8 or 10 national banks with a network of branches; local banks would be confined to a specific region, rural banks should be confined to rural areas only. The RBI should permit setting up of new banks in the private sector. There should be a uniform treatment between the public sector banks and the private sector banks. RBI should follow a liberal policy of allowing foreign banks to open branches in India in line with the requirements as applicable to Indian banks.

Reduction of Cash Reserve Ratio

Cash reserve ratio is drastically reduced from 15 percent in 1989 to 8 percent in 2000. The CRR was fixed at 7.5 percent with effect from May 2001. The ninth plan remarked that the level of the cash reserve ratio that is to be maintained by the Indian banks is considerably higher than the international levels. There has been a significant reduction in the CRR from 15 percent to 4.5 per cent still the RBI has a view to reduce the cash reserve ratio to 3 percent. The RBI could to use the instrument in either direction, for liquidity management, taking into account the liquidity conditions, inflationary trends and other macro economic developments.

Reduction of Statutory Liquidity Ratio

As per the RBI rule every banking company in India has to invest 25 percent to 40 percent of their deposit amount in approved government securities. Under section 24 of the Banking Regulation act, 1949, banks had to maintain in India liquid assets in cash, gold or UN encumbered approved securities amounting to not less section (2A) in section 24, requiring all banks to maintain a minimum amount of liquid assets equal to not less than 25 percent of their demand and time liabilities in India. The amendment of the Act in 1962 ensured that with every increase in the cash reserve requirements, the overall liquidity obligations were also raised. Since 1970 the SLR has been gradually raised from 25 percent to 35 percent effective fro October, 1981 to 38.25 percent in the beginning of 1993 and thereafter the SLR has been gradually declined to 25 percent in 1997. Further reduction can carried out only with reduction in the fiscal deficit.

Liberalised Interest Rates

Public procurement and distribution agencies had a four tier interest rate structure, 12 percent for food grains, 15 percent and 16 percent of sale of non food grains on commercial basis. There were two categories of interest rates on commodities coming within the preview of selective credit control. Six categories of interest rates for pre shipment credit. Five categories for post shipment credit, one for duty draw back scheme, six categories for agriculture, four categories for loans to small scale industry, two categories for loans to state level corporations engaged in assisting weaker sections and cottage industries.

Apart from that, other categories of advances such as differential rates of interest advances, retail trade advances (3 categories), educational advances, priority sector advances. For the term loans interest rate categories for the small scale industries (SSIs), Agriculture, Housing and road transport operations.

Interest rate reforms were undertaken in money, credit and government security markets, since 1992-93, interest rate in the government securities market was deregulated with the introduction of auction system. The structure of interest rates for the commercial banks was changed. The existing six categories of lending rates were reduced to three in 1993. Interest rates on loans above Rs. 2 lakh were freed, banks were permitted to determine their prime lending rates.

Interest rates slabs have been reduced from 20 to 3. the prevailing interest rates have been deregulated on the high slabs of bank rates to promote competition among banks and their operational efficiency. Scheduled banks have been permitted to fix annual interest rates on deposits between 4.5 percent and 11 percent.

The prime lending rates of banks for commercial credit are with in the purview of the banks and are not set by the RBI. The domestic interest rates which are still subject to regulation at rate of interest on savings accounts and rates of interest on export credit. The RBI reduced the bank rate from 8 percent to 7 percent effective from April 2000. Rate of interest on savings deposit of commercial banks was also reduced from 4.5 percent to 4 percent. At present, the interest rate in India has come closer to the international interest rates charged by developed countries.

The cut in the bank rate from 6.5 percent to 6 percent in April 2003 was sobering impact on the structure of interest rates. The one day and 14 days repo rates were reduced from 6 percent to 5 percent with effective from March 2003. More over, in view of the macro economic and overall monetary conditions, one day repo rate was reduced to 4.5 percent on August 2003.

Differential Rates of Interest Scheme

The differential rate of interest scheme was introduced in 1972, being implemented by all commercial banks. Under the scheme, bank finance is provided at a concession rate of interest of 4 percent annum to weaker sections to improve their economic conditions. Banks are required to lend a minimum of one percent of their aggregate advance under the scheme. It is about 67 percent of the total DRI advances should be routed through the rural and semi urban branches.

Abolition of Selective Credit Controls

Selective credit control measures were introduced in India in 1956, certain regulation of credit for specific purposes include fixing minimum margins for lending against securities, ceiling on maximum advances against stocks of certain commodities, and minimum rates of interest for certain kinds of advances. The selective credit controls have been used mainly to prevent the speculative holding of essential commodities like food grains to prevent price rise. Selective credit controls have been abolished in the post liberalization period.

Other Measures

Credit restrictions for purchase of consumer durables have been removed/relaxed. Like that, coverage of priority sector has been enlarged by the inclusion of software, agro processing industries and venture capital.

Policy Regarding Public Sector Banks

Competition among the commercial banks has increased with the entry of private sector banks, permission to foreign banks to open up to 12 branches and relaxation of various restrictions of public sector banks which inter-alia are now allowed to access the capital market to raise funds. The competition in the banking sector has so evolved in the recent years that the market structure of the banking sector has tended to be oligoplistic. While the number of banks is large, the dominance of public sector blanks and a few large banks continues. Such banks may face challenges in the future and face competition, and the restructuring and reengineering processed processes by both foreign and private sector banks.

Non-Performing Assets in Banks

As per Reserve Bank of India presidential norms, a credit/ loan was facility in respect of which interest/principal has remained overdue for more than 180 days is defined as a *Non-Performing Asset*. Substandard Assets are those where interest and/or principal remain overdue interest and/or principal remains overdue for more than 180 days but not exceeding 18 months. Where asset remained as an NPA for period exceeding 18 months the assets are classified as doubtful Assets.

In the nineties, non-performing assets (NPAs) cause greater to the banking industry. It has been characterized by unsetting changes in India. The structural reforms of deregulation initiated in the banking sector, shift of funds to liquid assets, loans which promised a fixed rate of return of investment with no credit risk, funds flow from the private sector to the Government sector etc.

The Narasimham Committee recommended the introduction of capital adequacy requirements based on risk weighted assets. By this, loans and advance other than the guaranteed by Government carry a risk weight of 100 percent. Investments in Government and other approved securities carry zero risk weight. This prompted revised guideline applicable to public sector banks cover NPAs relating to all sectors for compromise settlement of NPAs. Guidelines for special one time settlement scheme for small and marginal farmers were also issued by the a RBI in the case of loans up to Rs. 50000/-

Private Sector Banks

Private sector banks are registered as companies under the Companies Act, 1956. The RBI also permitted the new private sector banks. With the liberalised process, the RBI has permitted private sector banks in India to do their banking services. They confirm to the minimum start up capital and other requirements and the prudential norms of accounting, provisioning and other aspects of operations. There should not be any difference in treatment between the public sector banks and private sector banks.

The RBI has issued guidelines for entry of new private sector entrants in the Indian banking industry in 2001. The RBI granted licenses to Centurion Bank, HDFC Bank, IDBI Bank, Indus land Bank, Bank of Punjab and UTI Bank.

Banks as Authorised Dealers

The RBI permits specific banks as authorized dealers (AD) for undertaking foreign exchange transaction. At present, 92 banks are functioning as authorized dealers through 27762 branches. The RBI also authorized companies to transact in foreign exchanges through two other channels-full fledged money changers and restricted money changers.

Local Area Banks

The RBI issued guideline in August, 1996 for setting up of Local Area Banks to provide institutional mechanisms for promoting rural savings and for the provision of credit for viable economic activities in the local areas. The RBI guideline stipulates the minimum paid up capital of the local area banks will be Rs. 5 crore with promoter contribution of Rs. 2 crore.

The banks are registered as public limited companies under the Companies Act, 1956 and granted licence under the provisions of the Banking Regulation Act 1949. The Local Area Banks have been included in the second schedule of the RBI Act 1934. The promoters of the banks may be individuals, corporate bodies, trusts and societies. They have to comply with the prudential norms and capital adequacy of 8 percent of risk weighted assets from the beginning.

The RBI permitted to establish local area banks in specific regions to dispense the banking functions. There are five local area banks are in operation.

(1) Coastal Local Area Bank Ltd. in Andhra Pradesh.

(2) Capital Local Area Bank Ltd. in Punjab.

(3) South Gujarat Local Area Bank Ltd. Gujarat.

(4) Krishna Bhima Samruddhi Local Area Bank Ltd. in Andhra Pradesh.

(5) The Subhedra Local Area Ltd. in Karnataka.

Lok Adalats

The Reserve Bank has issued guidelines to commercial banks and financial institutions to enable them to make increasing use of Lok Adalats. They have been advised to participate in the Lok Adalats convened by various Debt Recovery Tribunals/ Debt Recovery Appellate Tribunals for resolving cases involving Rs. 10 lakh and above to reduce the stock of NPAs. As on June 30, 2003, the number of cases filed by banks in Lok Adalats stood at 272793 involving an amount of Rs. 1193.3 crore and the amount recovered in 87907 cases was Rs. 190.5 crore.

Corporate Governance is introduced in banks to promote corporate fairness, transparency and accountability of banks services. The Corporate Governance as the system by which business corporations are directed and controlled. Banks follow the best practices in the area of corporate governance. Corporate governance facilitates effective management and control in turn, enables the banks to deliver optimum results to all its stakeholders.

The Objectives of the corporate governance of the banks are:

- To enhance shareholder value.
- To protect interest of shareholders and other stakeholder, customers, employees and society at large.
- To ensure transparency and integrity in communication and to make available full and accurate information.

- To ensure accountability for performance and to achieve excellence at all levels.
- To provide corporate leadership of highest standard to make socially responsible investment while creating assets.

MAJOR REFORMS-EXECUTED

The major reforms introduced so far may be broadly classified into five areas

- There are overall monetary policy issues relating to interest rates and exchange rates, reduction in SLR and CRR, modifications in refinance facilities, development of alternative system of monetary controls, development of securities and capital markets, etc.
- There are measures for strengthening banks by way of transparency in the financial statements of banks, clearing up of balance sheets by way of prescription of prudential norms for income recognition, asset classification and provisioning for impaired assets, and improving the risk absorption capacity by adopting prudential norms for capital adequacy. Computerisation of banking transactions, reorganisation of individual institutions to enhance competitive capabilities and to facilitate provision of better services to customers, autonomy to public sector bank managements in managing the affairs of individual banks, machinery for customer grievances redressal, etc. fall into this category.
    - The most important is the move towards complying with the Bank of International Settlements (BIS) capital adequacy norms (CAN) or what is also known as capital-to-risk assets ratio (CRAR). Banks were expected to achieve the required CAN of 8 per cent by March 31, 1997. CAN has been further raised; as of now this ratio should be 10 percent.

  - In order to enable the banks to reach the prescribed norms, a programme of recapitalisation of banks has been undertaken by infusing more capital. Likewise, commercial banks have also been permitted to tap capital market through equity issues.
  - The Assets Reconstruction Company was set up in January 2002 with a corpus of Rs. 350 crores. It will help the banks to reduce their NPAs.
  - The Securitisation, Reconstruction of Financial Assets and Enforcement of Security Rights Act has been enacted. It would strengthen rights of banks and financial institutions to foreclose loans and enforce securities and could improve recovery from overdue accounts.

- There are steps to enhance competition in the financial sector by allowing entry of private Indian and foreign banks with state of the art technology, giving more freedom to expand the operations of existing private banks, and widening the scope of activities of banking and non-banking institutions.
- There are issues relating to strengthening the regulation and supervision over banks and more particularly over the very large number of non-banking financial institutions. The emergence of a few financial conglomerates had raised serious issues in conducting integrated supervision.
  - The RBI has set up the Board for Financial Supervision (BFS) in an effort to streamline banking operations and make it more transparent. The board will have sweeping powers to keep an eye on financial transactions in public sector banks and other financial institutions. It will ensure compliance with regulations in the areas of credit management, asset classifications, income recognition, capital adequacy, provisioning and treasury operations.

- Liberalisation of interest rate regime is an important part of financial reforms. There is progressive freeing of interest rates, and banks have been given freedom to accept CDs to any extent while the borrowers have been given the further option for choosing alternative forms of finance in the form of CDs.
- Administered savings rates have been aligned to give yields of equivalent maturity in the secondary market. Savings rate, hanceforth, would become more market determined. This linkage would give flexibility to banks to make downward adjustment in their interest rates.
- A number of steps have been taken to ensure balanced development of various segments of the financial market as also to preserve its integrity and transparency. The operationalisation of the Clearing Corporation of India Limited (CCIL), The negotiation dealing system (NDS), introduction of collateralised borrowing and lending obligation (CBLO), prudential limits on uncollateralised call/notice money market and encouragement of collateralised repo transactions, and introduction of interest rate options would increase the depth of the financial market. This process would get a further boost with the operationalisation of the real time gross settlement (RTGS) system.

Beginning July 7, 2003, foreign currency options made their debut in the Indian currency markets. These options enhance the flexibility of a corporate to manage its exposures and tailor its risk profile in line with its risk policy—more specifically allowing it to buy protection against unexpected and volatile market moves.

Appraisal

The outcome of the various reform measures so far has been impressive and banks have responded to the deregulation and the increasingly competitive environment by restructuring their operations and upgrading performance standards.

Introduction of a more transparent balance sheet format, capital adequacy and prudential norms have helped to bring out the true strengths and weaknesses of each bank. The reforms have created strong compulsions for improvement in the working of banks. Some of which were making cash losses in successive years have achieved a turnaround.

POSITIVE ACHIEVEMENTS

- There has been a steady decline in the level of resource pre-emption from the banking system.
- The changing competitive environment in the banking sector has made a significant difference to banking practices and disclosure requirements.
- Reporting has become more reliable and uniform as more strict standards have been introduced. However, there is large room for improvement in transparency and disclosure.
- The attitude of the authorities remains quite supportive to banks in financial need.
- The banks, in general, have responded well to the changes brought by reforms and their financial strength has improved.
    - — The trend in erosion of profit and capital base has been reversed.
    - — The gross NPAs of public sector banks as per cent of total assets have declined from about 12 per cent in 1992-93 to about 4.0 per cent in March 2004.
    - — As of March 1999, all public sector banks except one had achieved capital adequacy ratio exceeding the prescribed norm of 8 per cent. Most of them now are on the threshold of the prescribed 10 per cent ratio.
    - — The improved performance has enabled most of the banks to meet their capital requirements from internal resources and the market without dependence on budgetary support.
    - — A positive externality of the reform process has been the building up of the institutional architecture in

terms of markets, and creation of enabling environment through technological and legal infrastructure and improving the managerial competence, etc.

CRITICISMS

- Operations of new private sector banks have tended to encourage myriad unhealthy practices in competition with foreign banks, concentration on elite banking, dominance of treasury, money market and capital market operations rather than genuine supply of production credit and competitive mobilisation of surplus funds of corporates through CDs or otherwise at unusually high rates of interest, etc.
- Free-market philosophy has tended to subvert the accepted goals of regional and functional reach of banks and other financial institutions in an equitable manner.
- Prescription of capital adequacy norms had pushed banks and DFIs into the market place for equity and debt capital, in competition with the real sectors of the economy. It involves massive cost and diversion of savings which are avoidable.
- Elimination of the apex role of the IDBI among development finance and investment institutions has induced unhealthy competition and absence of focus and priorities in project finance.
- Free-market philosophy has inflicted on the economic system as a process of financial engineering and dominance of finance capital, with layers of non-functional transactions, arbitraging and prohibitively expensive cost of capital. This has already begun to hurt the process of capital accumulation and real sector development.

Above all, the approach to financial reforms is based too heavily on introducing changes at a pace gauged exclusively against domestic comparisons with the past rather than international comparisons applying tot he present. Financial reforms will always lag behind the needs of India's reforming economy of Government's sights are set on where the system is coming from, rather than where it is to go, and when. Domestic restraints on the pace of change obviously need to be noted, but they cannot be surrendered; the whole issue of reform pivots around loosening restraints.

Recent economic upheavals in south-east Asia have given us two important lessons that are valuable for charting the future direction of reforms in India. *One,* a financial boom, unless matched by real sector expansion, remains fragile. *Two,* with deregulated finance, it becomes harder on the part of the monetary authority to provide a package of policies which can avert a financial crisis.

AREAS OF FUTURE FINANCIAL REFORMS

- It is necessary to continue with the process of strengthening prudential, provisioning and capitalisation norms and bring them in line with international standards.
- It is important to continue with efforts to introduce maximum transparency, disclosure, and accountability so that investors and counter parties to financial transactions can take their decisions based on full information and their own assessment of market and other risks.
- The level of NPAs is still too high. A vigorous effort needs to be made by banks to strengthen their internal control and risk management systems, and to set up early warning signals for timely detection and action.
- The issue of legal reforms requires urgent consideration. There is an urgent need to institute a proper legal framework to ensure expeditious recovery of debt and give adequate legal powers to banks to effect property transfers.
- Banks need to increase their capitalisation quite substantially in the next few years. There seems to be a strong case for raising the legislative ceiling for market participation in equity capital of public sector banks.
- While there has been progress in developing various segments of the markets including money and debt markets, the depth of these markets remains low and the volumes as well as the number of participants are not very

large. An important priority for the future is to develop the depth and breadth of these markets and to allow multiplicity of intermediation possibilities with different risks and leverage profiles.

- The on-going financial sector reforms have brought about a major cohesiveness in the three markets—bank credit, money and security markets at the domestic level. The changed financial architecture has significant implications for corporate strategy, organisation and performance necessitating a move for banks to become 'one stop financial shops'.
- The process of covergence needs to be carefully pursued by banks through changes in products, technology, structure, processes and introduction of advanced management concepts and practices to successfully introduce new financial strategies and instruments, and new and cheaper delivery, trading and settlement mechanisms.
- The strategy for change management requires accent on 24 hour banking, tele-banking, Internet banking, corporate banking, merchant banking, investment banking, treasury and forex functions, internal checks and controls and transparency.
- Forces unleashed by the IT revolution are fast transforming the banks and banking business. IT dramatically brings down distribution costs. Banks incur 50 percent of their costs in the distribution of their products and services, and it is here that IT can save costs dramatically and boost the bottom lines of banks in a significant manner. Studies in the US have shown the banks incur an expenditure of $ 3 per transaction, if the customer visits the branch; $ 1 if he transacts it over the telephone and a mere 5 cents if it is on online. There is no way out now, but to make increasingly more use of new technology in banking business. Sooner the banks can shift over to the new systems, better would it be for long-run health of the banking industry.

- For achieving organisational transformation and dramatic improvements in performance, banks must accord the highest priority to HRD. Training should focus, in addition to specific tasks and procedures, on the business visions and goals of organisations. It should provide an impetus for change in work culture.
- The market of the future will largely be unstructured and competition in the future may not be an extrapolation of the past. In such a scenario the real winners will be those organisations who challenge and question 'accepted practice' and redefine market segments and set new price-performance expectations. Redesigning some of banking organisations and a re-look at work processes will be necessary. Poor customer service will reflect in clearly discernible fallout of clientele. Banks must make sincere attempts to move from mere customer satisfaction to customer delight.
- World over it is agreed that a direct need of our times is the strengthening of the internal control systems in banks. The internal control systems in banks provide continuous feedback to the management.
- Deregulation of interest rates has led to a situation very similar to what has come to be known as the 'prisoner's dilemma' in the Game Theory. The essence of the prisoner's dilemma applies to banks in situations of rivalry for deposits. A lack of communication and coordination between banks with conflicting self-interest can lead to a situation in which all banks are worse off compared with the outcomes that would have been obtained, had there been communication and co-ordination between them. This invariably happens when there is strategic interdependence. This can bring to focus the need for some concerted action on the part of banks.

The outcome of these reforms will hopefully be a financial structure that moves India to a higher and stable growth path, while remaining subject to strict market discipline. In short, in the new environment, financial institutions have to appreciate and be prepared for what Dick Fredrick has called 'Darwinian Banking', i.e., survival of the fittest.

REFERENCES

—(2005), Economic Times- August and September.

—(2004-2005), GOI, Economic Survey.

—Business World.

—Banking Theory-Law and Practice.

I.C. Dhingra-The Indian Economy.

R.J. Chelliah-Essays in Fiscal and Financial Sector Reforms in India.

Vijay Joshi-India's Economic Reforms.

S.P Gupta-Post-Reform India: Emerging Trends.

CHAPTER 12

IMPACT AND FUTURE AGENDA OF BANKING AND FINANCIAL SECTOR REFORMS IN INDIA

Kamini Jha

INTRODUCTION

For most of its independent history, India has adhered to a socialist-inspired approach, with strict government control over private sector participation, foreign trade, and foreign direct investment. Since the early 1990s, India has gradually opened up its markets through economic reforms by reducing government controls on foreign trade and investment. The regime of economic planning began five decades ago with a vision of a resurgent India marching firmly on the path of progress while ensuring an equitable distribution of the nation's wealth. Until July 1991, the government had pursued a package of conservative macro-economic policies, fiscal policies that aimed at mobilising resources from the private sector to finance development programmes and public investment in infrastructure. Monetary policy sought to regulate financial flows in accordance with the needs of the industrial sector and keep the rate of inflation under control. Foreign trade policy was formulated to protect domestic industry and keep the trade balance in manageable limits.

These macro-economic policies achieved many of its objectives but economic imbalances grew to critical levels. In order to bridge the gap between the vision and the reality it took the economy towards the misguided alternative of deficit financing. The monetary deficit worked itself through the foreign trade multiplier into a current account deficit in the balance of payment. As a rising BOP deficit cannot be financed beyond a point, it would result in a haemorrhage of the foreign exchange reserves which then makes it necessary to adopt measures to adjust for the monetisation of the budget deficit. The fiscal adjustment requires a slow down of the economy as the public sector, given its role as a prime mover, inevitably reduces its activities. Thus over the past five decades, the tyranny of the twin deficits held sway and any sustained revival of the growth was quickly punctured as the fiscal expansion would reflect in a monetisation which in turn would result in a widening of the current account deficit. Thus the economy was caught in the vice of the twin deficits.

THE ECONOMIC CRISIS

A country's financial system includes its banks, securities exchanges, pension funds, insurers, central bank and regulators-all of the firms and institutions that provide a framework for carrying out economic transactions and help to channel savings into investment. The financial system has to play a crucial role in the mobilization of funds and their allocation to most productive use to fulfill its role as an essential adjunct to economic growth. A sound financial system is an essential prerequisite for economic growth. Financial system malfunctions can create financial difficulties for an economy with its result and bad impact on the monetary policies, financial institution and in the process will lead to capital flight. Financial weakness of an economy will lead to its falling into the 'vicious circle of economic recession'.

The financial crisis of the 1990s underscored the linkages between macroeconomic developments and financial system soundness. Weak financial institutions, inadequate bank regulation, supervision and lack of transparency were at the heart of these crises. Despite impressive quantitative achievement, several distortions had crept in India's financial sector especially in respect of allocation of resources. Productivity and efficiency had suffered due to the system still working with outdated work technology. With the transaction cost escalation profitability had suffered erosion. Banks and financial institutions were unable to meet the challenges of a competitive environment.

The dimensions of the crisis which ensued got reflected in the macro-economic imbalances which grew to critical proportions. The most visible sign of the country's economic crisis was its extremely low foreign exchange reserves. Trade deficit, external debt, fiscal deficit, budgetary deficit and total public debt were increasing. Situation further worsened with the international agencies lowering the country's credit rating. Government response was to relieve the economy of the macro economic imbalances by adoption of certain short term, medium term and long term measures.

TWO STAGES OF ECONOMIC REFORMS

Operation 2-G, the new wave of reforms had two stages. The first stage involved changes in trade, finance and fiscal areas. The priorities were to reduce inflation, dismantle institutions of protectionism and statism and restore growth. It used instruments like price liberalisation, trade and foreign investment liberalisation, tax reforms, private sector deregulation, easier privatisations and budget cuts. The typical strategy adopted was reduction of macroeconomic rules and state role. Its impact on the economy was instant.

The second stage involved issues of equity, regional and sectoral allocation, good governance, institutional changes etc. The focus was on improving social conditions, increase international competitiveness and maintenance of macro economic stability. The priorities were to be achieved with the help of typical instruments like labour market reforms, restructuring of government and upgrading of regulatory capacities. The reform aimed at long term impact.

This strategy of reform can find its parallel in USSR of the 1920s when with the 'New Economic Policy' major changes were brought to "reform, reconstruction and revival" of the economy from the depressed state it had fallen into during the era of war communism. Indian reforms involved structural adjustments and stabilisation programmes. The announcement of the new reforms was a prelude to the appointment of a high level committee on financial system that would examine all the aspects relating to the structure, organisation, functions and procedures of the Indian financial system. Financial reforms have received special attention as part of the economic reforms because of the perceived interdependent relationship between the real and financial sectors of the modern economy. The competitive efficiency in the real sectors of the economy cannot be realized unless the allocative efficiency of the financial sector was improved.

FINANCIAL SECTOR REFORMS

Indian financial sector includes all financial institutions, all financial markets and the financial instruments and services which facilitate transfer of funds. Reforms was needed in all these sectors viz. banking, insurance and capital market, to streamline the functioning of the financial system and increase the efficiency of capital usage. The term 'Financial system' implies intimately related but still different terms-Money, Credit and Finance.

Goals

The objective of reforms in general is to accelerate the growth momentum of the economy, defined in terms of per capita income. Typically, improvements in the growth rate can be effected through three, not necessarily mutually exclusive, channels; improving productivity of capital, through investments in human capital and raising Total Factor Productivity (TFP).

Chile and Indonesia hosted the first and second seminar on financial systems reforms in Asia and Latin America. It was realized that financial reforms does not come easy or without pain. The number of banks and branches mushroomed in the euphoria of the time. But banks had not prepared the necessary infrastructure to cope with the volume of credit that followed. Economic history provides support for the fact that financial development makes fundamental contribution to growth. Proper resource mobilisation encourages large investment but for all this to happen the where with alls is a necessary. The required infrastructure should be able to efficiently and effectively handle the growing financial needs of the dynamic economy.

The Indian Government on 14th August in 1991 appointed a committee under the chairmanship of Shri Narasimham to study the different aspects of Indian financial system. The committee submitted a report on 16 November, 1991.

Measures

As for the recommendations of the Narasimham Committee the Government has undertaken various measures for the reforms of its financial sector. These include:

(a) Reduction in liquidity ratio

(b) Abolition of direct credit programmes

(c) Free determination of interest rates.

(d) Necessary improvement in the banking account system.

(e) Making provisions for non-performing assets (NPAs).

(f) Establishing speedy recovery of loans by special tribunals.

(g) Reconstitution of banking system for the establishment of a few banks of international standard national banks, local banks, rural banks, private sector banks, etc.

(h) Liberal treatment to foreign banks.

(i) Abolition of branch licensing system.

(j) Giving more freedom to banks and ending dual control of RBI and Finance Ministry, and

(k) Reform of the financial institutions related to development financing and establishing special cell in RBI to look after the functioning of the financial institutions consisting financing companies, merchant banks, mutual funds etc. and

(l) Introducing capital market reforms.

LIBERALISATION

In general, liberalization refers to a relaxation of previous government restrictions, usually in areas of social or economic policy. Liberalization of autocratic regimes may precede democratization. In the arena of social policy it may refer to a relaxation of laws restricting for example divorce, abortion, homosexuality or drugs. Most often, the term is used to refer to economic liberalization, especially trade liberalization or capital market liberalization, policies often referred to as neo-liberalism. Although economic liberalization is often associated with privatization, the two can be quite separate processes. For example, the European Union has liberalized gas and electricity markets, instituting a system of competition; but some of the leading European energy companies (such as EDF and Vattenfall) remain partially or completely in government ownership. Liberalization is one of three focal points (the others being privitatization and stabilization) of the Washington consensus's trinity strategy for economies in transition. Liberalizaed and privatized public services may be dominated by just a few big companies, particularly in sectors with high capital costs, or high sunk cost, such as water, gas and electricity. In some cases they may remain legal monopolies, at least for some part of the market (e.g. small consumers).

INDIA AND LIBERALISATION

Economic liberalisation in the country since 1991 has led to reduced government interference and has removed unnecessary restrictions on economic activities and has been encouraging privatisation of the economy. Under this liberalisation wave, the financial sector is facing the challenges to rationalise its activities. The reforms of the last 15 years have gone a long way toward freeing up the domestic economy from state control. Since liberalisation the government has approved significant banking reforms. Some relate to nationalised banks to increase their profitability and competitiveness and some reforms have opened up the banking and insurance sectors to private and foreign players.

PAIN OR PANACEA

The impact of the Financial Sector Reform was evident from the relatively cleaner balance sheet of the banks. But without doubt it can be said that it is an attempt to imitate the trends of abroad i.e. it lacks normative approach and suffers from ideological overload. It is not spontaneous. It would be wrong to say that reform was all pain and no pleasure. When assessing the reform in financial sector, commercial and economic criteria are not enough. The broader aspects of socio-political and economic criteria if analyzed show a significant improvement.

The situation of operating profit, capital adequacy ratio improved. There was also a sizable reduction in non-performing asset. Financial liberalisation intensified the competition among the financial institutions. The competition led to the banks entering new venues like para-banking and other financial services, insurance companies entered into banking and other fields and manufacturing corporate entering into financial activities besides their own. This development has led to the emergence of a "universal banking" concept that would lead to the emergence of financial giants with tremendous economic power but difficult to control.

Liberalised economy has opened up the Indian economy and integrated it with the rest of world. Due to the free market based exchange rate system there is severe external pressures leading to a certain amount of loss of autonomy of domestic monetary policy. The financial reform has had its impact on the shift of savings from the informal to formal financial markets without a considerable increase in the total savings. This is not a good trend as, informal markets have lower overhead costs but suffer from narrow information base and limited capacity for risk-pooling.

Another argument is that less control and state interference would lead to the formation of a "capital market based" financial system dominated by the principle of short term profitability.

FUTURE PROSPECT

The future banks need to adjust itself to the new future market that is emerging to be unstructured. Competition would be rampant, so it would not be enough to adhere to "accepted practice", but to set new goals and device innovative ways to achieve these goals. Restructuring of work process is needed. 'Customer Delight' should replace 'Customer Satisfaction'.

What is required are reform measures that would give the financial structure of India the required strength that would help India to achieve higher and a sustained growth path, subject to strict market discipline.

Some Areas of Future Financial Reforms are:

(1) Financial institutions should be prepared for the "Darwin banking that is survival of the fittest. Due to the deregulation of interest rates the banks have fallen into the prisoners' dilemma of the game theory where rivalry for deposit is concerned. The cut throat competition is due to lack of communication and coordination between the banks and their mutual interdependence. The need is for a more concerted action on part of banks.

(2) There should be a proper internal control system in banks that would keep the management informed about the changing scenario and expectations of the future MPA level is still high so the internal control and risk management should be strengthened to realize the warning signal and timely detection would lead to appropriate action taken on issue.

(3) IT revolution has dramatically brought down the distribution cost of the banking business thus increasing usage of new technology will help the banking industry in becoming cost effective and a profitable business.

(4) Work culture needs to be redefined HRD needs to be given the highest priority to achieve organisational transformation and high performance level.

(5) Considering the market of the future and its growing needs the bank should try to achieve the ones top financial shop status.

(6) The strategy for change management requires accent on twenty four hour banking, tele-banking, internet banking, corporate banking, merchant banking, investment banking, treasury and forex functions internal checks and controls and transparencies.

(6) Considering the market of the future and its growing needs the bank should try to achieve the ones top financial shop status.

(7) An important priority for the future is to develop the depth and breadth of the money and debt market. This is possible only with allowing multiplicity of intermediation possibilities with different risks and leverage profiles. Bank needs to increase their capitalisation.

(8) Private sector led growth is the only sustainable means of economic development. The harnessing of the entrepreneurial energies however requires institutions that can provide efficient financial intermediation and then deploy the mobilized capital for productive use.

(9) Legal reforms are required for a proper legal frame work to help the banks for expeditious recovery of debt and effect property transfer.

The Union Budget 2001-2002 mentioned rightly, "While economic reforms have placed the country on a much more secure and sustained growth path, we still have some serious concerns and cannot afford to be complacent "Thus in future the financial sector will have to be dealt with different at four levels :

(1) Public regulation of financial institutions,

(2) Organisational structure should be made more efficient,

(3) Technological upgradation to make it cost effective and a profitable, and

(4) A change in the attitude and psyche of the employees to help them survive in this highly competitive environment.

The more efficient the financial system in resource generation and its allocation the more enhanced is its role in the productivity growth and an economy's wide development. Thus the quality at functioning of the financial sector affects the functioning and productivity of all sectors of the economy. An efficient financial sector and timely reforms to it with the changing times can bring about a spectacular improvement in resource allocation which in turn would generate and promote growth. Financial sector no doubt in today's monetized economy is essential to promote both extensive and intensive growth.

REFERENCES

Government of India (1998), Report of the Committee on Banking Sector Reforms (Chairman, Shri M. Narasimhan) New Delhi.

Mohan, R. (2005), "Financial sector Reforms: Policies and Performance Analysis" Economic & Political Weekly, Special Issue on Money, Banking and Finance, March, 1106-1121.

Mohan, R. (2005), Reforms, Productivity and Efficiency in Banking: The Indian Experience, 21st Annual General Meeting and Conference.

Bhole, L.M.: "Financial Institutions and Markets" Fourth edition, structure growth and innovations.

Dhingra, Ishwar C.: "The Indian Economy" Environmental and policy.

—http:/ www.webindia.com/budget/indsecfs.htnl.

CHAPTER 13

BANKING SECTOR REFORMS IN INDIA–AN OVERVIEW

S.K. Khandelia

Banks play an important role in the economy of the country. Banking, when properly organized, aids and facilitates the development of trade and industry and hence of national economy. In the modern economy, banks are to be considered not as dealers in money in the money markets but as the leader of the factors for the development of the economy. Banks are not just the store houses of the country's wealth but are the resources necessary for economic development.[1]

BANKING SECTORS REFORMS

In the post-liberalization era, it has been recognized that the Indian banking system should be in tune with well laid down international standards of capital adequacy and prudential norms. The Reserve Bank has initiated several measures to ensure safety and soundness of the banking system and at the same time, encouraging banks to play an effective role in accelerating the growth process. Progressive reduction of reserve requirements to correct the impact of directed investment on the profitability of banks, deregulation of complex and administered interest rate structure to move to market determined rates, and introduction of prudential norms for assets classification, income recognition and provisioning in order to remove subjectivity were some of the major steps taken in the direction of banking sector reforms.[2] Accounting practices had been prescribed in consonance with internationally accepts standards with the objective of enhancing transparency and credibility and ensuring accuracy of financial statements. The Indian banking facilitated the much awaited paradigm shift from a highly regulated one to market-oriented one. They are grouped under three phases:

FIRST PHASE REFORMS: 1991-96

The Government of India implemented the following reforms in the Banking Sector:[3]

- The deregulation of entry of new private sector banks, both domestic and foreign in 1992-93.
- Liberalization of branch licensing policy-allowing banks more freedom of plan branch expansion in response to market needs, subject to certain minimum performance requirements.
- Phase-wise deregulation of interest rates on both deposits and advances.
- Introduction of capital adequacy norms of 8% in line with the norms set by the banks for international settlement (BIS).
- Institution of transparent prudential and income recognition norms.
- Allowing public sector banks to access the capital market to raise equity.
- Gradual reduction of CRR and SLR.

SECOND PHASE REFORMS: 1997-2000

The major changes in macro-economic environment and institutional structures called for a critical evaluation of policy initiatives already undertaken. Accordingly, the Government implemented the following reforms:[4]

- Strengthening of capital adequacy including explicit capital for market risk.
- Tightening of the prudential and disclosure standards in line with international best practices.
- Consolidation of banking system (Mergers and Acquisition).
- Restructuring of weak public sector banks.
- Dilution of government equity of 33 percent in public sector banks and providing functional autonomy to government banks.
- Technology improvements to modernize Indian banking.
- Adoption of scientific tools for management of risk emphasis on management asset/liability and NPAs.
- Legal reforms for expedite recovery of bank's dues.

(a) Equity Diluting: On 16th November 2000, the government allowed to reduce its equity stake form 51 percent to 33 percent as announced by the finance minister in the union budget for 2000-01 through the issue of fresh equity. This would provide the much-needed funds to banks for their expansion plans rather depending on budgetary support from the Government.

(b) VRS Package: Public sector banks are over-staffed roughly with the average of 20 percent. In banking sector, wage cost is the second largest item of expenditure; it is two times of gross profits and heavy amount in the restructuring, PSBs are involved in finalizing their VRS packages. The number of bank employees seeking voluntary retirement scheme is swelled to 90,000 at an average of 7 lakh per employee, the total compensation amount comes out to the tune of Rs. 6300 crores. Except Corporation Bank, all others have announced their VRS packages.

(c) Technology Upgradation: In the changing scenario, only those banks shall survive who can provide consumers–oriented services using latest technology. Information technology can spruce sophistication in financial engineering. Computerization process and inter-connectivity of computerized

branches reduced the transaction costs with brand consumer base. Now a variety of different configuration in banking technology is available such as ATM Cards, tele banking, Mobile and Internet banking, electronic fund transfer, etc.

(d) Bank Assurance: This term of French origin refers to integration of banking and insurance services. With an advantage of brand name along with the strength of their exponential branch network, banks can attain a commanding position in this challenging sphere after the entry of ICICI Prudential Life, HDFC-Standard Life, Royal Sundaram General and Birla Sun Life into Insurance Sector. Now it is turn of commercial banks. SBI, the largest commercial bank in the country has also received a clearance from RBI to promote an insurance company with BNP Paribas Insurance, the subsidiary of France Cardiff Insurance as a joint venture.

THIRD PHASE REFORMS: AFTER 2000-01

Banking sector reforms during 2000-2001 emphasized on building the health of banks and financial institutions, improving their asset quality, strengthening prudential norms and supervision and monitoring development with a view to securing the soundness and stability of the Indian Banking System comparable to international standards. The segment-wise status of the reforms is provided as under:[5]

(a) Capital Adequacy and Provisioning: In a move towards consolidated supervision, banks are to voluntarily build in the risk-weighted components of their subsidiaries into their own balance sheet on a national basis and assign additional capital in phases from 2000-02 onwards.

(b) Exposure Norms: Fresh norms on the concept of capital funds measurement of credit exposures and level of exposure limits to individual group borrowers were announced. The exposure ceiling for commercial banks in respect of individual borrower is reduced from 20 per cent to 15 per cent of capital funds in March 31, 2002. With effect from April 1, 2003, the non-fund based exposure is reckoned at 100 per cent and banks are required to include forward contracts and other derivatives in determining individual/group exposure. Within the overall exposure, a bank's exposure to the capital market in all forms

was set at 5 percent of its outstanding advances (including commercial paper) as on March 31, 2005.

(c) Prudential Accounting Norms: Valuation norms applicable for banks' investment portfolios were modified to reflect market movements. Commercial banks were required to classify their entire investment portfolio under three categories viz., held to maturity, available for sale or held for trading. Investments were required to be marked to market periodically.

(d) Entry Norms for New Private Sector Banks: The entry norms for new banks in the private sector were revised in January 2001 and guidelines for conversion of non-banking financial companies to scheduled bank also issued. The minimum capital for entry was set at Rs.200 crores to be raised to Rs. 300 crores within three years from commencement of business. A minimum CRAR of 10 percent was prescribed for new private sector banks.

(e) Norms for Banks and NBFCs Entering Insurance: Banks and registered NBFCs have been permitted to enter the insurance business under the Insurance Regulatory and Development Authority (IRDA) Act, 1999. Certain eligibility criteria have been prescribed for entry of banks and NBFCs into insurance business through the above routes.

(f) International Standards: The standing committee on International Financial Standards and Codes (Chairman: Dr. Y.V. Reddy) was constituted by the Reserve Bank and Government of India for identifying the development in global standard and codes with a view to consider the applicability of these standards and codes to the Indian financial system.

(g) Technological Developments: The process of finalizing the Real Time Gross Settlement design specifications covering the entire gamut of policy, operational and implementation issues were completed by RBI. The Indian Financial Network, which initially comprised only the PSBs, was opened up for participation by other categories of members. 26 PSBs achieved the level of 70 percent of business captured through computerization by June 2001. Further, the Information Technology Act, 2000 has given legal recognition to creation,

transmission and retention of an electro magnetic data to be treated as valid proof in a court of law.

The worldwide trend towards economic liberalization prompted the Indian authorities also, to go in for banking sector reforms as part of general economic structural adjustment program. The philosophy behind the banking sector reforms was claimed to be to promote a diversified, efficient and competitive banking sector with the ultimate objective of improving the allocative efficiency of available resources, increasing the return on investments and promoting an accelerated growth of the real sector of the economy.

REFORM EXPERIENCE

Starting from Chakraborty Committee, the financial reform began and this has been pursued step by step, with the recommendations of several other committees of which Narasimham Committee I and II and Vaghual Committee reports are prominent. The recommendations and implementation of those may be classified as follows:[6] (a) ownership of financial institutions and banking structure, (b) functional improvements of banks, (c) structural and functional change of the money market, (d) global participation, and (e) supervision and regulation. The objective of the LPG programme in the financial sector was aimed at improving the functions of the financial institutions through privatization and competition.

As per ownership and privatization, the Narasimham Committee recommended partial privatization of nationalized banks and dilution of their public ownership to 33 percent. Government has allowed the nationalized banks to raise funds from the capital market through public issues. New private sector banks are allowed to function and the financial institutions like UTI have set up banks. This is aimed at inducting competition among the banking system and to improve efficiency.

A number of measures have been adopted for functional improvements of commercial banks and to improve their functional efficiency and profitability. External constraints on liquidity utilization of resources have been removed and CRR and SLR have been reduced substantially; interest rates on lending and deposit rates have been partly relaxed and competitive lending rate has been adopted beyond 2-lakh advances. Prudential norms have been changed by imposition of capital adequacy norm on the lines of Basel Committee recommendation of the World Bank. Measures have been taken for reclassification of the NPA and improvement of the soundness of commercial bank functions. Assets have been classified in four categories- standard, sub-standard, doubtful and loss. However, advances guaranteed by government are not classified as NPA even if income is not being recognized on accrual basis. Banks were asked to complete classification of borrowals below Rs. 25000 by March 1998. The Narasimham Committee, of course, has recommended that asset classification norm should apply even to government guaranteed advances in the same manner as for any other advance. For strengthening prudential norms, investment portfolio of banks have been examined and all new private sector banks were required to mark to market their entire investments in approved securities from March 31, 1997. Generally, banks had to mark to market 70 percent of the investments in government and approved securities by March 31, 1999 and in the next three years the entire portfolio.

To induce competition in the banking sector, Narasimham Committee suggested that foreign banks should be allowed to set up subsidiaries/joint ventures in India. In the real sector, along side RRBs, Local Area Banks should be allowed to compete with other banks. In fact, India made commitments in WTO under the General Agreements on Trade in Services to grant licenses every year to new and existing foreign banks. As stated above, relaxation of interest rate has introduced a little competition among banks regarding big loans.

Other important issues in respect of functional improvement of nationalized banks are credit delivery system, priority sector lending or directed credit and risk management. As for the credit control/credit delivery system, a number of measures have been introduced. Banks have been given freedom to decide on their own the levels of holdings of inventory and receivables of various industries while assessing credit requirements of borrowers. The amount consortium lending has been raised from earlier Rs. 50m. to Rs. 5000m. Considerable flexibility with regard to credit delivery system for borrowers has been introduced. Some simplification of procedure in regards to agriculture and small industry has been brought about mandatory requirements on formation of consortium for loans of Rs. 500 million and above from more than one bank has been withdrawn in 1997. Except for sugar, all selective credit controls on sensitive commodities have been abolished. In a sense some advances have been made to build market-oriented control and delivery system, which will not be easy for medium and small sector.

This is far more serious in case of directed credit/priority sector lending. Narasimahm Committee has pointed the necessity for redefining the priority sector and limiting the bank credit limit to 10 per cent for the redefined priority sector. The redefined priority sector includes advances to software industry, transport operators, housing, and plantation crops (tea, coffee, rubber, and cardamom) investment on special bonds of SIDBI, NABARD, HUDCO, SFCs and Rural Electrification Corporation. This extension of priority sector credit has facilitated banks to make loans on commercially viable terms. This has been partly to support the NPA problem of commercial banks. However, this reorientation of priority lending will hardly provide relief to the commercial banks from the NPA burden.

However, simply changing the priority sector lending will not reduce risk of the commercial banks. Narasimham Committee II has elaborately examined this risk issues in the context of market-oriented lending. Banks are advised to introduce effective risk management system to cover credit risk, forex risk, market risk and operational risk. Comprehensive Asset Liability Management Systems are being introduced to take care of these risks. An expert group on foreign exchange market (O.P. Sodhani Committee) and Malhotra Committee on capital account convertibility have examined the forex risk and suggested measures for orderly management of forex risk. In order to reduce the operational risk, a number of measures have been introduced. Implementation of Jilani Committee recommendations for strengthening of internal inspection and audit system in banks is a part of that measure. In addition to that, intensive monitoring of inter branch, inter bank accounts have been introduced, setting up of compliance officers and setting up of Audit Committee of Board are also important steps in that direction. Money market reform is another area of consideration, which is to be followed by global issues and the question of supervision. RBI has recently taken measures to develop the money market through issues of new instruments such as commercial paper and Certificate of Deposits in which Banks and FIs are allowed to operate on a limited scale. Money Market Mutual Funds is another addition to the money market structure. In the government securities market, important changes have been introduced. Tap-T Bills were replaced by 14 days intermediate T-Bills and 182 days T-Bills were withdrawn. A new set of Primary Dealers was licensed and a set of Satellite Dealers was also registered. Along with that some policy measures were also implemented. Instruments eligible for repo/reverse repo transactions were expanded, non-bank entities were permitted to enter into reverse repo transactions and Foreign Institutional Investors (FIIs) were permitted to enter the government securities market. These efforts are in the line of making the government securities market and debt market competitive as suggested by Chakraborty Committee. Government securities market is very important segment of debt market as it sets the benchmark in the financial market and serves as an important transmission channel for control of liquidity. Two other segments of the debt market are bond market and corporate securities market. The importance of government debt market is used from the magnitude of transaction. As on March 31, 1998 the outstanding securities of the Central and State Governments amounted to over Rs. 4000 billion and the major part of this volume was held by commercial banks.

The bond market and corporate securities markets are also coming up. Some important PSU bonds and other bonds are traded in this market whereas the Securities and Exchange Board of India (SEBI) regulates the non-government securities in the secondary market through stock exchange. The debt market development is therefore, a significant part of the financial reform, since it plays a very important role in the financial flow of the economy and this investment pattern.

Another development in the financial market is the regulation of non-banking financial companies (NBFCs). A comprehensive regulatory framework for NBFCs have been introduced in January 1998 in order to determine their prudential norms and deposit acceptance activities.

In the reform wave, the foreign exchange market is an important segment where a number of changes have been introduced. Indian forex market has been integrated with global financial system. Banks have been allowed to invest up to 15 percent of their capital in foreign countries. But a significant development is the rupee forex swap, which enable the banks to hedge risk and exchange market volatility. Since August 1996, cross currency options and derivative products have been made available and authorized dealers (A-D) have been allowed to offer interest rate swaps, currency swaps, coupon swaps, purchase of interest rate caps/collars and forward rate agreements to their corporate clients. Since September 1996, ADs have been accorded freedom to offer to their customers cost reduction strategies and risk reduction option strategies like Range Forwards, Ratio Range Forwards, etc. ADs have also been permitted from April 1997 to borrow from their overseas office as well as to invest funds in overseas money market instruments up to 10 million dollars. ADs have also been permitted to book forward cover for exporters and importers. Forward contracts have been allowed for remittance of dividend in respect of direct foreign investment.

This is the current status of the recommendations of the Committee on Capital Account Convertibility. The committee has suggested to allow forward markets, derivatives and futures and prominent role of the primary Dealers and Satellite

Dealers. The Committee has also suggested development of T-Bill market and participation of FIIs in it. India has, by now, covered some of these recommendations and has been closing to capital account convertibility and global capital market. However, the financial sector liberalization comprises opening of capital market and allowing foreign financial institutions to participate in insurance, banking and share market. With the Authorized Dealers permission of derivative markets and allowing FIIs in T-Bill market we have to make a small beginning in this direction. SEBI panel headed by L.C. Gupta has suggested phased introduction of derivative products in the country.

We must remember that the CAC has asked to shape the macro-economic issues before going for capital account convertibility. These issues are sufficient foreign exchange reserve, fiscal consolidation, the mandated rate of inflation for three years period at about 3-5 percent and a stable exchange rate. We shall later assess the current state of macro-economic response and the implication of this reform and liberalization.

REFORM ASSESSMENT[7]

(a) The area of banking and financial reform has been, as yet, mainly confined to functional aspect of the institutions. Sickness of commercial banks has been tried to be corrected by reducing their irrational lending and restricting the directional credit. The improvement of functioning of the nationalized commercial banks is recently evident from their regaining strength in respect of capital norm and profitability. A few of nationalized banks have turned round currently.

(b) The interest rate flexibility has not induced any sufficient competition in the system. Interest rate, exchange rate and capital asset yield rate are important components of interest rate syndrome. Low interest rate discourages intermediation and ultimately reduces investment via reduction of savings. This repression hypothesis is supported by fiscal compulsion of the government.

Over last few years, the external value of Rupee in terms of dollar has been sliding. The alignment between exchange rate and the other trade and capital account variables are not convincing. The trade and capital account variables are not convincing. The trade account of the country shows no sign of improvement and the export growth is disappointing. On the other hand, the capital flow has been quite unsatisfactory, after an initial spurt. In our balance sheet account, capital account convertibility has made no progress although expectation of foreign capital for economic development has been one important factor for globalization.

(c) Financial reform has two components – fiscal policy and monetary policy. Government has to make budgetary balance so that it does not depend much on market borrowing or ad hoc finance from the banking system. It frustrates the objectives of monetary policy of liquidity control in our country; government budgetary position is yet to be compressed.

(d) As for the approach to external sector reforms, Report of the High Level Committee on Balance of Payments (Chaired by C. Rangarajan) is relevant. It has recommended the market determined exchange rate, current account convertibility and regulation of commercial borrowings. On the recommendations of this committee, the capital loss has been managed and there has been a gradual move from administered exchange rate to market determined exchange rate. But, as stated above, capital flow has been sluggish and exchange rate has been unfavourable. Compared to China, another big foreign capital recipient, capital flow in India has been very insignificant. As against the recommendations of the Rangarajan Committee, the exchange rate volatility has become an endemic feature even with incipient capital flow and RBI appears to be shaky against the uncertainty of international currency markets.

(e) This leads to the central macro-economic issue of foreign investment and economic crises of Asian and Mexico type.

In view of these experiences, the slow process of our financial sector reform, particularly in the external sector, is a step in the right direction.

(f) Compulsion of external sector and financial sector globalization generally comes from two sources–the private multinational debtor and the IMF-World Bank. However, if the country continuously avoids too much borrowing from these sources, the crises from MNC investment and IMF compulsion can be avoided. This requires reform in a big way on the domestic front, which we are lacking.

REFORM LAGGING

There are three important areas where financial sector reform is lagging:[8] (a) the rural financial sector, (b) the fiscal connection and (c) the personnel management.

(a) If the financial sector reform on the external front has shown wisdom, then on the domestic front it lacks wisdom and courage. The entire rural financial sector requires radical reform, both in respect of structure and function of the financial institutions. At present, six agencies are operating in the rural credit market: (i) Cooperatives, (ii) RRBs, (iii) branches of commercial banks, (iv) Self-Help Groups and NGOs, (v) indigenous banks and (vi) money lenders of various descriptions including employers.

The Narasimham Committees have advised reduction of credit to the priority sector. As we have seen, the definition of redefined rural sector leaves many people below poverty line. The growth of NGOs and the so-called Self-Help Groups are now filling the vacuum. The sickness of RRBs, rural branches of commercial banks and cooperatives have to be corrected. It is to be remembered that India's biggest productive potential lies in the rural sector and the rejuvenated rural financial structure is the biggest push factor for expansion of growth.

(b) The fiscal drag in our reform attempt needs urgent care. Fiscal decentralization is important. State and Central finances have to be redesigned so that they do not distract growth, generate financial instability and encourage corruption and black money. Monetary reform will not be successful as long as revenue lapses in the government persist which is largely due to over centralization of fiscal structure.

(c) Financially, there has been no progress in the personnel management of financial institutions. The entire nationalized banking structure, which accounts for more than 80 percent suffers from low customer service and inefficiency. Present attempt to induce efficiency as a result of external competition will not be successful and if the external agencies thrive then the nationalized banks will lose in all respect and it will be difficult to support those derelict and decaying banks by simply budgetary support. It is, therefore, essential to pay serious attention to the personnel management so that services to the customers, improve and banks can turn sickness to efficiency. At present, the customer's service is the first casualty and corruption is rampant. While measures have been taken for supervision and correction of NPA, the personnel management and improvement has been completely neglected.

PROBLEMS STILL PERSIST

In spite of these achievements, problems still persisted in the following ways:

- Narasimham Committee has ignored the implications of the existence of a vast unorganized sector. As late as 1987-88, about 40 percent of the rural labour households were indebted and 43 percent of their debt was contracted with the traditional sources of moneylender/ indigenous bankers, while relatives and friends financed another 14 percent of it. The end use of these borrowings is equally revealing with half the debt incurred being for personal consumption and ceremonials.[9] As it seems, the present package of financial sector reforms does not address the relation between organized and unorganized segments. The unorganized segments have continued to dominate in the credit market in spite of the reforms in financial sector.

- Narasimham committee has considered directed credit as one of the factors for the growing volume of NPAs in banks. But this is not true in all cases. The NPAs in banks are a problem due to growing size of sick industrial units. Unlike the small borrowers turning defaulters, these sick borrowers are strong enough to obtain nursing programmes one after the other with benign support of the operating agencies. Export credit is another area where the NPAs are growing while very little collateral support is available. Hence, it is the 'misdirected credit' and not the directed credit, which contributes to the gravity of the NPA muddle.[10]
- The committee has stressed the need for converting DFI's into commercial banks. The process has already been initiated by UTI and LIC. The future role of DFI turned bank is not elaborated in the report. Are they exposed to open retail outlets all over, duplicating the work done by the existing commercial banks? Should they dilute the expertise in term lending nurtured over the years.[11]
- The committee in its first report recommended for the merger of RRBs with sponsoring banks. But now in its second report, the committee maintains silence about the future of RRBs. The committee has evidently viewing the need for allowing the RRBs to continue to co-exist with other banks in the realigned banking pattern. At the same time, the committee has gone to the other extreme of emphasizing the need to facilitate the evolution and growth of micro-credit institutions.

The committee recommends that, 'third-tier banks should be promoted and strengthened to be autonomous, vibrant, effective and competitive in their operations' (Narasimham, 115). There is an apparent contradiction here. It is not clear whether the committee treats some of the nationalized banks, which would be operating at the regional level on par with tiny banks. Or it may classify the micro-credit institutions as the 'fourth-tier banks'.

- The committee has recommended for the setting up of the Board for Financial Supervision and Regulation (BFSR). All rural credit institutions are expected to be brought under the supervision of the board. Besides in due course it is proposed to bring FI's, NBFC's foreign banks, urban cooperative banks under the supervision of BFSR. Considering the enormity of the work involved in supervising the work of such diverse financial institutions spread over a wider geographical area, one wonders as to what should be the size and shape of BFSR. Can a monolithic organization of this type discharge its duties effectively under such circumstances? We have had several experiences in the past.

Narasimham Committees–I and II seek to place commercial banks with greater footing and sounder objectives for catering to the needs of growing population who will be depending largely on banks (for everything added) in the present millennium. It seeks to overhaul the inherent contradictions and operational drawbacks by promising greater work efficiency, transparency in management, competitiveness and improved profitability. Before the turn of the century, the banks are required to follow the prescribed guidelines of the banks strictly on the one hand and to remove all those contradictions, which form a part of the recommendations on the other.

CONCLUSION

Economic crisis of 1991 has paved the way for financial and real sector reform with greater emphasis on the former. The weaknesses manifested under state intervention, bureaucratic controls and political interferences in the banking sector were corrected by financial and banking sectors reforms with emphasis on prudential norms, capital restructuring, efficiency and competitiveness in banks. Besides, there was also the stress for reducing non-performing assets (NPA's) and improving profitability of banks under financial and banking sector reforms, the commercial banks have progressed significantly in several directions. They are now guided more by market environment than by financial repression and controls. However, the government does not guarantee full autonomy as is expected from market economy by banks because intimately the state is responsible to the general public for the wrongs committed by banks.

REFERENCES

1. Radhaswamy, M. and S.V Vasudevan (1979), A Text Book of Banking Law Practice and Theory of Banking, S. Chand & Co., p.521.
2. Kumar, R. Shashi (2006), "Financial Reforms and the Performance of Indian Banking Sector" in Indian Banking and Financial Sector Reforms (Ed. Ravishankar Kumar Singh), Abhijeet Publications, Delhi, pp. 284-288.
3. *Ibid*
4. *Ibid*
5. *Ibid*
6. Banerjee, Amalesh, "Macro-Economic Aspects of Financial Reform" in Banking and Financial Sector Reforms in India (Ed. Banerjee, A. and S.K. Singh), Deep & Deep Publication Pvt. Ltd., New Delhi, pp. 8-16.
7. *Ibid*
8. *Ibid*
9. Mishra, S.N. and Sriram Mishra, "Development of Commercial Banking Under Financial and Banking Sector Reforms: Problems, Achievements and Prospects" in Banking and Financial Sector Reforms in India (Ed. Banerjee, A. and S.K. Singh), Deep & Deep Publication Pvt. Ltd., New Delhi, pp. 119-121.

10. Om Prakash, G., (1997), Financial Development, Review of Development and Change, Vol. II, No.2, July-December.

11. Thingalaya, N., (1999), "Narashimham Committee Reports: Some Contradictions and Compromises", The Journal of Indian Institute of Banking, January-March, Bombay.

CHAPTER 14

IMPACT OF GLOBALISATION ON BANKING REFORMS IN INDIA WITH SPECIAL REFERENCE TO USE OF ATM

Bipin Kumar

In any economy, the financial sector plays a major role in the mobilisation and allocation of savings. Financial institutions, instruments and markets which constitute the financial sector act as a conduit for the transfer of financial resources from net savers to net borrowers, i.e. from those who spend less than they earn, to those who earn less than they spend. In the late seventies and eighties financial sector reforms had been an integral and complementary part of the overall structural adjustment programme of the economies of several countries. Reforms in the financial sector obviously need to increase the efficiency in the financial sector and attempt to improve the efficiency and productivity of the real sector of the economy. Apart from this, reforms are called for making the sector capable of serving the emerging multiple needs of the growing real sector. The financial sector reforms currently underwent in India must also be seen as a component of the overall scheme of structural reforms. The overall package is aimed at enhancing the productivity and efficiency of the economy as a whole and also increasing international competitiveness. The reforms are comprehensive in scope covering several other components of economic policy (besides financial sector reforms) including liberalisation and deregulation of domestic investment, infrastructure, foreign investment, Public sector, foreign trade, tax system, etc. All these reforms are closely interrelated and progress in one area helps to achieve objectives in others. Structural reforms in areas such as industrial and trade policy can succeed only if resources are redeployed towards more efficient producers which are encouraged to expand under new policies. This reallocation is possible only if the financial system plays a crucial supportive role.

In the period 1991 following nationalisation in 1969, the Indian banking system made phenomenal strides in the volume of its business and it diversified its activities.

(1) Between 1969 and 1990, there was almost a sevenfold expansion in the number of bank branches.

(2) Especially noteworthy was the spread of banking to rural areas.

(3) The banking sector now has to its credit 300 million deposit accounts.

(4) A considerable amount of money and effort was spent on the cooperative credit movement for the agricultural sector.

(5) Social banking catering to priority and vulnerable sectors played a notable part in the lending protfolio of the nationalised banking sector.

By and large, the major objectives of bank nationalisation have been fulfilled. These achievements are reflected in some broad statistical indicators as given below.

Indicators	*June 1969*	*March 1990*
Share of priority sector advances to net bank credit (in per cent)	14	43
Number of Commercial Bank Officers	8262	60294
Number of Rural branches	1833	34940
Per cent of rural branches	22	57
Average population served per bank office	65000	12000
Aggregate Deposits (in crores)	6460	171648
Share of Bank Deposits to national Income (In crores)	15.2	50
Total Bank Credit (in crores)	3599	103835

A number of reform initiatives have been taken to remove or minimize the distortions impinging upon the efficient and profitable functioning of banks. These include the following :

(i) Reduction in SLR and CRR whereby the lending capacity of the banks has been gradually augmented. The reduction of SLR to 25 per cent as recommended by the Committee has been by and large, achieved. The medium target of 10 per cent in CRR has also been achieved though the Committee recommended that it should be reduced by 3 to 5 per cent of the total deposits of the banks. The incremental CRR of 10 per cent was abolished.

(ii) Transparent guidelines or norms for entry and exit of private sector banks have been stipulated. A few private sector banks have already started functioning.

(iii) The nationalized banks have been allowed direct access to capital markets to mobilize funds from the public although they will continue to remain in the control of the Government which will retain 51 per cent of the equity.

(iv) The regulated interest rate has been rationalized and simplified. The banks' deposit rates have been deregulated subject to a ceiling rate. The number of lending rates has been reduced from six to three rates with two concessional rates and a floor rate for all advances above rupees two lakhs.

(v) Movement of interest yield on Government Securities towards market related rates has been allowed subject to prudential guidelines since the reform initiatives in this area in India are in the formative stage.

(vi) Branch licensing policy has been liberalized.

(vii) Accounting and prudential norms related to income recognition, provisioning and capital adequacy, in line with the accepted international standards, have been implemented since 1992-93 to ensure safety of the financial system.

(viii) The Recovery of Debts due to Banks and Financial Institution Act, 1993 was enacted for setting up of dedicated tribunals for expenditious adjudication and recovery of debts. A new Tribunals have been set up in a number of cities and an Appellate Tribunal has also been set up in Mumbai.

(ix) The implementation of the new norms under the reform measures will lead to a considerable impairment of capital in some of the nationalized banks which have to be recapitalized. Hence the Government has been making provision for such recapitalization since the budget of 1993-94.

(x) A Board for Financial Bank Supervision has been established to strengthen the supervisory system of the RBI.

These and other measures that have been taken would help the highly regulated and directed banking system to transform itself into one characterized by openness, competition, prudential and supervisory discipline. They will also make the Commercial Banks in the country to successfully respond to the new challenges particularly to the growing demands from the customers for high quality service.

In recent years, the Indian Economy has been subjected to massive doses of reforms, the foundations of which were laid more than a decade ago. The present paper contains some reflections on the process of banking sector reforms and uses of ATM in India. These reform measures have had major impact on the overall efficiency and stability of the banking system in India. The present capital adequacy of Indian banks is comparable to those at international level. There has been a marked improvement in asset quality with the percentage of gross non-performing assets (NPS) to gross advances for the banking system reduced from 14.4 per cent in 1998 to 7.2 per cent in 2004.

Globalization has benefited the banking sector by enhancing competition and efficiency. The days are not far off when India will emerge as a major international banking centre. The process of globalization which begins in 1970s and gained momentum in 1990s is of considerable significance for the world economy in general and India in particular. Globalization implies expansion of market for goods, services, labour and capital beyond national boundaries. Globalization of economy means globalization of production, trade, services and finance. Globalization has brought new challenges for the Indian business and more particularly the banking sector, due to structural change in the financial market, increased competition, increased market volatility, technological advancement, deregulation, customer awareness and expectations. Globalization of the Indian economy has brought in its way fierce pressure on the Indian banks from International Banks. In order to complete with new entrants, dramatic changes have been made over the years. The Indian banking system is undergoing a metamorphosis. Several significant transformations have taken place in the history of Indian banking sector. Reforms introduced in the banking sector represent a continuous process aimed at improving financial strengths and functional efficiency of banks and bringing them up to the international standards. The banking sector reforms pave way for globalization. Foreign banks were set up in India. After the economic reforms in 1991, the liberalisation, privatisation and globalisation (LPG) have been applied to all sectors in India and the banking sector is no exception to it.

The banking service today has become highly competitive. LPG have changed the scenario in banking dramatically. The introduction of prudentional norms in the banking industry in early 1990s and the efforts by the banks to make the balance sheet more transparent, created a new necessity for banks for reengineering their business objective and profit maximisation. The primary source of comparative advantage of nations today is skills and the ability to adopt changed. We have to transform our banking system from being a largely domestic one to a truly international standard. The growing competition and growing expectation have led to increased awareness among banks about the role and importance of technology in banking.

The arrival of private and foreign banks with superior state-of-the-art technology based services pushed Indian Banks also to follow suit by going in for the latest technology to meet the competition and retain the customer base. Global measures brought in a completely new operating environment to the bank services and products like anywhere banking, ATMs, Tele banking, Smart cards, Internet banking, Internet cards, web banking, e-banking, etc. are the order of the day and banks are coping with the competition, offering innovative technology-based service to the customers.

The banking industry all over the world is experiencing a sea change in the following areas:

(a) Consolidation of market players through mergers and acquisition;

(b) Globalization of operations; and

(c) Development of new technologies.

The banks also experience vast development in the following aspects, viz. structure and ownership pattern, corporate governance, management structure, traditional banking pattern, bank-lending operation, human resource development, international trading and risk management. One of the most significant future challenges to banks would be set rigorous credit standard, raising global competition, increasing deregulation, introduction of innovative products and delivery channel. These have pushed risk management to the fore front of today's banking landscape. Banks are now faced with the challenges of increased risk caused by liberalization. One major management challenge is identified as managing human resources. Choosing the right business model, taking up competition and adoption of appropriate technique to manage the business is given top priority by the bank management.

International happenings have changed the role of the Indian banks from traditional banking to commercial and social banking. The organisational structure of the Indian banks is so unwieldy that the time has come to trim its shape, to weed out the non-profit making branches and to tone up the operational efficiency. Branches that are not viable are to be either merged with other branches or the operations have to be completely stopped.

In the liberalised economy, the computer is occupying the centre stage of the banking function. With the introduction of computers, costumer service has become very easy and convenient Day-to-Day house keeping work of the banks has been improved and the delivery system has been modified. Information system has helped the banks in maintaining and improving the internal control system for taking timely decisions. Risk management and assets-liability management are some of the areas where IT will be of immense used to the banks. Information technology helps the banks in the area of optimally using the ATMs for quick transfer of funds and for optimising the profit. The banking sector in India is facing challenging times with advent of globalisation, privatisation and liberalisation the competition in the banking sector has gone up and the customer service has become focal point. At the same time customer's expectations have gone up in terms of global standards. Hence, bank need to manage their operations efficiently and profitably and design innovate means of attracting and retaining customers. Modern India is exploiting all the benefits of technological advancements. There are radical changes in banking field. Customers require ratting services and they should feel splendid. More numbers of access points in market, residential and travel areas are installed, then the banks can see higher turnover and better customer satisfaction at all levels. Explosion in the field of (IT) information technology, security systems and encryption models have brought in significant changes in modern banking services in India. Many more value added services in banking sector have been introduced to satisfy billions of customers without increasing the paper related work load of clerical staff in banks. These days banks have to follow altruistic principle, which is unselfness as principal of action, to increase customer satisfaction in this competitive banking field. This in the long-run will pave way for significant growth in service sector. Once upon a time, people have to spend three to four hours to go and do bank transactions. Some times the cost of transaction was more than that of the money deposited or withdrawn. But now billion of customers are being handled with care and caution by providing advanced technology based services without scarifying the concepts of secrecy and reasonable care. ATM's have relieved the customers and bankers from tense circumstances and are enabling them to have good relationship to certain level. In future, people have to transact using remote banking and virtual banking facilities.

What is ATM? ATM (or) Automatic Telling Machines are a means of convenience for customers. So much that most of the people have changed the acronym to any time money. The story of the humbly cash dispensing machine started around three decades back. In India, HBSC set the trend and set up the first ATM machine here in 1987. Since then they have become a common sight in many of our metros. With more than 8,00,000 machines world wide. ATMs have made hard cash just seconds away all through out the day at every concern of the globe. ATMs are self service vendor machines help the banks to provide round the clock banking services to their customers at convenient places without visiting to the bank premises. They enable the banks to transact more business by offering various services in cost effective way on the one side and to get more customer satisfaction on the other. To avail the ATM services customers are provided with ATM card, which is small plastic card with magnetic strips, containing information about the name of the bank, name of the customer, card number, validity period an signature panel. The magnetic strips contains information about the customer, which enables the bank to verify the identify when the card is inserted at the slot provided in ATM. ATMs were allowed to set up by the RBI from the year 1996-97 at the bank branches, extension counters in special centers at convenient locations, shops and establishments.

REASONS FOR PREFERRING ATMs

Plethora of banking institutions is engaged in operating ATMs. Traditional banking services are felt as otiose by many customers. Invective scenes are common in banks in busy hours. Occasionally, services are also lamentable in physical banking areas. Hence some bankers may have insisted the customers to use ATMs. Sometimes the customers themselves may have opted to use ATMs due to their pattern of banking aspects. The reasons included any time banking, any where banking, safety, avoid bank conventional services or others.

STATEMENT OF PROBLEM

In modern India, mass of people can not revert to atavism due modern sophisticated processes. In the lack of awareness and proper education people do not want to avail the modern technology. Some people think that ATMs satisfy corny aspects of customer. Some say that customer may become a squander, further many customers are ticklish to handle. There are some trumpery cards which are rubbish. Some customers may be strum in ATM usage. It is to be noted that even though some agreements in ATM use are impudent or impertinent, people with centrist views also use ATMs. Some customers practice pleonasm but many officials are showing obeisance to customers may prefer ATM for the purpose of safety in transactions. Under these circumstances, some of the observations made by banking experts about the significant role of ATMs in banking services are shown here under. 'Keith Taylor' senior vice president, financial solutions division, NCR corporation, expressed that "India is one of the world's lowest users of ATMs". He says that people still prefer cash and cheque transaction. He pointed out that the worldwide installed base of ATMs is over 1.1 million units. In India form a small installed base of 500 ATMs in 1998. It has grown to nearly 7,500 ATMs. He also expressed that ATM penetration in India is only 7 per million, while 'Lonnie Anthony', Euronet India's managing director, expressed that over 5,000 ATMs to be installed during financial year 2004 which would work to Rs.750 crore. He also says that over 400 ATMs added every month. There are 18 members ATM card in the country. In comparison, China has 470 M cards. He also suggests that we need to have 30-40 M ATM cards.

'Swadhan' is the name given to the ATM network of public sector banks and some private banks. Over the past year up to 44 banks in Mumbai, vashi and thane have become a part of 'swadhan', a system of shared payments networks, introduced by the Indian bank association (IBA). The 44 members between them have 85 operational branches whose clients could swap the existing ATM card of our member's bank for the 'Swadhan Card' to access the teller machines of this retail chain. A Self evident testimony to the demand for ATMs from customers which was first triggered off over a decade ago in 1987 when the Hong Kong and *Shanghai* bank first introduced ATMs in Mumbai. With *'Swadhan'* it was hoped that Indian banks customers would be able to benefit from an ATM pool that solved the problems of single-ATM outlet banks and its attendant problems of limited access, distance and time.

P.C.Narayan, President of Global Trust Bank, classifies shared ATM networks into two kinds viz. "parent child" and "peer to peer". A good example of parent child would be a large sized bank, which has a lot of ATMs and which it could offer to smaller banks to share the network. Peer to peer would be a large bank coming together to build a national ATM network. Generally, All ATMs have the sharing network with other banks. A shared payment network is that where in ATM card holders of one bank can have the access to avail the ATM services from the ATM of their bank and also from the ATM of their bank. It means, different ATM card holders belonging to different banks, which are under the shared network basis. It helps the customers of both the banks to have accessibility of ATM services from different banks.

CONCLUSION AND SUGGESTIONS

(a) All banks can issue ATM cards to all customers to avoid unnecessary crowding and unpleasant scenes in banks during banking hours.

(b) Inter bank adjustments may be made so that the card of any bank can be used in all other bank ATM points. Charges should be done away with so that there is overall clearing is done only in electronic manner.

(c) Instead of having concentration of more number of ATM access points in one single place by all the banks, more number of ATM access points at various places may be installed so that the customers can have access to any ATM within one or two kilometers within city limits.

(d) Bank charges should be pellucid. Charges levied for services should not lead to pathos in using ATMs. More number of semi-urban are as may be covered by installing ATM access points so that the banking habit develop Now-a-days, modern India is exploiting all the benefits of technological advancements. There are radical changes in banking field. Customers require ratting services and they should feel splendid. To-day, the nation is having 24 hours entertainment, transport, internet warehouse facilities and so on. These days physical banking system cannot withstand the pressures of more than one crore strong population in India. Hence, 24 hours banking facility can not be easily side lined. But it is true if more numbers of access points in market, residential and travel areas are installed, then the banks can see higher turnover and better customer satisfaction at all levels.

REFERENCES

Banerjee Amlesh and Singh Shrawan Kumar (Eds.) (2002), "Banking and Financial Sector Reforms in India", Deep & Deep Publications Pvt. Ltd. New Delhi, pp. 3-15.

Das, Uday Kumar (2002), "Banking Reforms and Lead Bank Scheme" Deep and Deep Publications pvt. Ltd. p. 112.

Kumar, Sanjeev (Ed.) (1995), "Economic Reforms and Management of Change: Some Reflections" Deep & Deep Publications, New Delhi, p-V.

Kumar, Dr. Revathi (2006), Impact of Globalization on the Banking Sector, Business and Economic Facts for you, November, pp. 40-42.

Laxman, G. (2005)', ATM Services and perceptions of Users: A Case Study of Andhra Bank', Southern Economist, October, PP-16-20.

Leeladhar, (2006), 'Indian Banks and Global Challenges Speech, RBI Bulletin, February, Vol. LX No.2, P.-233.

—Management Series, Discovery Publishing House, New Delhi Mohan Rakesh, "Reforms, Productivity and Efficiency in Banking: The Indian Experience", Speech, RBI Bulletin, March Vol. LX No.3, p.279.

Ramakrishna, G. And Bhargavi, T.S. (2005), 'Move Forwards Consolidation of Banking Sector in India' Southern Economist, August, pp. 11-12.

Reddy, Y.V. (2005), 'Progress of Reforms & Features of Reforms, Speech RBI Bulletin, August 15, PP-27-31.

Readdy. Y.V. (2006), 'Progress of Reforms & Features of Reforms', Speech, RBI Bulletin June, Vol. LX No.6, PP-641-643.

Singh, Ravishankar Kumar (Ed.) (2006), "Indian Banking and Financial Sector Reforms," Abhijeet Publication, Delhi, P. 6416.

Singh, M.K. & Bhattacharya, A. (1990), "Banking Sector Management Modern Management Series, Discovery Publishing House, New Delhi.

Vallabhan, S.V. Srinivasa (2005), 'Virtual Banking-ATM Usage, Southern Economist, August, PP.27-31.

CHAPTER 15

STRUCTURAL ISSUES OF BANKING SECTOR IN INDIA WITH REFERENCE TO EFT SYSTEM

Meera Ranjan Lal

INTRODUCTION

In 1995, the Reserve Bank had set up the Committee headed by Smt. K.S. Shere for proposing Legislation on Electronic Funds Transfer and other Electronic Payments. The Shere committee had recommended a set of EFT Regulation by the Reserve Bank under the Reserve Bank of India Act, 1934 and amendments to the Banker's Book Evidence Act, 1881 as short term measures and promotion of a few Acts like the Electronic Funds Transfer Act, the Computer Misuse and Data Protection Act etc. as long term measures. The Reserve Bank has already initiated steps for framing of EFT Regulations.

The proposed Information Technology Bill, 1999 and Electronic Commerce Bill, 1999 are intended to be general; purpose legislation covering mainly issues like secure electronic records and signatures, acceptance of digital signatures, duties of certification authority, liability of network service providers, computer crime and data protection. Both the bills deal with electronic contracts and they are being promoted by the Government of India primarily to facilitate introduction of Electronic Data Interchange in the commercial sector. However they are equally applicable for electronic funds transfer already launched by the Reserve Bank and going to be increasingly resorted to by the user banks of the VSAT Based network the INFINET. However, there is still a need for separate Act for Electronic Fund Transfer because certain transactional issues like payment finality, rights and obligations of the parties evolved in electronic funds transfer and payments. The EFT Regulations will, however cover only the credit transfer related transactions and not debit clearing transactions. A separate legislation on the lines of Electronic Funds Transfer Act of USA is, therefore, required which should be consumer protection oriented and would at the same time address transactional issues like execution of payment order, settlement finality, etc.

EVOLUTION OF THE LEGAL, LEGISLATIVE AND STRUCTURAL SYSTEM

The advent of electronics in banking has brought about a sea change in the nature of banker-customer relation and perception of customer service in the banking business. The Indian banking industry is on the threshold of a computer/ information revolution. Payment system is *one* area where electronic and information technology can bring about salutary innovations. Realizing the need for giving greater impetus and priority to adoption of technological innovations in Payment system the Reserve Bank of India had constituted a Committee on Technology issues headed by Shri W.S. Saraf, Executive Director, Reserve Bank of India (Saraf Committee), to look into among other things, technological issues relating to Payment System and to make recommendations for widening the use of modern technological advancements in the banking industry.

PRESENT STATUS OF PAYMENT SYSTEM IN INDIA

Payment system in India is primarily paper-based. Currency notes and paper instruments like cheque, draft, dividend and interest warrants, refund order, gift cheque, travelers cheque and stock-invest etc. are the commonly used methods of setting payment transactions. Use of computer and communications technology in payment system in India is not a very old phenomenon. Although computers are in use in some banks right from late sixties, they were used mainly for corporate database maintenance and statistical analysis. In nineties, front office of bank/branches was computerized in a large scale. Telegraphic Transfer of funds is the only popular mode of paperless funds transfer in payment system. Fund transfer through EFTPoS, Home Banking, Debit Card, etc. are still to strike roots in India. Even the available ATMs are used mainly as cash dispensers and not for funds transfer and utility bill payments as elsewhere.

- *Telegraphic Transfer:* In early eighties, major banks installed in-house telex/communication systems and employed them for routing funds transfer messages. This marked an advent of electronic technology for inter-branch funds transfer within a bank. However, a funds transfer mechanism involving inter-bank funds settlement at the national level is conspicuous by its absence. The Reserve Bank has a Remittance Facilities Scheme for Banks which caters to their limited needs for currency chest operations and Government transactions but the ordinary customers of banks do not enjoy may such facility.
- *MICR Clearing:* Till recent past, the focus of technology upgradation in payment system has been on improving productivity and efficiency in processing of paper based instruments. As a result, we have had rationalization of draft issuance procedures, courier arrangements for collection of inter-city cheque, computerization of the service Branches and the Clearing section of the large branches and computerization of clearing houses etc. Under the MICR Clearing, unlike in the manual system, debits to individual banks were raised on the basis of the data captured mechanically during the cheque sorting process.

- *Electronic Credit Clearing:* A scheme called Electronic Clearing Service (Credit clearing) was launched by the Reserve Bank in April 1995. The scheme envisages presenting of payments data on magnetic media by a Corporate body to its banks who in turn will forward the same to the Clearing House with an authorization to debit its accounts and credit the accounts of the beneficiaries as recorded on the magnetic media.
- *Electronic Debit Clearing:* This operates on the principle of "Authorised Debit".
- *Floppy Input Clearing:* Floppy Input Clearing is another mode of electronic clearing introduced at clearing houses managed by Reserve Bank. Banks sort the cheque bank-wise, exchange the same amongst themselves and lodge a claim through the clearing system for the amounts for which they had present cheque to other banks through a claim statement.
- *Total Branch Computerisation:* After signing of the agreement between the unions and IBA in 1993, the pace of computerization in the banking industry has quickened. Now branches may receive the data electronically and process them without use of paper documents. Banks having a good number of TBC branches have already started products like "Any Branch Banking" and electronic fund transfer between selected branches. Banks are increasingly using technology to enhance their competitive strengths. The foreign banks and newly established private sector banks have relatively superior technological infrastructure and fully computerized banking environment.
- *SWIFT:* India joined the society for Worked-wide Inter-bank Financial Telecommunication (SWIFT) banks in 1991 as the 74th country. Initially 41 banks in India participated. SWIFT is not a payment system per se, but has helped considerably in the transmission of international payment messages.

- *BANKNET:* A communication Network called BANKNET has been setup in 1991, connecting four metropolitan centers of Mumbai, Delhi, Chennai and Calcutta along-with Bangalore, Hyderabad and Nagpur. The Communication switches (X.25) are located at the four metro centers and at Nagpur. Communication software called COMET had been designed primarily for templates based applications. This software was further supplemented by communication software named RBInet. This software had additional features such as dialup connectivity, facility of ASCII file transfer and message tracking facility. However, due to major technological advancement in telecommunication system and information transmission system VSAT based networking of financial system (INFINET) has been set up by Reserve Bank.
- *INFINET:* In order to upgrade the coun·ry's payment and settlement systems, the Reserve Bank of India took initiative of providing a communication backbone in the form of a satellite network based on VSAT technology to the Banking and Financial Sector and entrusted the work to IDRBT. As the bandwidth at present on INFINET is limited it may have to be optimally used. This would need allocation of bandwidth to various users and appropriate configuration of ports for dealing with different type of applications viz. Bursty, transaction oriented and streams by employing appropriate Access mode.

A Financial Network in the form of reliable communication backbone facilities running different application/services which eventually result in:

- Banking and Financial services independent of their location;
- Extended banking business reach and hours as well as increased business volume and better fund utilization thereby facilitating reduced operational cost'

- Increased security;
- Reduction/elimination of payment risks;
- Efficient Housekeeping;
- Improvement in decision-making process;
- Innovative customer-oriented delivery mechanisms;

EVOLUTION OF ELECTRONIC FUND TRANSFER SYSTEM

The Saraf Committee recommended institution of Electronic Fund Transfer (EFT) System in India. The term "Electronic Fund Transfer" means any transfer of funds, other than a transaction originated by a cheque, draft or similar type of paper instrument or computer or magnetic tape/media, so as to order, instruct or authorize a financial institution to debit or credit an account. Such terms includes, but is not limited to Point of Sale transfers, Automated Teller Machine transactions, direct deposit or withdrawals of funds and transfers initiated by telephone. This means a wired transfer Network, Automated clearing house or other communication system of a clearing house or other association of banks through which a payment order by a bank may be transmitted to the bank to which order is addressed. In other words the fund transfer in which one or more of the steps in the process that were previously done by paper-based technique are now done by electronic technique. In brief in essence there are three types of transactions that can be performed by electronic means:

(i) Debiting or crediting one's own account viz. ATM transactions.

(ii) Transferring funds between two accounts by issuing a credit instruction to one's own institution and

(iii) Transferring funds between two accounts by authorizing a debit authorization to another party.

However, there is no act or legislation specifically addressed to the issue of Electronic Fund Transfer. Since, the bank at destination centers would be required to credit the accounts of their customers entirely on the basis of electronic messages received through electronic information channels.

Therefore, the responsibility and the accountability of the concerned parties at each stage, have to be prescribed and agreed upon by the participating institutions with adequate legal banking. In this background, it is imperative to enact a suitable legislation suitable to Indian conditions at the earliest, along the lines of Electronic Fund Transfer Act of 1978 in USA and Data protection Act of 1984 in United Kingdom.

Each revolution in the history of payment system, had brought with it new concepts and issues. In the case of cash, new rules and concepts were to be first put in place to introduce the system. Law was instrumentality of change in the case. But in the case of negotiable instruments, the legal principles followed the law Marchant and the market practice. Introduction of legal principles was more by way of a response to emerging usage and practice. Further, a payment system, by its very nature has a direct implication on the Monetary and Credit System. There are also public interest issues like consumer protection and issues of competition among a regime of multiple systems. Again transactional aspects refer to the rules to establish the predictability and certainty to a given transaction. The Regulatory and Transactional issues are complementary to each other and inseparable if the payment has to function as a concomitant to overall economic and developmental objectives of the society.

A study of the EGT Systems in advanced countries shows that the need for Central Bank's empowerment for overall control and supervision of electronic payment systems was being increasingly felt in these countries. These issues arise mainly due to following aspects:

- Possible risk transfer to Central Banks through float or daylight overdrafts (as in most cases the central bank manages clearing and settlement), since EFTs are generally believed to increase the level of float.
- Risk of systemic failure increased efficiency in terms of speed would increase the systemic risk, especially when the system is linked to securities transactions. Issues of accountability, soundness and safety of the banking system are central in any EFT system.

- Electronic payments are prone to uncontrolled increase in money and credit supply. If central bank is not used for settlement, the system may also lead to inefficient use of bank balances.
- Electronic Payments have greater potential for abuse of banking system for money laundering, tax evasion and other unlawful fund transfers.

Law making is a long process in which policy formulation normally precedes to fill the contents of legislation. An examination of the nature of issues would clearly show that transactional issues need to be addressed immediately, as without this it may be extremely difficult to implement/adopt any EGT system. Since, an efficient payment system is crucial for growth and productivity in a developing economy. Electronic Communication system enables fast funds movement between two places, by way of message transmissions as against the conventional way of transferring funds through paper-based instruments. On the other hand the substantive issues need a very detailed probe not only legal angle but also from the regulatory and monetary policy angles.

In this background, the Governor Reserve bank of India constituted a committee headed by Mrs. K.S. Shere, Principal Legal Advisor, Reserve Bank of India to study all aspects relating to Electronic Fund Transfer and proposes appropriate Legislation. The main objectives of the committee were as under:

- Define the scope of "Electronic Fund Transfer" and determine the responsibilities and liabilities of the participants arising out of contractual obligations.
- Define the trigger events that determine the finality and irrevocability of the transfer of funds at different stages like sender finality, settlement finality, receiver finality, etc including the scope for countermanding and money back guarantees.
- Define measures to ensure operational security, integrity and efficiency of communication network linkages (e.g. Checksum, encryption, firewall etc.)

- Procedures to be followed in consequences of bank failures and other systemic events.
- Admissibility of electronic media for the purpose of evidence, preservation period of electronic media etc.
- Cheque truncation.
- A comprehensive fresh legislation to deal not only EFT, but also for bringing changes requires in existing acts such as Negotiable Instruments Act, Bankers Books of Evidence Act, Securities and Control Regulation Act (SCRA) etc.
- Any other matter related to EFT such as securities transfer and other cash/credit/debit transactions through electronic fund transfer at Point of Sales (EFTPoS) devices and computer/communication networks.

EXISTING LAWS IN INDIA-EFT ISSUES

Payments systems, in all forms have a direct bearing on the financial sector in general and banking sector in particular. There is growing recognition that at a particular stage of development, electronic fund transfer system supports sound financial market development through improved certainty and timeliness of payments. But, every new system would bring a new crop of problems for the regulators. EFT system, especially due to their potential for generating unaccounted credit and money supply, have been viewed as a close concern of the central banking authorities.

MONETARY AND CREDIT POLICY CONSIDERATIONS

In EFT Systems, where the central bank acts as an intermediary or takes on itself the clearing and settlement responsibilities, the central bank is exposed to the risk through float (daylight overdrafts) and unless this is regulated an excessive volumes of money gets pumped into the system. In card operations, the float may create an unaccounted increase in the volume of credit in the system. Further, because of the speed in the EFT System, systemic risk due to a bank failure would get an expedited transmission into the banking system. This will be more so when EFT Systems are organized without the involvement of Central Bank's settlement machinery. Apart from these, there are also the supervisory concerns relating monitoring the volume and pattern of transactions in the payment system. Misuse of the EFT System for evading exchange control, tax liability or for money Laundering and other unlawful purposes needs special and specific attention.

In India, the powers and functions of the Reserve Bank are contained in the Reserve Bank of India Act, 1934, the Banking Regulation Act, 1949, Foreign Exchange Management Act, 2000 and Public debt Act. The existing provisions of the RBI Act do not specifically empower the Reserve Bank to make regulation for defining rights and obligations of participants in an EFT transaction, Section 17 (6), however, empowers the Reserve Bank to operate remittance system for transfer of funds payable at its own offices or agencies. Section 58, which deal with the regulation making power of the Central Board of Reserve, empower the Reserve Bank to make regulation "consistent with the Act to provide for all matters for the provisions of the Act". The Preamble of the Act provides that the Reserve Bank is constituted among other things, "to secure monetary stability and generally to operate the currency and credit system of the country to its advantage". But except for the provisions dealing with currency notes, there is no substantive provision in the Act specifically dealing with payment system as such. Sub-section (2) of Section 58 Lists at clause (p), "the regulation of Clearing Houses for the banks including post-office saving bank as one of the items for which the Central Board may make Regulations.

As far as banks alone are concerned, the Reserve Bank has adequate powers, under the Banking Regulation Act of issuing directions binding on them. However, in the growing and fast changing technology the need for improving the payments system to be in tune with the overall financial sector development, need may arise for permitting one or more banks to organize different/multiple type of payments system to cater to the requirements of different sector. In such a scenario, special powers of monitoring and controlling the multiple EFT Systems in the country may be required to be exercised by the Reserve Bank. This would need an amendment to the RBI Act.

CONSUMER PROTECTION

Legal issues consumer protection in regard to EFT operations center around the following concepts:

- Transparency of charges (protection by proper disclosure).
- Access to information in case of disputes
- Confidentiality, unfair conditions, frauds, mistakes and errors.

The consumer movement in India has gained momentum after the enactment of the Consumer Protection Act, 1986. "Banking Services" have been brought within the purview of the Consumer Protection Act. EFT may also be regarded as a banking service for the purpose of Consumer Protection Act. Further Consumer protection issue is addressed to a great extent by the Banking Regulation Act also Reserve Bank is empowered to pursue any policy in the interest of the banking system or in the interest of monetary stability or sound economic growth and Reserve Bank's regulatory power under the Banking Regulation Act takes care of the consumer protection issues in EFT like reasonableness of terms of services, pricing, disclosure norms, transparency in operations etc.

COMMERCIAL BANK'S POWER TO TRANSACT EFT BUSINESS

EFT as prevalent in other countries is basically an additional payment or fund transfer mechanism through the banking system. In India, under Section 6 (1) of the Banking Regulation Act, business which the banking companies can undertake includes collecting and transmitting of money and securities. This covers every type of EFT operations.

However, the Income Tax Act, 1961 will have some bearing on the fund transfer through the EFT System. Section 40 A of this Act, dealing with deductible expenses, restricts the benefit only if the payment of more that Rs. 10,000/- is made by a crossed cheque or crossed bank draft. Similarly, Chapter XX-dealing with acquisition of immovable properties requires payments in excess of specified limits to be made only by a crossed cheque/bank draft. Chapter XX-B dealing with "mode of acceptance, Payment or repayment" in certain cases requires payment in excess of Rs. 20,000/- to be made only by cheque/draft crossed "A/C Payee". If the EFT is restricted to funds transfer from a designated account to a designated account within the banking system that would, by itself serve the same purpose for which requirement of crossed cheque or crossed "A/C Payee". Cheque is stipulated under the Income Tax Act.

BANKER-CUSTOMER RELATION

The nature of contractual relation between banks and their customers differs depending upon the particular service provided by the banks. When a bank extends to a customer an EFT facility for transfer of funds from his account, a relation of principal and agent would come into existence between the banks and its customer. Funds remittance and payment on behalf of customers is basically an agency function. Depending on the funds availability arrangement made between a bank and its customer, EFT may result, especially in card-based transactions, in credit being extended to the customer. In that case a creditor debtor relation may also ensue between the bank and the customer.

In an EFT, the bank may have to execute the customer's payment instructions through another bank and in some cases an intermediary bank may also come into the picture. Here, if the banker-customer contract does not expressly provides otherwise, there is every possibility of an intermediary and beneficiary bank being regarded as substituted agent of the customer. If the transaction results in a substituted agency, then in law a direct privities between the customer and the intermediary or as the case may be, the beneficiary's bank would come into existence. The question, which should bear the loss on account of insolvency or suspension of payment, before the beneficiary's account is credited by the beneficiary's bank or the intermediary bank in such cases revolve on the incidence of substituted agency. The customer cannot make his bank liable for the loss in such case. A further question which would be of considerable significance is about the status of beneficiary's bank and the relation between the beneficiary and the beneficiary's bank in relation to the EFT transactions. When a beneficiary's bank execute a payment order receive by it form another bank, it credits the beneficiary's account. Does the bank in such case act as an agent of beneficiary? If so, it would be only a receiving hand. The bank however, assumes an obligation to the sending bank by committing itself to the payment order at the instance of the sending bank. It would appear that the mechanism of execution of payment order is by substitution of the obligation of the sender by an obligation of the beneficiary's bank. In this case it would be more appropriate to regard the beneficiary's bank as an agent of the sending bank rather than its own customer. This position, however, will have a direct bearing on the bank's right to recover money from the beneficiary by reversing the credit given to his account, if there was an error in crediting his account. The law relating to recovery of payments made under mistakes is contained in Section 72 of the Indian Contract Act. The Supreme Court has held that when the bank is acting only as agent of its customer in receiving funds to the credit of his account it will not have any right to unilaterally correct an error in the account without the consent of the customer. On the other hand if the bank acted as an agent of the person who made the payment, it will have every right available under section 72 for recovery of payment made under mistake. The existing provisions of Contract Act, however, do not provide a clear and unambiguous answer about whether the beneficiary's bank acts as an agent of the beneficiary in regard to an EFT.

FINALITY OF PAYMENT

Payment in Law is the discharge or satisfaction of an obligation. Payment by cash does not require acceptance by the payee.

All other methods of payment involve an element of acceptance by the payee. Law, however, provides the default rule. Section 85 of Negotiable Instruments Act provides discharge to the bank when it puts in due course. Section 128 similarly provides the default rule in regard to payment of a crossed cheque. A distinguishing feature of a cheque is that it needs to be presented by the payee to the paying banker. Presentment of a cheque, especially when the cheque is paid in clearing cannot obviously take place without the express or implied consent of the beneficiary. Based on these default rules, courts have held that payment of a cheque is conditional when the cheque is delivered. But once the cheque is honored, the payment relates back to the date of delivery of the cheque to the beneficiary. Even in the case of a post dated cheque, the payment time, when the cheque is eventually honored, would be the earliest point of time when the cheque could have been in-cashed, irrespective of the actual date of payment.

Unlike a cheque in an EFT, funds are credited to the account of a beneficiary without an apparent consent of the beneficiary. By banking practice, it can be safely assumed that bankers have the implied authority of the customers to receive payments to the credit of the customer. Credit to an account in any case is a tender of a payment. Section 38 of Contract Act also gives some clue about the default rule in Law in regard to tender of a payment. As between the customer who initiates an EFT and the beneficiary of the EFT, the credit to the latter's bank account can be regarded as discharging such customer's obligation if the conditions stated in the section are complied with. To give a valid discharge, section 38 requires a tender to be unconditional and for the full amount of obligation. A tender of part payment does not qualify for discharge under Section 38, so is the case if the tender is made before the due date.

Depending on the contractual arrangement in a credit card scheme, a card holder would be liable to pay to the card issuing company, whether or not, that company had paid to the supplier, Payment by credit card in such an event was an absolute, not a conditional discharge of the buyer liability and the card's holder obligations to the supplier were absolutely discharged by the supplier accepting the voucher signed by the card holder. Thus if the credit card issuing company goes into liquidation before making payment to the supplier, the supplier had no remedy against the cardholder.

The above analysis of the existing law in India shows that the question, as to what point of time a payment can be deemed to have been made in an EFT, is not answered by the existing provisions of the law. Unless defined by a rule of law or by contract between the parties the following interpretations are possible:

- Payment is made when the beneficiary is advised of the credit from his bank.
- Payment is made when the beneficiary's bank dispatches credit advice to the beneficiary.
- Payment is made when the beneficiary's banks credit the beneficiary's account.
- Payment is made when the beneficiary's bank receives the payment order for credit to the beneficiary's account.

Which of the above interpretation would apply as a default rule depends on how a funds transfer is to be construed in law. As with other payment systems, the EFT payment is a transfer of funds from the payer's account at his bank and a corresponding credit in the payee's account at the beneficiary's bank. There could however a time gap between the point of time when the originator's account is debited and the point of time when the beneficiary's account is credited. If the irrevocability rule is applied at the stage of receipt of the payment instruction by the originator's bank, can this be regarded as an assignment of a debt? In such a situation, if the payment instruction is regarded as equitable assignment, obviously all the conditions of a valid assignment referred to in section 131 of Transfer of property Act should apply.

The existing laws, does not provide any satisfactory clarification to the exact nature of a funds transfer instruction and the exact point of tie of applicability or nature of default rule of payment. It would therefore, Leave considerable uncertainty, unless this aspect of the transaction is specifically covered by express agreement between the parties or through a separate provision of law on the lines of Section 85 of the Negotiable Instruments Act. In the UK, EFT is not treated as an assignment or trust. It is simply treated as a matter of agency contract. Even in the USA, where the finality principles are defined by statute, an EFT is not treated as arising under as assignment or trust. The basic principles of agency are applied in the statute, to define the principles of finality.

IRREVOCABILITY–FINALITY OF PAYMENT ORDER

Generally, the issue of irrevocability refers to the point of time up to which a payment instruction could be changed or canceled by the issuer. In the case of payment by the cheque, the implied contract between the banker and the customer obliges a bank to honor any stop payment order received from the customer, until a cheque is actually paid. Thus in the case of cheque, finality of payment and irrevocability are one and the same. This may mot be the case in EFT. In the absence of an express contract, the default principle of Laq that would appear to apply is the *Law of Estoppels.* Under this principle, if the sending banker has altered his position (by executing the payment order), on the basis of the customer's Payment instruction, it will not be open to the customer to bind thee bank with any cancellation or any revocation even though at the time of such cancellation or revocation, the beneficiary's account may not have been actually credited. Depending on the system compatibility and considerations of fairness as also the need for making EFT a user-friendly system, the irrevocability rules should be adopted out of the following principles, as applied abroad:

- A payment order becomes irrevocable once it is issued by the originator;
- A payment order becomes irrevocable when the sending bank issues it or executes it;
- A payment order becomes irrevocable when the beneficiary's bank receives it;

- A payment order becomes irrevocable when the beneficiary's bank credits the beneficiary's account with the amount of the payment order.
- A payment order becomes irrevocable when the beneficiary's bank commits itself irrevocably by issue of advice of credit to the beneficiary.

AUTHENTICATION OF PAPERLESS PAYMENT ORDER

Verification of authenticity in relation to paper-based payment is verification of customer's signature. Where the instruction become paperless, the question that would arise is when a banker can bind the customer with the payments made electronically to him or on his behalf. The signature is replaced by what is known as security procedure. Certain electronic devices like encryption, identification numbers or other procedures like call back are established to determine/verify the authenticity of the instructions received by the bank purporting to be that of the customer. The existing legal provision in India does not have any specific provision either permitting or prohibiting authentication procedure otherwise than by signature. This, therefore, con be established by a contract between the parties. The important point which is established either stature or by decided cases is that the authentication procedure, if established at the instance of the bank should be commercially reasonable. The concept of "commercially reasonable security procedure" has developed considerably both in English law and American jurisprudence. Further, even after establishing the security procedure, there are issues like when and under what circumstances and to what extent the customer is not liable to pay the bank even if the bank had executed payment order in good faith complying with the security procedure.

SECURITY OF SECURITY PROCEDURES

An issue closely connected with authentication is regarding confidentiality and safety of the system. Security procedure established by agreement between the parties needs to be kept secured. Any unauthorized access to security procedure by a third party, popularly known as *interloper fraud*, can result in EFT being execute by the bank without actual authority although the payment instruction may comply with the security procedure. The design of the computer-to-computer transmission system and the automated data Processing assumes significance in considering issues of interloper frauds and bankers' responsibility of maintaining secrecy of the customers' data. It is in this context that the UNCITRAL Legal Guide on Electronic Funds Transfer, pointed out that banks may have to assume a broader duty to establish a security system for the transmission of funds transfer instructions and their storage which limits the possibility of such access. Operational security becomes more relevant in EFT.

ERRORS AND SYSTEM MAL-FUNCTIONING

The UNCITRAL Legal Guide on Electronic Funds Transfer lists the following circumstances in which an error may affect the electronic fund transfer:

- Non-standardisation of message format between the various electronic fund transfer systems resulting in re-keying of messages.
- Re-creation of messages.
- . Non-standardisation of procedures particularly in relation to international transfers.
- Equipment failure or software error.

The loss arising on account of errors may be different from loss arising on account of negligence though at times negligence may lead to error. The rules for allocation of loss arising on account of errors are generally based on the principles of Contract and Tots. If the chain of legal relation between the bank and the customer and other participants in the system are based on the principles of agency, the existing provisions of agency law in India rea sufficient to regulate allocation of loss arising on account of errors. Generally, if the loss can be attributed to the conduct of a party to the transaction, that party becomes liable for it. Where neither party is directly liable under the principle of *"party at default"*, the equity rule provides that party, whose conduct led to fraud to take place or caused an error to take place, must bear the loss. In the case the case of cheques, the problem is specifically dealt with in Negotiable Instruments Act. Section 85 and 128 read with Section 10 of this act give statutory protection to a paying banker in regard to loss by interloper fraud subject to the conditions that the payment must have been made in good faith and in due course etc. Similarly Section 131 protects a collecting banker. Although by analogy, these provisions seem capable of providing useful tests by determining liabilities in an EFT context, the concept of collecting banker and paying banker does nit appear to be strictly applicable in EFT. In the United States and some European countries, negligence invites astronomical measures of damages. Exemplary damages in contract are exceptions in India. Even in the actions based on Tort, the quantum of compensation awarded by courts is not something for which a new rule would be required to be made in regard to EFTs. The parties to the contract have a right to quantify the extent of loss at the time they make the contract. If the parties quantify the loss (liquidated damages) in the contract, court cannot award compensation for breach of contract for an amount greater than the amount quantified. If the parties have not quantified the loss by contract, the compensation for breach of contract would be decide in accordance with the principles laid down in Section 73 of the Contract Act. Section 73 entitles p party who suffers a breach of contract, to receive "compensation for any loss or damage caused to him thereby, which naturally arose in usual course of things from such breach, or which the parties knew when they made the contract to be likely to result from the breach of it. This provision ordinarily restricts damages to actual loss. However, compensation for consequential loss is also payable if notice of special circumstances giving rise to consequential damages was given at the time of the contract. Having regard to the uncertainty about the extent of liability for consequential damage, the question that needs to be considered is whether special rules are required for limiting the liability of the banks and customers involved in EFT.

INCIDENCE OF INSOLVENCY

EFT, as we have noticed earlier, is a method or means. But the incidence of insolvency of any bank involved in an EFT could be substantially different from those arising in paper-based payment. In EFT, there could be a float between the point of time a payment order is issued by a customer to the point of time when payment is complete. The issue that needs to be focused here is, if payment is suspended by any bank participating in the EFT before setting its payment obligation on whom does the loss fall? Should the beneficiary bear the loss? Should the initiator of the payment order bear the loss? Or, should the sending bank or beneficiary's bank bear loss? Under the English Law, on which most of Indian Banking law principles are based, the following position is stated:

- If a bank having given a commitment to pay becomes insolvent before discharging its obligations, the bank to whom that commitment was given has no claim to any funds. It will only have a mere claim in the insolvency in competition with other creditors, while the creditor customer for who the commitment constituted conditional payment has a right to demand payment from the debtor customer.
- Where the receiving bank becomes insolvent after the payee's account has been credited, the creditor customer has to bear the loss.
- If a bank goes into liquidation before it has collected a cheque, it has no right to borrow the sum in question back from the customer.
- A credit transfer, once initiated, may be reversed by the paying back upto midnight on the day of the transfer (but not later), even though the credit has not been communicated to the beneficiary. There is no reason to distinguish an in-house transfer from an external payment in this respect.

The Companies Act or the Banking Regulation Act in India do not provide any satisfactory solution. In practice, by operation of Clearing House Rules, netting of transactions (clearing inward and clearing outward) on the date of suspension of payment by a bank is resorted to and surplus, if any is treated as money held in trust in the hands of the liquidator. In the EFT, apart from the nature of legal relationship of the parties, the point of time at which settlement between banks takes place may have significance for considering the incidence of insolvency. The following option could be considered:

- Establishment of a contingency fund
- Distribution of loss among the participants
- Provision for collateral
- Provision of insurance

Which of these alternatives may have to be pursed, will ultimately have a bearing on a suitable clearing and settlement procedures to be adopted.

CONFIDENTIALITY AND DATA PROTECTION

In the absence of specific statutory provision, the law relating to banker's secrecy law in India has, by and large followed the English decisions. The special concern of the banker's secrecy obligations in EFT would arise, inter-alia, on account of the following:

- EFT will create new records of transactions.
- EFT will result in an increase in the amount of information available in new records.
- Because these are electronically readable, records will be more easily accessible.
- More institutions might gain access to an individual's financial records.
- The place where a person operates a terminal will be precisely located.

A clear understanding of the risk involved in transmission of payment data through a communication network and keeping records of transactions in computers and other electronic devices is necessary. The possibility of unauthorized access by third parties, of the vitas data, may depend on the design of the network system, its dependence on general communication facility etc. A dedicated communication network may be less prone to unauthorized access. The Council of Europe had adopted in 1981, a convention for the protection of individuals with regard to automatic processing of personal data. This Data Protection Act, 1984 enacted in the UK was pursuant to this convention. This Act basically provides that personal data must not be disclosed in any way incompatible with purpose for which the data is held. The Cat establishes a system of Registration of Data Users and Computer Bureaux and prohibits holding by any person of personal data on electronic media unless he is registered under the Act. Although, the principles provided in the Data Protection Act cannot be considered as a necessary concomitant to introduction of EFT, as a long term perspective, the question, whether a similar legal framework may have to be provided in India to cope up with the pressure on the banker's secrecy obligations due to increasing computerization of banking business, needs to be considered.

DISPUTE RESOLUTION

One of the important issues considered in most the countries where EFT has been in operation, is the provision for a separate investigation and dispute resolution mechanism. This is felt necessary especially in regard to high value fund transfers. In the USA, in regard to EFT of all types, specific statutory provisions are made to provide for an effective mechanism for investigation and resolution of disputes. This assumes special significance in India, as EFT transactions are highly technical and need a clear understanding of the concepts and technological aspects in investigating and resolving disputes. Under the existing framework of India law, the band customers have the following remedies:

- To approach civil courts by way of suit for damages, injunction or specific performance.
- To approach Consumer Forums established under the Consumer Protection Act.

- To avail Customer Grievances Redressal Machinery provided within the banking system (such as complaint to Banking Ombudsman, complaint to Reserve Bank's Grievance Cell, etc.

Civil courts are bound by the technical rules of evidence and procedure and the process of dispute resolution by resort to litigation in courts could be extremely expensive and tie consuming, which may not be suitable to EFT disputes. All banking services come within the purview of Consumer forums. EFT being a "services" would also come within the purview of the jurisdiction of consumer forums. However, the National Consumer Disputes Redressal Commission has repeatedly held that even in disputes of general nature, if the case involves complicated questions of law or elaborate evidence the consumer forums should decline to exercise jurisdiction. In this view of the matter, to make EFT more user friendly, the question, whether a separate system of dispute resolution needs to be provided requires to be considered.

The existing system under Banking Ombudsman Scheme 1995 for banking sector in India is mixture of principles of conciliation, mediation, and adjudication. The remedy through Ombudsman is an additional remedy and not exclusive. The Ombudsman award becomes enforceable only if the complainant accepts it. The question whether a separate system of arbitration or other form of adjudication of disputes between banks and their customers, arising under the EFT would be necessary, can be better considered when a clear idea about the type of disputes are known. Resolution of disputes between bank customers and banks may have to be treated differently.

CHOICE OF LEGAL FRAMEWORK

The existing legal framework on most of the regulatory and consumer interest issues may be considered as adequate, at least in the short term, these would be inadequate in regard to evidence and investigation issues. Most of the transactional issues could be covered by contractual framework. A contractual model has the advantage of maximum flexibility. But when unregulated, it may lead to exploitation, especially when there is an inherent inequality in the bargaining power. Further the growth of sound legal principles may be hampered if uniformity in the rights and obligation are not brought in. Choice by contract may lead to divergent incidence leading to considerable confusion and lack of uniformity.

A legislative model has the advantage of maximum certainty, uniformity and predictability. But in considering the formulation of a detailed and comprehensive legislation one has to bear in mind the rigidity that will be brought in by legislation. Legislation making is a slow process. Changing the legislation once made is much slower. In an area where the technology is growing and fast changing, a comprehensive legislation ay hamper the development. EFT is an evolving field. By its very nature, maximum flexibility is needed to allow the system to grow in a market responsive environment. At the same time, the substantial issue does indicate that some form of basis regulatory framework and statutory rules to define the trigger events may have to be provided to ensure certainty and predictability of the transaction. The experience in other counties shows that statutory rules were called in at some stage to prevent system providers from excluding by contact every conceivable source of liability. Therefore, while a comprehensive legislation may hamper the development of evolving technology, leaving it completely to an unregulated contract regime may create chaos. A regulatory model properly molded, provides the certainty and predictability associated with statute law and at the same time leaves enough flexibility allowing growth and development of technology. The need for some measure of EFT regulation is urgent enough to override the cautionary argument for delay until EFT system has developed further. But the caution should be kept firmly in mind; it will be of prime importance to limit any proposals to what is seen as absolutely necessary, and to frame them in such a way as will not hamper the design and development of future EFT systems. A 'two tier' approach that restricts statute law to a few key issues common to EFT systems, reserving for standards of best practice those more detailed issues that bear specific systems or technologies, should help to preserve flexibility.

CONCLUDING OBSERVATION

Since the Reserve Bank is embarking on large electronic schemes such as the nation wide RTGS, it is time that efforts are made to bring about necessary legislative framework that synchronises and synthesizes with the initiatives taken by the Government of India, Department of Electronics for promotion of the Information Technology Bill, 1999 and /or the Electronic Commerce Bill, 1999.

The proposed Information Technology Bill, 1999 and Electronic Commerce Bill, 1999 are intended to be general purpose legislation conversing mainly issues like secure electronic records and signatures, acceptance of digital signatures, duties of certification authority, liability of network service providers, computer crime and data protection. Both the bills deal with electronic contracts and they are brings promoted by the Government of India primarily to facilitate introduction of Electronic Data Interchange in the commercial sector. However, they are equally applicable for electronic funds transfer already launched by the Reserve Bank and is going to be increasingly resorted to by the user for a separate Act for Electronic Funds Transfer because certain transactional issues like payments finality, rights and obligations of the parties involved in electronic funds transfer etc. cannot be covered in general purpose Electronic Commerce Bill. The EFT Regulations being framed by the Reserve Bank would address only the specific type of EFT system that the Reserve Bank would be involved with as a service provider as also a regulator. The EFT Regulation would, moreover, cover only credit transfer related transactions and not Debit Clearing transactions. A separate legislation which would be consumer protection oriented and would at the same time address transactional issues like execution of payment order, settlement finality, etc.

The Reserve Bank has taken the help of a consultant in drafting a new legislation on electronic Funds Transfer System and proposing amendment to the Reserve Bank of India act 1934. The Committee, after a careful examination of the issue, has endorsed the view that proposed Electronic Funds Transfer

Act should cover all forms of electronic payments. The Committee supports the view that the Reserve Bank, at an appropriate time, considers operating the inter bank payment systems through an agency or subsidiary so that its regulatory role is rendered distinct from its supervisory role. Retail payment systems such as the ECS and the EFT Remittance Processing Scheme presently operational may be managed by a group of large banks with country wide branch network and technical capability, with settlement assistance from the Reserve bank. This would help the RBI to focus its efforts only of large value time critical funds transfers to be settled on an RTGS basis. In the ongoing debate on the roe of central bank in payment systems, the trend is towards distinguishing the central bank role as a regulator from that of service providers which could be commercial banks themselves or the entities under the control of commercial banks. The Committee has considered it necessary that the legal framework for payment system takes into account this international trend.

REFERENCES

—(1996), Report of Committee for Proposing Legislation on Electronic Funds Transfer and Other Electronic Payments, Jan, (Chairman: Mrs. K.S.Shere Committee), RBI, Mumbai.

Raj Bhalla, (1995), "Towards A Payments System Law for Developing and Transition Economics", World Bank Discussion Papers, The World Bank Washington.

Cliford Chance, (1995), "People's Bank of China Payment Systems Project" A World Bank Assistance Paper.

—(1987), UNCITRAL, Legal Guide on Electronic Funds Transfers, United Nations, New York.

Pagets (1989), 'Law of Banking' Tenth Edition Butterworths, p. 415.

Edward L.Rubin & Robe Cooter (1989), The Payment System, American Casebook Series, West Publishing Company, p. 736-741.

—(1967), Jammu and Kashmir Bank Vs Attar-UI-Nisha, 37 Comp Case 62.

A.R. Krishnaswamy Vs. V.M.N. Ramkrishna (1945), 15 Comp Case 134.

Anil Kumar Sawhney Vs. Gulshan Rai (1994), 79 Comp Case 150 (SC).

—Re Charge Card Services Ltd. (1988), 3 ALL ER 702.

—(1971), W.J. Alam & Co. Ltd. Vs. EI Naser Export & Import Co. 1 Lioyd's 'Reb 401.

—(1991), M/S Special Machines, Karnal Vs. Punjab National Bank, 1CPJ78.

—(1991), Teresa Vs. Motor Superior: 2CPR 53.

—Jack Committee Report.

—Proposed Information Technology Bill and other Amendments in Related Act/Laws.

—(1999), Committee on Technology Upgradation in the Banking Sector (July).

—(1992)), The Computer Misuse Act of Singapore.

—(1995), Quoted in 'the Regulation and Prevention of Economic Crime', Editor: Jonathan Reuvid, Kogan, p.

CHAPTER 16

TECHNOLOGICAL INNOVATIONS IN PUBLIC SECTOR BANKS IN INDIA

Reeta Kumari

A key element of financial sector reforms in India has been building the appropriate technological infrastructure for the smooth functioning of the financial system. The Indian financial system comprising the commercial banks, the financial institutions and the capital markets, has undergone a very rapid transformation in the past three decades.

A study of the technological progress in the banking sector is important because bank play an important role in providing financial and mobilizing saving, especially in emerging market as compared to mature markets, where such functions are performed by the well developed capital markets. Technological efficiency can result in lower transaction cost and increased revenue for banks. The use of technology can improve/enhance system for administrative control such as enabling better management of risk, which if disclosed in regulatory reports to supervisors and in annual report to investor, can improve bank transparency and enable the banks to reduce their cost of capital (Basel Committee, 1998; Healy and Palepu, 2001). Hence, the use of technology can be the key to differentiation, competitive edge, and institutional survival.

The Indian banking functions under the regulatory and supervisory guidelines issued by the Central Bank. The Reserve Bank of India can be broadly classified into the following three categories: a) Public sector banks or PSBs (State Bank of India & its associates and nationalized banks); b) Private sector banks (old and new): (c) foreign banks.

The expansion of branch banking of public sector banks in the late 1950s and the resulting growth in the sheer volume of transactions necessitated the first move towards mechanization in the Indian Banking Sector. It was at this time that the SBI introduced Column punched card equipment to help with the reconciliation of the large volume of inter-bank transactions in its Calcutta office. In the early 1960s the SBI bought its first computer (an IBM 140) supported by 80 column punched card machines) to assist in the reconciliation of accounts between branches. The example of the SBI was soon followed by most other large nationalized banks.

The first wave of technology adoption was literally a move to computerize operations by PSBs to increase efficiency in retail banking operations. Banks rapidly installed Automatic Led posting machines (ALPMS) and mini computers and began an aggressive program of training programmers and data entry terminal operators.

The financial sector reforms of the 1990s, as outlines by the Narasimham Committee (1991), liberalized the Indian Banking industry and opened it to competition from within and outside. Given the weight of PSBs in the banking sector, it is worthwhile examining the PSB union response to competition and the push toward mechanization as a cost saving device.

At the core of this drive is the development of a sound and efficient payment and settlement system. To strengthen the payment system in public sector banks following technologies were introduced:

(1) Real Time Gross Settlement (RTGS) – This system was significant development in this field. A payment system which operates as "a gross settlement system in which both processing and final settlements of

funds transfer instructions can take place continuously (i.e. in real time)" is termed as Real Time Gross Settlement System. This system lessens settlement risk because inter bank settlement happens throughout the day, rather than just at the end of the day.

KEY ELEMENTS OF THE SYSTEM

- Orderly queuing messages and their disposal are intrinsic to the design of RTGS.
- Avoidance of gridlock by providing for intraday liquidity to the participants. (Gridlock may arise when series of the interdependent payment are stalled due to insufficient funds to settle the primary transaction).
- The risk inherent in net settlement system namely settlement risk, principal (credit) risk and systemic risk resulting in default by one bank leading to "Knock on" or domino effect on the system is avoided.

RTGS system leads to optimization of use of available resources in the banking sector in addition to faster movement of funds and information among various constituents of financial sector. It is a secure electronic fund transfer system, providing real time on-line settlement for inter-bank transactions and customer-based inter-bank transactions of any amount across the country.

The coverage of Real Time Gross Settlement (RTGS) system has increased significantly. Connectivity is now available in 16,000 bank branches at 700 cities. By end-March 2006, the number of monthly transaction of the system is expected to expand from one lakh to two lakh.

NATIONAL ELECTRONIC FUNDS TRANSFER SYSTEM

It has been in existence since 1997 covering 1.5 centres where the Reserve Bank manages the clearing houses. In order to increase the coverage of the scheme and to provide for funds transfers in a quicker manner, a variant of EFT called the special EFT was introduced with effect from April, 2003. SEFT is available across branches of banks that are computerized and

Table 1
Month-wise RTGS Transactions 2005
(Value in Rs. Crore)

Months	*No. of Participant*	*Inter Bank*		*Customer*		*Total*	
		Volume	*Value*	*Volume*	*Value*	*Volume*	*Value*
January	109	49,389	5,23,134	10,348	33,180	59,737	5,56,314
February	109	49,9895,	20,214	13,050	40,768	63,039	5,60,982
March	109	51,590	5,06,704	17,426	75,863	69,016	5,82,567
April	109	53,165	5,27,315	15,901	57,415	69,066	5,84,730
May	109	71,622	5,71,514	22,925	59,043	94,547	6,30,557
June	109	79,503	7,40,482	28,678	90,338	1,08,181	8,30,820
July	109	82,422	7,16,966	31,479	95,696	1,13,901	8,12,662

Source: Annual Report 2004-05 (RBI)

connected through a network so that electronic messages can travel to the receiving branch in a straight thorough manner. In the case EFT, all branches of banks in the 15 locations are part of the scheme irrespective of whether they are networked or not. In order to broad base the facilities of EFT and to provide for integration with the structured Financial Messaging Solution (SFMS) of the Indian Financial Network (INFINET), it was decided to implements a new variant of the EFT called the National EFT.

NEFT would be an electronic deferred net settlement funds transfer product. In order to increase the coverage of NEFT to a wider section of bank customers in Semi-Urban and rural areas, an enhancement of the NEFT called the NEFT-X (National EFT-Extended) is now proposed where the last leg connectivity would continue to be either through electronic mode or paper based.

NEFT started live operation on November 21st, 2005. The objective is to establish and Electronic Funds Transfer System to facilitate an efficient, secure, economical, reliable and expeditious system of funds transfer between banks in the banking sector using structured financial messaging solution (SFMS) backbone. NEFT will be the major clearing system for all retail payments. The eight banks who are participating in the first phase are: Canara Bank, Bank of Baroda, Punjab National Bank, Dena Bank, ABNAMRO Bank, HSBC, ICICI Bank and HDFC Bank.

RETAIL PAYMENT SYSTEMS

Retail Payment System recorded considerable increase in volume and value during 2004-05. These systems include the cheque clearing systems. The predominant mode for retail payments both the (MICR and Non–MICR Clearings) – electronics system i.e., the special EFT (SEFT) and card based system (credit, debit, ATM and smart cards). ECS is now available at 44 centres. In order to facilitate electronic modes of payments, banks are providing innovative/product to their customers by developing new product and integrating them with ECS/EFT/SEFT.

Table 2
Retail Electronic Payment Transaction 2004-05

Type	*Volume of Transaction (000's)*	*Growth in Volume (%)*	*Value of Transaction (Rupees Crore)*	*Growth in Value %*
Ecs-Credit	40.001 (22,654)	76.6	20.310 (10.228)	98.6
Ecs-Debit	15,299 (7,987)	93.7	4,466	98.2
EFT	1,365 (719)	89.9	49,123 (14,820)	231.5
SEFT	407 (82)	396	5,577 (2,305)	142.0

Note: Figures in brackets are data for 2003-04
Source: Annual Report, RBI (2004-05)

CARD BASED PAYMENTS SYSTEM

The popularity of card based transactions, especially debit cards, has increased significantly in recent years. The increased use of cards and their growing share in the payment system turnover highlights in the need for introduction of suitable regulatory measures. Such measures would have to ensure that rules, regulations, standard and practice of card issue are in alignment with the best customer practices.

Table 3
Card-based Payments (2004-05)

Type	*No.of Transactions (in 000s)*	*Growth in Transaction %*	*Value Rs. Crore*	*Growth in Value %*
Credit cards	129,975 (100,179)	29.7	25,682	45.4
Debit cards	230,480	166.8	51,226	176.7
Smart cards	1,585 (1,717)	7.7	212 (89)	138.2

Note: Figures in brackets are data for 2003-04
Source: Annual Report, RBI (2004-05)

CHEQUE TRUNCATION

In order to increase efficiency in the existing paper-based instruments, the cheque Truncation System (CTS) has been undertaken in the National capital region on a pilot basis. The cheque is currently the most visible and significant mode of payment in India. In view of the large volume of cheques to be processed, Magnetic Ink Cheque Recognition (MICR) technology enabled the banking system to handle the growth in volume of cheques and to provide faster and efficient clearing services to customers and to do straight through processing using MICR data over a period of two decades, a number of MICR clearing houses have evolved. Cheque Truncation is one of the ways to compress the clearing cycle to provide for faster clearance of local and intercity cheque truncation is the process by which the physical of cheques with a bank, between banks and the clearing house is curtailed or eliminated, being replaced in whole or in party by electronic records of their content for further processing and transmission.

Cheque Truncation Model for India

The working groups set up by RBI deliberated on the following issues:-

(a) Point of cheque Truncation, whether to be at presenting bank, clearing house or drawee bank.

(b) Truncation of whole cheque or MICR code only.

(c) Preservation period of paper instruments.

(d) Storage of cheque images.

(e) Type of images.

(f) Introduction of check digit in MICR line.

(g) Security over network.

Depending on the level of technology, banks are expected to adopt the best suitable model for their implementation. The major vendors providing the cheque truncation solution are NCR Corporation, Unisys and BCSIS. The vendor for SBI is NCR Corporation and has adopted Branch Model for the pilot project.

NATIONAL FINANCIAL SWITCH

The National Financial Switch (NFS) to facilitate apex level connectivity of other ATM switches has been set up by the institute for development and research in Banking Technology. The NFS started operation from August 28th , 2004. The NFS enables customers of banks connected to it to withdraw cash and obtain information from ATMs of any of those banks.

INTERNET BANKING

With technology advancements in computers and communications, Banks have launched "Internet Banking product, which is an alternative banking delivery channel. It aims to provide any where any time banking.

Functionalities: Various functionalities include, basic services like obtaining account statement, request for issuance of cheque book, demand draft, stop payment of a cheque and transfer of funds from one account to another account of the account holder. All the above services can happen at a click of the mouse.

With strong competition Banks margins have come down drastically, forcing it to cut down on cost. With advancement of technology, penetration of internet to rural and semi-urban areas is on the increase.

Table 4
Cost Comparison with Other Delivery Channels

Name of the Delivery Channel	*Cost Per Transaction (US $)*
Teller	1.00
ATM	.45
Phone	0.35
Debit Card	.25
Internet	.10

Source: India Research May 29th, 2000, Kotak Securities

A recent study by Meridien Research sums up the landscape today: "Internet banking is no longer a competitive advantage but a competitive necessity."

One of the major challenges faced by banks is the impact of competition and the falling margins in the transactions undertaken by them. With this profit margins being the order of the day, the solution to this would perhaps lie in increasing volumes so as to result in better operating results for banks. This is best achieved by exploiting the benefits of technology which facilitates increased volumes at higher levels of efficiency. A customer is no longer of a branch but a customer of the bank.

SINGLE WINDOW SYSTEM/CONCEPT

Single window concept is a system of delivery of all services offered by the Bank, at a single window counter. The single window concept envisages that all the needs of the customer are taken care of at a single point of delivery i.e. at a single window, as compared to the existing system where a customer has to approach different product specific counters for completion of his work. The single window system will provide quicker and more efficient customer service.

The transaction handled at single window counter is divided into core activities and non-core activities.

Core Activities

(a) Savings Bank Accounts
(b) Current Account
(c) Term Deposits
(d) Drafts issue/payment
(e) Bankers cheque issue/ payment
(f) T. T. inward/outward remittances.

Non-Core Activities

(a) Government payments/Receipts (including PPF Accounts)
(b) Travellers cheques and gift cheques issue and payments.
(c) Passbook issue/updating.
(d) Cheque book issue and recording of stop payment instructions.
(e) Recording of standing instructions.

BPR TECHNOLOGY: (BUSINESS PROCESS REENGINEERING)

There have been fundamental changes in competition, technology and customer expectations. Also there have been many changes in the delivery systems of products and services of the Bank. But the business process (i.e. the banks procedures, documentation etc) remained the same. The change of business processes is called reengineering; the business processes must be aligned to the new technology.

Reasons to Adopt BPR in Banks

- Globlisation and competition have intensified.
- The bank has to increase its market share in the high network customers/youth segment.

Benefits of BPR

- World class processes can be adopted.
- State of the art infrastructure will put in place.
- Customer expectation will be fulfilled.

DANGERS OF NEW TECHNOLOGICAL INNOVATIONS

The most prominent challenge/danger arising from these innovations related to the concept of security with the delivery channels relating to funds based services such as movement of funds electronically between different accounts ofcustomers –taking place with the use of technology, the requirements relating to security also need to undergo metamorphosis at a rapid pace. Various concepts such as digital signatures, certification, storage of information in a secure and tamper proof manner assume significance and have to be part of the practices and procedures in the day to day functioning of banks of tomorrow.

REASONS FOR NOT PICKING UP

"More than a lack of regulatory framework, it is the lack of zeal and a mindset attitude towards resisting any new technology that is holding back the nationalized banks". As per industrial analysts, other reasons are that the average customer, comprising of senior citizen 50+ age group/Semi-urban/Rural background, who is comfortable with traditional banking system, and is not too keen on adopting an online model.

SUGGESTIONS FOR SOUND PAYMENT SYSTEM

- The system should have a well – founded legal basis under all relevant jurisdictions.
- The system's rules and procedures should enable participants to have a clear understanding of the systems impact on each of the financial risks they incur through participation in it.
- They system should provide prompt final settlement prompt final settlement on the day of value, preferably during the day and at a minimum at the end of the day.
- The system should ensure a high degree of security and operational reliability and should have contingency arrangements for timely completion of daily processing.
- The system should provide a means of making payments which is practical for its users and efficient for the economy.
- The system's governance arrangements should be effective, accountable and transparent.

CONCLUSION

IT use in Indian banking has come a long way since the days when banks were perceived only as instruments of social change. However, despite its importance there are no significant studies that have closely examined technological change in the Indian banking system. This article has attempted to address this limitation by providing some relevant information on technology adoption in India. As highlighted in the article, in the early twenty first century, the Indian banking system is in the midst of technological revolution. As a result, PSBs have launched voluntary retirement schemes in an effort to bring down their wage costs. The focus on retail banking and other fee based services such as guarantees and commissions on drafts is expected to improve profitability. Yet, PSBs have still to cover a lot of ground with respect to implementation of technology in all their branches.

The Narsimham Committee (1991) rightfully suggested that the PSBs had to adopt technology to become more competitive and to enhance their internal workings. As on 2004, the scheduled commercial banks have been given the freedom to open new branches and upgrade extension counters, after meeting capital adequacy norms and prudential accounting standards. However, they are now permitted to close non-viable branches, except in rural areas.

Indian PSBs possess some unique advantage over their competition. But it is their use of technology that will enable PSBs to build up their strengths. PSBs also have a vast network of branches within rural and semi-urban India and can effectively employ technology to tap into under served markets with significant social returns.

Finally, it is worthwhile to note that the late Rajiv Gandhi's encouragement to IT in the late 1980's was very controversial because computers were seen as a substitute for manpower and viewed as an icon for "jobless". A decade and a half later, India has assumed the "lead" in developing software in the world. At a time when India is synonyms with the 'IT' revolution of the early twenty-first century, it is hard to see how banks can resist technology in their day-to-day operation for long.

REFERENCES

Basel Committee (1998), 'Report on Enhancing Bank Transparency' Paper No. 41

Dutt, R. and Sundharam, K. P. M. (2004), Indian Economy, S. Chand and Company Ltd., New Delhi

—(2004), Accounting Business & Financial History, November, p. 339.

—(2004), Banking Digest, Book No. 4 August, pp. 39-40

—(2005), State Bank of India, Monthly Review, October, p. 470

—(2004-05), RBI, Report on Trend and Progress of Banking in India.

— (2004-05), RBI, Annual Report.

CHAPTER 17

THE NPA OVERHANG–MAGNITUDES, SOLUTIONS AND LEGAL REFORMS

Rashmi Akhoury

INTRODUCTION

Economic reforms initiated in 1991 by the then finance Minister Dr. Manmohan Singh would have remained incomplete without the overhaul of the Indian banking sector. The process, which began on the basis of recommendations of the Narasimham Committee Report (first report), is still continuing, though many of the sick banks have been able to come out of the red after repeat doses of fund infusion. A few of them, however, are still in the red but the efforts are on to resuscitate them. However, the bigger challenge at the moment is to deal with the worsening financial health of the financial institutions. The other aspect of the banking sector reforms relates to liberalisation of norms and guidelines for making the whole sector vibrant and competitive.

This was a gradual process undertaken with utmost care least it should disrupt the banking sector. Slowly, the Reserve Bank of India (RBI) freed interest rates, both on the deposit and the lending sides. At the same time it relaxed the Cash Reserve Ratio (CRR) and Statutory Liquidity Ratio (SLR) unlocking more and more funds. On the deposit side, a bank is free to offer any rate depending upon its asset-liability position. Only savings rate are mandated by the RBI. Similarly, banks can charge any rate on lending operations depending on risk perception. It would be wrong to say that there are no controls, but they are much less as compared to the controls that existed before the initiation of the banking sector reforms.

Reduction of NPAs

The most important dimension of the banking sector reforms was reduction of the non-performing assets (NPAs). In fact the whole effort to reform the banking sector would collapse if the banks are not able to contain and reduce their NPAs. It would be impossible for a bank with high NPAs to be either vibrant or competitive. What are these NPAs? These are the assets that do not yield any return. It is like owning a vast field where nothing grows, though the field was purchased at high rates.

Indian banks functionally diverse and geographically widespread have played a crucial role in the socio-economic progress of the country after Independence. Development of agriculture culminating in green revolution and proliferation of small scale industries across the country with huge employment and export potential, growth of a large number of medium and big industries and above all, blossoming of entrepreneurs in diverse fields led to the expansion and diversification of banking activities. The rapid growth, however, led to stallions in the operational efficiency of banks and the accumulation of Non-performing Assets in their loan portfolios. The high level of non performing assets, however, is a cause for worry and it should be brought down to acceptable levels for creating a vibrant and competitive financial system.

Non-performing assets are a serious strain on earning profits. Poor credit decisions taken by the bank management are cited as reasons for mounting non-performing assets. Priority sector lending and out-dated legal system not only encourage the incidence of non-performing assets but also prolong their existence by placing a premium on default and delay.

The recent efforts such as establishing more debt recovery tribunals and setting up of settlement advisory committee in banks would help to bring down the level of non-performing Assets. However, there is an urgent need to, "institute a proper legal framework to ensure expeditious recovery of debt and give adequate legal powers to banks to affect property transfers." The absence of quick and efficient system of legal redress constitutes an important "moral hazard" in the financial sector as it encourages imprudent borrowing.

It is not possible to have no non-performing asset and therefore, the best norm would be to bring non-performing assets down to 1 to 2 percent. Towards this, a corrective action is to be initiated by the authorities for external factors and individual banks for internal factors. Otherwise, "the iceberg of non-performing asset might get converted into a grave situation and results in a national crisis." Bank supervision assumes a considerable importance in the context of maintaining stability and soundness of banking operations. The periodical review with-in-built checks throw light on solvency, liquidity, quality and sound management of banking system. The new policy directions aim at attaining the objectives of banking sector on healthy basis through means of sound structure and operations.

CONCEPTUAL FRAMEWORK

Balance Sheet provides an opportunity which highlights the strength and does not disclose the weaknesses. Perhaps, it is a common saying that the balance sheet is one which hides more than it reveals. On the introduction of prudential norms such as income recognition, assets classification and provisioning, the very thrust of balance sheet has changed. This not only discloses the quantity in terms of assets and liabilities at the end of the year but also reveals the quality in terms of sound functioning as well. Assets classification can be done on the criteria of recovery of interest and installment. The assets of the banks can be classified into (a) performing assets, (b) Non Performing Assets.

Since the deposits received from the depositors have to be repaid to them by the bank, they are known as bank's "Liabilities" and as the loans given to the borrowers are to be received back from them they are termed as bank's "Assets". So, "Assets" are Bank's Loans and Advances.

WHAT IS A PERFORMING ASSET AND A NON-PERFORMING ASSET

As mentioned above, it is imperative for maintaining bank's income that the borrowers not only pay due interest on the loans but also repay the loans fully. Further, it is also imperative that both the interest and the loan repayment installments are paid in time i.e. within the time fixed therefore. If the borrower does so and continues to do so, the loan is called a "Performing Asset" i.e., it is earning income for the bank.

In case, however, the borrower fails to pay in time, the loan/its periodical installments or the periodical interest thereon, the loan will, strictly speaking, not be a Performing Asset. However, in many cases the borrowers are late by a short period only in repaying either their installments or the interest due. Banks in the past used to account for interest income on such loans, on accruals basis, despite not actually receiving any funds from the borrowers at that point of time. Thus, they credited their income heads with the amount of interest due from the borrowers in the belief that the borrowers will eventually make the payment. This artificially inflated the banks' actual income in the particular period and some times when the borrowers did not actually make the payment for a long time, the income booked had to be reversed.

From the year 1992, RBI started tightening the Banks in this respect and put forth guidelines so that income remaining unrecovered for invariably long periods may not be included in current period's income and also the banks may, in turn, tighten the borrowers to maintain discipline and make payments of installments/interest timely. RBI has fixed time-norms before which the installment/interest due must be received from the borrowers otherwise the income accrued on these loans will not be recognized or included as income and these loans will be termed as 'Non-Performing Asset'. The current RBI time norm is 90 days. The circumstances that will render the various types of loans non-performing assets, as per RBI guidelines, are as under –

(i) *Term Loan*: If interest and/or installment of principal remains overdue for a period of more than 90 days.

(ii) *Overdraft/Cash Credit*: If the account remains 'Out of Order' for a period of more than 90 days.

(iii) *Bills Purchased & Discounted*: If the bill remains overdue for a period of more than 90 days.

(iv) *Loan for Short Duration Crop:* If the installment of principal or interest thereon remains overdue for two crop seasons.

(v) *Loan for Long Duration Crop:* If the installment of principal or interest thereon remains overdue for one crop season.

(vi) *Other Accounts:* If any amount to be received remains overdue for a period of more than 90 days.

NPA CLASSIFICATION NORMS

Banks are required to classify non-performing assets further into the following three categories based on the period for which the asset has remained non-performing and the realisability of the dues:

(a) Sub-standard Assets

(b) Doubtful Assets

(c) Loss Assets

- An asset is classified as *Sub-standard* when it remains an NPA for a period less than or equal to 12 months.
- An asset is classified as *doubtful* if it remains an NPA for more than 12 months (With effect from 31.03.2005).
- An asset is classified as *loss asset* where the value of security available is less than 10% of the outstandings.
- Asset classification will be borrower-wise and not facility or account-wise.

- Restructured NPA accounts become eligible for upgradation after a period of one year after the date when first payment of interest or of principal, whichever is earlier, falls due, subject to satisfactory performance of the unit.

PROVISIONING NORMS

Provisioning in sub standard assets is made at a uniform fixed percentage, in doubtful assets, it is made on the basis of age of the NPA and security available, and loss assets are to be fully provided for.

SPECIAL MENTION ACCOUNTS

In addition to the above, in line with the best International practices, an asset category between standard and sub standard categories called "Special Mention Accounts" has been created for close monitoring and follow up of Potential NPAs, i.e. those where (a) Interest and/or Installment is overdue for a period of 30 days or (b) early warning signals are visible. These assets are those that have not been classified as NPAs as yet, but have been placed in a special category to give them focused attention so that they may not become NPAs.

An asset becomes non-performing when it ceases to generate income for the bank. A non-performing Asset (NPA) is defined as a credit facility in respect of which the interest and/or installment of principal has remained 'overdue/out of order' for a specified period of time.

EFFECTS OF ASSETS TURNING INTO NPAS

The effects of assets turning into NPAs are two fold:

(1) Firstly, the income accruing on such assets cannot be recognized by the bank i.e. it can not be treated or included as income of the bank.

(2) Secondly, since the recovery of the principal amount outstanding is also in doubt, Provision is required to be made for the same–out of the bank's profits–which reduces the profits by such amount.

In the circumstances, since the non-recovery or late-recovery of installments of the principal and/or interest turns the banks' loans and advances into NPAs, which has a very adverse impact on the banks' profits, it is imperative that both the installments as well as interest are recovered from the borrowers timely.

CURRENT SITUATION AND TREND IN NPAs

A proper system of income recognition and provisioning is fundamental to the preservation of strength and stability of the banking system. The non performing assets share in total bank loans is an important indicator of banking health. In this paper an attempt has been made to study the impact of Non-Performing Assets (NPAs) on the profitability of the Commercial Banks in India during the post reform period.

Banking Policy and Trends

With liberalisation and growing integration of the Indian financial sector with the international market, the supervisory and regulatory role of RBI has become critical for the maintenance of financial stability. RBI has been continuously fine-tuning its regulatory and supervisory mechanism in recent years to match international standards. Migration to new capital adequacy framework (Basel-II) based on a three-pillar approach, namely, minimum capital requirements, supervisory review, and market discipline, involves implementation challenges for both RBI and banks. RBI has taken a number of initiatives to make migration to Basel-II smoother. Banks have been advised to undertake a self–assessment of the existing risk management systems and to simultaneously initiate suitable measures to upgrade them to match international standards. Banks have also been asked to prepare a road map and to review the progress on a quarterly basis.

During the year 2003-04, the banking sector witnessed strong growth in deposits and advances. Aggregate deposits of scheduled commercial banks (SCBs) grew by 17.5 per cent compared to 13.4 per cent in 2002-03. Credit and investments by SCBs increased by 15.3 per cent and 25.1 per cent, respectively in 2003-04 compared to 16.1 per cent and 23.3 per cent respectively in 2002-03. These developments coupled with a decline in gross NPAs enabled SCBs to improve their financial performance, despite a lower income growth consequent upon low interest rates. Ratio of net profits to total assets of SCBs improved marginally from 1.0 per cent to 1.1 per cent, Ratio of operating profits to total assets improved from 2.4 per cent in 2002-03 to 2.7 per cent in 2003-04.

Total income of SCBs increased by 6.6 per cent to RS.1,83,767 crore in 2003-04 as compared to an increase of 14.0 per cent in 2002-03. The lower income growth was on account of lower growth of 2.4 per cent in interest income in 2003-04. Income growth in 2003-04 came mainly from other income, which increased by 25.5 per cent. Total expenditure of SCBs grew at a lower rate of 4.0 per cent in 2003-04 compared to 11.3 per cent in 2002-03.

The lower growth of total expenditure was entirely on account of a decline in interest expenditure from Rs.93,596 crore in 2002-03 to Rs.8,567 crore in 2003-04. As a proportion of total assets, interest expenditure declined from 5.5 per cent to 4.4 per cent. Expenditure on provisions and contingencies witnessed an increase of 28.8 per cent in 2003-04 on top of increases of 29.3 per cent in the previous year. The financial performance varied across bank groups. Increase in the income of the SCBs varied from 2.4 per cent for old private sector banks to 8.1 per cent for foreign banks. The income of the public sector banks (PSBs) grew by 7.1 per cent in 2003-04. Among income, the growth of interest income was the highest for new private sector banks followed by old private banks, PSBs and foreign banks. The growth of other income was in sharp contrast with the growth in interest income. Growth of other income was the highest in case of foreign banks and the lowest for the old private sector banks. Growth of expenditure was the highest in the case of foreign banks and lowest in the case of old private sector banks. Expenditure on interest declined for all bank groups, following the reduction in deposit rates. The decline in expenditure on interest was the highest for foreign banks

(15.5 per cent) and lowest for old private sector banks (5.5 per cent) and PSBs (5.9 per cent).

The ratio of net profits to total assets was the highest for foreign banks (1.77 per cent) followed by old private sector banks (1.2 per cent), PSBs (1.1 per cent), and new private sector banks (0.8 per cent). The ratio of operating profits to total assets followed more or less a similar pattern with foreign banks performing the best (3.7 per cent), followed by PSBs (2.7 per cent), old private sector banks (2.6 per cent) and new private sector banks (2.0 per cent). There has been an overall improvement in the efficiency of SCBs as evident in the declining ratios for operating expenses to net total income (total income – interest expenditure). For SCBs as a whole the ratio declined from 53.0 per cent in 2001-02 to 48.3 per cent in 2002-03 and further to 45.2 per cent in 2003-04.

The profitability of SCBs, though still high, showed a declining trend in the first half of 2004-05 on account of a fall in treasury income. The ratio of net profit to total assets (annualised) was lower at 1.1 per cent in the second quarter of 2004-05 compared to 1.3 per cent in the corresponding previous quarter.

Interest spread is an important indicator of efficiency of banking operations. The growth of spread in recent years clearly establishes that banks have not fully passed on the benefit of falling interest rates to their customers. Despite the initiatives taken by the RBI, lending rates of banks have exhibited considerable downward rigidity. Net interest income (annualised) of SCBs as a proportion of total assets improved to 3.1 per cent in the second quarter of 2004-05 compared to 2.9 per cent in the corresponding quarter of last year.

NON-PERFORMING ASSETS OF THE BANKING SECTOR

There was a significant decline in the non-performing assets (NPAs) of SCBs in 2003-04, despite adoption of 90 day delinquency norm from March 31, 2004. The gross NPAs of SCBs declined from 4.0 per cent of total assets in 2002-03 to 3.3 per cent in 2003-04. The corresponding decline in net NPAs was from 1.9 per cent to 1.2 per cent. Both gross NPAs and net

Table 1
Working Results of Scheduled Commercial Banks

Rs. Crore

Items	Public Sector Banks		Foreign Banks		Old Pvt. Sector banks		New Pvt. Sector Banks		SCBs	
	2002-03	2003-04	2002-03	2003-04	2002-03	2003-04	2002-03	2003-04	2002-03	2003-04
Income	128464	137602	120346	13012	11279	11551	20567	21602	172345	183767
Interest Income	107232	109496	8958	8990	8920	9120	15633	16421	140742	144028
Other Income	107232	28106	3076.95	4022	2359	2431	4934	51806	31603	39739
Expenditure	116169	121055	10210	10769	10047	10105	18843	1956701	155270	161436
Interest Expended	69853	65765	505501	4272	6327	5982	12361	11548	93596	87567
Intermediation Cost	28895	32363	3251	3752	2147	2374	3774	5041	38067	43530
Provisions and contingencies	17422	22928	1904	2744	1573	1749	2708	2978	23607	30400
Operating Profit (A-Bi-Bii)	29716	39475	3728	4987	2805	3196	4433	5013	40682	52671
Net Profit (A-B)	12295	16546	1824	2243	1232	1446	1725	2035	17075	22271
Net Interest Income (Spred)	37379	43732	3903	4718	2593	3139	3272	4873	47146	56462
Total Assets	1285411	1471428	116661	136316	104956	120700	192170	246576	1699198	1975020
As Per cent of Total Assets										
Income	10.0	9.4	10.3	9.5	10.7	9.6	10.7	8.8	10.1	9.3
Interest Income	8.3	7.4	7.7	6.6	8.5	7.6	8.1	6.7	8.3	7.3
Other Income	1.7	1.9	2.6	3.0	2.2	2.0	2.6	2.1	1.9	2.0
Expenditure	9.0	8.2	8.8	7.9	9.6	8.4	9.8	7.9	9.1	8.2
Interest expended	5.4	4.5	4.3	3.1	6	5	6.4	4.7	5.5	4.4
Intermediation Cost	2.2	2.2	2.8	2.8	2.0	2.0	2.0	2.0	2.2	2.2
Provisions and contingencies	1.4	1.6	1.6	2.0	1.5	1.4	1.4	1.2	1.4	1.5

Contd.

Items	*Public Sector Banks*		*Foreign Banks*		*Old Pvt. Sector banks*		*New Pvt. Sector Banks*		*SCBs*	
	2002-03	2003-04	2002-03	2003-04	2002-03	2003-04	2002-03	2003-04	2002-03	2003-04
Operating Profit	2.3	2.7	3.2	3.7	2.7	2.6	2.3	2.0	2.4	2.7
Net Profit (A-B)	1.0	1.1	1.6	1.6	1.2	1.2	0.9	0.8	1.0	1.1
Net Interest income (Spred)	2.9	2.97	3.35	3.46	2.47	2.60	1.70	1.98	2.77	2.86
Total Assets	1.0	1.1	1.6	1.6	1.2	1.2	0.9	0.8	1.0	1.1
Memo Item										
Operating expenses as per cent of net income	49.3	45.0	46.6	42.9	43.4	42.6	46	50.1	48.3	45.2

Source: GOI, Economic Survey, 2004-05.

Table 2
Non-Performing Assets of Scheduled Commercial Banks

Items	Gross NPAs (Rs. Crore)			Percentage to Gross Advances				Percentage to Total Assets			
Items	*2001-02*	*2002-03*	*2003-04*	*2001-02*	*2002-03*	*2003-04*	*2004-05*	*2.001-02*	*2002-03*	*2003-04*	*2004-05*
Bank Group											
Public Sector	56473	54090	51538	11.1	9.4	7.8	5.53	4.9	4.2	3.5	2.74
Private Sector	11662	11782	10355	9.6	8.1	5.8	4.44	4.4	4.0	2.8	2.05
Foreign	2726	2845	2894	5.4	5.3	4.6	2.85	2.4	2.4	2.1	1.42
SCBs (1+2+3)	70861	68717	64787	10.4	8.8	7.2		4.6	4.0	3.3	
Items	*Net NPAs (Rs. Crore)*			*Percentage to Net Advances*				*Percentage to Total Assets*			
Public Sector	27958	24867	18860	5.8	4.5	3	2.06	2.4	1.9	1.3	0.99
Private Sector	6676	6882	4857	5.7	5.0	2.8	2.17	2.5	2.3	1.3	0.97
Foreign	920	921	900	1.9	1.8	1.5	0.86	0.8	0.8	0.7	0.42
SCBs (1+2+3)	35554	32670	24617	5.5	4.4	2.9		2.3	1.9	1.2	

Gross NPAs to Gross Advances March 2004 - 7.4
March 2005 - 5.2

Net NPA to Net Advances March 2004 - 2.9
March 2005 - 2.0

(Calculated on the basis of above table)
Source: GOI, Economic Survey, 2004-05

NPAs declined in absolute terms. While the gross NPAs declined from Rs.68,717 crore in 2002-03 to Rs.64,787 crore in 2003-04, net NPAs declined from Rs. 32,670 crore to Rs.24,617 crore in the same period. There was also a significant decline in the proportion of net NPAs to net advances from 4.4 per cent in 2002-03 to 2.9 per cent in 2003-04. The significant decline in the net NPAs by 24.7 per cent in 2003-04 as compared to 8.1 per cent in 2002-03 was mainly on account of higher provisions (up to 40.0 per cent) for NPAs made by SCBs.

The decline in NPAs in 2003-04 was witnessed across all bank groups. The decline in net NPAs as a proportion of total assets was quite significant in the case of new private sector banks, followed by PSBs. The ratio of net NPAs to net advances of SCBs declined from 4.4 per cent in 2002-03 to 2.9 per cent in 2003-04. Among the bank groups, old private sector banks had the highest ratio of net NPAs to net advances at 3.8 per cent followed by PSBs (3.0 per cent) new private sector banks (2.4 per cent) and foreign banks (1.5 per cent).

Asset Quality

The declining trend in gross and net NPAs for scheduled commercial banks that set in during 2002-03 continued during 2004-05 with the net NPA ratio going below two per cent for the first time. The fact that the provisioning for NPAs was much lower during 2004-05 indicates that the decline was due to increased recovery and overall reduction in asset slippage. An improved industrial climate also contributed to better recoveries. Only four banks had net NPAs in excess of 10 per cent of their net advances (Table–3). Similarly, the net NPA to capital ratio steadily declined from 21.3 per cent at end-March, 2004 to 14.4 per cent by end-March, 2005 reflecting the increase in capital, coupled with rapid decline in net NPAs.

In India a high level of NPA is a major cause of weakness and poor performance of commercial banks in India. A major change reported by RBI, as a result of the decision to adopt the net NPAs as the measure, is in the number of banks with varying levels of NPAs.

Table 3
Net NPAs to Net Advances of Scheduled Commercial Banks

Year	*Public Sector Banks*		*Private Sector Banks*		*Foreign Banks*
2000-01					
Up to 2 per cent	0	0	0	1	22
Above 2 per cent and up to 5 per cent	1	5	4	5	5
Above 5 per cent and up to 10 per cent	7	8	12	3	4
Above 10 per cent	0	6	6	0	11
2001-02					
Up to 2 per cent	0	0	1	1	20
Above 2 per cent and up to 5 per cent	4	4	2	3	4
Above 5 per cent and up to 10 per cent	4	12	13	5	1
Above 10 per cent	0	3	6	0	14
2002-03					
Up to 2 per cent	1	3	1	3	21
Above 2 per cent and up to 5 per cent	6	6	4	2	2
Above 5 per cent and up to 10 per cent	1	8	13	4	5
Above 10 per cent	0	2	2	1	8
2003-04					
Up to 2 per cent	6	5	2	4	19
Above 2 per cent and up to 5 per cent	2	9	9	5	4
Above 5 per cent and up to 10 per cent	0	4	7	0	3
Above 10 per cent	0	1	2	1	7
2004-05					
Up to 2 per cent	7	10	4	5	22
Above 2 per cent and up to 5 per cent	1	8	11	3	2
Above 5 per cent and up to 10 per cent	0	2	5	1	2
Above 10 per cent	0	0	0	0	4

P: Provisional
Note: Data as on March 31,2006 are un-audited and provisional
Source: Off-site supervisory returns submitted by the banks pertaining to their domestic operations.

As many as 19 out of 28 private sector banks continued to have NPAs upto 2% at the end-March 2005. Two out of that had NPAs level of above 5% and upto 10% only 4 out of 20 old private sector banks and 5 out of nine new private sector banks had an NPAs upto 2%. Analysis shows that NPAs level is higher in private sector banks in comparison to public sector banks in the range of above 5 and upto 10%. This implies that NPA management in the Indian banking system results in better management of advanced port-folio of all SCBs.

Over 90% of NPAs pertain to PSBs as share of business as well as share of NPAs in the total advances of these banks is high. Therefore, NPA management in the Indian banking system results in better management of advances portfolio of PSBs.

Table 4
Distribution of Scheduled Commercial Banks by Ratio of Net NPAs to Net Advances

(Number of Banks)

	As at End-March				
Bank Group	2001	2002	2003	2004	2005
Public Sector Banks	27	27	27	27	28
Upto 2 per cent	1	–	4	11	19
Above 2 and upto 5 per cent	5	0	14	13	7
Above 5 and upto 10 per cent	16	15	7	3	2
Above 10 per cent	5	3	2		
Old Private Sector Banks	23	22	21	20	20
Upto 2 per cent	1	2	2	2	4
Above 2 and upto 5 per cent	4	2	4	9	12
Above 5 and upto 10 per cent	11	13	13	7	4
Above 10 per cent	7	5	2	2	-
New Private Sector Banks	8	8	9	10	9
Upto 2 per cent	1	1	3	4	5
Above 2 and upto 5 per cent	5	3	2	5	3
Above 5 and upto 10 per cent	2	4	3	–	1
Above 10 per cent	–	–	1	1	–
Foreign Banks	42	40	36	33	31
Upto 2 per cent	21	21	20	21	23
Above 2 and upto 5 per cent	6	4	2	3	3
Above 5 and upto 10 per cent	4	1	6	3	2
Above 10 per cent	11	14	8	6	4

Source: GOI, Economic Survey, 20004-2005.

The quality and performance of advances have direct bearing on the profitability and viability of banks. Despite the credit appraisal and disbursement mechanism, the problem often tends to manifest itself in an accretion to the stock of non-performing assets (NPAs). Although the net NPAs of the commercial banks in India have witnessed a decline over the past several years, they are still high as compared to developed country standards of around 2 per cent. Prompt remedial actions are, therefore warranted in this regard.

In market–driven systems, the seeds of credit excesses are often sown in an upswing when boom conditions prevail. Once financial excesses are unwound, however, there can be a tendency for loans to go bad, at the expenses of the lender and the health of the financial system. In order to counter the benefits of faster credit growth in a boom against the costs of volatile economic cycles once the movements reverse, it is important that banks are not only equipped with balanced prudential norms, but also have forward-looking or dynamic provisioning so as to build-up a protective cushion in good times that can be drawn down in exigencies. The cumulative provisions against loan losses of PSBs in India amounted to 42.5 per cent of their gross NPAs for the year ended March 31, 2002. This is low compared to the international standards, where provisions against impaired assets are often as high as 140 per cent. There is, therefore, need for banks to improve their provisioning practices, full provisioning towards already impaired assets needs to be a priority corporate goal.

The public sector bank (PSBs) in India have made significant contributions to almost all the sectors of the Indian economy such as agriculture, industries of various categories, trade, employment and infrastructure. The ever increasing trends in deposits and credits speak volumes for the performance of Indian banks. With over Rs.968,749 crore as deposits and over Rs. 4,80,681 crore as loans, the public sector banks command the heights of the Indian economy. However, the non-performing assets (NPAs) in the credit portfolios of the PSBs have become a thorn in the flesh during the last one decade or so. NPAs have not only affected the productivity and the profitability of the banks, but also sullied the image of Indian banking and a drain on the very value system of the society. Is it not a bounded duty of the borrower to repay what he took away from the bank as a loan? If bank loans turn to be bad and are irrecoverable, does it not amount to defrauding the society? Hence, the all round cry over the staggering volume of NPAs which have risen to an alarming level of over Rs.70,000 crore caused mainly because of willful defaulting on the part of borrowers.

Table 5

Gross and Net NPAs of Scheduled Commercial Banksj Bank Group-wise Amount in Crores (As at End March)

		Gross NPAs				Net NPAs		
Bank Group/Year	*Gross Advance*	*Amount*	*Per cent to Gross Advances*	*Per cent to Total Assets*	*Net Advances*	*Amount*	*Per cent to Net Advances*	*Per cent to Total Assets*
Public Sector Banks								
2002	509368	56473	11.1	4.9	480681	27958	5.8	2.4
2003	577813	54090	9.4	4.2	549351	24867	4.5	1.9
2004	661975	51638	7.8	3.5	631383	18860	3.0	1.3
2005	836128	47325	5.7	2.8	807293	16642	2.1	1.0
2005#	877825	48541	5.5	2.7	848912	17490	2.1	1.0

Source:

1. Balance Sheets of respective banks.
2. Returns submitted by respective banks.

Including the impact of a non- banking entity into a banking entity.

Data, made available periodically by RBI, bring out the multiple dimensions of NPAs in the Indian banking system.

(1) The Non-performing Assets of all the Public Sector Banks together (both in Gross and Net terms) only continue to increase right from the introduction of Banking Sector Reforms (Phase 1) in 1992. This ever increasing trend speaks of the sad state of affairs prevailing in the banks for well over a decade. Statisticians may try to convince us by saying that the percentage shares of both Gross and Net NPAs in respective advances have tended to decline during the same period; this is, however, due to the simple fact that advances have increased at a faster rate (Table– 5).

(2.) Priority sector's contribution to NPAs has actually declined (50 per cent in 1995 to 44.5 per cent in 2002) in spite of its increasing share in the total advances (33 per cent in 1995 to 43 per cent in 2002); contrary to this, non-priority sector's contribution to NPAs has increased (46.5 per cent in 1995 to 53.54 per cent in 2002) despite its declining share in the total bank advances. This points to the fact that priority sector is not the sole culprit, as it is often feared, responsible for the staggering accumulation of NPAs in the PSBs.

Table 6
Priority Sector Advances of PSBs–Impact on NPAs

Year March-End	*Priority Sector Advance over Total Advances (%)*	*Priority Sector NPAs over Total NPAs (%)*
1995	32.8	50.0
1996	32.9	48.3
1997	34.2	47.7
1998	42.0	46.4
1999	39.2	–
2000	40.2	–
2001	43.0	–
2002	43.15	44.5

Source: RBI, Report on Trend and Progress of Banking in India, 2005-06.

Table 7
NPAs of Public Sector Banks – Sector wise
As at the End-March 2005

(Amount in Rs. Crore)

	Priority Sector		*Non-Priority Sector*	
	Amount	*% to Total*	*Amount*	*% to Total*
Public Sector Banks	23397.38	49.05	2384861	50%

Source: RBI report on trend and progress of Banking in India 2005-06.

(3) While both the PSBs and Indian private sector banks are the victims of NPAs, the incidence of NPAs is obviously greater in the PSBs than in the private sector. Even the foreign banks (40 out of 48 banks) have fallen prey to the defaulting borrowers.

Table 8
Level of NPAs Among Scheduled Commercial Banks March, 2002

	Public Sector	*Private Sector*		
Net NPA Net Advance	*Banks*	*Indian*	*Foreign*	*Total*
Nil	–	–	8	8
Upto 10%	24	25	26	75
Above 10%-Upto 20%	3	3	5	11
Total	27	30	48	105

Source: RBI Report on Trend and Progress of Banking in India

Trends in NPAs

The gravity of NPAs in use in banks and financial institutions is measured in terms of percentage of net/gross overdues to net/gross advances at a point of time. The NPAs of public sector banks showed a marginal decline where as, a little increase is noticed in all other bank groups. A look at Table –7 reveals that the number of Public Sector Banks (PSBs) with net NPAs upto 10 per cent increased from 19 in 1996 to 24 in 2002 and the number of banks with net NPAs in the range of 10% and 20% declined from 6 in 1996 to 3 in 2002 with none continuing to show NPAs above 20%. The data further show that the number of old private sector banks with the net NPAs below 10% declined considerably between 1996 and 2002 whereas the number of banks with 20% and above recorded a

Table 9
Distribution of Net NPAs (1996-2000)

No. of Banks

	End of March						
NPAs/NetAdvances (in per cent)	*1996*	*1997*	*1998*	*1999*	*2000*	*2001*	*2002*
Public Sector Banks							
Upto 10,00 per cent	19	17	17	18	22	22	24
Above 10,00 to 20,00 per cent	6	9	9	8	5	5	3
Above 20,00 per cent	2	1	1	1	–	–	–
Old Indian Pvt. Sector Banks							
Loan than 10 per cent	22	22	21	17	18	16	17
10-20 per cent	3	3	4	5	5	4	3
Above 20 per cent	Nil	Nil	Nil	3	1	3	2
New Indian Pvt. Sector Banks							
Less than 10 per cent	9	9	9	9	8	8	8
10-20 per cent	Nil	Nil	Nil	Nil	Nil	Nil	Nil
Above 20 per cent	Nil	Nil	Nil	Nil	Nil	Nil	Nil
Foreign Banks in India							
Less than 10 per cent	30	36	34	27	31	31	26
10-20 per cent	1	1	6	11	7	6	5
Above 20 per cent	Nil	2	2	3	4	5	9

Source:
1. RBI Bulletin, December 1999, p.70.
2. RBI, Report on Trend and Progress of Banking in India, 2001-02, p.67.

significant increase from 1999 onwards. The position of new private sector banks and foreign banks in India is slightly better than that of the PSBs. However, the number of foreign banks with more than 20% NPAs increased from 2 in 1997 to 9 in 2002.

An analysis of NPAs of different bank groups showed that with the exception of PSBs, the other bank group (i.e., private sector banks and foreign banks) experienced an increase during 1998-99. In the case of PSBs, marginal decline in NPAs ratio mainly was aided by an increase in the share of standard assets and commensurate decline in the share of doubtful and sub-standard assets. However, the declining trend of NPAs of SCBs witnessed till the year 1997-98 could not be sustained in 1998-99. The gross NPAs to total assets of PSBs, however, declined from 6.4 per cent in 1997-98 to 4.6 per cent in 2001-02 and net NPAs to net total assets also declined from 3.0 per cent in 1997-98 to 2.3 per cent in 2001-02. In brief, this analysis indicates that the ratio of NPAs to loans and advances is not under check.

As on March 31, 2005, gross NPAs of all scheduled Commercial Banks is 57546.1 crores, gross advances are 1171210.3 crores and gross NPA Ratio % is 4.9. Gross NPAs to gross advances of Commercial Banks of India in March 2004 and in March 2005 is 7.4% and 5.2% respectively while net NPA to net advances in the same period is 2.9% and 2.0% respectively.

IMPACT, CAUSES AND IMPLICATIONS

Impact of NPAs on Banks' Profits and Lending Process

The efficiency of a bank is not always reflected only by the size of its balance sheet but by the level of return on its assets. NPAs do not generate interest income for the banks, but at the same time banks are required to make provisions for such NPAs from their current profits.

NPAs have a deleterious effect on the return on assets in several ways-

- They erode current profits through provisioning requirements.

- They result in reduced interest income
- They require higher provisioning requirements affecting profits and accretion to capital funds and capacity to increase good quality risk assets in future, and
- They limit recycling of funds, set in asset –liability mismatches, etc.

There is at times a tendency among some of the banks to understate the level of NPAs in order to reduce the provisioning and boost up bottom lines. It would only postpone the doomsday effect as happened in some of the banks with disastrous consequences, like getting branded as weak and losing credibility internationally, besides subjecting the senior management to vigilance and CBI process.

In the context of crippling effect on a bank's operations in all spheres, asset quality has been placed as one of the most important parameters in the measurement of a bank's performance under the Camels supervisory rating system of RBI.

Impact of NPAs on Balance Sheet Quality

- Increasing provisioning requirements each year.
- Adverse impact on Capital Adequacy Ratio
- ROE and ROA goes down because NPAs do not earn.
- Bank's rating gets affected.
- Bank's cost of raising funds goes up.
- RBI's approval required for declaration of dividend if Net NPA ratio is above 3%

Movement of NPAs Over the Years

A glance through the statistics on the movement of NPAs of public sector banks since introduction of prudential norms in 1992-1993 will help us to understand the extent to which the public sector banks have made progress in reducing their NPA levels.

Table 10
Movement of NPAs
(1992-93 to at the end of March 2005)

	Gross NPAs		*Net NPAs*	
Year	*Amount (Rs. Crore)*	*As a percentage to Total Advances*	*Amount (Rs. Crore)*	*As a percentage to Net Advances*
1992-1993	39253.14	23.18	*Not Compiled*	
1993-1994	41041.33	24.78	19690.74	14.46
1994-1995	38385.18	19.45	17566.64	10.67
1995-1996	41660.94	18.01	18297.49	8.90
1996-1997	43577.09	17.84	20284.73	9.18
1997-1998	45652.64	16.02	21232.13	8.15
1998-1999	51710.50	15.89	24211.49	8.13
1999-2000	53294.02	14.02	26187.60	7.42
2000-2001	54773.16	12.40	27968.11	6.74
At the end March 2004	52880.00		18859.00	
At the end March 2005	47325.00		17490.00	

The level of gross and net NPAs has been sliding down over the years. Gross NPA had come down from 23.18% in 1992 –93 to 12.40% in 2000-01. Net NPA also moved down from 14.46% in 1993-94 to 6.74% in 2000-01. Still the NPA level can be considered of staggering magnitude in absolute terms costing the public sector banks more than Rs.5000 crores annually by way of loss of interest income, besides servicing and litigation costs.

It will be interesting to have a look at the movement of NPAs (gross and net), as a percentage of advances, group-wise over the last four years. This will give an idea of where banks, as different groups, stand in regard to their NPAs.

A significant improvement in recovering the NPAs combined with a sharp increase in gross loans and advances for SCB led to a sharp decline in gross NPAs to gross advances ratio to 5.2% at end March 2005 from 7.2% at end-March 2004. The decline in gross and net NPAs was evident across all bank groups.

Table 11
Gross and Net NPAs of Scheduled Commercial Banks -Bank Group- wise

(As at the End–March)

	Percent of Gross/Net NPAs to Total Advances As At End March							
Bank Group	1998	1999	2000	2001	2002	2003	2004	2005
Public Sector Banks	16.0	15.9	14.0	12.4	11.1	9.4	7.8	5.7
	(8.2)	(8.1)	(7.4)	(96.7)	(5.8)	(4.5)	(3.0)	(2.1)
All Private Sector Banks	8.7	10.8	8.2	8.5				
	(5.3)	(7.4)	(5.4)	(5.4)				
Old Private Sector Banks	10.9	13.1	10.8	11.1	11.0	9.4	7.8	5.7
	(6.5)	(9.0)	(7.1)	(7.3)	(7.1)	(5.5)	(3.8)	(2.7)
New Private Sector Banks	3.5	6.2	4.1	5.1	8.9	7.6	5.0	3.6
	(2.6)	(4.5)	(2.9)	(3.1)	(4.9)	(4.6)	(2.4)	(1.9)
Foreign Banks	6.4	7.6	7.0	6.8	5.4	5.3	4.6	2.8
	(2.2)	(2.9)	(2.4)	(1.9)	(1.9)	(1.8)	(1.5)	(0.9)
All Commercial Banks	14.4	14.7	12.7	11.4	10.4	8.8	7.2	5.2
	(7.3)	(7.6)	(6.8)	(6.2)	(5.5)	(4.4)	(2.9)	(2.o)

Note: Figures in parenthesis denote percentage of net NPAs to net advances
Source: Balance Sheets of respective Banks.

Need for Building up of Loan Loss Provisions

The net NPAs, i.e., that portion of NPAs which is not provided for, pose a major concern for solvency of the bank. To the credit of the Indian banking system's ability to provide for loan losses over a period, though not fully, the level of unprovided for NPAs i.e. net NPAs in public sector banks has been continuously declining from 14.46% in 1993-94 to 6.74% in 2000-01 and to 2.1% in the month of March, 2005. This is still not at a level of comfort and it must be noted that the percentage of net NPAs to net advances in developed countries is around 2%.

The cumulative provisions made for NPAs at the end-March, 2005 were lower the respective levels at end-March, 2004 in respect of all bank groups except old private sector banks. However, in view of decline in gross NPAs, the cumulative provisions made to cushion the NPAs increased to 59.7% at end-March 2005 from 56.6% at end–March 2004. The cumulative provisions as % of gross NPAs was the highest for foreign banks followed by public sector banks, old private banks and new private banks.

Table 12
Movements in Provisions for Non-Performing Loans Bank Group-wise

Particulars	*Scheduled Commercial Banks (87)*	*Scheduled Commercial Banks (88)#*	*Nationlised Banks (19)*	*State Bank Group (8)*	*Public Sector Banks (27)*	*Public Sector Banks (28)#*	*Old Private Sector Banks (20)*	*New Private Sector Banks (9)*	*Foreign Banks (31)*
Provision for NPAs									
As at end-March 2004	35.735	36.199	20.619	9.030	29.649	30.113	2.060	2.431	1.585
Add: Provision made during the year	11.498	11.630	5.946	1.977	7.923	8.055	568	2.364	642
Less: Write-off, write back of excess during the year	12.070	12.297	5.380	2.797	8.177	8.404	441	2.601	852
As at end-March, 2005	35.162	35.531	21.185	8.210	29.395	29.764	2.197	2.195	1.376
Memo:									
Gross NPAs	58.300	59.516	31.709	15.616	47.325	48.541	4.206	4.576	2.192
Ratio:									
Cumulative Provision to Gross NPAs (percent)	60.3	59.7	66.8	52.6	62.1	61.3	52.2	48.0	62.8

#: Including the impact of conversion of a non-banking entity into a banking entity.
Note: Figures in brackets indicate the number of banks in that group for the year 2004-05.
Source: Balance Sheets respective banks.

Table 13

Sector-wise NPAsj Bank Group-wise

Country	*Public Sector Banks*		*Old Private Sector Banks*		*New Private Sector Banks*		*All SCBs**	
Priority Sector	23,840	23,397	1,802	1,782	681	407	26,323	25,586
Agriculture	7,240	7,254	288	304	171	161	7,699	7,719
Small Scale Industries	8,838	7,835	859	792	404	172	10,101	8,719
Others	7,762	8,308	655	686	106	73	8,523	9,067
Public Sector	610	450	8	8	66	34	684	493
Non-Priority Sector	25,698	23,849	2,591	2,444	5,205	4,125	33,494	30,417
Total (A+B+C)	50,148	47,696	4,401	4,234	5,952	4,566	60,501	56,496

*: Excluding Foreign Banks.

Sources: Based on off-site returns submitted by banks.

NPAS–CAUSES

Incidence and Impact of Directed Lending to Stock of NPAs

In all forums of interactions the global multilateral institutions and rating agencies had with RBI and the Government, directed lending concept gets quoted as an important attribute and a contributory factor for the build up of NPAs in banks in India. It is a different matter that RBI and the Government are accused of soft attitude towards banks which do not fulfill the prescribed targets for priority sector lending, particularly agriculture and small scale sector.

NPAs of public and private sector banks are classified in three broad sectors, viz., priority sector, public sector and non-priority sector. The share of NPAs in the priority sector to total NPAs of public sector banks increased marginally to 48.9 per cent at end-March 2005 from 47.5 per cent at end-March 2004. However, the share of NPAs of small scale industries in respect of PSBs declined. While the share of NPAs of public sector undertakings declined.

As regards private sector banks, the share of NPAs on account of all the three components of priority sector, viz., agriculture, small scale industries and other priority sector increased during 2004-05 as compared with 2003-04. The absolute amount of NPAs in each of these sectors, however, registered a decline during the year. The share of non-priority sector NPAs in total NPAs of private sector bank remained steady at 75.0 per cent during 2004-05.

Recovery of dues by banks is directly related to the performance of the borrowal unit/industrial segments. An internal study conducted by RBI shows that in the order of prominence, the following factors contribute to NPAs.

Internal Factors

- diversion of funds for
  - Expansion/diversification/modernization
  - Taking up new projects
  - Helping/promoting associate concerns

- Time/cost over run during the project implementation stage
- Business (product, marketing, etc) failure
- Inefficient management
- Strained labour relations
- Inappropriate technology/technical problems
- Product obsolescence, etc.

External Factors

- Recession
- Non-payment in other countries
- Inputs/power shortage
- Price escalation
- Accidents and natural calamities, etc.
- Changes in government policies in excise/import duties, pollution control orders, etc.

Contribution to NPAs by factors like siphoning off funds through fraud/misappropriation was less significant in comparison with other factors.

Incidence of NPAs on account of deficiencies on the part of banks such as delay in sanction and disbursement of funds whereby borrowing units are starved of funds when in need, and delay in settlement of payments/subsidies by the Government bodies was on the low side in proportion to other factors.

One of the most prominent causes for NPAs, as often observed by RBI Inspectors, is the slackness on the part of the credit management staff in their follow up to detect and prevent diversion of funds in the post-disbursement stage.

Supervisory Action that may arise on Account of High Level of NPAs

One of the trigger points in the proposed prompt corrective action (PCA) mechanism is the level of net NPAs.

When the trigger point mechanism is activated by the performance of a bank, the mandatory actions would follow by way of restriction on expansion of risk-weighted assets, submission and implementation of capital restoration plan, prior approval of RBI for opening of new branches and new lines of business paying off costly deposits and special drive to reduce the stock of NPAs, review of loan policy, etc.

The most important business implication of the NPAs is that it leads to the credit risk management assuming priority over other aspects of bank's functioning.

As already mentioned earlier, a bank with high level of NPAs would be forced to incur carrying costs on a non –income yielding assets. Other consequences would be reduction in interest income, high level of provisioning, stress on profitability and capital adequacy, gradual decline in ability to meet steady increase in cost, increased pressure on net interest margin (NIM) thereby reducing competitiveness, steady erosion of capital resources and increased difficulty in augmenting capital resources.

MANAGEMENT OF NPAs

The approach to NPA management by the banks has to be multi-pronged, necessitating varied strategies suited to different stages of the passage of credit facility. Close monitoring of the account, particularly the larger ones, is of prime importance. Emerging weakness in profitability and liquidity of corporates, recessionary tends, recovery of instalments/interest with time lag, etc. should alert and caution the banks. The loan review mechanism is to be adopted as a tool to bring about improvements in credit administration. Banks should also adopt their own risk – rating systems to assess the risk of lending. Sanctions above certain limits should be through a Committee, which can assume the status of an 'Approval Grid'. Exchange of credit information among banks would be of immense help to avoid possible NPAs. The banking system ought to be so geared that a defaulter at one place is recognised as a defaulter by the system. The system will have to provide a mechanism to ensure that the unscrupulous borrowers are unable to play one bank against the other.

Measures taken to reduce NPAs include re-schedulement, restructuring at the bank level, corporate debt restructuring, and recovery through Lok Adalats, Civil Courts, and debt recovery tribunals and compromise settlements. The recovery management received a major fillip with the enactment of the Securitisation and Reconstruction of Financial Assets and Enforcement of Security interest (SARFAESI) Act, 2002 enabling banks to realise their dues without intervention of courts and tribunals.

In view of several options available to banks for dealing with NPAs, banks have been able to recover a significant amount of NPAs (Table –14). An improved industrial climate contributed to a better recovery position. The recourse to aggressive restructuring by banks in 2004-05 also helped in reducing the level of NPAs.

Table 14
NPAs Recovered by Scheduled Commercial Banks through Various Channels

(Amount in Rs. Crore)

	2003-04			2004-05		
Item	*No. of Cases Referred**	*Amount Involved*	*Amount Recovered*	*NO. of Cases Referred**	*Amount Involved*	*Amount Recovered*
One-time Settlement/ Compromise Schemes*	139562	1510	617	132781	1332	880
Lok Adalats	186100	1063	149	185395	801	113
DRTs	7544	12305	2117	4744	14317	2688
SARFAESI Act	2661#	7847	1156	39288#	13224	2391
Asset Reconstruction Companies (ARCs)						

-: NIL Negligible

#: Number of notices issued under section 13(2) of the SARFAESI Act.

*: The scheme was operational upto July 31, 2004 and the last date for processing of application was October 31,2004.

The setting up of the Asset Reconstruction Corporation of India (ARCIL) has provided a major boost to banks' efforts to recover their NPAs. During 2004-05, several banks and certain FIs sold their NPAs to the ARCIL to the extent of Rs.15,33 crore.

In view of the future consequences an attempt is made to suggest a strategy for reducing the NPAs in the financial sector.

Table 15
Details of Financial Assets Acquired by ARCIL
(As on March 31, 2005)

Bank/FIs	*No. of Cases*	*Principal Debt Acquired*	*Interest and Other Charges*	*Total Dues Purchased*
Public Sector Banks	314	2,584	2,920	5,504
Old Private Sector Banks	11	153	84	237
New Private Sector Banks	132	4,436	4,329	8,765
Financial Institutions	12	386	450	837
Total	368	7,559	7,783	15,343

Note: Figures in Brackets are percentage variations over the previous year.

Chart I
Causes and Consequences of NPAs

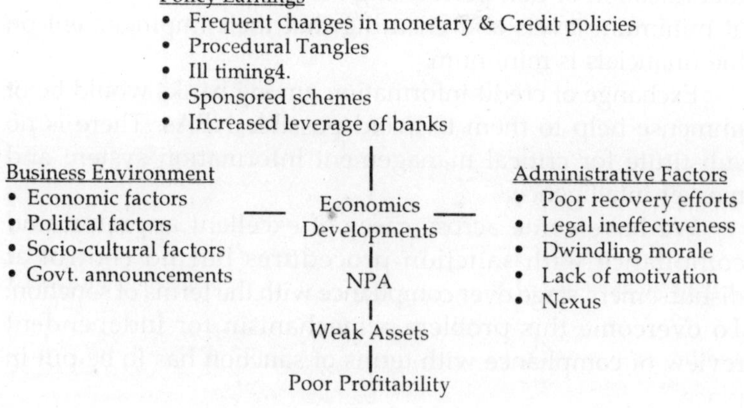

NPA Management Policy: Objectives

- To bring down gross NPA ratio to less than 5% and Net NPA ratio to less than 1.75% by March, 2006.
- Early identification of Special Mention Accounts and proper review of the same to avert their slippage into NPA category.
- Creation of Stressed Assets Management Group has led to increased focus on high value NPAs. Our top priority at

this hour revolves around arresting new NPAs and reducing existing level of NPAs.

- Prompt finalisation of CDR packages, Rehabilitation packages and their timely implementation.
- Targets to beset on recovery, write off, rephasement or recourse to CDR/ARCIL.
- Formulating a policy defining Exit Route for weak Standard Assets, such as Special Mention Accounts, before they turn non-performing.

The quality and performance of advances have a direct bearing on the profitability and disbursement mechanism; problems can still arise due to various factors. The essential component of a sound NPA management system is quick identification of non-performing advances, their containment at minimum levels and ensuring that their impingement on the financials is minimum.

Exchange of credit information among banks would be of immense help to them to avoid possible NPAs. There is no substitute for critical management information system and market intelligence.

We have come across cases of excellent appraisal and compliance with sanction procedures but no control at disbursement stage over compliance with the terms of sanction. To overcome this problem a mechanism for independent review of compliance with terms of sanction has to be put in place.

Banks should ensure that sanctioning of further credit facilities is done only at higher levels. A quick review of all documents originally obtained and their validity should be made. A phased programme of exit from the account should also be considered.

Measures Initiated by Resume Bank and Government of India for Reduction of NPAs.

The first crucial step towards meaningful NPA management is to accept that recoveries are one's own responsibility. To keep the Bank's operating cycle going smoothly, it is essential that this realisation of one's duties be transformed into deeds by resorting to various methods of recovery.

Compromise Settlement Schemes: The RBI/Government of India have been constantly goading the banks to take steps for arresting the incidence of fresh NPAs and have also been creating legal and regulatory environment to facilitate the recovery of existing NPAs of banks.

- The broad framework for compromise or negotiated settlement of NPAs advised by RBI in July 1995 continues to be in place. Banks are free to design and implement their own policies for recovery and write-off incorporating compromise and negotiated settlements with the approval of their Boards, particularly for old and unresolved cases falling under the NPA category. The policy framework suggested by RBI provides for setting up of an independent Settlement Advisory Committees headed by a retired Judge of the High Court to scrutinise and recommend compromise proposals.
- Specific guidelines were issued in May 1999 to public sector banks for one time non discretionary and non discriminatory settlement of NPAs of small sector. The scheme was operative upto September 30,2000. [Public Sector Banks recovered Rs.668 crore through compromise settlement under this scheme].
- Guidelines were modified in July 2000 for recovery of the stock of NPAs of Rs.5 crore and less as on 31 March 1997. [The above guidelines which were valid upto June 30, 2001 helped the public sector banks to recover Rs.2600 crore by September 2001].
- An OTS Scheme covering advances of Rs.25000 and below continues to be in operation and guidelines in pursuance to the budget announcement of the Hon'ble Finance Minister providing for OTS for advances up to Rs.50,000 in respect of NPAs of small/ marginal farmers are being drawn up.

NEW OTS SCHEME FOR SME

This scheme will cover;

- All NPAs in SME sector which have become doubtful for loss as on March 31, 2004 with outstanding balance of Rs.10 crore and below.
- NPAs classified as sub-standard as on 31st March 2004, which have subsequently become doubtful or loss where the outstanding balance was Rs.10 crore and below.
- Cases on which the banks have initiated action under the SARFAESI Act and also cases pending before Courts/DRTs/BIFR, subject to consent decree being obtained from the Courts/DRTs/BIFR.
- Cases of willful default, fraud and malfeasance will not be covered.

Advantages

Saves Money, Time and Manpower

Banks are mainly concerned with recovery of dues, to the maximum possible extent, at minimum expense. By entering into compromise settlements, the objective is achieved. Also, a lot of executive time is saved because most of the usual problems/delays associated with court action are avoided.

(i) *Projects a Helpful Image of the Bank:* A well-concluded compromise settlement, which results in a WIN-WIN for the Bank as well as the borrower, is a strong positive propaganda for the Bank. The impression generated is that the Bank is capable not only of sympathy, but also empathy.

(ii) *Expedites Recycling of Funds:* Compromise settlements aim at quick recovery. Recovery means funds becoming available for recycling and, additional interest generation.

(iii) *Cleanses Balance Sheet:* With the NPA level going down, and the additional funds becoming available for recycling as fresh advances, the asset quality of the Bank is bound to go up. Improved asset quality signifies higher profits by reduced provisions and increased interest income. With additions to the reserves, the capital position also improves, improving the Capital Adequacy position.

Besides the above, compromise offers the best option when:

(i) the documents are defective and cannot be rectified

(ii) security is not enforceable

(iii) forced sale is extremely difficult, or would result only in realising a paltry amount and

(iv) the borrowers become untraceable and recovery can be only though guarantors.

Disadvantages

(i) Compromise involves loss, since full recovery is not possible. In fact, full recovery is not even envisaged, but sacrifice is.

(ii) It may be viewed as a reward for default, especially if chronic default cases are settled by negotiations.

(iii) It may have a demonstrative effect, and so may vitiate the culture of repayment.

iv) There is also the possibility of misuse or, even, malafides, since assessment of situation is highly subjective.

Special Mention Accounts (SMAS)

- *Special Mention Accounts (SMAS)* is a Preventive Measure.
- Action is initiated for identification & Prevention of account from slipping to NPA status.

Genesis: The concept arose out of the findings of an analysis of NPAs done by the RBI as suggested by the Board For Financial Supervision (BFS), RBI recommended that an 'Early Alert System' or 'Early Warning System' (EWS) (which captures early warning signals) should be an integral part of a bank's risk management process.

RBI also advised that banks should introduce a new asset category between 'Standard' and 'Sub-Standard' i.e. Special Mention Accounts (SMAs).

- For own internal monitoring & follow-up – in line with international practice.
- It was decided to designate accounts as SMA under two categories.

Measures for Faster Legal Process: Lok Adalats: Lok Adalat institutions help banks to settle disputes involving accounts in "doubtful" and "loss" category, with outstanding balance of Rs.5 lakh for compromise settlement under Lok Adalats. Debt Recovery Tribunals have now been empowered to organize Lok Adalats to decide on cases of NPAs of Rs.10 lakhs and above. The public sector banks had recovered Rs.40.38 crore as on September 30, 2001, through the forum of Lok Adalat. The progress through this channel is expected to pick up in the coming years particularly looking at the recent initiatives taken by some of the public sector banks.

Debt Recovery Tribunals: The Recovery of Debts due to Banks and Financial Institutions (amendment) Act, passed in March 2000 has helped in strengthening the functioning of DRTs. Provisions for placement of more than one Recovery Officer, power to attach defendant's property/assets before judgement, penal provisions for disobedience of Tribunal's order or for breach of any terms of the order and appointment of receiver with powers of realization, management, protection and preservation of property are expected to provide necessary teeth to the DRTs and speed up the recovery of NPAs in the times to come.

Circulation of Information on Defaulters: The RBI has put in place a system for periodical circulation of details of wilful defaults of borrowers of banks and financial institutions. This serves as a caution list while considering requests for new or additional credit limits from defaulting borrowing units and also from the directors / proprietors/ partners of these entities. RBI also publishes a list of borrowers (with outstandings aggregating Rs.1 crore and above) against whom suits have been filed by banks and FIs for recovery of their funds, as on 31st March every year.

Asset Reconstruction Company: The gross NPAs in the Indian banking system are reported at about Rs.90,000 crore. A year-on-year analysis shows that while net NPAs have been decreasing, the gross NPAs have remain steady, indicating high level of provisioning but limited progress on recoveries by the banking system.

In order to accelerate NPA resolution process, Government of India enacted Securitisation and Reconstruction of Financial Assets and Enforcement of Securities Interest Act, 2002 (SARFAESI, Act 2002). The Act empowers the lenders to enforce their security interest without judicial intervention and provides for establishment and empowerments of Assets Reconstruction Companies (ARCs).

ARCs are meant to resolve NPAs acquired from the banking system by deploying specialized skill sets. Isolation of NPAs from the balance sheets of the banks/FIs enables the banks to concentrate on normal banking activities.

Asset Reconstruction Company India Ltd. (ARCIL) is the first ARC to obtain license from Reserve Bank of India. Arcil has been sponsored by State Bank of India, ICICI Bank Ltd., Industrial Development Bank of India Ltd. Punjab National Bank. ARCIL is the only operational ARC at present in India.

Legal Reforms: The Honourable Finance Minister in his recent budget speech has already announced the proposal for a comprehensive legislation on asset foreclosure and Securitisation. The Act permits banks and FIs to transfer their NPAs to Securitisation and Asset Reconstruction companies (registered under Indian companies act) RBI will be the regulator for the asset reconstruction companies as well. Asset Reconstruction & Securitisation companies will acquire the financial assets of banks/FIs by issuing bonds/debentures/securities.

Under the Act, the secured creditor can

(1) take possession/management of the secured asset for transfer by sale or lease or assignment for realisation of dues from the secured asset.

(2) appoint any person to manage the secured asset so taken.

(3) prevent transfer by sale, lease or otherwise any asset by the borrower after receipt of notice.

Corporate Debt Restructuring: Corporate Debt Restructuring mechanism has been institutionalized in 2001 to provide a timely and transparent system for restructuring of the corporate debts of Rs.20 crore and above with the banks and financial institutions. The CDR process would also enable viable corporate entities to restructure their dues outside the existing legal framework and reduce the incidence of fresh NPAs. The CDR structure has been headquartered in IDBI, Mumbai and a Standing Forum and Core Group for administering the mechanism had already been put in place. As announced by the Hon'ble Finance Minister in the Union Budget 2002-03, RBI has set up a high level Group under the Chairmanship of Shri Vepa Kamesam, Deputy Governor, RBI to review the implementation procedures of CDR mechanism and to make it more effective. The Group will review the operation of the CDR Scheme, identify the operational difficulties, if any, in the smooth implementation of the scheme and suggest measures to make the operation of the scheme more efficient.

Credit Information Bureau: Institutionalization of information sharing arrangements through the newly formed Credit Information Bureau of India Ltd. (CIBIL) is under way; RBI is considering the recommendations of the S.R. lyer Group (Chairman of CIBIL) to operationalise the scheme of information dissemination on defaults to the financial system. The main recommendations of the Group include dissemination of information relating to suit-filed accounts regardless of the amount claimed in the suit or amount of credit granted by a credit institution as also such irregular accounts where the borrower has given consent for disclosure.

Proposed Guidelines on Willful Defaults/Diversion of Funds: RBI is examining the recommendation of Kohli Group on willful defaulters, it is working out a proper definition covering such classes of defaulters so that credit denials to this group of borrowers can be made effective and criminal prosecution can be made demonstrative against willful defaulters.

Corporate Governance: A consultative Group under the chairmanship of Dr. A Ganguly was set up by the Reserve Bank to review the supervisory role of Boards of Banks and financial institutions and to obtain feedback on the functioning of the Boards vis-à-vis compliance, transparency, disclosures, audit committees etc. and make recommendations for making the role of Board of Directors more effective with a view to minimising risks and over-exposure. The Group is finalising its recommendations shortly and may come out with guidelines for effective control and supervision by bank boards over credit management and NPA prevention measures.

Integrated approach to review and management of Stressed Assets (SMAs, NPAs & AUCA):

Stressed Accounts comprise SMAs, NPAs & AUCA. A review of problem Loans/ Special Mention Accounts (SMAs) and the approach to restructuring of such Stressed Assets was undertaken. It was decided to streamline the multiple review processes and to integrate the Bank's approach to management of Stressed Assets including their restructuring.

The new integrated approach would supercede all existing instructions (Non-BIFR/ Non-CDR) on review of Problem Loans/SMAs/ NPAs (including AUCA). The new integrated approach, for review of captioned accounts, will hereafter comprise two separate tracks, as under;

(i) Review of stressed assets (which comprise of SMAs and sub-standard assets) with focus on restructuring of loans to viable units wherever feasible.

(ii) Review of Doubtful/ Loss assets and AUCA with focus on quick recovery action

CONCLUSION

The change in the policy frame work was aimed at the complete removal and or reduction of internal and external constraints in the way of smooth and efficient functioning of the banking system in achieving maximum profit. Though there are problems in effecting recoveries and write-offs and in compromise settlements, it is of utmost importance that necessary changes are brought about in the related legislation for making recovery process more smooth and less time consuming and loans create other alternative agencies for reduction of non-performing advances.

To Conclude with

Firstly, NPAs are better avoided at the initial stage of credit consideration by putting in place the rigorous and appropriate credit approval mechanism.

Secondly the mindset of the borrowers needs to change so that the return of proper utilisation of credit facilities and timely repayment is developed.

Finally, extending credit involves lenders and borrowers and both should realise their role and responsibilities. They should appreciate the difficulties of each other and should endeavour to work towards contributing to a healthy financial system.

Corporate entities must put their best foot forward in creating an environment where a healthy, vibrant and sound financial system can be built up and sustained.

REFERENCES

Ahluwalia, Montek S. (2002), *Economic Reforms in India since 1991: Has Graduatism Worked?* Journal of Economic Perspectives 16, No.3 (Summer 2002), Pages 67-68.

—(2004-05), *Reserve Bank of India Bulletin* .

—(2002), Reserve Bank of India, *"Report on Trends and Progress of Banking in India"* Mumbai.

—(1991), Ministry of Finance, Government of India, The Narasimham Committee Report; *The Banking Sector Reforms*: by Sri M. Narasimham.

N.A. Mazumdar (1996), *Financial Sector Reforms; An Exercise in Introspection,* Economic and Political Weekly, March, 23.

—(2003), Yojana, Vol.47, Oct. , No.10.

—(2002), Yojana, Vol. 46 July.

Das, Uday Kumar (2002), *Banking Reforms and Lead Bank Scheme,* Deep & Deep Publication.

Banerjee, Amlesh, & Singh, S.K.; (2002), *Banking and Financial Sector Reforms in India*, Deep & Deep Publication Pvt. Ltd..

Reddy, B. Ramchandra (ed.); (2004), *Management of Non-Performing Assets in Banks and Financial Institutions*, Serials Publication, New Delhi.

CHAPTER 18

FSRs AND INVESTMENT SCENARIO IN INDIA: EMERGING TRENDS

Mahesh Chandra Prasad

BACKGROUND

Developing countries like India suffer due to a low level of income and low level of capital formation. Despite these shortages, these countries have developed strong industrialisation and economic development programmes. Since the domestic resources to carry out such programmes have been entirely inadequate, India has had to depend on foreign capital. In India, foreign capital has been allowed in two main forms, i.e., private foreign investment and foreign aid. The improvement in FDI reflects the recent initiative taken to create an enabling environment for FDI and inclusion of new technologies and management practices.

Globalization is the absence of borders and barriers to trade between nations, but it has also been described as a shift in traditional patterns of international production, investment and trade. Globalisation is characterized by: growing worldwide interconnections, rapid, discontinuous change, growing numbers and diversity of participants and greater managerial complexity.

Financial sector reform is a broader concept. Reform consists of macro stabilization and structural reform. Macro stabilization ideals are related with the demand side of the economy whereas structural reform has to deal with the structural side of the economic problem. Foreign Direct Investment (FDI) has been considered as one of the important sources of non-debt finance. It is being sought as a means of technology inflow and of establishing inter-firm connection in a World of Multinational Corporations (MNCs) operating primarily on the basis of a network of global interconnections. The IMF definition of FDI includes as many as twelve different elements–equity capital, reinvestment earnings of foreign companies, inter-company debt transactions, short-term and long-terms loans, financial leasing, trade credits, grants, bonds, non-cash acquisition of equity, investment made by foreign venture capital investors, earnings data of indirectly held FDI enterprises, control premium and non-competition fee.

Steps of financial sector reforms and globalization undertaken need to be supplemented by public action to enhance human capabilities through investment in health, education and gender empowerment and creation of opportunities for the poor. This alone will give human face to our economic reforms as Dr. Amartya Sen has given to the welfare economics. Opening the new economy was not an easy task. Communist countries had faced severe financial crisis. This was en eye opener for India. With the tight rope walking of the Finance Minister, Dr. Man Mohan Singh, Indian Economy opened and became a partner of Globalization. Thus, capital in-flow reform, full convertability and financial sector reforms have already been introduced. Foreign investors are gaining confidence, foreign reserve is swelling and state control is gradually diluted as disinvestments.

The question arises what should India do at this juncture? There are political compulsions too. The last regime lost power because they could not bring palpable micro economic changes. Even among the urban mass unemployment and discouraging measures on savings were the signals that Indian rulers had to face in implementation of financial sector reforms. Some political parties, now having a say in present government do not want financial sector reforms at all.

THE 1991 CRISIS

During 1950-80, the economy grew just at 3.4 per cent per annum. But in the sixth and seventh plans (1980-85 and 1985-90) this figure rose to 5.3 per cent and 5.8 per cent. Total factor productivity also increased, and the 1980s saw a reduction in poverty from 40 per cent to 19 per cent of the population. But this was followed by certain adverse developments, that included the following:

Government saving deteriorated since the mid-1980s. In 1990-91, it amounted to 2.8 per cent of GDP; the fiscal deficit in the sixth plan was 8 per cent of GDP and in the seventh plan. 2 per cent revenue deficits also increased.

Through the 1980s, the balance of payments situation deteriorated and matters came to a head when, in 1990-91, international price rose sharply as a result of the Gulf war. The trade balance deteriorated sharply by $2 billion and remittances from West Asia fell. This resulted in a $3 billion decline in foreign exchange reserves, which dipped to $1.1 billion by June 1991. This had several serious consequences for the economy. There was a crisis of confidence in international economy that took the following forms. NRI deposits were heavily withdrawn. International banks stopped accepting letters of credit for imports. To revive confidence in the international arena, drastic steps had to be taken, such as the transfer of gold held by the RBI to the Bank of England to get credit.

The Government had to adopt several measures to overcome the crisis. There were in the nature of stablization policies, to control inflation and structural adjustment policies. These constituted the New Economic Policy. There was neither gradualism nor a shock therapy. This Middle path, Dr. Sen Gupta called a state driven market economy rather than a market economy with a diminishing role for the state.

The Government adopted the following additional measures: Substantial devaluation of rupee; reduction of the

Centre's fiscal deficit from the highs of 8.3 per cent of GDP in 1990-91. The government also initiated structural reforms in 1991-92. The stabilization measures led to severe import compression and recessionary conditions.

The savings rate of household sector at around 19 per cent of GDP over the last few years has been stagnant mainly due to increased inflation rates and a tapering off of the level of growth of savings. This stage of growth is called "low level equilibrium trap." Even so, the average rate of growth of around 6 per cent over the last two decades should be considered as a good achievement by the Indian planners. Besides, the other achievements of planning in India are rapid growth in the public sector and a mixed economy with a contribution of public sector of around one-fourth in the total production. The basic and capital goods industries which were well developed since the Second Five Year Plan have led India into one of the leading industrial producers in the world with a diversified industrial base and structure. It should also be noted that India has developed a high level of infrastructural facilities such as transport, communications, irrigation, railways etc. and entered into a number of high-technology industries like computers, I.T., satellite communication and non-conventional energy. The commendable performance of these industries, particularly transport, communications, energy, etc. have helped the industrialisation process in India. During the second half of the Nineties the growth of infrastructure industries was stagnant. These achievements are in no way insignificant and can be attributed mainly to the growing role of financial intermediation in India during the eighties and nineties. In recent years, more varieties of financial institutions have come up like Venture Capital Fund, factoring agencies, securities firms etc. The new economy of the new millennium is characterised by the growth of knowledge based industries, e-commerce, I.T., multi-media, bio-tech industries, etc. Poverty ratio was brought down to 26 per cent of the population due to a number of poverty alleviation programmes. India became a leader in I.T. software and

Table 1
Selected Investment Avenues (2005)

Name of Security	*Rate of Interest Per Annum*	*Income-tax Concession*
Post Office Saving Bank accounts	3.5%	Exempt under Sec.10(15)(ii)
Saving deposits of banks	3.5%	- do -
Public Provident Fund Accounts (PPF)	8.0%	Exempt under Sec.10 and 88 upto Rs. 60,000 P.A.
Post Office Time Deposit Accounts	6.25 to 7.5%	- do -
Bank Fixed Deposits	4.5 to 6.25%	- do -
Post Office Recurring Deposit Accounts	7.5%	- do -
National Savings Scheme (NSS), 1992	8.0%	Investment and income completely exempt (Section 88 and 80L)
6-year Post Office Monthly Income Scheme	8.0% (Payable monthly)	Qualifying for deduction under Sec.80L within limit of Rs. 12,000
Indira Vikas Patra@ (period 7.25 years)	@	No
Kisan Vikas Patra (Period of 8 years & 7 months)	N.A.	No
NSC VIII Issue	8.0%	Eligible under Section 88L
Units of UTI/Schemes of mutual funds	Variable	Included in 80L exemption
Equity shares of companies	Variable	1. Dividend in the hands of investors is tax-free 2. Provision for a tax rebate at 20% on any investment in eligible quity linked schemes of Rs.10,000 maximum j a rebate of Rs.2,000
Convertible Debentures	Variable	Taxable
Non-Convertible Debentures	- Do -	Taxable
Fixed deposits of companies	11 to 14%	Taxable
Preference Shares (Redeemable or cumulative)	14 j 15%	Dividend exempted under Sec. 80L
Comulative Convertible Preference Shares (CCP)	10%	- do -
Bonds of Public Sector Companies (PSU)	9% - 10.5%	Taxable
Senior Citizens Saving Scheme	9%	Taxable

@ This Scheme was discontinued in July 2000. Rates on savings schemes of P.O. were lowered by one-half per cent from March 2002, and lowered again 2003.

Source: Investment Management, V.A. Avadhani, Himalaya Publishing House.

knowledge based services. India has build up huge foreign exchange reserves and enough foodstocks. Inflation rate was brought down considerably to 4-5 per cent annum. These achievements cannot be set aside as small and insignificant, at the time of the beginning of Tenth Plan.

The data in Table 1 presented show that the various instruments can be classified by risk-return characteristics and that the returns are variable on these instruments as also the tax treatment given by the Government in respect of these instruments. In January 2000, the interest rates on Savings media of the Govt. were lowered to reduce the cost of borrowing by the Govt. The interest rates in general were sought to be brought down to be in tune with lower inflation rates. In October 2001, Bank rate was lowered to be the level of 6.5 per cent and further to 6 per cent by stages in 2003. The deposit and lending rates also fell accordingly in respect of banks.

GROSS DOMESTIC INVESTMENT AND GROSS DOUBLE SAVINGS

The Household Sector Savings rate was 15.7 percent during the eighties and increased to 19.1 per cent during 1992-93 to 1996-97 and stood at 19 per cent in 1997-98 and at 24.3 per cent in 2003-04.

Table 2
Savings and Investment (As Percentage of GDP)

	1997-98	*1999-2000*	*2003-04*
Gross Domestic Saving			
Household Sector	19.0	19.8	24.3
Private Corporate Sector	4.3	3.8	4.1
Public Sector of which	1.4	–	- 0.3
– Public Authorities	(-) 2.1	(-) 1.2	–
– Non-Dept. Enterprises	3.5	–	–
Total	24.7	22.3	28.1
Net Capital Inflow	2.6	1.0	-1.8
Gross Domestic Investment	26.2	23.3	26.3

Source: Investment Management, V.A. Avadhani, Himalaya, Publishing House.

The rise on this account was mainly due to a large increase in the Household sector savings in financial form in the form of bank deposits; P.F. and Small Savings due to financial reforms. Similarly, there was a sharp rise in the savings and investment in the private corporate sector from below 2 per cent during the Eighties to 4.3 per cent in 1997-98 and stood at 3.4 per cent in 2002-2003. The investment rate was 4.4 per cent in the Eighties and savings rate was less than 2 per cent. In the Nineties, the investment rate rose to of 7.4 per cent. The public sector savings rate was low both in the Eighties and Nineties. The rate of public savings declined from 2.8 per cent during the Eighties to 1.6 per cent during 1991-92 to 1996-97, but stood at -0.3 in 2003-04. The public sector investment rate similarly declined from 10.3 per cent in the Eighties to 8.4 per cent to 7.5 per cent during 1993-94 to 1997-98. Gross Domestic Investment as a percentage of GDP was 24.8 per cent during 1993-94 to 1997-98 and stood at 26.2 per cent in 1997-98 and 23.3 per cent in 1999-2000. The Savings and Investment rate declined in 1999-2000, as seen from the attached Table, despite the rise in GDP at constant prices to 4 per cent in 2002-03 and 8.5 per cent in 2003-04 as compared to 5 percent in 1997-98 and around 4-6 per cent in last three years.

MARKET CONDITIONS AND ITS IMPACT ON INVESTMENT

Investment is motivated by market conditions. The primary market conditions are depicted over a period of five years both in respect of public issues and right issues. The principles of investment in any market are as follows: (Avadhani, 2004)

(i) Buy low and sell high. Buy low and sell only when the purchase price plus some gain is available, when the market is declining, buy lowest and sell at least to cover the purchase price.

(ii) When trading, a margin of 10 per cent gain or less or stop, loss order can not be set at 10 per cent to get into investment.

(iii) In a portfolio of shares, sell only overpriced share of which the fundamentals have weakened and bottomlines are expected to decline.

(iv) Sell, to start with, upcoming companies in the portfolio even when no profit can be booked. Short-term losses can be booked to show against short-term for tax purposes.

Indian economy today is characterized by an environment of confidence, positive business expectations, a renewal of rule-based fiscal consolidation, stable and orderly financial markets and institutions and progressive integration with the global economy. Real GDP growth for 2005-06 has been conservatively projected at around 7 per cent and more recently, revised upwards to a range of 7 to 7.5 per cent. Despite the sustained strength of export performance, the merchandise trade deficit is expected to be somewhat higher in 2005-06 than in the previous year, mainly on account of substantially higher oil prices and non-oil import demand for investment.

For the year as a whole, while invisibles may finance a large part of the enlarged trade deficit, the current account deficit is expected to widen during 2005-06 but to remain within acceptable limits that can be financed by normal capital flows. The inflation is expected to lie in the range of 5.0–5.5 per cent. Consolidation of Central Government finance is the goal of fiscal policy at the centre–the targets are : the gross fiscal deficit of 3 per cent of GDP and the elimination of the revenue deficit by 2008-09. The fiscal position of State Governments also continues to undergo slight correction in terms of key deficit indicators. (Dr. Y.V. Reddy, Governor of RBI, In an International Symposium).

Sri P. Chidambaram, Honorable Finance Minister, focuses on the investments in the various sectors to sharpen our economy:

"The policies adopted since 1991 have brought considerable benefits and strengths to the Indian economy. What the new Government will do now and what I will do now, is to factor in the experience gained during the last thirteen years. I have reason to believe that the economy is in a resilient mode–in terms of growth, inflation and balance of payments. And I am confident that there is great scope for consolidating the growth momentum with special emphasis on agriculture, the manufacturing sector and employment. These three sectors require and other sectors also require, massive investment–both public investment and private investment. It will be my endeavour to promote investment which, I believe is the key to growth, to jobs and to incomes."

FOREIGN FINANCIAL INVESTMENT

The Indian capital market has undergone significant changes under the liberalization and globalization policies adopted by the government. Opening up of the economy for foreign investment, liberal import technology, lowering the tariffs and other tax rates, giving greater role for private sector, measures to control fiscal deficits, decision on conversion of rupee on current account, limiting the FERA restrictions and amendment of MRTP Act are the major components of the changes affected by the Government.

FDI is permitted in India in the forms through financial collaborations, joint ventures and technical collaborations, capital market via Euro issues and through private placements. Similarly in some of the industrial sectors the FDI is not permitted in India such as arms and ammunition, atomic energy, railway transport, coal and lignite and mining of iron, manganese, chrome, gypsum, sulphur, gold, diamonds, copper and zinc and the like. Generally in India, foreign investors are attracted by many of the opportunities which indicate FDI performance index over the years improved investment climate and better growth prospects. The following are some of the opportunities for foreign direct investors to invest in India :

(i) Largest developing economy in the world.

(ii) Place for access to the vast domestic and South Asian Market.

(iii) No restriction to using foreign brand name.

(iv) Corporate tax holidays for 5 years for 100 per cent export oriented units in export processing zone.

(v) English is widely spoken and understood.

(vi) Changes for growing consumer market.

(vii) Opportunies for getting skilled managerial personnel at competitive price.

(viii) Scope for well developed rural development infrastructure

(ix) Liberal government policy environment i.e., freedom of entry on investment and choice of technology.

(x) Sophisticated financial sector covers wide capital market transactions.

The efforts in this direction have paved the way to get the Indian economy integrated with international market. This has also resulted in breaking the age old structure of the capital market and improving the competitive spirit of industrial and service sectors. The active role assigned to the Foreign Institutional Investors (FIIs) is to be justified from the point of view of economic development. The domestic savings will not be sufficient enough to achieve this target. It has become imperative in this situation that the economy shows interest in attracting maximum foreign investments.

The investment from abroad can be of two types: (i) Direct Investment, and (ii) Portfolio Investment. The Direct Investment flows into the economy through RBI automatic route, SIA/FIFs route and NRIs. Foreign direct investment is possible under two categories i.e. upto 40 per cent in selected industries and upto 100 per cent in export oriented industries and stock companies. Portfolio Investment is managed through Foreign Institutional Investors, Euro-equities and Offshore funds.

The foreign investment in India started gaining momentum with the permission granted by SEBI, to operate foreign financian institutions in India in 1993. These foreign institutions like pension funds, mutual funds, investment trusts, assets management companies and Institutional portfolio managers have been operating in all instruments in the money and capital markets abroad.

Foreign investment flows moderated during May-July 2004, but bounced back in the second half of the year (Table-3). The slowdown in the first half was on account of global uncertainties caused by hardening of crude oil prices and the upturn in the interest rate cycle. The resumptión in the next FII in –flows to India from August 2004 continued till the end of 2004-05.

Table 3
Foreign Investment Flows to India

US$ Million

Item	*2004-05*	*2003-04*	*2002-03*
Direct Investment (I+II+III)	5536	4673	5035
Equity (a+b+c+d+e)	3363	2387	2764
(a) Government (SIA/FIPB)	1062	928	739
(b) RBI	1259	534	739
(c) NRI	–	–	–
(d) Acquisition of shares	930	735	916
(e) Equity capital of unincorporated bodies	112	190	190
Re-invested earnings	1816	1798	1833
Other capital	357	488	438
Portfolio Investment (a+b+c)	8909	11377	979
(a) GDRs/ADRs	613	459	600
(b) FIIs	8280	10,918	377
(c) Off-shore funds and others	16	–	2
Total (A+B)	14445	16050	6014

Source: Annual Report 2004-05, RBI, Mumbai.

FDI POLICY IN INDIA

India has one of the most transparent and liberal FDI regimes among the emerging and developing countries. By FDI regime we mean those restrictions that apply to foreign nationals and entities but not to Indian nationals and Indian owned entities. The differential treatment is limited to a few entry rules, spelling out the proportion of equity that the foreign entrant can hold in an Indian company or business. There are a few banned sectors and some sectors with limits on foreign equity proportion. The entry rules are clear and well defined and equity limit for foreign investment in selected sectors is quite explicit and well known.

Most of the manufacturing sectors have been for many years on the 100 per cent automatic route. Foreign equity is limited only in production of defence equipment (26 per cent), telecom (49 per cent), civil aviation (49 per cent), insurance (26 per cent), oil and gas pipelines (51 per cent), banking (49 per cent), airports (74 per cent), Govt. owned petroleum refineries (26 per cent), print media (26 per cent), and diamonds and precious stones (74 per cent). India also has a clear policy of FDI in services, with 100 per cent automatic entry into many services such as construction, townships, resorts, hotels, tourism, films, business services and consultancy, medical health, and courier services etc. In case of infrastructure, highways and roadways, ports, inland waterways and transport etc. are on the 100 per cent automatic route.

Given the above foreign equity conditions, a foreign company can set up a registered company in India and operate under the same laws, rules and regulations as Indian-owned company would. Unlike many countries including China, India extends national treatment to foreign investors. There is absolutely no discrimination against foreign invested companies registered in India.

DOMESTIC POLICY IN INDIA

The domestic policy framework affects all investment, whether the investor is Indian or foreign. Among the policy problems that have been identified by surveys as acting as additional hurdles for FDI are laws, regulatory systems and Govt. monopolies that do not have contemporary relevance. For example, labour laws, rules and procedures have led to a deterioration in the work culture and the comparative advantage that is even beginning to be recognised by responsible trade unions. Further, SSI reservations limit the possibility of entering labour intensive sector for export. These two policy constraints are particularly relevant for export-oriented FDI. More flexible labour laws that improve work culture and enhance productivity and SSI de-reservations will help attract employment generating FDI inflows of the kind seen in South East Asia in the 70s and 80s and in China since the 90s. Likewise, the Outdated Food Price Order (FPO) and Prevention of Food Adulteration Act are a major hurdle on FDI in food processing. The latter makes even a technical or minor violation subject to criminal liability. The Essential Commodities Act adds to the difficulty of entering the food processing industry by making the procurement, storage and transport of agricultural produce. The Urban Land Ceiling Acts and Rent Control Acts in States are serious constraint on the entire real estate sector. This is another sector that has attracted large amounts of FDI in many countries including China. These Acts need to be replaced if a construction boom is to be initiated that would reverse the decline in overall investment, attract FDI, and generate employment. Rent control is a state subject and each state would have to reform its Rent Control Act. Similarly, strategy and implementation problems connected with disinvestment created greater uncertainty and increased policy/regulatory risk, resulting in a lack of interest of FDI investors in bidding for these companies. Likewise, Special Economic Zones (SEZs) are still not fully at par with the Export Zones of China with respect to labour intensive production.

GROWTH AND PATTERN OF FDI IN INDIA

In the post-reforms period, policies have emphasized upon greater encouragement and mobilization of non-debt creating private capital inflows for reducing reliance on debt flows as the chief source of external resources. Progressively liberal policies adopted in this regarded have led to increasing inflows of foreign investment in the country, both in terms of FDI as well as portfolio investment. Table-4 gives the composition of foreign investment inflows in India.

In India, annual aggregate foreign investment inflows varied between US $ 4 to 6 billion during the period 1993-94 to 2001-02 except for 1998-99 when due to Asian crisis foreign investment inflows virtually stopped. As far FDI is concerned, its share in total foreign investment inflows was 96 per cent during 1991-92, which declined to 43 per cent during 1995-96, but increased to 65 per cent during 2001-02. Hence, we find a fluctuating trend of FDI's share in total foreign investment inflows. Table-4 shows the trend of FDI inflows by host region/economy during 1994-2004.

Table 4
Country-wise FDI Inflows to India

(Rs. in Crores)

Name of the Countries	2002-03	2003-04	2004-05	% of FDI on Total Inflows	% of Increase/ Decrease (2002-05)
Mauritius	534	381	820	35.34	53.56
USA	268	297	469	20.21	75.00
UK	224	157	84	3.62	62.50
Germany	103	69	143	6.16	38.83
Netherlands	94	197	196	8.45	108.51
Japan	66	67	122	5.26	84.85
France	53	34	44	1.90	16.98
Singapore	39	15	64	2.76	64.10
Switzerland	35	5	64	2.76	82.86
South Korea	15	22	14	0.60	6.67
Others	227	218	300	12.94	32.16
Total	1658	1462	2320	100.00	39.93

Source: Yojana, July 2006

Global FDI inflows went down by 41 per cent in 2001 and a further 21 per cent in 2002 to $ 651 billion which is the half the peak in 2000. Some of the important factors responsible for this significant downturn are weak economic growth, crumbling stock markets and institutional factors such as the winding down of the privatisation in several countries (WIR-2003). The United States and United Kingdom alone accounted for 54 per cent of the fall in the countries with reduced inflows. In 2002 inflows in developed world declined by 22 per cent, while decline in the developing countries was 23 per cent. However, inflows in Asia and Pacific fell only a little due to higher flows to China. As far as India is concerned, share in global FDI inflows is very much insignificant and it varies between 0.1-0.7 per cent during 1991-02. Likewise among developing countries, India's share varies between 0.9-2.1 per cent of total FDI of developing countries and among South East Asian economies between 1.6-3.8 per cent. However, total FDI inflows in India was at a peak level during 1997. Table gives FDI inflows in some of Asian economies. In 2002, developing economies of Asia accounted 13.6 per cent of total global FDI inflows. China has been the largest recipient of FDI inflows among developing economies of Asia with its share in total FDI of these economies. India, though way behind China in attracting FDI inflows, has marginally improved its share in total FDI inflows of developing economies from 1.1 per cent during 1991-96 to 2.1 per cent during 2002. A sharp rise in volume of FDI inflows in the Indian economy in 2001-02 shows its growing attractiveness as an investment destination.

In comparison to other competing countries, India's measured FDI as a per cent of GDP is quite low. In terms of GDP based on purchasing power parity (PPP) India is the 4th largest economy in the world, but unfortunately share of its FDI stocks in GDP is only 5.1 per cent during 2002. On the other hand, Singapore has attracted, highest FDI inflows which is equal to 137 per cent of its GDP, followed by Malaysia (59.4 per cent), Vietnam (50.2 per cent), China (36.2 per cent), Indonesia (32.2 per cent), and so on during 2002.

Table 5

FDI Inflows and Its Trends in India (Million Dollars)

Year	*FDI Inflows*	*% of Increase/ Decrease*	*Trend*
1994-1995	1314	–	1574
1995-1996	2144	63.16	1987
1996-1997	2821	31.57	2400
1997-1998	3557	26.09	2813
1998-1999	2462	-30.78	3225
1999-2000	2155	-12.46	3638
2000-2001	4029	86.96	4051
2001-2002	6130	52.14	4464
2002-2003	5035	-17.86	4877
2003-2004	4673	-7.18	5290

Source: Yojana, July 2006

REASONS FOR LOW FDI IN INDIA

In general any new investment decision goes through four stages in the decision-making process and action cycle namely, screening, planning, implementing, operating and expanding.

The biggest barrier for India is at the first, screening stage itself in the action cycle. Often India loses at the screening stage itself. This is primarily because we do not get across effectively to the decision-making stage of corporate entities where a final decision is taken. China and India are the giants of the developing world. Both enjoy healthy rates of economic growth. But there are significant differences in their FDI performance. FDI inflows to China grew from $3.5 billion in 1990 to $52.7 billion in 2002. Those to India rose from $0.4 billion to $5.5 billion during the same period. China attracted seven times more FDI than India in 2002, 3.2 per cent of its GDP compared to 1.1 per cent for India. In UNCTAD's FDI performance index, China ranked 54th and India 122nd in 1999-2001. In India, FDI has been much less important in driving India's export growth, except in information technology. FDI in Indian manufacturing has been and remains domestic market-seeking. FDI accounted for only 3 per cent of India's exports in the early 1990. Even today, FDI is estimated to account for less than 10 per cent of India's manufacturing exports (WIR-2003).

One important reason of low FDI inflow is the development strategy followed in India. India for a long time followed an import-substitution policy and relied on domestic resource mobilization and domestic firms as a strategy of industrial development (Bhalla 2002), encouraging FDI only in higher technology activities. Also, India allowed FDI long before but did not take comprehensive steps towards liberalization until 1991 (Nagaraj 2003). In India, a tradition of entrepreneurship has spawned a broad based domestic enterprise sector (Huang and Khanna 2003). This combines with the necessary legal and institutional infrastructure and a restrictive FDI policies followed until the 1990s. As a result, TNC participation in production has often taken externalized forms such as licensing and contractual arrangements. Even after a significant liberalization of FDI policies, internalization is not necessarily dominant. The time taken for application / bidding/approval of FDI projects in India was too long. However, this leads to loss of investors' confidence despite promises of a considerable market size (Mckinsy, 2001). Further, poor infrastructure affects the productivity of the economy as a whole. It also reduces the comparative advantage of industries that are more intensive in the use of such infrastructure. Inadequate and poor quality roads, railroads and posts however raise export costs vis-à-vis global competitors having better quality and lower cost infrastructure. On this ground India is handicapped in attracting export oriented FDI. Laws, rules, regulations to infrastructure are sometimes missing or unclear e.g. LNG and the power sector is beset with multiple problems such as State monopoly, bankruptcy and weak regulators (Mckinsy 2001).

CONCLUSION

Foreign direct investment brings in investible resources to host countries, introduces modern technologies and provides access to export markets. The MNCs are the driving force behind FDI. They have large internal markets, access to which is available only to affiliates. They enjoy considerable advantages in creating an initial export base for new entrants. FDI directly impacts on output growth in India by augmenting the available investible capital. However, one important impact of FDI is externalities leading to higher efficiency and productivity. FDI services to increase competition in markets, bring new technology into India, and foster skill acquisition amongst domestic labour. FDI provides a platform for global production chains which enhances export growth rate in our country. However, on the policy front India has one of the most transparent and liberal FDI regimes among the emerging and developing countries. In most of the manufacturing sectors 100 per cent FDI is permitted under the automatic route. Even then, India's share in global FDI inflows is very insignificant and varies between 0.1 to 0.7 per cent of global FDI only. Among South Asian economies its share varies between 1.6 to 3.8 per cent and among developing economies it varies between 0.9 to 2.1 per cent.

There has been significant change in the direction of FDI in India. Industries such as computers, engineering, services, and electronics and electrical equipment are dominating in attracting FDI, while domestic appliances, food and dairy products are less attractive activities for FDI. However, in India FDI has been less important in driving India's export growth except in information technology. The manufacturing sector has been domestic market-seeking. On the other hand, FDI has contributed to the rapid growth of China's merchandise exports, at an annual rate of 15 per cent between 1989 and 2001. Hence, it is required that the existing strategy for attracting FDI should be overhauled. The relative emphasis must shift from a broad approach to one of targeting specific companies in specific sectors. At the same time, the SEZs should be developed as the most competitive destination for export related FDI in the world as found in China. On the policy front, there is a need for careful design of FDI policies. Ideally policies should be designed to attract sufficient FDI, extract all benefits offered and to ensure that they operate with a framework similar to international best practices (Jeromi, 2003). At the same time, there is the need of real sector reforms, development of infrastructure and privatization of public enterprises for the larger flow of FDI in India. Once an atmosphere is created for the economic principles to guide investment activity, the FDI will naturally flow to the country.

PROBLEMS PERSIST

The above measures, being more comprehensive than ever before, changed the macroeconomic picture considerably. Consequently, there was impressive and significant progress in all sectors. But some problems persist, such as budgetary deficits and current account balance and a debt burden which is 32.9 per cent of GDP. The strong points of the socialist experience which worked to the country's benefit are : The rates of savings and investment have been much higher than earlier, but the investments in infrastructure have to be stepped up to considerable desire to the full benefit of liberalization.

It is also needed to eliminate the fear of indigenous companies that the entry of multinationals with specialized management skill and technologies would adversely affect their working, through appropriate measures.

It is also desirable to ensure that the funds flown from outside is channelised to raise the standard of living of the masses and bring the economy at par with other developed economics. The initiative of the government in building up adequate infrastructural facilities including skilled labour, power, transport, communication and raw materials would result in creating a favourable environment for foreign investors. The decision to implement capital account convertibility may also result in creating a favourable atmosphere for the Indian companies to make the Global Depository Receipts route conducive to reaching the international capital market.

REFERENCES

Avadhani, V.A., (2004), *"Investment Management"*, Himalaya Publishing House, Mumbai.

Bagchi, A.K. (1999), *"Globalisation, Liberalisation and Vulnerability of India and Third World"*, EPW, 34 (45), Nov. 6.

Baker, Chris (2000), *"Opportunity and Danger: Globalisation, States and Politics in 1990s Asia"*, Conference on 'Globalisation, Income Distribution and Structural Change', Chennai, 14-17 Dec.

Bhattacharyya, B. (1994), *"FDI in India"*, Foreign Trade Review, pp.308-09.

Confederation of Indian Industry (2002), *"From Crumbs to Riches: Reorienting Foreign Direct Investment in India"*, New Delhi.

Dutt, R. and Sundharam, KPM (2003), *"Indian Economy"*, S. Chand and Company Ltd., New Delhi.

FICCI (2001), *"The Experience of Foreign Direct Investment in India'*, April, New Delhi.

Gandhi, Jagdish (2001), *"Dynamics of Global Economy"*, Southern Economist, May, pp.11-14.

Gopinath, T.(1997), *"Foreign Investment in India: Policy, Issues, Trends and Prospects"*, RBI Occasional Papers, Vol.18, Nos. 2&3, June-Sept.

—(2003), Government of India, *"Economic Survey-2002-03"*, Ministry of Finance and Company Affairs, Economic Division, Government of India, New Delhi.

—(2003), Government of India , *"Report of the Steering Group on Foreign Direct Investment"*, Planning Commission, Academic Foundation, New Delhi.

Jain, Rajiv (1994), *Guide on Foreign Collaboration: Policies and Procedures, Indian Investment Publication*, New Delhi.

Jeromi, P.D. (2003), *"FDI in India: Policy, Trends and Impact"*, in Raj Kapila & Uma Kapila (ed.), Economic Development in India, Vol.62, Academic Foundation, New Delhi.

Khor, M. (1996), *"Globalisation: Implications for Development Policy"*, Third World Resurgence, No.74.

Kumar, Nagesh (2002), *Globalisation and the Quality of FDI*, Oxford University Press, New Delhi.

Kurien, C.T. (1994), *Global Capitalism and the Indian Economy*, Orient Longman, Hyderabad.

Majumdar, Chhibber (1998), *"Are Liberal Foreign Investment Policies Good for India"*, EPW, Feb.7, pp.267-70.

Misra, S.K. and V.K. Puri (2003), *"Indian Economy"*, Himalaya Publishing House, Delhi.

Nayyar, Deepak (1998), *"Globalisation: What Does It Mean for Development/"*, Bibek Debroy (ed.), *Challenges of Globalisation*, Konark Publishers Pvt.Ltd., Delhi.

—(1998), NCAER, *"Foreign Direct Investment in India"*, March, New Delhi.

Paul, M. Thomas and Jamkhandi (1999), *Role of FDI in Developing Countries*, National Institute of Bank Management, Pune.

Prasad, H. and Ashok Chandra (1994), *"Foreign Investment in India: Some Basic Facts and Issues"*, Foreign Trade Review, pp.331-53.

Ray, Alok (1993), *"External Sector Liberalisation in India"*, EPW, Oct.2, p.2161.

—(2001), RBI , *"Handbook of Statistics on Indian Economy"*, Bombay.

—(2002), RBI , *"Report on Currency and Finance"*, Bombay.

Schuuman, F.J. (2001), *"Globalisation and Development Studies: Challenges for the 21st Century"*, Vister, New Delhi.

Singh, Kavaljit (1998), *"A Citizens' Guide to the Globalisation of Finance"*, Madhyam Books, Delhi.

Singh, R.K. (2005), *"Globalisation and Contemporary Economic Scenario"*, article by S.M. Jawed Akhtar, Globalisation and FDI- the Indian Experience, Abhijeet Publication, New Delhi.

Sinha, Yashwant (2000), *"India has Emerged as an Attractive Destination for FDI"* in Raj Kapila & Uma Kapila (ed.), Economic Developments in India, Vol.30, Academic Foundation, New Delhi.

Subramanian, K.K. et al. (1996), *"Foreign Collaboration Under Liberalisation Policy*- Pattern of FDI and Technology Transfer in Indian Industry Since 1991", Development Research Group, Study No.14, RBI, Mumbai.

Thomas, T. (2000), *"Stepping Up FDI"*, Business Standard, Vol.VII, No.115, Aug.30, New Delhi.

—(2003), UNCTAD, *"World Investment Report"*, Bookwell, Delhi.

—*(1996), World Bank*, "India: Five Years of Stabilization and Reform and the Challenges Ahead", Washington, D.C.

—(2002), World Bank, *"Globalisation, Growth and Poverty"*, The World Bank Policy Research Report, Washington, D.C.

—(2004), World Bank, *"World Development Report", Washington, D.C.*

CHAPTER 19

EMERGING DIMENSIONS OF FINANCIAL INNOVATIONS IN INDIAN BANKING SECTOR

M.M. Nazri
Md. Imteyaz Hassan

INTRODUCTION

The banking sector in India has undergone a remarkable change over the last few years due to the changes in economic policies and with the implementation of the financial sector reforms in India. The landmarks in banking reforms were the introduction of prudential norms, partial deregulation of interest rates, reduction in directed lending and the entry of private sector banks.

The initial reforms in 1992-93 aimed at bringing in transparency in the banking system. Introduced in April 1992, the prudential norms involved a new look at asset classification, income recognition, provisioning of bad debts, capital adequacy, etc. Income is now viewed in terms of realization rather than on accrual basis. The weaknesses of Banks and non-banking financial institutions in terms of low competitive efficiency, productivity and low profitability of their assets have forced them to enter into new areas of non-bank financial services since the early eighties.

The Chakravarty Committee (1985) and Narasimham Committee (1991) have recommended the need for market-oriented financial system, where banks and non-banking financial institutions can function with greater autonomy accountability and efficiency. The Narasimham Committee was of the opinion that there should be prudential guidelines granting greater autonomy so that these institutions operate with adequate precautions.

As per the international norms, a capital adequacy ratio of 8% of the risk-weighted assets was advised partial privatization of nationalized banks is yet another revolutionary step taken by the government. Rather depending on government infusion of funds to meet adequacy ratios, these banks can now tap the capital market. With a view to improving operational efficiency and profitability of public sector banks, in January 1993, the doors were thrown open to private players. In addition, new vistas such as leasing, project finance and securities trading were now opened to banks. These new private sector banks have shown encouraging results.

The banking sector has thus undergone a major change in the Indian economy. The dormant sector has shown great vibrancy in absorbing the changes of the reforms. Public sector Banks like the State Bank of India and the Oriental Bank of Commerce have successfully tapped the capital market in pursuit of capital adequacy. In addition, with some amount of capital infusion by the government, 14 out of the 28 public sector banks have achieved this adequacy. Banking reforms have not yet completed a full circle, there is much more to go. Further, deregulation in interest rates, freedom to offer new products and enter new businesses, offer more investment avenues.

PRIVATE SECTOR BANKS

Special importance on banking efficiency and better customer service, the key recommendations of the Narasimham Committee has resulted in the entry of new players in the banking arena. The new private banks, which their customer friendly approach, have been able to win many clients and have started making profits in the very first year of operation. These banks operate in a highly sophisticated environment and their presence is confined to the metros and semi-metros.

Once the banking reforms were announced, majority of the financial institutions like ICICI, IDBI, UTI, HDFC, etc. made a foray into banking. Even among the NBFCs, while 20th century finance has set-up Centurion Bank. These institutions, with their influence, easily get corporate clients and the corporates are more than willing because of the quality of service, highly professional approach and capability to offer innovative products.

INNOVATIONS IN BANKING SERVICES

It is no longer limited to borrowing and lending of funds by banks. In recent years banks have been seen diversifying into new areas to widen their business horizons. In the changing economic scenario, with increase in financial deregulation and industrial liberalization, the role of the financial sector is increasing manifold. The financial service sector has thus emerged as the fastest growing sunrise industry. With the onset of liberalization process, several new institutions have appeared on the financial scene. These institutions like merchant banks, leasing companies, venture capital companies, factoring companies and mutual funds, etc. have expanded the range of financial services available.

Banks, investment companies, accounting firms, financial institutions offer numerous financial services to business concerns. A few financial innovations, which are emerging as potent instruments at the disposal of commercial banks and investment financing institutions in India, are:

(1) Mutual Funds

(2) Leasing

(3) Merchant Banking

(4) Factoring

(5) Credit Cards

(6) Credit Rating

(7) Commercial Paper
(8) Housing Finance
(9) Venture Capital
(10) Merchant Banking

Merchant banking is financial intermediaries. They act as intermediaries in the process of transfer of capital from those who own it to those who use it. However, they do this with a difference. The main strength of merchant bankers is not provision of finance but providing the whole range of inputs of innovative financial services, technical and managerial knowledge and competence and expert advice on legal and industrial matters needed by the user of funds for establishing a new industrial unit or for diversifying/modernizing a running industrial unit or for merger/acquiring another industrial unit or for entering into a foreign collaboration/launching of a joint venture abroad.

Merchant banking business in India developed on the traditional European pattern and remained till recently an adjunct to the main business of loan operations of Commercial/Development banks. After that many other institutions joined, notably, the State Bank of India, Bank of Baroda, Canara Bank, ICICI and some of leading brooking firms. Merchant banking divisions of commercial banks have been active in a narrow range of traditional merchant banking activities akin to or arising out of their major commercial banking business. The availability of funds temporarily at lower cost attracts banks to act as manager to the new issues. The commercial banks are also engaged in underwriting business. They are also actively, involved in arranging Euro-currency loans and export finance. Some of them (notably the State Bank of India) act as advisers to major borrowers during major foreign loan negotiations.

With a view to strengthening the organizational and managerial capabilities, broad base the resources position, enlarge the scope of operations and activities and to offer more specialised services with professional expertise and skills, the erstwhile Merchant Banking Divisions of the emotionalized banks have started forming independent subsidiary companies. State Bank of India (SBI) Finance; Indian Bank-Ind Bank Finance, Canara Bank-Canfin; Punjab National Bank-PNB CAPS, etc. formed the first of such subsidiary company.

Development banks, i.e. IDEL, IFCI and ICICI are involved in the primary securities market due to their function of underwriting of issues of new industrial projects financed by them. They also subscribe to shares and debenture issues supporting expansion and diversification plans of companies. While development banks are active in the primary market, the GIC, LIC and UTI operate in the secondary market. These institutions inspite of their more than two decades of existence are neither a dominant outlet for savings of the household sector nor a major source of finance for industrial units.

MUTUAL FUNDS

Mutual Funds originated in the U.K. during the last century essentially as a means of mobilising household savings for housing finance. Now these are important elements in the development of capital markets world over. Mutual Fund is an ideal alternative for a small saver who is handicapped with inadequate resources for diversified portfolio, lack of time, expertise and market knowledge.

A mutual fund organization is a little more than a collection of small investors; however, own not the pool of shares but the shares of the fund, sharing costs, profits and losses of the fund. The first Mutual Fund in India was established in 1964 by UTI, but the movement gained momentum only in 80s. Now the Indian money market is flooded with mutual funds catering to the needs of varied interest of savers. These includes SBI MF; Can Bank MF, UCMF (Dhamasri-Dhjanaraksha Dhanavrithi) and Mutual Funds of Bank of Baroda Punjab National Bank and GIC Mutual Funds.

The Abid Hussain Committee recommended opening of mutual funds to the private sector in tune with the experience of the Western Countries. As a result, various mutual funds set-up by the private sector include Twentieth Century Mutual, Tata Mutual Fund, and JM Mutual Fund besides foreign tie-ups for inland schemes are by Alliance Capital Mutual Fund of U.S.A. and ICICI Mutual Funds with J.P. Morgan Investment Management of U.S.A., etc. The enormous growth of mutual funds compelled the government to set-up SEBI to regulate the same for their healthy growth on prudential norms.

With a view to providing an additional short-term avenue to investors and to bring money market instruments within the reach of individuals and small bodies, the RBI has proposed a scheme for a new type of Mutual Fund by scheduled commercial banks and their subsidiaries. The new money market mutual funds are a special genre of funds investing only in high quality money market instruments of a short-term nature. In an increasingly tightening money market, the few existing MFs and nationalized banks-owned MFs are out-doing each other in offering higher discounts to gain the investors attention towards their tax saving scheme. RBI and SFBI (MF) Regulation, 1993, are governing the Mutual Funds. SEBI has revised its guidelines for money market investments by mutual funds to give it more flexibility.

LEASING

Recently the tendency of the commercial banks and other financial institutions to act as leasing intermediaries and to dominate the lessors market is increasing dramatically. The important reason, perhaps is the ability of the financial institutions (because of their high profitability and relatively high tax brackets) to exploit the attractive tax concessions.

The modern concept of financial leasing was pioneered in India during the year 1973 by setting up of "First Leasing Company of India Limited" in Madras, which remained "monopoly" for a period of six years. During that period, the company had a business of Rs. 26 crores and gross profit of the company formed 93 per cent of its total income.

With the entry of "Sundaram Finance Limited" (incorporate in 1953) into leasing business, many other companies like MGF Limited, Goodwill India Limited, The New Indian Industries Ltd. etc. diversified their finance and hire purchase business by starting leasing activities. Several financial institutions also started taking keen interest in leasing operations.

Apart from the private leasing companies, the banks and financial institutions also started participating in the leasing business. With a view to encouraging healthy growth of lease financing activity in India. RBI has issued policy guidelines in respect of the role of commercial banks in this regard. The Industrial Reconstruction Bank of India (IRBI} and Industrial Credit and Investment Corporation of India (ICICI) entered the lease market during August 1982 and March 1993 respectively.

The Industrial Development Bank of India (IDBI) also entered the leasing venture in the year 1987-88. On November 1, 1987, the Industrial Finance Corporation of India (IFCI) launched a new scheme for leasing and hire purchase concerns in the corporate and cooperative sectors.

On April 1, 1988, the commercial banks were also permitted to transact leasing business through their subsidiaries.. Several banks have decided to enter the field of leasing by promoting leasing subsidiaries or by making portfolio investment in existing or newly set-up private leasing companies. The banks are in an advantageous position to recover lease rentals in time which is not so in case of other leasing companies.

FACTORING

RBI constituted a study group in January 1988 to examine the feasibility of starting factoring organizations in India. RBI accepted its recommendations in principles in 1989. Vaghul Committee and Kalyana Sundaram Committee recommended the introduction of Factoring services in India. Factoring is a business activity where in the Factor (a bank) purchases the receivables of the sellers of Goods (clients) and reimbursement is obtained later on from the buyer of goods. This service is intended to provide much critical input of credit to both buyers and sellers of small scale and medium industries. The first factoring company in India was SBI Commercial and Factoring Services Limited (July 1991). Canbank Factoring Ltd. was set-up in August 1991 followed by PNB Factoring Ltd. With the introduction of factoring services, it is expected that the commercial banks factoring services will be able to meet the requirements of the small-scale sector and exports units in the country.

CREDIT CARDS

Under Credit Card, system credit is accommodated to the card holders for a specific period without obtaining any security. The credit card service has been introduced as an integral part of better customer service and the bank is able to make increased earnings by way of commission from dealers and interest on credit offered.

A Credit Card organization enters into an agreement with several establishments of the different parts of the country and even of other countries to provide goods and services to the Credit Card holders. This service also provides emergency cash facilities through banks or Automatic Teller Machine (ATM). The ATM facility is popular with the customers as all-time money facility. Central Bank of India was the first Bank of India to introduce Credit Card System in August 1980, and was followed by several other banks.

CREDIT RATING

Establishment of Credit Rating Agencies forms an important step in the process of financial reforms. In India during the last five years, two rating agencies have been set-up. These are:

(1) The Credit Rating Information Services of India Limited; and

(2) The Investment Information and Credit Rating Agency of India Limited (ICRA).

The Industrial Credit and Investment Corporation of India (ICICI) and Unit Trust of India (UTI) promoted the CRISIL in 1987. Other shareholders include the Asian Development Bank (ADB), UC, SBI, HDFC, GIC and 20 other Banks. The rating provides a guide to the investor. However, it is not a recommendation to invest or not to invest. CRISIL rates debentures, fixed deposits, short-term instruments like commercial paper and the preference shares.

The Industrial Finance Corporation of India (IFCI), Life Insurance Corporation of India (LIC), SBI and 17 other banks, promoted the ICRA in 1991. The primary objective of ICRA is to provide guidance to the investors/creditors in determining the credit risk associated with a debt instrument/credit obligation. The ratings are recommendations to buy or sell Securities. The ICRA rates instruments including Debentures, Bonds, Preference Shares, fixed deposits and short-term instruments like commercial papers, etc.

Setting up of the two credit ratings agencies by various financial institutions and commercial banks is a new development to give boost to the capital market.

COMMERCIAL PAPER

Financial disintermediation has been gaining momentum in the Indian economy. The Reserve Bank has been giving a definite direction to this trend through its policy initiatives. The introduction of Commercial Paper (CP) from January 1, 1990 has been one of the important policy initiatives of the RBI and it intends to bring the high credit worthy corporate borrowers and the investors into direct contact through the scheme of Commercial Papers (CPs). The public utilities, insurance companies, bank holding companies and finance companies, etc. issue Commercial Papers. Purchasers of CPs are banks and non-banking and financial institutions. The position is quite significant in the market for commercial papers because in addition to being an important buyer, they also acts as agents in issuing, holding of commercial papers and provide credit to firms, which issue commercial papers. The non-banking institution investors like LIC, GIC and UTI are not substantial buyers of commercial papers because the government decides their investment requirements and funding strategies. With the money market Mutual Funds opening up, the potential of CP will increase further. However, CP is said to be highly liquid because of its transferability, but in the absence of highly developed secondary markets, its liquidity could be greatly affected.

HOUSING FINANCE

Commercial banks have entered into Housing Finance to facilitate middle and low income groups, purchase or construct houses or flats. Setting up of NHB in 1988, an apex body for housing finance has given a boost to banks. Banks like SBI, Canara Bank, PNB, have already set-up separate subsidiaries for housing finance. Housing Finance while opens up a new era for business so far as the banks are concerned, it is also of great significance from the point of view of social justice.

The Canara Bank sponsored a Housing Finance Company, Can Fin Homes Ltd., in 1988, it has its branches in more than 22 cities and it operates the home loan account scheme of NHB, GIC set-up a company in July 1990 GIC Grih Vitsa Ltd. in joint venture with its subsidiaries UTI, ICICI, IFCI, HDFC and SBI Capital Market. The purpose of setting up there companies is to help people to own their homes. LIC set-up a Housing Finance Company, namely Housing Finance Limited in 1991 with its two schemes, namely, Jeevan Kutir and Jeevan Nivas. The primary business of UCHFL is granting housing loans to individuals. It also provides finances to agencies engaged in construction of houses/flats for residential purposes. It has floated various schemes for group housing loans being targeted towards development authorities, builders, developers, employer organization for construction of employee's quarters, etc. LICHFL has 93.5% market share and along with HDFC control 82% of the market. Other Commercial Banks have set-up their housing finance companies, namely, PNB Housing Finance Limited and SBI Home Finance Limited.

VENTURE CAPITAL

Venture capital is the response to capitalize on an opportunity to earn very high returns as compared to conventional security backed lending, by enabling high risk but high promise projects to realize their full potential.

The growth of venture capital is typically the response to demand created for more risk bearing funds to finance commercialization of new technologies and innovative market solutions. Venture capital industry in India is for recent origin.

In 1986, The Government of India enacted Research and Development Cess Act, prescribing collection of a cess of 5 per cent on all payments for import of technology with the idea that the funds thus collected will be used for venture capital to be operated by the Industrial Development Bank of India (IDBI).

Almost around the same time, ICICI set-up a venture capital scheme, In 1988 ICICI established the Technology Development and Information Corporation of India Ltd. (TDICI). Similarly, the Industrial Finance Corporation of India established the Risk Capital and Technology Finance Corporation. Later, some of the state-level developmental financial institutions also promoted venture capital units like the Gujarat Venture Finance Corporation of India. Later some of the state-level developmental financial institutions also promoted venture capital units – the Gujarat Venture Finance Ltd, APIDC Venture Capital Ltd., etc. (APIDC, 1991 GVFL, 1988). The Can Bank Venture Capital Fund was established by Can Fin and Canara Bank. The Credit Venture Fund (CCVF) was the first private sector venture capital fund to be set-up, followed by the Twentieth Century Venture Finance.

Some public sector banks also have undertaken Venture Capital financing through their subsidiaries. Can Bank Financial Service Ltd. (Canfina), a subsidiary of Canara Bank. SBI Capital Markets Ltd. (SBI Caps), a subsidiary of State Bank of India and India Investment Funds and Financial Projects of Grindlays Bank has started operation in this direction.

EMERGING CHALLENGES

Since the volume of international business and capital flows are increasing, hence, the commercial banks are likely to be exposed to different types of risks and there is a need to hedge these exposures. The emerging derivatives in foreign countries are increasingly used by banks to bring variations in the sensitivity of their funds and the underlying portfolio. It is the right time that forex dealers, especially the commercial banks, in India, familiarize with the complexity of these instruments and acquires skills to manage these challenges.

Establishments of foreign banks and non-banking companies have played a key role in introducing the technology cult in the financial sector in India. In the light of the diversified product range, the banks and other financial institutions are offering to public the various types of financial services in a global perspective. Hence, in the aspiration towards becoming major player in the modern financial service sector, commercial banks and various investment institutions will have to evolve appropriate strategies for technology integration for providing faster and efficient financial services.

The pension funds are playing a very important role in U.S.A. and other European Countries in ensuring channelising of savings into fruitful diversified investment portfolio. Different types of financial services are being provided by these pension funds. The aim of financial sector reforms in India has been to encourage the foreign institutional investors to invest in India and it is hoped that in the changing global business scenario, more and more pension funds will enter in India to provide wide variety of financial services. Presently some of the investment schemes in the name of pension funds investments have been started by IDBI, ICICI and by some other financial institutions.

CONCLUSION AND SUGGESTIONS

Over the year, with the changing scenario in Indian economy, new challenges are emerging before the Financial Sector. The major challenges before Banks relating to financial services are likely to be in growth of the corporate sector, development of capital markets and its impact on commercial banks, development of commercial paper and factoring services and the need for disintermediation in the foreign trade.

Much of the existing finance theory is based on the assumption of perfect capital market (with or without uncertainty). However, the existence of a few large agencies of financial services in India characterizes an oligopolistic market structure. This opens up new opportunities and challenges to finance professionals to devise new theory of finance, which will be relevant in the present day context.

Banks and term lending financial institutions like LIC and GIC have been doing a commendable task in the field of merchant banking services especially for large and medium size units. These agencies can also provide services to bigger projects for entering in joint venture abroad besides promotion and syndication of projects, investment management and advising services. The Merchant Banking activities may change in description or coverage in line with changing needs. The training and professional development programmes have to be reshaped to enable Merchant Banks to render more specialised services. Financial Institutions in India should actively contribute towards venture capital facilities for accelerating economic activity, particularly by the small corporate firms having assessed prospects for their future growth potential.

Several Banks and Financial Institutions have diversified into services like merchant banking, leasing venture capital, factoring, mutual funds, consumer credit cards and housing finance either directly or through subsidiaries. Merchant banking activity encompasses managing of public issues, loan syndication, financial and management consultancy services, project counseling and appraisal, arrangement of technical consultancy, mergers and acquisitions, etc.

Mutual Funds through their investment schemes provide benefits of diversified portfolio and expert investment advice to a large number of investors. The setting up of the National Housing Banks as an apex institution has provided further impetus to banks and financial institutions to meet the funding requirements of the housing sector. Travel-related services are emerging as an important avenue for the banking sector. As capital market expands both internally and externally, the scope for advisory services will be immense for commercial banks and term lending institutions in future.

Along with increasing integration of financial markets, there has been a remarkable growth in the types of new financial services. The task before the financial institutions in accommodating these changes assumes added significance in the wake of deregulation in the domestic financial markets and lesser controls over cross-border flow up of capital. With these perceived changes, banks and financial institutions besides retaining their traditional activities will have to provide wider range of financial services entailing more competition and declining margin.

REFERENCES

—(2002-03), Government of India, Economic Survey.

Jalan, Bimal (2002), Indian Banking and Finance: Managing New Challenge, RBI Bulletin.

Kumbhakar, Subual and Subrata Sarkar (2003), Deregulation, Ownership and Productivity Growth in the Banking Industry. Evidence form India, Journal of Money, Credit and Banking, Vol. 35.

Mohan, Rakesh (2003), Transforming Indian Banking: In Search of a Better Tomorrow, RBI Bulletin, January.

Rangarajan, C and Narendra Jadhav (1992), Issues in Financial Sector Reforms, in Bimal Jalan (ed.). The Indian Economy, Delhi.

Reddy, Y.V. (1988), Financial Sector Reform: Review and Prospects, RBI Bulletin, December, Reserve Bank of India (2001), Report on Currency and Finance, 1999-02. Mumbai, RBI.

CHAPTER 20

COMMERCIAL BANKS AND AGRICULTURAL CREDIT WITH REFERENCE TO BIHAR

Bhagwan Prasad Singh

In this paper, an attempt has been made to highlight the role of banks in economic development, and to evaluate policy changes having bearing on allocation of bank credit to different sectors. Before 1991 i.e. reforms in banking sector, banks were assigned crucial role in promoting economic development by increasing flow of credit to important but neglected sectors like agriculture, small scale industries, self-employed persons, etc. With introduction of economic reforms measures in India, there had been a shift in banking policy a more liberal market-oriented policy is being pursued with increased emphasis on efficiency and productivity and virtually to the neglect of agriculture and other such segments of the economy.

The present article is divided in three sections. In Section One, the role of banks in economic development has been highlighted. In Section Two, an idea of branch expansion policy in pre and post reforms period has been provided. The issues of credit allocation and credit dispersal have been dealt with. In Section Three, conclusion and suggestions have been made.

SECTION I

Historical experiences show that banks have played significant role in economic development of both developed and developing economics[1]. They help in mobilization of savings and their channelisation in productive sectors and activities. They are the link between savers and investors. Schumpeter highlighted the role of bank credit in economic development and in promoting innovations. He regarded credit as 'an indispensable adjunct to entrepreneurship and innovations'. Gurley and Shaw highlighted the important role of finance in promotion of savings and investment and, therefore, in economic development[2]. Banks being important financial intermediary help in institutionalization of savings and investment, which quickens the growth rates of income and wealth.

Admittedly, rise in the levels of savings and investment and efficient allocation of resources in investment channels are indispensable pre-requisites for a faster economic development. As the process of economic development proceeds, not only commercial banks but many other financial intermediaries develop and help in speeding up the process of development. Resource mobilization is important and tapping savings and their channelization for productive purpose is equally important. Banking Commission (1972) clearly mentioned that "Ever since the initiation of planned economic development in India, and more particularly in recent years, a high degree of emphasis has been placed on deposit mobilization by banks as one of the main ways in which resources for the development of the economy can be enlarged"[3]. The resources mobilized should be channelised in the socially desired direction for while planning and control is needed. Banks when in private sector, generally did not allocate credit in conformity with the priorities of planning to the desired extent. For serving social and national purpose in a better way banks were nationalized in 1969 to play a more growth stimulating role, serve social purpose in a better way. H.J. Patrick's analysis of role of banks is apt as regards serving the purpose in underdeveloping countries. He made distinction between ' demand following' and 'supply leading'[4] role of Banks. In demand following phenomena financial institution play passive role, they respond to financial requirement in the course of development. As development proceeds demand for financial services emerge, evoking supply response in the form of the development of financial system. Finance follows development in supply leading phenomena. On the other hand, there is creation of financial institutions and their assists and related financial services in advance of demand for them. Here finance leads development Supply leading finance presents an opportunity to induce real growth by means of finance in underdeveloped countries. Like Indian financial institution including banks are required to play supply-leading role to give a fillip to development process.

In our country since 1969, the aim is to ensure that the banks do play a dynamic role in the development process of rural and backward areas and for the uplift of the poorer sections of society[5]. Banks must allocate credit in accordance with the requirements of economic development and ensure flow in the directions intended. But with announcement of economic reform measures, measures for financial and Banking reforms were undertaken. There has been a paradigm shift and emphasis was laid on efficiency in banking and improving productivity. A Committee under the chairmanship of M. Narasimham was constituted to advise on financial sector reforms and later on banking sector reforms. In the support of the Committee on Financial System (1991), it has been clearly stated that financial services industry should operate" on the basis of operational flexibility and functional autonomy with a view to enhancing efficiency, productivity and profitability"[6]

The Committee felt that there has been decline in productivity, and efficiency and erosion of the profitability of the banking sector because of a) directed investments and b) directed credit programmes, Erosion in profitability was due to massive expansion of branches particularly unremunerative in rural areas, considerable degree of overmarking and inadequate progress in updating work technique- therefore it suggested that statutory liquidity ratio (SLR) be brought down in a phased manner to 25 percent over a period of about five years. Cash reserve ratio be progressively reduced and directed credit should be phased out the credit for redefined priority sector comprising small marginal farmers, the tiny sector of industry, small business and transport operators, village and cottage industries, rural artisans and other weaker sections should hence forth be fixed to 10 percent of aggregate credit. Committee on Banking sector reforms (1998, chairman M. Narsimham) suggested that capital adequacy requirement needs to take into account market risks. Accordingly, the Committee recommended a 5 percent weight for market risk for Government and other securities. The minimum capital to risk ratio be increased to 10 percent from its present level of 8 percent. The directive of the banking sector reforms was to promote a diversified, efficient and competitive financial system. The Committee recommended that banking industry should be made more competitive by removing restriction in entry and expansion of private banks, and by reducing those on expansion of foreign banks. Thus, the ultimate objective was improving the allocative efficiency of resources through operational flexibility, improved financial viability and institutional strengthening. According to Rakesh Mohan, Deputy Governor, R.B.I. "The whole policy reform process has been designed to make the banking system more market oriented to enable efficient price discovery and to induce greater internal efficiency in the resource allocation process. Thus whereas the efforts in the 1960s, 1970s and 80s were essentially developed to financial deepening, the focus of reforms in the past decade and a half has been gendering greater efficiency and productivity in the banking system in particular, and in financial sector as a whole"[7] By making changes in policies and initiatives taken thereafter, no doubt, there has been improvement in efficiency and productivity of banks but spread of banking in rural areas and flow of credit to agriculture and rural people have suffered.

SECTION II

In our country since bank nationalization in 1969, branch expansion ws made fastly in rural areas and credit flow to agricultures, small scale industries, artisans etc. increased. Data in Table 1 clearly demonstrate that there was faster expansion of branch network in the country during 1969-1980 but slow down in branch expansion started since early 1990s and faster declaration since mid-nineties has taken place.

Table 1
Bank Offices of Scheduled Commercial Banks in India and Bihar

	June 1969	*June 1991*	*March 1993*	*June 2000*	*June 2002*	*March 2003*
INDIA Number of Bank Offices	8262	60190	60884	65340	66186	66638*
Population per bank office (in '000)	65	11	11	15	16	16
BIHAR						
Member of Bank Offices	273	4845	4876	4992	3550	Not
Population per bank office (in 1000)	207	14	14	20	21	24

Source:
(a) Trend and progress of Banking in India, RBI
(b) Economic and Political weekly, March 19, 2005, p.l265.

In this phase, we witness rapid branch expansion in metropolitan cities. The phase of high-street banking started and branch expansion in urban and metropolitan areas galloped. Growth of urban-centric banking has taken place. Rural people suffered both in terms of banking facilities and credit. The states like Maharastlra, Gujarat, Karnataka, Tamil Nadu, Andhra Pradesh are well-banked states while Bihar remains a poorly banked state which is clearly reflected in high population per bank office there. The national average of population per bank office was 15 thousand in March 2003 whereas in Bihar it was 24 thousand per bank office. Table -2 provides an idea of deposit mobilization and credit disbersal.

Deposit mobilization has increased in the country but credit dispersal has been relatively slow. Banks have achieved remarkable success in deposit mobilization but they have not been extending credit at a desirable pace and level"[8].

Table 2
Deposits and Credits of Scheduled Commercial Bank

(Rupees in Crores)

	June 1969		*March 2001*		*March 2004*	
Level	*Deposits*	*Credits*	*Deposits*	*Credits*	*Deposits*	*Credits*
India	4646	3599	989141	529272	1517200	890866
Bihar	186.03	50.56	2680.0	554.2	36130	9244

Source: Basic statistical Returns, March 2001 & 2003

The poor flow of credit as ratio of deposits is reflected in low credit deposit ratio in the country. Figures in Table-3 speak for themselves. The C-D ratio has been well above national average in states like Tamil Nadu, Maharashtra, Karnataka, Andhra Pradesh. It means that banks have shown interest there and made advances for different purposes but in poor states like Bihar it has remained nearly half of the national average right from 1969 to 2003. In a poor state like Bihar due to non-availability of resources productive activity suffer whereas reverse transfer of resources has been going on from the state. Resources mobilized in the state are not deployed in the state, non-availability of credit to people of the state is impeding the process of economic development. Out of deposits of rupees one hundred only paise 25 were being advanced as credit in the state, now this has reached to 30. C-D ratio is about 30 percent. Banks have became highly safety-conscious and want to play safe. They have scant concern for development, even the genuine needs of agriculturists and poorer sections are not being met, they had to suffer due to non-availability of bank credit. Relatively backward states like Bihar are neglected and its people do not get credit for even genuine and productive activities.

So far as credit to agriculture by Commercial Banks is concerned, the position is not different In the post-reform period they have shown less interest in financing agriculture and rural poor because they find serving the vast numbers of small accounts both deposit and borrowing-costly and cumbersome. They prefer instead the safer (and remunerative) alternative of meeting targeted level of lending to agriculture, investing in RIDF. They did not reach RBI stipulated 18 percent of their net bank credit to agriculture. They are ready to provide funds to ventures which are less risky or which has government support. That is why they prefer investing in Rural Infrastructure Development Fund.

Table 3
State-wise Credit-Deposit Ratio of Scheduled Commercial Banks (As Per Sanction)

(Percent)

States	*June 1969*	*March 1994*	*2000*	*2001*	*2002*	*2003*
Bihar	30.8	34.7	22.5	20.7	21.3	23.1
Haryana	46.9	50.1	42.4	41.0	43.7	43.6
Punjab	27.0	42.0	39.4	41.1	41.8	41.6
Maharashtra	100.9	69.9	86.4	86.4	92.3	93.2
Gujarat	48.6	46.3	49.0	48.5	44.1	45.2
Andhra Pradesh	100.8	73.3	64.2	64.4	61.9	62.6
Kamataka	76.1	72.7	63.3	61.0	61.6	60.9
Tamil Nadu	135.5	87.0	88.6	90.6	85.4	97.6
All India	88.0	57.5	56.0	56.7	58.4	59.4

In case of scheduled Commercial Bank credit to agriculture (Table-4) there is clear bias in credit to states which are relatively developed. Andhra Pradesh,Maharashtra, Karnataka, Tamil Nadu, Gujarat, Punjab states received more credit for agriculture but states like Bihar were unable to get the required amount for development of agriculture, a crucial sector on which depends development of the state. Figure in Table -4 vividly demonstrate this trend.

In the post-reform period i.e after 1991, there has been marked change in banking resource allocation policy. There has been increased flow to industry and services sector, but reduction in percent credit to agriculture.(9) This Report of the expert committee on Rural credit, NABARD, July 2001, pp 7980 is clear from figures presented in Table-5 .

During the period 1980 to 1985, there was rapid rise in bank credit from scheduled commercial Banks to agriculture, which rose from 14.8 in 1980 to 17.6 percent in 1985. But since 1990 it started declining, from 15.9 percent in 1990 to 9.8 in 2002 with

Table 4
Scheduled Commercial Banks Credit to Agriculture

(Rs in Crores)

States/India	*June 1968*	*June 1969*	*1996 to 1997*	*1998 to 1999*	*1999 to 2000*	*2000 to 2001*	*2001 to 2002*	*2002 to 2003*
Bihar	0.7	1.34	1492.53	1482.03	1422.75	1338.30	1487.08	1631.93
Andhra Pradesh	4.56	19.8	4178.25	5204.62	5690.57	6360.48	7575.08	8640.71
Maharashtra	5.31	40.86	3244.68	3977.24	4749.49	4979.98	6524.98	7461.66
Gujarat	0.8	7.54	1531.29	2232.59	2377.83	2608.11	3757.19	4084.33
Kamataka	4.50	18.64	3226.68	4310.77	5281.34	5254.59	6695.03	7768.58
Tamil Nadu	8.47	51.81	3695.53	4222.59	4325.05	4656.13	5054.66	6235.95
Punjab	0.38	1.84	2825.26	2552.58	3096.81	3546.16	4022.70	4736.25
ALL-INDIA	44.58	188.42	31634.15	40889.26	45638.27	51730.35	64008.55	75935.22

Source:
1. Report on Currency and Finance, RBI
2. CMIE, Agriculture, March 2005

Table 5
Distribution of Outstanding Credit of Scheduled Commercial Banks according to Occupation

(Percent Total)

Item	*June 1980*	*June 1985*	*March 1990*	*March 1995*	*March 2000*	*March 2001*	*March 2002*	*March 2003*
Agriculture	14.8	17.6	15.9	11.8	9.9	9.6	9.8	10.0
Direct	11.3	14.7	13.8	10.2	8.4	8.1	7.2	7.8
Indirect	3.4	3.0	2.1	1.7	1.5	1.5	2.5	2.2
Industry	48.0	41.3	48.7	45.6	46.5	43.9	41.4	41.0
Transport	4.3	4.8	3.2	1.9	1.8	1.6	1.4	1.2
Personal Loan & Professional Services	2.2	6.4	9.4	11.3	14.4	15.8	16.8	19.6
Trade	22.2	23.4	13.9	17.1	15.6	16.6	15.4	13.8
Financial Institution	0.8	1.2	2.1	3.8	4.8	4.9	5.9	6.7
Miscellaneous/All others	7.6	5.3	6.8	8.5	7.1	7.5	9.5	7.7
Total	10.0	100.0	.100.0	100.0	100.0	100.0	100.0	100.0
Memo: services	24.2	26.3	30.5	31.9	31.9	32.8	35.6	36.8

Source: Report on Currency and Finance 2003-04, R.B.I., p.162 . ..

marginal improvement in 2003 to 10%. Scheduled commercial bank credit to industry ranged between 41 % to 48%. There was continuous upward trend in credit to person for purchase of consumer durables and for housing. Credit to resources rose at a faster rate, it rose from 24.2 percent in 1980 to 36.8 percent in 2003.

From the above one thing is amply clear that bank credit to non-agricultural sector has risen but to agriculture and rural poor it has declined. Still agriculture contributes about 22% of national income and provides employment to nearly 60 percent people. In this context there is need for increasing flow of credit to agriculture and help agriculturists for undertaking genuine and productive activities. Majority of farmers come in the category of small marginal farmers and they need institutional credit support for modernization, technological break through in agriculture and undertaking more remunerative areas of production viz. animal husbandry, horticulture, floriculture, fishery etc. Increased flow of credit to agriculturists for this purpose will help in diversification of agriculture, raise the incomes of farmers and help them in alleviating, poverty in rural areas.

SECTION III

We have discussed, in brief, the main developments and policy since 1991 in banking sector in our country. There was a time when private sector banks were nationalized to serve social purpose, curbed misdirection of resources and channelise credit in hitherto neglected but important sectors like agriculture, small scale industries, arts etc. But in the post-reform period there has been a paradigm change and more emphasis was laid on efficiency and productivity in the allocation of resources improving profitability of banks and increase their competitiveness. No doubt these goals are important for health and economic strength of banks but equally important is the social purpose providing more and more facilities, mobilization of savings and increasing flow of funds for productive purposes. Any change in policy should be for betterment of majority of people, poorer and vulnerable sections. Admittedly, due to policy changes efficiency has improved, costs have declined, improving working results of banks. But there has been marked slow down in branch expansion, particularly in rural areas, but on the other hand there has been rapid expansion of branches in the metropolitan cities. There has been growth of urban centric banking and we have reached the phase of high-street banking. Due to this trend rural population has suffered in terms of banking facilities and flow of credit. C- D ratio in rural areas has declined. This trend is also seen in terms of banking facilities in states. Developed states are well-banked states, enjoying better banking facilities while poorer states like Bihar remain under banked which is reflected in population per bank office being highest in the country. C-D ratio in developed states is relatively high, above national average, but in poor states like Bihar it is quite low. Even resources mobilized in the state are not deployed, only about 1/4th of resources mobilized are being provided as credit. This has clearly impeded the growth of states like Bihar, as there is causality between credit and development. Agriculture sector has suffered in the country due to continuous decline in capital formation in agriculture (both public and private) and declining flow of credit to the sector. This trend does not well for agricultural growth and for poor frustrated farming community in the country. Poor farmers will be forced to go again in the hands of moneylenders. In a state like Bihar if bank do not change their mind set and come in a big way to finance genuine and productive activities, development in general and agricultural development in particular, will suffer. In Bihar over 80 percent farmers come in the category of small/marginal farmers, agriculture contributes nearly 40% of state domestic product. Bihar, being nearly industryless state, will suffer, if flow of funds to agriculture does not rise perceptibly. C-D ratio should rise to at least 40 percent and genuine productive activities entrepreneurs and agripreneurs, agriculturists should be not to stimulate process of overall rural development and help the poorer people of the state overcome poverty syndrome. Banks should play active and supply- leading role at least in agriculture sector. There is urgent need for flexible and innovative approach rather than play safe attitude. Broker scrutiny and follow up should be done in case of credit proposals and banks should not be reluctant and over safety conscious in their behaviour and attitude.

REFERENCES

1. Kurihara, K.K.(1959), The Keynsian Theory of Economic Development, p. 134
2. Gwrley, J. S. and Shaw, E.S., (1985), Financial Aspect of Economic Development, The American Economic Review, September, p. 516
3. Report of the Banking Commission (1972), Government of India, p. 85
4. Patrick, H. J. (1966), "Financial Development and Economic Growth" Economic Development and cultural change, January, pp. 174-189.
5. Report of the Committee to Review Arrangements For Institutional Credit.
6. (1981), Agriculture and Rural Development, R.B.I., Bombay, p. 24.

   Narasimham, M. (1991), Report of the Committee on Financial System, (summary) November, 1991.
7. Rakesh Mohan (2006), Reforms, Productivity and Efficiency in Banking. The Indian Experience, RBI Bulletin, March, p. 2847
8. (2004), EPW Research Foundation- Scheduled Commercial Banks in India, March 20.

CHAPTER 21

EVOLUTION OF FINANCIAL SECTOR REFORMS AND CREDIT MARKETS IN INDIA

Arjun Kondamani

The Indian economy has seen a phased liberalization of socialist-era banking and finance laws and is gearing itself towards world-class capitalistic performance in tune with its emerging place amongst leading world economies. In this paper, we will travel some of the roads of liberalization and highlight the financial aspects that have improved meaningfully as well as address areas of work in progress.

BACKGROUND

India has made remarkable economic strides in the past two decades as its industries have become world-class entities, competitive in the global market place. The rapid growth has come mainly from service industries, like software and outsourcing and as the economic boom seeped through to the consumers, domestic demand has spurred other industries as well. As has often happened with sudden spurts of growth in other countries, infrastructure development has often lagged (the talented and growing pool of technical graduates being one of the exceptions) the positive trends set by the first movers in industry.

As India emerges into economic superpower status, industry watchers, investors, and rating agencies, to name a few, will be concerned not just with growth but its sustainability and hence the ability of infrastructure to support and enhance future growth. We are quick to point out that India has strong democratic institutions that have demarcated functions and are functionally-on paper-compatible with the best sovereign peers worldwide. However, as readers are already aware, the World Bank and other agencies have cast many of India's infra-structure in a poor light-as being "caught in time", as being crisis-ridden and rudimentary, and not geared to allow the Indian economic engine to expand at its best pace. India's roads and electricity generation remain pitifully inadequate, the lack of a uniform civil code adds to some doubt in observers' minds, and the Indian judicial system is well known to be mired in paperwork and hapless in its ability to execute decisions quickly.

India is admired to have a working finance system, one that is comprehensive and funnels funds from a large pool of savings into industries and projects. It enjoys a liquid stock market and a working debt market, entities that are essential to formation of capital and which many countries lack. (As an aside, impartial market observers award India better marks over China because India has working democratic institutions and that it has put in place a developed, working capital markets system)

Much has been written about the different financial sector reforms and their history and impact. In this paper, we will limit ourselves to debt capital markets within the finance realm and examine aspects of Indian banking and capital markets that can have a meaningful impact on taking the debt capital markets to the next level.

ROLE OF INVESTMENT IN GDP

The development of investment in the economy is as important as (net) exports and consumer spending to a nation's Gross Domestic Product (GDP). Even in the US, where consumer spending is 60% or more of the GDP and much greater than

Investment spending, Investment Spending is sometimes called the "tail that wags the dog" and is important in maintaining a stable GDP or in growing the economy. Investment spending is comparatively a decided, planned effort to invest in growth versus consumer spending that can sometimes be fickle in the face of higher interest rates, housing slowdowns (as in the US currently) or wage meltdowns. Investments made by government (commonly referred to as "government spending" involving road building, defense spending to name a few) or by the private sector (as in plant overhauls, R&D, new store purchases, real estate etc) help spur the economy and create jobs, fuel wages and bolster confidence-all of which in turn create greater consumer spending and higher tax receipts - hence the tail wagging the dog.

To bankroll this investment or spending, Investments are made from existing pools of funds (government from taxes, private sector from retained earnings and cash) but very often private and public entities raise funds for this spending through capital markets (debt/credit and equity). The Indian economy is growing at a blistering 8% or so with nominal inflation. To maintain this growth will require strong debt markets and better financial intermediaries to provide a steady source of liquid capital.

ROLE OF CREDIT MARKETS IN INVESTMENT

From the Oxford English Dictionary, credit, n: "Trust or confidence in a buyer's ability and intention to pay at some future time, exhibited by entrusting him with goods, etc. without present payment."

Credit markets facilitate "loans" to entities (often called "issuers of debt") from return-seeking investors (who are paid "coupons" or "interest") and are fundamental components of capital markets in developed economies to provide the range and scale of funds needed for capital-seeking entities. In the US for example, credit markets are composed of a matrix of bank lending, repo, treasury, agency, corporate issuance, mortgage issuance etc. These markets provide the gamut of funds ranging from days to years to issuers of debt (or capital seekers) like the government, agencies (public sector enterprises), corporations, municipalities and the like. An entity like Reliance Industries can thus tap this credit framework for short-term funds needed to pay suppliers all the way to long-term funds it needs to invest in the next technology or factory in Pune.

In the Indian context, credit markets are still incipient. Although India possesses many of the structural pawns needed to develop a healthy credit market, there are still some road blocks. Indian firms should be able to avail credit more cheaply, far more easily and abundantly. This can help them plan their growth rate better, grow their business faster with efficient investment, and reward investors better since the investing public has more venues of deploying their savings and investment to generate returns. And their returns translate into higher consumer spending. This overall cycle feeds on itself (as it has in the US) and can transform the GDP visibly upward for India.

What financial sector reforms has India invested in to develop its capital markets? But before that, what constitutes an efficient capital market system?

As an investor seeking to lend money profitably to an entity, we would look for, among a few:

Visibility of Corporate Actions: Is the entity's purpose honorable and its existence verifiable? Is it an ongoing concern and do we have access to its past actions, future course of action and its structure?

Balance Sheet Transparency: To what extent is the true financial picture of the corporation available? Are all its bad debts listed? Are there strange off- balance sheet transactions or hidden option costs?

Financial Regulation: What kind of government scrutiny is in place to prevent fraudulent transactions? What systems exist to dis-incentivize corporate scandals, protect investors and oversee bankruptcies?

Liquidity: What liquidity does the system provide through intermediaries and/or exchanges to permit easy entry and exit? What kinds of transparent information exchanges can be present for participants to know the value of a security and to prevent collusion amongst intermediaries[i] (TRACE system)

Rating Agency Participation: What independent metrics are available to rate entities by their credit worthiness and provide a roadmap for investors to assess risk and return?

On the other hand, an entity or debtor would seek an efficient market with the lowest i1t cost of capital. This would be tied to the Indian Government keeping its finances in order, therefore attracting strong debt ratings; and in association with a well-run Gilt market to provide a low cost of funding for the sovereign entity (Republic of India). Added to the Indian Government's cost of capital (relatively risk-free), debtors would then incur an additional cost or "spread" over the Gilt curve depending on their credit metrics (revenue flow strength, cash flow, debt to capital etc). Also, depending on how they manage liquidity by providing the right depth of float and number of issues, they can attract a large, diversified investor base for the broadest participation and subscription.

Given our knowledge of how important credit markets are to India's development into an economic superpower, and armed with what is crucial to nurture and sustain these markets, let us examine areas of financial sector reform that have taken place vis-a-vis these requirements.

BANKS-THE TRADITIONAL PROVIDERS OF CREDIT

In any economy, banks are the backbone of credit markets. Lending is a primordial profession where capital is allocated from savers to debtors who invest for capital expenditures and ventures related to growth, profit generation and returns. A bank functions to earn a spread between collecting interest on loans and paying its depositors on term deposits. Banks tap most layers of savings and deposits by its very business of providing safety, liquidity and a savings growth.

Indian banks operated in a normal mix of private and public entities until the late 60's, when they underwent a large phase of government-owning/controlling to fall in line with the then government's nobler purpose of:

- attracting deposits at a high rate to encourage saving at a grass-roots level and

- disbursing these deposits to loans/investment that bolstered "social" needs in the then-nascent Indian economy (primarily agriculture and small industries).

It was believed that only government-controlled entities could effectively police this socio-economic corridor since their actions would not be motivated by profits alone nor answerable to shareholders focused on growth and dividends. (A similar argument exists for nations' proclivity to maintain state-owned postal systems).

On the upside, Indian banks have become very comprehensive and tap most geographic areas of the subcontinent (perhaps, a favorable outcome of nationalization?). On the downside, government ownership has led to bureaucracy, bloating, and an inability to efficiently perform their dictated socio-economic function of allocating funds to the targeted capital seekers (aside from reduced profit generation).

Indian banks are saddled with several issues that make them inefficient providers of liquidity and credit. Chief among them:

The Problem of NPAs: Banks have non-performing assets (NPA[1]) that have grown to somewhat unmanageable proportions.[2] These NPAs are a result of having an inadequate system to assess the creditworthiness of the debtor and with having poor post--disbursement supervision. In the case of bad debt recognition and subsequent liquidation, the asset disposal process is riddled with a host of bureaucratic delays and legal issues -mostly tilted against banks.

The NPAs result in a bank having no income versus the NP A account but at the same time having to make a provision on these assets as per the Reserve Bank of India (RBI) rules. Therefore, these NPAs eat up balance sheet but provide little or no income. And, as the RBI eases on the system and provides liquidity (like lower reserve requirements), banks are hesitant to pass the liquidity. By engaging in further lending, banks fear even more NP As - again, a result of having an inadequate system to assess credit risk and poor disposal processes. Thus, liquidity provided by the RBI stagnates somewhat within the banking sector.

Better Risk Management of Capital: Following the Basel reforms on addressing capital standards (or lack thereof) at banks, the Narasimhan[3] Committee on financial sector reforms recommended similar capital adequacy standards for Indian banks. The ensuing capital to risk-weighted metric of 8% has been enforced for banks, with 26 of them having complied by 1999. Fuller enforcement will promote the visibility of banks' risk management and elevate their standards to G-10 standards and consequently, decrease bank failures in crisis situations.

Credit Growth vs. Savings Growth-An Anomaly: Another issue facing Indian banks is their inefficiency in attracting deposits and making capital investments. Currently, Indian banks earn a spread of approximately 3% between collecting deposits and making loans. This number has been static over the past decade and in the current global context, high compared to other banking peers worldwide. The spread is by tradition-high- and somewhat necessary to maintain the cost of sustaining the large, bloated infrastructure of the system.

Banks ideally, should increase the rate paid to depositors and increase their efficiency (with better systems and practices and fewer staff) so that they are more profitable in spite of the lower spread. And this would augur well for India also: with a current account deficit of 3.5% of its GDP, India would be wise to attract local funds with higher savings rates[2] to fund its deficit versus "flighty" foreign capital that has to be paid out of forex reserves. As we stand now, strong economic growth in India has mushroomed demand for more credit whereas bank deposit growth has lagged[4] credit growth.

EVOLUTION OF THE INDIAN BOND MARKET

Although banks provide funding across all maturities, a bond market is essential to directly raise public funds. The efficiencies of directly reaching the public and piquing their interest helps in creating bonds a formidable avenue of capital raising and exerts the necessary competitive pressure on banks.

The biggest user of the bond market is of course the Government. Over the past decade, the Indian Government, particularly the RBI, has labored hard to create liquidity. and elongate the Gilt yield curve. The process has been supported with a more broad- based market, an efficient auction process, and a more active secondary market. Liquidity has been enhanced by measures such as:

- uniform T + 1 settlement cycle for Gilts
- rollover of repos
- access to repo markets by listed companies and non-scheduled urban cooperative banks

In spite of these advances, the market remains highly concentrated (few, large buyers that "buy and hold") and thus suffers from bursts of asset volatility from lack of float. The lack of liquidity (albeit, improved given the gradual financial reforms) of the secondary market does not help as well in mitigating asset volatility. Let us look at some ways that can address these factors.

The development of *repo markets* is essential to enhancing liquidity. Bond market players require repo to enhance liquidity without resorting to liquidating their positions itself. Repos are currently possible only with Gilts and not yet available for corporate bond markets. This crowds out participants with large asset hoards who are unable to tap the repo markets for liquidity.

Another aspect of poor liquidity has been the absence of *short positions.* A healthy bond market allows participants to express their views on interest rates and the market by maintaining long or short positions. The absence of a mechanism to short-sell bonds (even Gilts) constrains liquidity and forces participants to use swaps and other mechanisms to arrive at a short position. The introduction of short-selling measures with adequate safeguards (risk-based capital requirements to name one) would allow fixed income players to take the commensurate amount of short positions without creating a credit meltdown.

Overall, liquidity has now improved and is comparable with most developed markets, with bid-ask spreads in the range 1-3 bps for liquid Gilts. The secondary market has particularly benefited from insurance and pension funds supporting the longer end of the curve, much like the US where liability matching and immunization strategies have created natural demand for long paper from insurance and pension funds

Much of these benefits have stemmed from reforms over the past decade, the opening up of the insurance sector to a more diversified set of players, and development of mutual funds. Banks still are big players in the primary and secondary markets but their influence has waned with the emergence of the newer players in the sector. And as reforms continue, newer entrants will emerge and the size and liquidity of debt as an asset class will build on itself As the table below of the Merrill Lynch Indian Government Index shows, although Gilts may seem like they have the heft that developed countries' Treasury markets do, the liquidity is still thin by global standards.

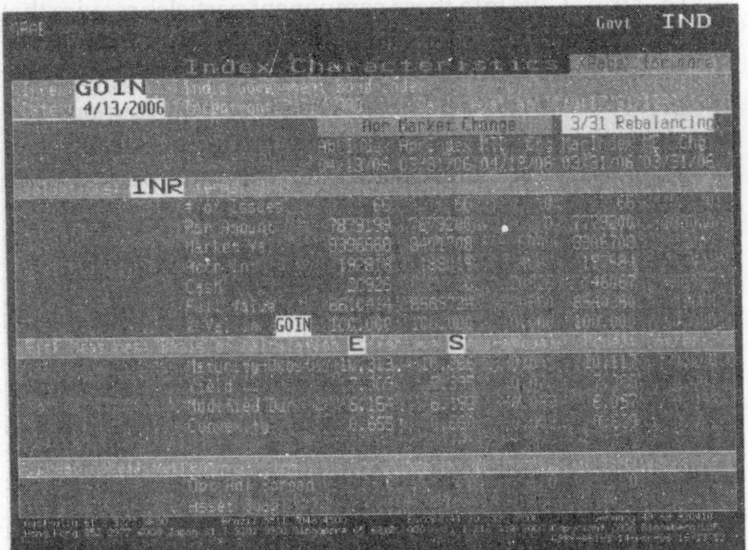

Creating a More Uniform Yield Curve - The Role of STRIPS

STRIPS, standing for separate trading of registered interest and principal of securities are portions of Gilts that are "stripped" of coupons and become distinct zero coupon bonds. They have a useful role in creating a smooth, transparent yield curve-the development of which spills benefits into security valuation, risk management, derivatives, capital finance etc. The reason STRIPS are useful is that inconsistencies in coupon rates can drive demand for lower coupon issues (priced closer to par) against lower demand for legacy, higher coupon paper. The Government dips for funds in debt markets with coupons that are reflective of the current interest rate and as interest rates fluctuate, coupons change with the times. Therefore, a natural set of buyers will emerge who will seek certainty of return, eschew reinvestment rate risks (associated with coupons) and take on higher fluctuations of the STRIP. Also, STRIPS will be attractive to a set of traffickers who want to replicate a set of cash flows accurately (as in a corporate finance project or pension funding) and can do it with STRIPS in a more precise manner.

To "strip" Gilts into these component particles require that Government funding be carried out with uniformity of funding viz. consistency of coupons, maturity of funding, coupon payments falling around fixed dates etc so that coupons and principal can be stripped into standard time buckets and securitized. Also, an infrastructure must be put in place to price these STRIPS and create an effective market place.

GROWTH AND NECESSITY OF A CORPORATE CREDIT MARKET

In the US, the corporate market is the 2nd largest segment of the market, eclipsed only by the mortgage market. Both these segments overshadow the Treasury market in size. Corporations efficiently use the debt markets as vehicles to draw funding across the maturity spectrum Markets are characterized by ease of primary issuance, competition amongst a large number of intermediaries, research and liquidity in secondary markets, and a rating system maintained by independent agencies (Moody's, S&P, Fitch to name a few).

The development of a corporate market is essential to creating an efficient capital market system because free-market forces in debt markets exert a competitive pressure on banks and their lending practices and force the system to clean itself up. Additionally, given that equities can be more frothy, corporations need a stable source of funding that is found in debt markets. The corporate market in India is still nascent, thus denying corporations efficient ways to tap into a potential pool of funds. The nascence has arisen from lack of local rating agencies to guide market participants, poor secondary market research, overwhelming private placements (to concentrated, informed buyers), and hoarding of issues (by block players holding to maturity)-killing liquidity in the bargain.

There is always a class of risk-takers in the investment spectrum that will lend to corporations to be rewarded with an appropriate "spread" over Gilts. This spread is mostly a function of economic conditions, inflation, sector risks, company outlook, management performance, and so on. Investors are often guided through this judgment process by a combination of independent rating actions on a company's bond and by brokerage houses analyzing a credit.

Creating independent rating agencies in the Indian markets is an important first step in establishing a ladder of credits ranging from very strong (high investment grade) to weak (high yield or junk) as well as developing credibility. Rating agencies will initially need to be funded by the government to sustain themselves and provide credibility before the volume of corporate issuance grows to accommodate privatization and stand-alone stature for the rating entities through corporations paying fees to have their bonds rated (like a Moody's or S&P). The very fact that there is such a huge private placement market in India tells us that there is a selective few (buyers) who know the debtor entity well and are able to accurately assess the risk/reward appropriately. The knowledge is there-it just remains to be disseminated to a larger group of investors through rating agencies and brokerage house research.

Along with this would be steps to enhance corporate visibility by establishing norms for financial actions, balance sheet controls, transparency of corporations, bankruptcy handling etc. With India's new stature come these responsibilities anyway; (irrespective of the development of credit markets) as India woos the global investor with tales of clean, well-run corporations whose actions are transparent and not shrouded in secrecy. Courts must efficiently deal with company scandal and enforce Sarbanes Oxley-like norms on companies. Bankruptcies must be expediently dealt with and investors protected. A detailed discussion on the current problems of corporate governance and the judicial system is beyond the scope of this paper but they play an ever-increasing part in sharing up confidence in corporations.

With education in risk/reward and with a renewed confidence in the corporate sector, the demand for corporate bonds would then be not from a knowledgeable-few but be across the board. Different customer segments would be the harbinger of demand for different types of corporate bonds as well as injecting much-needed liquidity in the system.

Growth of Provincial Markets

The 12th Finance Commission[5] enacted reforms under debt relief and corrective measures to include the recommendation that the Central Government not act as an intermediary for most State Governments. States now can tap markets for debt in the first step towards developing healthy provincial markets as in the US, Canada where agency issues trade in a liquid manner with small spreads to Gilt issues and are almost proxies for Sovereign debt depending on the creditworthiness of the entity.

Much of what we discussed for corporations is equally true for State markets. A state like Karnataka would potentially command a better credit rating than say, Rajasthan, given the strength of its local economy and the visibility of future earnings (tax receipts).

SUMMARY

To summarize, financial sector reforms in India are very commendable. Past administrations have helped put in place a working capital markets system that has many of the necessary legs needed to supply the economy with capital and provide investment vehicles. To catapult India to-the next step of being an economic superpower, current inefficiencies need to be eradicated and new reforms accelerated to bring financial institutions and corporate governance to G-10 standards.

The markets have always been receptive to change that makes them work better and the international community, already having heaped praise for India's financial institutions, are looking for the next wave of changes that transforms India's financial markets meaningfully and allows them to do business with India more efficiently as well.

We look forward to seeing India shape her destiny positively and developing a strong capital market system.

NOTES

1. The TRACE system developed in the US was provided to protect retail investors from gouging and collusion. The free (delayed) data allows participants to view historical data and ascertain price movements and context.
2. Muniappan GP (2002) "The NPA Overhang-Magnitude, Solutions, Legal Reforms" -. CII Banking Summit 2002.
3. M. Narasimhan (2000) "Report of The Advisory Group on Transparency in Monetary and Financial Policies", Reserve Bank of India.
4. Ashok K Nag, Abhiman Das (2002) "Credit Growth and Response to Capital Requirements Evidence from Indian Public Sector Banks", Economic and Political Weekly
5. Twelfth Finance Commission (2005), http://indiabudget.nic.in/es2004-05/chapt2005/chap25.pdf

SUB-NOTES

—An asset is deemed an "NPA" if interest payments or principal remains due for 180 days or more

—In a nation of increasing financial vehicles (mutual funds, healthy stock market, etc) with better advertising than banking products, why would a "saver" settle for substandard savings rates in the face of better returns elsewhere?

CHAPTER 22

FISCAL REFORMS, PLAN EROSION AND CRISIS IN FOODGRAINS PRODUCTION: A CASE STUDY FOR STRENGTHENING PLANNING IN INDIA

Indradeo Sharma
Renu Sinha

One major achievement of planned development in India over its first four decades (1951-91) is the achievement of self-sufficiency in foodgrains. From a chronic and large importer of food till mid-1970s, India emerged as a net exporter of foodgrains by the beginning of 1990s. Under the process of so-called fiscal reforms, however there has been a marked erosion in the role of the government as an investor including that in agriculture and irrigation, causing a marked deceleration and even declines in area irrigated. At the same time, price movements during reforms have been extremely unfavourable for foodgrains, especially in relation to such key agricultural inputs as diesel, electricity used in agriculture and fertilizer - causing sharp declines in real terms of trade of foodgrains in relation to these inputs. All these factors have connived to break the backbone of Indian agriculture, especially its foodgrains sector. The rate of growth of production of foodgrains has decelerated from 3 percent per annum during the pre reform planned period (1951-91) to around one per cent during the reform period (1991-2005) which is much below the population growth rate. As a consequence, the average annual production of foodgrains per person in India has come down from 208 kg in 1988-91 to 181 kg in 2002-05 which is much below the level needed for selfsufficiency (194 kg). Hence, the country has decided to import foodgrains to the tune of 30 lakh tonnes this year which is likely to go up to 50 lakh tonnes. Thus, the self-sufficiency in foodgrains which the country assiduously attained over its first 4 decades of planning has been lost during the process of reforms mainly due to plan erosion. It is to highlight this crisis in food production that this short note is devoted.

PLANNING AND ECONOMIC GROWTH

In a developing economy like India, the government has to play an active role in the process of economic growth by providing social and economic overhead capital, i.e. those basic services without which primary, secondary and tertiary economic activities can not function properly. These include all public services from law and order through education and public health to transportation, communications, power and water supply, as well as such agricultural overhead capital as irrigation, flood control and drainage systems (Hirschman, 1960). These are of vital significance for economic growth without which investments in different sectors can not be fully productive. They promote different areas (sectors) by generating large external economies to them. However, the economies they generate to other sectors are not reflected in their own rate of return. Hence, they seldom attract much of private investments. Therefore, in general, these services are provided by public agencies either free of charge or at nominal rates. They have been subjected to public control, regulation and support even when provided through private agencies. The most notable example in this respect is the growth of private railways during the nineteenth century in Europe and elsewhere with government guarantees of minimum returns. In addition to providing these services, the government in

Table 1

Sector-wise Expansion in Gross Domestic Product (At Factor Cost at Constant 1993-94 Prices) in India

Sector	*1950-53*	*1978-81*	*1988-91*	*2002-05*	*CAGR (1950- 53 to 2002-05)*
Agriculture and allied activities	82740	154058	216205	302728	2.53
(Agriculture)	(72219	(137810)	(198164)	(275155)	(2.61)
Industry and Mining	21501	93209	174101	386133	5.71
Services	40429	141540	264464	737245	5.74
All Sectors	144670	388806	654767	1426106	4.50

CAGR = compound annual growth rate

Source: Central Statistical Organisation, New Delhi, National Accounts Statistics of Relevant Years.

India, in order to initiate and accelerate the process of economic growth, has played a role in directly promoting a number of industries such as heavy engineering and steel industries which were necessary for economic development but could not be developed in the private sector on account of very large capital requirements and long gestation periods. And, to perform these roles better, India adopted economic planning which got deepened over time. Thus, the annual size of plan expenditure at constant 1981-82 prices rose from Rs. 3823 crore during 1951-61 to Rs. 41735 crore during 1990-05 which is around eleven times of the earlier amount. As a percentage to the net domestic product of India, it rose from 5.64 to 11.98 over the same period. In fact, this percentage was even higher at 14.31 during 1980-90. Economic planning in India has been associated with a significant acceleration in its economic growth. The value of its annual average gross domestic product at constant 1993-94 prices has expanded from Rs. 144670 crore during 1950-53 to 1426106 crore during 2002-95, recording an annual compound growth rate of 4.50 per cent which is 3.4 times of the rate of growth in national income of India recorded during the first half of the twentieth century (1900-1950 at 1.32 percent per annum). During the second half of the twentieth century, the population of India grew at 2.1 per cent per annum which is again 2.5 times of that during the first half of the twentieth century (at 0.84 percent per annum). Still over the period 1950-53 at 2002-05, the rise in gross domestic product per capita comes to 2.40 percent per annum which is 5 times of that recorded during the first half of the twentieth century (i.e. 0.48 per cent per annum).

AGRICULTURAL GROWTH AND POVERTY ALLEVIATION

The nature of poverty in the third world including that in India is primarily rural (UNDP,1993). Rural poor number over 76 per cent of the total both in the developing world taken together as well as in India. Such poor number as high as 83.33 per cent in the least developed world and around 92 per cent in Bihar and 88 per cent in Jharkhand.

In relative terms also, the incidence (ratio) of poverty is much higher in rural areas. Rural poor are mostly engaged in agriculture who derive their means of livelihood by working as agricultural labourers, marginal/small farmers or petty rural artisans (Todaro, 1981).Hence, more than the general per capita income (r=-0.52), it is the value of net agricultural product per worker which emerges as the most crucial variable (r=-0.72) explaining the spatial distribution of rural poverty across states in India (Sharma, 1998). In raising agricultural productivity through accelerated agricultural development, therefore, lies the major solution to the problem of poverty in developing countries like India. As most rural poor are engaged in agriculture, they stand to gain directly by way of higher income, wages and employment as agriculture grows. Even those who are not directly engaged in agriculture, they rely on non farm income and employment which are dependent in one way or the other on agriculture. Agricultural growth is particularly effective in reducing rural poverty because of demand spill overs to local markets in which non farm rural poor have a large stake. Increased farm incomes are mostly spent in rural areas, especially on consumption goods and services produced by the rural poor. Rural construction, personal services, simple manufacturing and repairs have been some major channels through which poor people have shared agricultural booms.

Again, agriculture's linkages to non farm economy generate considerable employment, income and growth in the rest of the economy. In most rural areas the generation of significant non farm income depends critically on having a dynamic agriculture. If regional agriculture stagnates the local economy has no engine to drive non farm activities. Hence agricultural growth has been a catalyst for broad based economic growth in most low income economies. Very few countries have experienced rapid economic growth without agricultural growth either preceding or accompanying it. Agriculture has, acted as the lead sector in the rapidly growing East Asian economies like Taiwan, South Korea, China,

Thailand and Malaysia. A review of East Asian economic growth experience since the 1950' s clearly indicates the catalytic role of agriculture in generating economic growth and reducing poverty. (Per Pinstrup-Anderson & Rajul Pandya-Lorch). Thus, in addition to the rate of economic growth, it is the regional and sectoral composition of growth that affects the national rate of poverty reduction. If growth bypasses poor regions, growth may lead to rising inequality and poverty. On the other hand, if growth is concentrated in sectors from which poor people are more likely to derive their income, such as agriculture, growth can be associated with declining income inequality and reduced poverty. Consistent with cross country evidence for developing countries, India's states tell a similar story of the importance of rural growth in poverty reduction. And within rural areas, growth in agriculture and services has been particularly effective in poverty reduction while industrial growth has not (World Bank, 2000-2001).

PLANNING AND AGRICULTURE

At the commencement of planning in India, agriculture formed its largest sector generating over 56 percent of the gross domestic product and employing over 70 percent of the total work force. However, the nature of agriculture was quite underdeveloped characterized by extremely low and erratic yields, and prevalence of pervasive poverty, hunger and under nutrition in rural areas. Rural poor still constitute over 75 percent of the total poor in India. In view of its vital significance, therefore, agriculture has been assigned a key place in the development planning of India. A sum of Rs. 169388 crore at constant 1981-82 prices has been spent as plan expenditure on agriculture and allied activities including irrigation, flood control and drainage over the plan period till 2004-05 which comes to 15.52 percent of the total plan expenditure on all sector over this period. As a consequence, Indian agriculture has recorded a long term growth in its gross domestic product at the rate of 2.61 percent per annum over the period (1950-53 to 2002-05). The achievement is no mean.

The rate of growth in agricultural product has been higher than the growth in agricultural workers. Hence, there has been a rise in the value of agricultural product per agriculture worker at the rate of 0.75 per cent per annum. The achievements are much more perceptible on the food front

FOOD SELF SUFFICIENCY

India got independence as a food dependent country. On account of partition, a major portion (31 %) of undivided India's irrigated area went to Pakistan. This share came to around 55 per cent in the case of area irrigated through government canals. On the other hand, the bulk of the population (82%) remained in India, causing an acute problem of food deficiency in it which continued for a long time. Also, on account of better health care over the plan period, population took an upward swing, (from 1.26 per cent per annum during 1941-51 to over 2 per cent during the subsequent period) aggravating further the problem of foodgrains deficiency. And, the problem assumed the nature of a crisis by the mid 1960s. The country experienced two unprecedented consecutive droughts during 1965-67, causing sharp declines in its foodgrains production from 89 million tonnes in 1964-65 to 72 million tonnes in 1965-66 and 74 million tonnes in 1966-67. To meet the situation, the country had to take recourse to large annual imports of foodgrains (largely from the USA under PL 480 Aid), averaging over 8 million tonnes during 1964-68 (RBI, 1970-71). During 1966-67, the import of foodgrains exceeded 10 million tonnes valued at Rs 586 crore which consumed over half of annual export earnings of the country. Besides being undesirable on economic grounds, such a large dependence on imports for foodgrains for a country like India became undesirable also on political grounds. After the Indo-Pak War in 1965, the United States made PL 480 Aid more stringent and tried to teach India a lesson for not aligning with its foreign policies and also because Pakistan happened to be one of its close strategic allies at that time. All these forced India to lay renewed emphasis on attaining the goal of food selfsufficiency.

Table 2
Dynamics of Population and Foodgrains Production in India

		Average Annual Foodgrains Production Total (in million tonnes)		*in Kg/Person*	
Period	*Population (in Crores)*	*Foodgrains*	*Pulses*	*Foodgrains*	*Pulses*
1948-51	35.66	52.77	8.39	148	24
1962-65	46.94	83.38	11.39	178	24
1973-76	59.87	108.50	11.10	181	19
1978-81	66.84	123.73	10.46	185	16
1988-91	82.84	172.45	13.66	208	16
1998-01	100.74	203.11	13.00	202	13
2002-05	108.94	197.43	13.13	181	12
(Annual Compound Growth Rate 1948-51 to 1998-01)	2.10	2.73	0.89	0.62	-1.23

Source: Ministry of Agriculture, Government of India and Director General of Census Operations, Government of India, New Delhi.

The mid 1960's marked a turning point in Indian agriculture. The unprecedented droughts and the resultant food crisis exposed the weakness of rainfed Indian agriculture and its utter vulnerability to droughts. It induced the government to lay more emphasis on irrigation, especially ground water irrigation, which gives quick results and is relatively free from the vagaries of rains. There is less fluctuation in ground water supplies than in precipitation because of the buffering effect of underground storage (Gasser, 1981). The period also marked the advent of green revolution (new technology) in agriculture comprising the use of high yielding seeds in association with enhanced use of fertilizers, irrigation and other modern inputs. The government adopted a number of measures to spread the new technology. All these have led to a sustained and substantial rise in the production of foodgrains in the country over the plan period. As shown in Table-2, the average annual production of foodgrains in the country has expanded from 52.77 million tonnes during 1948-51 to 203.11 million tonnes during 1998-01, i.e. at the rate of 2.73 per cent per annum. Over the same period, the population of India has increased from 35.66 to 100.74 crores, i.e. at the rate of 2.1 per cent per annum. Thus, the long term annual growth rate of foodgrains has been significantly higher than its population growth rate. Consequently, the annual production of foodgrains per capita in the country has risen from 148 kg in 1948-51 to 202 kg in 1998-01 which is marginally higher than that needed for selfsufficiency (i.e. 194 kg per capita as per 50th round NSS). This has transformed the nature of the Indian economy from that of a chronic importer of foodgrains to a net exporter since the beginning of 1990's. Thus, India exported about 8.5 million tonnes of foodgrains during 2002-03 valued at about Rs 95 billion which came to 3.75 per cent of its total export earnings. In a view of these achievements, it is often claimed that the country has achieved food security.

PLAN EROSION

The self-sufficiency attained in foodgrains in India is, however, more technical than real as it is based on market demand and not on actual requirements of the society. It is based on the fact that all are not getting enough of foodgrains to eat. Further, the self sufficiency in foodgrains is confined to cereals alone. The country is still dependent on large imports in matters of edible oils and pulses. The average Indian diet is extremely lopsided and lacks variety. It is extremely lacking in animal food which is not good from the point of view of nutrition. It is important to note that even now per capita annual production of foodgrains in India (around 200 Kg) is much below the world average (around 330 Kg). In future with rising share of animal food in place of plant food, more and more of foodgrains will be needed for cattle feed so as to produce more of milk, meat, eggs, etc., per person. All these call for an acceleration and diversification of agricultural production in the country which, inturn, is crucially dependent on enhanced public investment in agriculture. In India, the government has played a key role in providing these services in agriculture such as those of irrigation, flood control and drainage as well as those in agricultural research, etc. Under the new economic policy, in the name of privatisation and fiscal consolidation, however, there has been a perceptible decline in the role of the government as an investor. Firstly, there has been a decline in the level of public expenditure which has gone down from around 40 percent of the net domestic during 1985-90 to around 36 per cent of the net domestic product during 1990-05. The decline has been much more in plan expenditure. The plan expenditure as per centage to public expenditure has gone down from 39.25 during 1980-90 to 30.45 during 1990-05. Thus, the size of plan expenditure, as a percentage to the net domestic product in the country, has gone down from 14.31 during 1980-90 to 10.98 during 1990-05. The decline has been much more in that on agriculture and irrigation, including flood control and command area development. Their combined share in total plan expenditure over the same period has gone down from 16.11 to 12.62 per cent.

Table 3

Plan Expenditure on Agriculture and Irrigation in India (1951-05)

(in Rs. Crore at 1981-82 Prices)

Period	*Plan Expenditure*				*Plan Expenditure as % to*	
	Agriculture, Cooperation and C.A.D.	*Rural Develop-ment*	*Irrigation and Flood Control*	*All Sectors*	*Public Expen-diture*	*Net Domestic Product*
1951-61	4814 (12.59)	–	5128 (13.41)	38233 (100.00)	41.93	5.64
1961-69	8316 (14.18)	–	4452 (7.59)	58630 (100.00)	37.80	7.94
1969-80	15983 (13.69)	–	11068 (9.48)	116724 (100.00)	35.46	9.07
1980-90	18810 (7.47)	16952 (6.73)	21767 (8.64)	251939 (100.00)	39.25	14.31
1990-05	35353 (5.64)	48285 (7.71)	43697 (6.98)	626019 (100.00)	30.45	10.98

Figures in brackets indicate percentage share in total plan expenditure. CAD = Command Area Development.

Source: Computed by authors from data contained in Economic Survey, Govt. of India, of relevant years and from other sources.

ADVERSE TERMS OF TRADE

One major factor promoting better growth in Indian agriculture was the favourble terms of trade that this sector enjoyed during 1980s, i.e. agricultural prices rose higher that those of other commodities, especially in relation to key agricultural inputs like fertilizers, fuel, etc. Thus, with 1981-82 as the base (100) the whole sale price index of foodgrains rose to 179 in 1990-91, the same for fertilizer and diesel stood at 99 and 156. Data depicting movements in whole sale price index of some commodities are contained in table 5. It is clear from the table that price movements have not been favourable for agricultural commodities, during the period of reforms especially for foodgrains after 1999-00. Thus, between 1999-00 and 2005-06 (till December) while the price index for foodgrains rose by only 12 points, those of fertilizer, diesel and electricity in agriculture rose by 59, 345 and 221 respectively points. These price movements have adversely impacted the real terms of trade of agricultural produce, especially of foodgrains. The terms of trade (with 1990-91=100) of foodgrains during 2005-06 stood at 0.46, 0.57 and 0.84 in relation to diesel, electricity in agriculture and fertilizer respectively. The abnormal rise in the price of fuels (especially diesel and electricy) has really broken the backbone of Indian agriculture, as energy has become an important input in agriculture. It is needed for operating irrigation pump sets and other agricultural implements. Thus, the terms of trade have become very adverse for agriculture during reforms which have very adversely impacted its growth process. It has raised the cost of irrigation through ground water to abnormal heights and made agriculture unremunerative.

Table 4
Whole Sale Price Index (1990-91 = 100)

Year	*Food Articles*	*Foodgrains*	*Fertilser*	*Diesel*	*Electricity in Agriculture*
1994-95	160	167	212	152	186
1999-00	235	257	262	246	251
2000-01	242	253	290	319	317
2001-02	250	251	296	352	371
2002-03	254	254	308	381	409
2003-04	257	257	310	419	430
2004-05	264	258	313	503	433
2005-06 *	277	269	321	591	472

* till December, 2005.

Source: RBI, Handbook of Monetary Statistics of India, 2006.

CRISIS IN FOODGRAINS PRODUCTION

The decline in the leve l of public investment in agriculture has been followed by a perceptible decline in the growth of irrigation which has been the basis of agricultural breakthrough during the second half of the twentieth century. The annual rate of irrigation expansion in India has come down from 2.37 per cent during 1978-81 and 1988-91 to 1.60 per cent during 1988-91 and 2000-03. In fact, there has been an absolute decline in the net irrigated area in the country by about 2 million hectares since the closing years of the last century, mainly due to the decline in the area irrigated through government canal. This has been followed by a marked decline in the net sown area from 142.41 million hectares in 1988-91 to 138.42 million hectares in 2000-03. Again, there have been marked deceleration and declines in the use of chemical fertilizers in subsidies on them. The annual consumption of fertilizer has declined from 17.2 million tonnes during 1998-01 to 16.75 million tonnes during 2001-04. Over the same period, the average annual use of electricity in agriculture has gone down from 91 to 85 billion kwh. This is extremely disturbing in view of the fact that cheap electric supply to agriculture has played a crucial role in promoting ground water irrigation which has been the most dynamic element in irrigation-the basis of green revolution since the mid 1960s. Ground water has accounted for over 90 per cent of the net addition to the irrigated area in the country over the period 1962-65 to 2000-03. As a result of all these, there has been a sharp deceleration in the rate of growth of agriculture in the country. Thus, the annual compound growth rate of agricultural gross domestic product has gone down from 3.70 per cent during 1978-81 and 1988-91 to 2.37 percent during 1988-91 and 2002-05. The deceleration has been much more in the production of foodgrains which grew at the rate of only 0.97 per cent per annum during 1988-91 and 2002-05 against 3.38 percent per annum during 1978-81 and 1988-91. As a result, the per capita annual production of foodgrains in the country, instead of going up, has gone down from 208 Kg during 1988-91 to 181 Kg during 2002-05, which is much below the level needed for self sufficiency (194kg. per person per year). These trends are extremely disturbing from the point of view of food security which need to be corrected on a priority basis by making a quantum jump in the level of public investment in agriculture including those in irrigation, rural electrification, flood control and drainage. This needs to be supplemented by other suitable measures relating to pricing, marketing and subsidies needed for agricultural development. Otherwise, the way things are moving under the new economic policy, the country is limping towards food insecurity even in the limited sense of the term, i.e. se1f-sufficiency in foodgrains. Infact the government has already decided to important foodgrains to the tune of 3 million tonnes during 2006-07.

Table 5
Some Key Inputs in Agriculture

Area in Million Hectares

Period	*Net Irrigated Area*	*Gross Irrigated Area*	*Net Sown Area*	*Cropping Intensity*	*Fertiliser Use (Million Tonres)*	*Electricity Use in Agriculture (Billion Kwh)*
1948-51	19.99	21.52	110.59	1.13	0.05	0.15
1962-65	26.05	29.96	136.98	1.15	0.59	1.22
1978-81	38.43	49.10	140.63	1.23	5.30	13.32
1988-91	46.96	62.06	142.41	1.29	11.78	44.42
1998-01	56.22	76.08	141.59	1.34	17.19	90.95
2001-04	54.61@	75.61@	138.42@	1.33@	16.75	85.44

Source: Central Statistical Organisation, New Delhi, Statistical Abstract of India (various volumes) and Ministry of Agriculture, Govt. of India, Land Use Statistics of relevant years (@ relate to the period 2000-03).

Table 6
Sector wise Growth in G.D.P. at 1993-94 Prices
(Compound Annual gr. rate)

	Pre- reform Decade (1978-81 to 1988-91)	*Reform Period (1988-91 to 2002-05)*
Agriculture and Allied Activities	3.45	2.43
(agriculture)	(3.70)	(2.37)
Mining and Industry	6.45	5.85
Services	6.45	7.60
All sectors	5.35	5.72
Agriculture and Industry	4.67	4.14

Source: Computed by the author

CONCLUSION

To conclude, there has been a marginal acceleration in the overall annual rate of growth of the Indian economy during the period of reforms i.e. from 5.35 per cent during 1978-81 and 1988-91 to 5.72 per cent during 1988-91 to 2002-05. However, this acceleration is confined to the services sector alone which has grown at the rate of 7.60 per cent per annum during the reform period against 6.45 percent per annum during the pre reform decade. Over the same period, both industries and agriculture have witnessed deceleration in their growth rates. The industrial sector has decelerated from 6.45 to 5.85 i.e. by 0.60 percentage point. The deceleration has been extremely marked in the case of agriculture which has witnessed a deceleration in its growth rate from 3.70 to 2.37, i.e. by 1.33 percentage point. The picture is extremely depressing on the food front as the production of foodgrains has grown at a rate much below that in population. It is no wonder, therefore, if the government has decided to import food grains to the tune of 30 lakh tonnes this year. Thus, the self-sufficiency in foodgrains which the country assiduously attained over the first four decades of planning has been lost as a result of plan erosion during the period of so called reforms. And, in so far as growth in agriculture provides a natural solution to the problem of poverty (as has happened in Punjab), it can be safely said that the growth process during reforms is not promoting equity, i.e. growth with social justice. The country has really fallen into a deep crisis on its food front which needs to be remedied on a very urgent basis by undertaking suitable policy measures, especially by strengthenning the planning process and having a congenial price regime.

REFERENCES

Hirschman, A.a. (1960), *The Strategy of Economi Development*, New Haven, Yale University Press, pages, 83-84.

U.N.D.P. (1993), *Human Development Report-1993*, p 213

Todaro, M.P. (1981), Economic Development in the Third World, New York, London, Longman.

Sharma, I. (1978), "Rural Poverty in India: A Study in Regional Dynamics", *Bihar Economic Journal, Conference Vol.* 1998, p. 39

Per Prinstrup-Anderson & Rajul Pandya- Lorch, "The Role of Agriculture to Alleviate Poverty," Agriculture+Rural Development, DLG-Verlags-GMBH, Eschnormer, Landstrabe, 122, 60489 Frankfertam Main, Germany, Vol. 6. N 0.2, p. 53.

—(2001), World Bank, *World Development Report (200-01)*

—(1970-71), Reserve Bank of India , Report on Currency and Finance, Bombay, p.69, Table-3.

Gasser, W.R. (1981), *Survey of Irrigation in Eight Asian Nations,* National Technical Service, U.S. Department of Commerce, Washington D.C., USA, 20250, p. 14.

—(1996), National Sample Survey Organisation, *Nutritional Intake in India, Report No. 405,* p. 14, Dept. of Statistics, Govt. of India, New Delhi.

CHAPTER 23

FINANCIAL SECTOR REFORMS AND FINANCIAL VIABILITY OF REGIONAL RURAL BANKS IN INDIA

Bipul Vikash

Indian economy has been recording impressive growth rate since 1991. This can be partly attributed to the multi-sector structural reforms aimed at enhancing productivity, efficiency and international competitiveness of the economy. The reforms in the financial sector have been most effective. The main thrust of the financial sector reforms has been the creation of efficient and stable financial institutions and development of the markets, especially the money and government securities market. In addition, fiscal correction was undertaken and reforms in the banking and external sector were also initiated. The reforms have been undertaken gradually with mutual consent and wider debate amongst the participants and in a sequential pattern that is reinforcing to the overall economy. The financial markets have developed and are more integrated after the reforms and regulatory and supervisory institutions have been set up. The reforms, though slow paced initially but well synchronized have begun to yield results. The economy has recorded consistently high growth rates, avoided any adverse impact from the South East Asian Crisis, built substantial foreign exchange reserves, paid some of its external debt and restructured its domestic debt.

The performance of the Indian economy in the last decade has been remarkably strong. One of the reasons for the robust performance of the economy could be the ongoing financial sector reform which began in 1991.

Regional Rural Banks (RRBs) were set-up in 1976 as a result of disappointment with the progress of co-operative and commercial banks in extending credit to agriculture. The RRBs are not just banks; rather they cover millions of our poor farmers, particularly in the areas of poverty alleviation programmes. Each RRB in capitalized to the tune of 65 percent by the central and relevant state government and 35 percent by a "sponsor bank". RRBs were mandated to lend solely to people below the poverty line at concessional interest rates applying to small loans, significantly below a break-even rate. They could survive only with refinance from the National Bank for Agriculture and Rural Development (NABARD) and their sponsor commercial banks.

FINANCIAL PERFORMANCE OF RRBs

Banking sector reforms have brought about quantitative as well as qualitative improvements in the performance of RRBs. The policy measures undertaken in respect of RRBs, viz.; the permission to relocate loss making branches to better business centers and conversion of loss-making branches into satellite/ mobile offices without impairing the performance of branches in service area had salutary effect on the financial performance, especially in relation to profits and recovery of RRBs and decline in NPAs.

Significant improvement in the performance of RRBs is being witnessed in their improved bottom line. Over a period of three years (2002-04), aggregate reserves of RRBs increased significantly (74 percent) while the deposits and investments increased by 27 percent and 18 percent respectively. During the same period, loans and advances outstanding increased by 40 percent while loans issued increased by 47 percent. Table 1 shows the performance indicators of RRBs.

Table 1
Performance Indicators of RRBs
(As on 31st March)

(Rs. Crore)

Particulars	*2002*	*2003*	*2004*
Branch Network (No.)	14,390	14,433	14,446
Share Capital	195.81	195.85	195.85
Share Capital Deposits	2,080.62	2,112.74	2,134.98
Reserves	1,782.40	2,357.41	3,107.05
Deposits	44,539.15	50,098.34	56,350.08
Borrowings	4,524.37	4,798.69	4,595.48
Investments	30,531.73	33,063.42	36,135.40
Loans and Advances Outstanding	18,629.22	22,157.85	26,113.86
Loan Issued*	10,570.67	12,641.00	15,579.05
RRBs Earning Profit (No.)	167	156	163
Amount of Profit*	699.93	733.97	952.33
RRBs Incurring Losses (No.)	29	40	33
Amount of Losses	92.05	214.68	183.65
Accumulated Losses	2,694.06	2,752.25	2,725.35

*April-March

Source: NABARD, Annual Report, 2004-05, p.96

The net accumulated profit of RRBs as a group, as on 31 March 2004, increased by 48 percent over the previous year to Rs. 768.68 crores. In all, 163 RRBs showed improvement in their performance either by way of increase in profits or reduction in losses or by shifting from loss to profit at the end-March 2004, as compared to 156 at the end March 2003. The number of RRBs, which had wiped off accumulated losses and attained sustainable viability, increased to 106 (from 97) and together built up reserves to the extent of Rs. 3,099.86 crore and 57 RRBs attained current viability. The performance of RRBs, however, varied widely across the states.

RECOVERY PERFORMANCE

At the aggregate level as on 30th June 2004, recovery performance of RRBs improved further as compared to the previous year. In absolute terms, the amount of recovery increased from Rs. 8,274.34 crores (June 2002) to Rs. 13,712.78 crores (June 2004) i.e. by 66 percent. Table 2 shows the recovery performance of RRBs.

Table 2
Recovery Performance of RRBs
(As on 30th June)

(Rs. Crore)

Year	*Demand*	*Collection*	*Balance*	*Recovery (%)*
2002	11,569.82	8,274.34	3,295.48	71.52
2003	13,246.95	9,738.80	3,508.15	73.49
2004	17,656.08	13,712.78	3,943.30	77.67

Source: NABARD, Annual Report, 2004-05, p.96

NON-PERFORMING ASSETS (NPAs)

Constant follow-up by NABARD, RBI and sponsor banks created awareness among RRBs about the quality of lending. This was reflected from the declining trend in NPAs of these banks. RRBs showed steady improvement on this front as witnessed from the gradual decline in their gross NPAs as a percentage of loans and advances outstanding from 18.84 as at end-March 2001, to 12.63, as at end March 2004. However, in absolute terms, the NPAs of RRBs increased from Rs. 3,199.75 crores as at end-March 2003 to Rs. 3,298.83 crores as at end March 2004. Table 3 shows the state-wise working result of RRBs.

PRESENT SCENARIO

Now the RRBs have become a centre of hope to the rural people. Although this is the second phase of financial sector reforms there are some controls and restrictions on RRBs, which proves to be a major hurdle in the smooth running of these banks. RRBs deposit rates were controlled. Their freedom of operation was severely restricted even with regard to providing incentives to borrowers to repay on time. Refinance from NABARD is available at heavily subsidized rates of 6.5-8.5 per cent.

The network of RRBs grew rapidly. There are 196 RRBs with approximately 15,000 branches. Spread has not been matched by strength. At the beginning of 1994, 171 out of 196 banks were making losses and about three quarter of them had negative net worth. At the end of 2004, the result is satisfactory and loss making banks reduced upto 33. Their

Table 3
State-wise Working Result of RRBs
(As on 31 March 2004)

(Rs. Crore)

State	No. of RBBS	Profit Earning		Loss Incurring*		Net Accumulated		Loans & Advances	NPAs		Recovery %	
		No.	Amount	No.	Amount	Profit	Losses	O/s	Amount	%	June03	June 04
Andhra Pradesh	16	15	121.53	1	-3.36	118.17	29.18	3,452.03	279.28	8.09	70.96	77.14
Arunachal Pradesh	1	–	–	1	-2.18	-2.18	24.53	32.21	24.21	74.41	22.61	24.50
Assam	5	5	14.73	–	–	14.73	89.59	612.65	86.17	14.07	58.41	67.04
Bihar	16	7	48.52	9	-85.64	-37.12	611.98	1,409.13	265.79	18.86	60.92	63.54
Chhattisgarh	5	5	17.73	–	–	17.73	132.43	394.05	58.46	14.83	69.02	75.38
Gujarat	9	9	28.37	–	–	28.37	22.00	663.00	83.89	12.53	76.53	80.03
Haryana	4	4	57.37	–	–	57.37	4.05	823.07	44.33	5.39	84.73	87.89
Himachal Pradesh	2	2	9.16	–	–	9.16	–	175.22	12.99	7.41	80.79	82.53
Jammu & Kashmir	3	1	11.99	2	-10.85	1.14	81.98	201.57	22.49	11.16	63.85	75.37
Jharkhand	6	3	6.02	3	-11.61	-5.59	131.90	378.36	92.32	24.40	44.94	47.87
Karnataka	13	13	104.47	–	–	104.47	–	2,900.28	284.49	9.81	75.41	75.73
Kerala	2	2	38.33	–	–	38.33	–	1,456.07	109.54	7.52	84.99	86.80
Madhya Pradesh	19	14	35.86	5	-18.19	17.66	232.13	1,601.24	215.70	13.47	72.49	79.01
Maharashtra	10	9	16.36	1	-1.70	14.66	123.60	749.60	157.62	21.02	64.22	70.21
Manipur	1	–	–	1	-1.44	-1.44	15.68	16.49	6.32	38.32	51.80	50.17
Meghalaya	1	1	2.21	–	–	2.21	–	46.25	13.63	29.46	54.30	59.86
Mizoram	1	1	0.39	–	–	0.39	5.19	50.26	12.08	24.02	61.23	61.22
Orissa	9	5	16.14	4	-28.12	-11.98	485.64	7,732.31	242.06	13.97	67.38	71.37

Contd.

State	No. of RBBS	Profit Earning		Loss Incurring*		Net Accumulated		Loans & Advances	NPAs		Recovery %	
		No.	Amount	No.	Amount	Profit	Losses	O/s	Amount	%	June03	June 04
Punjab	5	5	39.73	–	–	39.73	–	427.35	20.40	4.77	91.66	93.48
Rajasthan	14	12	46.97	2	-7.05	39.92	179.69	1,587.96	133.14	8.38	80.05	83.17
Tamil Nadu	3	3	9.65	–	–	9.65	–	669.75	27.19	4.21	89.28	90.15
Tripura	1	1	6.43	–	–	6.43	135.01	213.70	58.85	27.54	44.56	51.30
Uttar Pradesh	36	35	295.27	1	-1.49	293.78	135.38	4760.98	795.84	16.72	70.04	73.15
Uttranchal	4	3	7.45	1	-0.98	6.46	2.95	187.69	22.26	11.86	79.30	88.26
West Bengal	9	8	1767	1	-10.63	7.04	280.45	1565.45	228.20	14.57	69.33	72.32
All India	196	163	952.33	33	-183.65	768.68	2,725.35	26,113.86	3,298.83	12.63	73.49	77.67

* During 2003-04

Source: NABARD, Annual Report, 2004-05, p.98

overdue performance is even worse than that of commercial and co-operative banks. The basic reason for the financial collapse of the RRBs is their total lack of commercial operation. Their administration costs are high; particularly important in this context is the fact that their employees have been given parity of wages with commercial banks. Identification of borrowers and projects is both lacking in care and highly politicized. Overdue are pervasive problems with willful default playing a major role.

STEPS TAKEN BY THE GOVERNMENT FOR THE IMPROVEMENT OF RRBs

Above mentioned facts have been known for a long time but there has been little action. Recently, some steps have been taken to improve the financial viability of RRBs.

- Restrictions regarding lending to target groups have been diluted. They have been given more flexibility both in managing their funds and in locating loss-making branches.
- The credit policy announced by RBI in October 2004 indicated that sponsor banks in consultation with state government would initiate steps for amalgamation of RRBs sponsored by them in each state.
- The Vikas Volunteer Vahini (VVV) Programme renamed as 'Farmers' Club' (FC) Programme. The essence of the programme is manifest in the principles of development through credit that envisages utilizing credit in an appropriate manner to enhance productivity and production leading to increase in income and repayment of loans for recycling of funds. The role of farmers clubs has been enlarged to cover technology transfer on farmers' field for higher productivity.
- NARARD provides financial assistance to banks, NGOs, Agriculture Universities, Krishi Vigyan Kendras, etc. During the year 2004-05, 3,649 clubs were launched. The programme has spread to 505

districts covering 31,108 villages through 13,664 clubs.

- An integrated plan to provide loans to the weaker sections through the banks has been initiated. It has been welcomed by all because so far big industrialists and businessmen had been taking advantage of bank loans. The bank has been warned that priority must be accorded to the weaker sections in loan disbursement and the bank branch target must be achieved, otherwise is would be a serious disobedience to the government order.

IDENTIFIED ISSUES

The RBI has been entrusted with the responsibility of supervision of all rural banks. Undoubtedly, RBI has discharged its responsibility very successfully. Apart from these, there has been a continuous decline in the profitability of these banks. The study reveals that:

(i) In the list of objectives of these poverty alleviation programmes, no mention was made of human resources in rural banks.

(ii) Impartial assessment of the requirements of the area and concern for selecting the right schemes are matters which have not always fructified

(iii) The RRB left the poor farmers completely in the void after granting them assets. They were not generating a sense of responsibility.

(iv) High levels of overdue - mostly chronic due to the poor quality of lending.

(v) The huge overdue represented the form of providing for bad debts.

(vi) Recovery of loans granted was low due to the lack of infrastructural facilities in most of the states, improper formulation and appraisal of schemes, inadequate follow-up action etc.

(vii) In reality, there are no comprehensive blue-prints for the reforms in RRB which have been uncoordinated.

CONCLUDING REMARKS

As India is an agrarian economy, the balanced economic growth of our country to a large extent, depends upon the development of rural India i.e. **"BHARAT"**. All the financial institutions involved in agricultural lending are weak or insolvent. This in itself indicates that the system is unhealthy. But this is not conclusive as regards the effects of directed credit on economic efficiency and a more direct test of the issue would obviously be desirable. Such a test is difficult to conduct in part because it is difficult to setup to counter factual case. There has been virtually no reform in the area of directed credit. The time has come to impose hard budget constraints on institutions lending to agriculture and small scale industries. Finally, Indian banks continue to have high spreads and are still extremely inefficient by international standards. They are massively overstaffed. In spite of all, India has made a good start with financial sector reform. But so far as RRBs are concerned, there is still a long way to go for a sophisticated modern economy.

REFERENCES

Joshi Vijay & Little I.M.D. (2002), India's Economic Reforms 1991-2001, Oxford University Press.

Tulsyan S.L. (2002), "Banking Sector Reforms: An Analytical Study of RRBs in North Bihar Looking upto the New Millennium" in *Banking and Financial Sector Reforms in India* (eds: Amalesh Banerjee & S.K. Singh), Deep & Deep Publications Pvt. Ltd., New Delhi.

RBI Bulletin, Various issues.

NABARD (2004-05), Annual Report.

INDEX

F